Death in England

Peter C. Jupp and Clare Gittings
———— editors ————

Death in England

AN·ILLUSTRATED·HISTORY

gift in memory of

Barbara Compton

Rutgers University Press
New Brunswick, New Jersey

First published in the United States 2000
by Rutgers University Press, New Brunswick, New Jersey

First published in Great Britain 1999
by Manchester University Press,
Oxford Road, Manchester M13 9NR, UK

Library of Congress Cataloging-in-Publication Data
Death in England : an illustrated history / edited by Peter C. Jupp and Clare Gittings.
    p. cm.
  Includes bibliographical references (p.   ) and index.
    ISBN 0–8135–2788–0 (cloth : alk. paper). — ISBN 0–8135–2789–9
(paper : alk. paper)
    1. Death—Social aspects—England. 2. Funeral rites and
ceremonies—England—History. 3. England—Social life and customs.
I. Gittings, Clare. II. Jupp, Peter C.
HQ1073.5.G7D427 1999
306.9′0942—dc21   99–42691

Printed in Great Britain

Contents

Illustrations

Figures

Plates

Contributors

Christopher Daniell has degrees in History, Medieval Studies and Computing from the University of York. He has been an archaeologist and historian and whilst working for York Archaeological Trust he undertook extensive historical research. He now works for Past Forward Ltd as a project manager and researcher. He is the author of *Death and Burial in Medieval England 1066–1550* (1997).

Clare Gittings is the author of *Death, Burial and the Individual in Early Modern England* (1984). She has also contributed to exhibition catalogues and collections of essays on death and to the journal *Mortality*. She works at the National Portrait Gallery, London, where she teaches, lectures and curates exhibitions.

Valerie M. Hope is a lecturer in the Department of Classical Studies at the Open University. Her main research area is in Roman social history focusing in particular on the organisation of the Roman cemetery and the construction of personal and familial identity through funerary monuments.

Rosemary Horrox is Fellow and Director of Studies in History at Fitzwilliam College, Cambridge. She is the editor of *The Black Death* (1994) and *Fifteenth-century Attitudes* (1994).

Ralph Houlbrooke is Professor of History at the University of Reading. He is the author of *Death, Religion and the Family in England 1480–1750* (1998) and editor of *Death, Ritual and Bereavement* (1989). He has also written on the family and on the church courts in late medieval and early modern England.

Pat Jalland is a Professor of History at the Australian National University. Her five books include *Death in the Victorian Family* (1996), *Women, Marriage and Politics* (1986) and *The Liberals and Ireland: The Ulster Question in British Politics to 1914* (1980).

Peter C. Jupp is a Founding Editor of the journal *Mortality* and a Visiting Fellow in the Department of Sociology, University of Bristol. He was Director of the National Funerals College (1992–97). His 1993 doctoral thesis constructed the history of cremation in England. He is currently minister of Corby United Reformed Church, Northamptonshire.

Philip Morgan is a historian at the University of Keele where he teaches courses on the Middle Ages, including the kingship of Edward II. His research interests centre on warfare, and on the English gentry of the late Middle Ages. He has published on Domesday Book and on medieval Cheshire.

Keith Ray has excavated on and has researched a variety of Neolithic and Bronze Age sites in England, Scotland and Wales. He has carried out field surveys of Neolithic cairns and barrows. He holds Cambridge University degrees in Archaeology to doctoral level, and works as County Archaeologist for Herefordshire Council.

Julie Rugg manages the Cemetery Research Group at the University of York, and is completing interdisciplinary research on the deposition of human remains. Her

1992 doctoral thesis comprised a study of early cemetery companies, and she has since that time published studies relating to cemetery history and contemporary cemetery management practices.

Victoria Thompson was brought up in Kenya and New York. She has degrees in English Literature and Medieval Studies from the Universities of Oxford and York. She is currently completing a doctorate at York on the understanding of death in England in the late Anglo-Saxon period, and works as a story-teller and guide.

Tony Walter, who lives in Bath, is Reader in Sociology at the University of Reading, where he has developed a new cross-disciplinary M.A. in Death and Society. Among his books are *Funerals and How to Improve Them* (1990), *The Revival of Death* (1994) and *The Eclipse of Eternity* (1995). He helped found the National Funerals College in 1992.

Acknowledgements

We thank Vanessa Graham of Manchester University Press (MUP) whose idea this book originally was. We thank Rosemary Horrox for recommending Peter's name to MUP as editor. In turn, he was glad to invite Clare to join him as co-editor, for which she is grateful. The order of names on the title page reflects this sequence of events. Work on the text has been equally shared throughout by both editors and Clare was responsible for overseeing the illustrations. *Death in England* has been published with the help of a grant towards the illustrations from the late Miss Isobel Thornley's Bequest to the University of London. We are grateful to Dr Pat Crimmin, Secretary, and members of the Isobel Thornley's Bequest Fund Committee for their generous support.

We thank our contributing authors for their enthusiasm and hard work. We have appreciated their good humour and endless patience as they have responded to requests for revisions as the book proceeded. We thank MUP's editorial team, especially our editor Louise Edwards; Michelle O'Connell conducted the picture research; Judith Ravenscroft copy-edited the text; Vivienne Robertson did the proof-reading; and Hazel Bell compiled the index. We thank all five for their dedication to the project. We would also like to acknowledge the perceptive comments of our two reviewers, Professor Roy Porter of the Wellcome Institute for the History of Medicine and Dr Jenny Hockey of the University of Hull, and the assistance of Dr Glennys Howarth of the Universities of Bath and Sydney.

Peter Jupp would particularly like to thank Clyde Binfield, Tom Clarke, Anne Eyre, John Faid, Carole Lambert, William MacQuitty, Katherine Riley, Christine Steele, Pat Sturdy and John Travell; and the staffs of the libraries of the Institute of Historical Research, the London School of Economics, the Wellcome Institute for the History of Medicine, and of Peterborough and Stamford Public Libraries. For continual support, he thanks Elisabeth Jupp to whom, with Edmund and Miles Jupp, he dedicates this book.

Clare Gittings would particularly like to thank her colleagues at the National Portrait Gallery for their help and encouragement, especially Lucy Clarke, Jacky Collis Harvey and Susie Foster of the Publications Department, and Bernard Horrocks, James Kilvington and Tom Morgan of the Picture Library. She also thanks Louisa Hearnden, Terri Sabatos and Tony Walter for their friendship and support. The greatest burden of living with this project has fallen on Malcolm Ramsay to whom Clare dedicates the book.

Peter C. Jupp and Clare Gittings

Introduction

This books charts the history of death from the earliest known humans in England to the close of the twentieth century. Although there have been many important books on death concentrating on different topics and eras, several of them written by contributors to this volume, this is the first time that the whole history of English death has been mapped out. The book does, however, restrict its geographical remit to the relatively modest terrain of England, rather than trying to cover the entire British Isles with its far greater diversity of cultural and religious history. The chronology of half a million years has been arranged into ten chapters to allow each author scope to explore changes, continuities and contrasts within their individual periods.

The study of death provides much fascinating insight into life in the past, adding to the wider historical picture. Sources permitting, every author has described and illustrated certain core aspects of death. These include demography and the causes of death, the process of dying, concepts of the afterlife, funeral rites, bereavement and commemoration. The relative emphasis placed on each of these themes, however, has been left to the discretion of the author. Where evidence exists, authors have looked at both sexes, all ages, different social classes or religious affiliations, and have noted regional variations within England (also making the occasional incursion into Wales). Authors have been invited to address the general reader, summarising existing knowledge and providing a select bibliography for their period.

This book explores how real people's deaths, and the arrangements made in response to them, have changed over the millennia. The strong visual record of death, often created in commemoration, provides the illustrations. For all but the most recent centuries little remains of the inner feelings either of the dying or of the bereaved, so inevitably the book focuses primarily on the public face of death. Where available, personal testimony has been invoked for the light it sheds on the unfolding history of death, rather than for the fame of the witnesses. Similarly, the deaths discussed are not generally of the famous, unless exemplifying particular ideas and practices. Death in literature would be a series of books in their own right and literary material is mainly drawn on here when it directly shapes or reflects behaviour and attitudes. Likewise, while an art-historical study would share several of the same illustrations, here they are used to illuminate historical, rather than aesthetic, developments. The changing deaths of Everyman and Everywoman – as far as they are currently knowable – are our prime concern.

With the study of the history of death in England in its infancy, as discussed below, authors have been encouraged to incorporate their own particular areas of research expertise, while still sketching in the broader general framework. Thus in Chapter 2, the reader can inspect Roman tombstones; in Chapter 5, tour medieval battle sites; in Chapter 6, attend funerals; in Chapter 8, visit cemeteries; in Chapter 9, watch at Victorian deathbeds; and in Chapter 10, probe belief in an afterlife, each in the company of an author who specialises in the topic. This provides individual chapters with a distinctive focus, ranging from intense, close-up studies of real human experiences to wider discussions of the distant, more impersonal forces shaping the history of death. The authors employ a variety of methodologies and represent a range of academic disciplines, including archaeology,[1] sociology and history. The book, therefore, both reveals the current state of historical death scholarship – some of its major themes and preoccupations – as well as providing a comprehensive outline of the history of death in England from earliest times.

Death and the historians

In Britain, while prehistoric and classical deaths have long been explored by archaeologists and historians from Sir Thomas Browne's *Urne Buriall* of 1658 onwards,[2] death has, until recently, received little attention from those studying later periods. In France, however, the *Annales* school of history began, from the mid-twentieth century, to examine mortality.[3] Of French historians, the most influential in Britain has been Philippe Ariès, in part because many of his compatriots have not been translated into English, but mainly for the breadth of his work and the model of change it proposes.[4]

Ariès produced the first extensive account, albeit somewhat impressionistically, of Western attitudes to death from the early Middle Ages to the late twentieth century. He drew in fact mainly on France and its Catholic culture. The overarching theme of his book, first published in English in 1981, was that Western individualism has shaped and indeed unhealthily distorted attitudes to death. His chronological structure of five collective *mentalités*, from 'tame death' to 'invisible death', has influenced both the interpretations and vocabulary of other historians. While some of the contributors to this book have previously differed with each other as to the value of his work,[5] several chapters here ascribe particular changes to greater individualism, without, however, according it the same degree of pre-eminence as Ariès.

French anthropologists, along with those from other countries, have also made a significant contribution to the study of death, particularly Hertz (1907) and Van Gennep (1909), neither translated into English until 1960.[6] Anthropological analysis vividly informs several historical and archaeological interpretations of death, as shown, in particular, by Chapter 1 of this book.[7]

In the United States, the first major historical study was made by David Stannard in 1977, exploring the culture of death in Puritan New England.[8] As yet, death in England in the period that he covers – the later seventeenth and eighteenth centuries – has not received such exclusive attention. Recently, historians have drawn on ideas from ground-breaking American research by sociologists and psychologists.[9] Several of these ideas have become established currency in the way we interpret death and dying, for example the differentiation between biological death and social death.[10] The pioneering work of these earlier American scholars was developed by the establishment of two inter-disciplinary journals, *Omega* (1969) and *Death Studies* (1977).

Scholars from different countries have shown a growing interest in the connection between death and sexuality. The biological and social necessities for this relationship have long been known.[11] In the twentieth century, their psychological connection was explored by Freud but made far more specific after 1980, in societies affected by AIDS and fascinated by the genre of horror stories. Ariès controversially suggested that death became morbidly eroticised during the sixteenth to eighteenth centuries. A few of the images in this book, for example *The Death of Chatterton* [**plate 14**], might give a certain credence to this theory, but the debate has not yet progressed sufficiently far to provide solid conclusions. Discussions most relevant to the present book include those of Baudrillard, Binion, Bronfen and Dollimore.[12] The debate has been developing in the histories of art and culture and in sociological analysis about the symbolism and language of the human body.

Although they probably would not have described themselves as such, there had been death scholars in Britain long before the explosion of death studies in the 1990s. Death was always a key issue for certain academic and professional disciplines. Historical studies of death have been enhanced by this interdisciplinary context. For archaeologists, graves and human remains often provide the foundation from which accounts of peoples and communities may be constructed, as the first three chapters of this book show. For anthropologists, too, death rituals provide keys to whole social structures. Art historians have studied, in monuments and tombs, the development of sculpture and the history of architectural style in miniature. Theologians can trace, in rituals of death and funerals, the ongoing interaction of beliefs, liturgies and pastoral practice which reveals concepts of God and of human nature. Death also has major implications for legal studies, especially those in inheritance and criminal law. Medical scholars have never been able to avoid mortality and its ethics. Medicine also stimulated the development of the hospice movement which interacted both with the 1960s counselling revolution and with psychological research on death and bereavement.

In late twentieth-century Britain, the initial impetus to study death in its own right came from the sociologist Geoffrey Gorer, wistfully comparing truncated contemporary mourning rituals with more lavish Victorian rites.[13] A very different response to Victorian death, emphasising its commercialism, appeared in the early 1970s in works by Morley and Curl and in the exhibition *Death, Heaven and the Victorians*.[14] Chapter 9 of this volume represents a much more measured view of the period.

A much earlier area of historical death research in England is demography, now spearheaded by the Centre for Population Studies at Cambridge (CAMPOP) which took its inspiration from the methodological success of the French *Annales* school. CAMPOP pioneered the technique of family reconstitution using parish registers, which were established in England in 1538.[15] A particular topic which has fascinated demographers is the impact of plague in early modern England, discussed in Chapters 6 and 7 of this book.[16]

Art historians such as Curl (1980) and Colvin (1991) produced studies of the styles of tombs, while memorial brasses have also received particular attention.[17] Such works have shown varying degrees of concern for the actual deaths which prompted these monuments. However, the cadaver tombs of the later Middle Ages, by directly confronting scholars with images of corpses, demanded explanation, as in the work of Boase (1966), itself partly inspired by Huizinga's *The Waning of the Middle Ages* (1919). Both Huizinga's book and cadaver tombs are also the starting point for Chapter 5 of this present book.[18]

The last two decades of the twentieth century saw a considerable growth in books on British death, several major works being written by authors who are contributors to this present publication.[19] Much of this research is distilled in the chapters which follow. Other important studies included collections of papers given at conferences on the history of death, or sets of essays, of which Whaley's *Mirrors of Mortality* (1981) was especially influential, particularly for its contribution by Cannadine on death in the twentieth century, discussed here in Chapter 10.[20] The founding of the interdisciplinary journal *Mortality* in 1996 provided a further outlet for historical studies, while the 1992 exhibition at the Victoria and Albert Museum, London, *The Art of Death*, increased interest in visual aspects of the subject.[21] Meanwhile, older attitudes to death were not extinct: the opening of *The Art of Death* was postponed because of fears for public morale during the Gulf War.

Summary

Archaeologists investigate the role of death and of mortuary practices among early populations using excavated evidence and analogy with traditional societies. As Chapter 1 shows, in some periods formal burial may have been exceptional rather than commonplace. For remote times, there is little evidence at all for burial. In the Neolithic period, human bone was an important constituent in ritual of differing kinds. Interment of corpses in chambers produced bones that could either reside in repositories or be circulated among locations. Complex rules were followed to associate such bones with pottery or with the bones of wild or domesticated animals. In the Bronze Age, individual burials more often retained their skeletal integrity, although cremation deposits could contain the mixed remains of several people. Interments still accumulated within cemeteries, while prominent barrows and rich grave items proclaimed the status of lineages. A closer link between living places and burial became evident during the second millennium BC.

Chapter 2 explores the evidence for death and burial in the Iron and Roman Ages. For the Iron Age relevant evidence is limited. How the majority of dead were disposed of often remains a mystery. Nevertheless it is possible to focus upon some striking funerary examples such as cart burials, cist cemeteries and warrior graves, although it is rarely possible to use this evidence to assert afterlife beliefs. For the Roman period the evidence is comparatively substantial as graves, cemeteries and tombstones survive. Furthermore, sources from elsewhere in the Roman world record aspects of funeral ritual and the death industry. But was there standardisation across the Roman world? In England, did distinctions between Roman and local practices persist? Whether the dead were cremated or inhumed is a critical issue. The shift to inhumation eventually created a common rite across England even though the original impetus for the change remains unknown.

Chapter 3 has two chronologically overlapping sections. The first describes the many diverse pagan Anglo-Saxon and Viking burial rites, drawing on archaeological evidence. The second section examines the impact of Christianity and the associated burial practices. Christianity fostered new written sources – wills, monastic records, charters, literary and religious works – which steadily increased throughout the Middle Ages. This early period also sees, in illuminated manuscripts and sculptures, the first surviving representations of the Christian afterlife in England. The chapter concludes by considering the impact of the Norman Conquest.

From the twelfth century, as Chapter 4 describes, the formalisation of the doctrine of Purgatory and its steady dissemination throughout society brought a significant shift in the way contemporaries thought about death and the afterlife. This led ultimately to the erection of a massive edifice of postmortem prayers and charitable works to help the souls of the dead towards salvation. In other respects, notably in ideas about the body after death and the status of ghosts, popular thinking was less clearly in step with official teaching. The impact of the Black Death at the end of the period covered by this chapter was initially to intensify existing ways of thinking about death rather than to transform them altogether. The emphasis on the macabre, often seen as characteristic of the post-plague world, was in fact well established by the beginning of the fourteenth century and the Church had long urged Christians to contemplate their own mortality by stressing the transience of life and the corruptibility of the body.

Chapter 5 asks whether there was a 'new' death in the late Middle Ages, a sensitivity to physical decay born of the experience of the Black Death and later plagues. If so, what were its parameters and how did contemporaries face its challenge? Whilst morbid depictions of death in the visual arts are undeniable, with death now seen as an attacker, most people seem to have approached death with hope rather than fear. Worms and cadavers notwithstanding, memorials and tomb sculpture offered an optimistic reading of death, whilst manuals of dying offered the prospect of a good death for many. Perhaps more challenging was the sixteenth-century attempt, articulated by the Henrician and Edwardian state during the English Reformation, to redraw the boundaries of death, severing the vital links between the living and the dead which had exemplified the social practice of the late Middle Ages.

Chapter 6 explores the impact of Protestantism on death in England from the accession of Elizabeth I to the Restoration. The new doctrine of the afterlife, in which the living could no longer assist departed souls by prayer, both made the deathbed a more irrevocable turning point and altered the balance of sacred and secular elements in funeral rituals, bringing greater prominence to secular aspects such as eating and drinking after the burial. The heraldic funerals of the aristocracy in Elizabeth's reign focused attention on social status while the night burials of the seventeenth century allowed for greater expression of the sorrow of bereavement. This sense of loss also appears in letters of the time and even in tomb sculpture. It was, however, during the Interregnum – a period comparatively meagre in historical sources – that Protestant doctrine was taken to its logical conclusion and burial briefly became a secular ceremony conducted by the laity.

The century between the Restoration and the accession of George III, surveyed in Chapter 7, experienced high mortality, at least until the 1730s, but also the dawn of a new confidence that disease could be curbed. It tolerated growing squalor in London slums, and the overcrowding of urban churchyards, yet cherished an ideal of decency – balance, harmony, restraint and seemliness – in respect of deathbeds, funerals and mourning rituals. This was the great age of classical funeral monuments and dignified prose epitaphs. Substantial headstones began to transform the appearance of churchyards. The testimonies of countless funerary inscriptions and funeral sermons are complemented by descriptions of individual reactions to death in some of the most intimately revealing of all English diaries and private correspondence. The apogee of 'rational religion' was followed by the beginnings of evangelical revival.

Chapter 8 covers the period 1760 to 1850. By 1850, the Church had begun to lose its hold on sepulchral matters. The centrality of the church building to death ritual was undermined by the increased use of secular burial places where pagan symbolism could hold sway; and a shift in attention to the feelings of the bereaved over the spiritual fate of the deceased reduced the importance of a clerical presence at the deathbed. Mass movements of thought and feeling also transformed attitudes towards death: the Enlightenment, Romanticism and Evangelicalism had a profound impact on beliefs relating to the afterlife and the experience of loss and bereavement. Large-scale urban mortality established the need for new ways of dealing with the dead, and class divisions infused increasingly commercialised death rituals. The secularisation of death was not achieved smoothly; the period also saw the beginnings of the Gothic Revival and its critique of a lack of spirituality in death ritual.

Chapter 9 suggests that the traditional Christian ideal of the 'good death' was still exceptionally powerful in 1850, though its realisation varied widely according to class, religion, age, gender and disease. Christian mourning rituals and the belief in family reunions in heaven helped to reconcile some parents to high infant and child mortality. Moreover, the solace of the private and social memory of the dead was complemented by visible symbols of remembrance such as paintings, photographs and death masks of the deceased, and mourning jewellery. Attitudes to death were transformed between 1850 and 1918 by the decline in religious beliefs and the significant fall in the death rate, which shifted the likely time of death from infancy to old age. The trauma of the First World War accelerated these changes since Victorian deathbed and mourning rituals were inadequate and inappropriate in the face of mass violent deaths far from home.

The tenth and final chapter shows how the Great War helped usher in an era of dramatically improving health. Death was increasingly deferred to old age. As dying became institutionalised and under medical control, control over funeral arrangements passed further from bereaved families to funeral directors, a process aided by the popularity of cremation. At the same time, greater liberal and secular attitudes led in the 1960s to legal reforms in capital punishment and suicide. The secular climate encouraged a wider range of beliefs about life after death, challenging traditional Christian beliefs. New models of 'the good death' were developed by the hospice movement. New attitudes to grieving slowly emerged, challenging the more private expression of grief formed by the two world wars. More open expressions of grief accompanied the series of highly publicised disasters in the 1980s and 1990s, notably with the death of Princess Diana.

This book does not attempt to frame a single, overarching hypothesis to account for changes in death attitudes and practices. Nevertheless, it has several major themes which are explored throughout the chapters. One is how the Church first established, during the first millennium AD, a monopoly over death rites and then lost it again under pressure from growing secularism after the Reformation. Another is the impact of demographic change, in particular increasing life expectancy, and the medicalisation of death. In all ages there have been notions of what constitutes 'good' and 'bad' deaths which vary over the centuries, including whether the dying should be conscious of their imminent decease. Similarly, views of the afterlife have undergone dramatic shifts, as have the ways death is visualised and portrayed, whether personified as a figure or represented symbolically.

All chapters discuss the links between death rites and social status, ranging from rulers to those on the margins of society or even excluded from it, such as paupers, children and criminals. The importance of the place where bodies are buried, whether intact or cremated, is explored. Changing expressions of grief through mourning rituals are traced, as are the connections between death and the other major moments of human transition, birth and marriage. The relationship between the living and the dead in different eras is another important theme. The gradual passing of authority for death from the dying and their kin to professional specialists such as undertakers and doctors is a development increasingly criticised in the later twentieth century. The growing interest in the history of death, of which this book is a part, can be seen as one facet in reversing this process and returning decision-making to the dying and bereaved.

Notes

In all references, place of publication is London unless otherwise stated.

1 For a representative survey, see, e.g., S. Bassett (ed.), *Death in Towns: Urban Responses to the Dying and the Dead 100–1600* (Leicester, 1994); A. Boddington, A. N. Garland and R. C. Janaway (eds), *Death, Decay and Reconstruction: Approaches to Archaeology and Forensic Science* (Manchester, 1987); M. Cox, *Life and Death in Spitalfields 1700 to 1850* (York, 1996); J. M. Lilley, G. Stroud, D. R. Brothwell and M. H. Williamson, *The Jewish Burial at Jewbury, The Medieval Cemeteries: The Archaeology of York 12/3* (York, 1994); C. A. Roberts, F. Lee and J. Bintliff (eds), *Burial Archaeology: Current Research Methods and Developments*, British Archaeological Reports, British Series 211 (1989); A. Woodward, *Shrines and Sacrifice* (1992).

2 T. Browne, *Hydriotaphia: Urne Buriall or a Discourse of the Sepulchrall Urnes Lately Found in Norfolk* (1658).

3 J. McManners, 'Death and the French historians', in J. Whaley (ed.), *Mirrors of Mortality: Studies in the Social History of Death* (1981).

4 For English-language contributions to French developments, see, e.g., J. McManners, *Death and the Enlightenment: Changing Attitudes to Death among Christians and Unbelievers in Eighteenth-century France* (Oxford, 1981); R. Cobb, *Death in Paris* (Oxford, 1978); T. A. Kselman, *Death and the Afterlife in Modern France* (Princeton, 1993). See especially P. Ariès, *Western Attitudes towards Death: From the Middle Ages to the Present* (Baltimore, 1974), and *The Hour of Our Death* (1981).

5 C. Gittings, *Death, Burial and the Individual in Early Modern England* (Beckenham, Kent, 1984), and R. Houlbrooke (ed.), *Death, Ritual, and Bereavement* (1989), chapters 1 and 2.

6 R. Hertz, *Death and the Right Hand* ([1907], 1960); A. Van Gennep, *The Rites of Passage* ([1909], Chicago, 1960).

7 For example, M. Bloch and J. Parry (eds), *Death and the Regeneration of Life* (Cambridge, 1982); R. Huntington and P. Metcalf, *Celebrations of Death: The Anthropology of Mortuary Ritual* (Cambridge, 1979); S. C. Humphries and H. King, *Mortality and Immortality: The Anthropology and Archaeology of Death* (1981).

8 D. E. Stannard, *The Puritan Way of Death: A Study in Religion, Culture and Social Change* (Oxford, 1977). Significant studies of later American periods include: J. J. Farrell, *Inventing the American Way of Death, 1830–1920* (Philadelphia, 1980); G. Laderman, *The Sacred Remains: American Attitudes towards Death 1793–1883* (New Haven, 1996); J. Mitford, *The American Way of Death Revisited* ([1963] New York, 1998); D. C. Sloane, *The Last Great Necessity: Cemeteries in American History* (Baltimore, 1991).

9 For a survey of pioneering American studies, see V. D. Pine, 'A socio-historical portrait of death education', *Death Education*, 1 (1977), 57–84.

10 B. G. Glaser and A. L. Strauss, *Awareness of Dying* (Chicago, 1965), and *Time for Dying* (Chicago, 1968).

11 W. R. Clark, *Sex and the Origins of Death* (Oxford, 1997).

12 J. Baudrillard, *Symbolic Exchange and Death* (English trans. 1993); R. Binion, *Love beyond Death: The Anatomy of a Myth in the Arts* (New York, 1993); E. Bronfen, *Over Her Dead Body: Death, Femininity and the Aesthetic* (Manchester, 1992); J. Dollimore, *Death, Desire and Loss in Western Culture* (1998).

13 G. Gorer, *Death, Grief and Mourning in Contemporary Britain* (1965).

14 J. Morley, *Death, Heaven and the Victorians* (1971); J. S. Curl, *The Victorian Celebration of Death* (Newton Abbot, 1972).

15 See, for example, E. A. Wrigley and R. S. Schofield, *The Population History of England 1541–1871: A Reconstruction* (1981); J. Landers, *Death and the Metropolis: Studies in the Demographic History of London 1670–1880* (Cambridge, 1993); M. J. Dobson, *Contours of Death and Disease in Early Modern England* (Cambridge, 1998).

16 See, for example, P. Slack, *The Impact of Plague in Tudor and Stuart England* (Oxford, 1985). Of particular and wider significance is C. Creighton, *A History of Epidemics in Britain*, 2 vols (1894).

17 J. S. Curl, *A Celebration of Death: An Introduction to Some of the Buildings, Monuments and Settings of Funerary Architecture in the Western European Tradition* (1980; rev. edn, 1993); H. Colvin, *Architecture and the After-life* (New Haven, 1991). For memorial brasses, see M. Norris, *Monumental Brasses: The Memorials*, vols I and II (1977), and *Monumental Brasses: The Craft* (1978); C. Gittings, *Brasses and Brass Rubbing* (1970).

18 J. Huizinga, *The Waning of the Middle Ages* (Harmondsworth, 1955); T. S. R. Boase, *Death in the Middle Ages: Mortality, Judgement and Remembrance* (1972).

19 Those contributing to this book include: C. Daniell, *Death and Burial in Medieval England 1066–1550* (1997); Gittings, *Death, Burial and the Individual in Early Modern England*; Houlbrooke (ed.), *Death, Ritual and Bereavement*, and *Death, Religion and the Family in England 1480–1750* (Oxford, 1998); R. Horrox, *The Black Death* (Manchester, 1994); P. Jalland, *Death in the Victorian Family* (Oxford, 1996); T. Walter, *The Revival of Death* (1994), *The Eclipse of Eternity: A Sociology of the Afterlife* (Basingstoke, 1995) and *The Social World of Bereavement* (Buckingham, 1999).

Other major books include: O. Anderson, *Suicide in Victorian and Edwardian England* (Oxford, 1987); S. M. Barnard, *To Prove I'm Not Forgot: Living and Dying in a Victorian City* (Manchester, 1990); P. Binski, *Medieval Death: Ritual and Representation* (1996); A. Borg, *War Memorials: From Antiquity to the Present* (1991); C. Brooks, *Mortal Remains: The History and Present State of the Victorian and Edwardian Cemetery* (Exeter, 1989); K. Charmaz, G. Howarth and A. Kellehear (eds), *The Unknown Country: Death in Australia, Britain and the USA* (Basingstoke, 1997); M. MacDonald and T. R. Murphy, *Sleepless Souls: Suicide in Early Modern England* (Oxford, 1990); R. Richardson, *Death, Dissection and the Destitute* (1987); L. Rose, *Massacre of the Innocents. Infanticide in Great Britain 1800–1939* (1986); E. Schor, *Bearing the Dead: The British Culture of Mourning from the Enlightenment to Victoria* (Princeton, N.J., 1994); L. Taylor, *Mourning Dress: A Costume and Social History* (1983); M. Wheeler, *Heaven, Hell and the Victorians* (Cambridge, 1994) (originally published as *Death and the Future Life in Victorian Literature and Theology* [Cambridge, 1990]); J. Winter, *Sites of Memory, Sites of Mourning: The Great War in European Cultural History* (Cambridge, 1995); J. Winter and B. Baggett, *1914–18: The Great War and the Shaping of the 20th Century* (1996).

20 Collections include: J. Whaley (ed.), *Mirrors of Mortality* (1981); Houlbrooke (ed.), *Death, Ritual and Bereavement*; D. Clark (ed.), *The Sociology of Death: Theory, Culture, Practice* (Oxford, 1993); Bassett (ed.), *Death in Towns*; J. Davies (ed.), *Ritual and Remembrance: Responses to Death in Human Societies* (Sheffield, 1994);

G. Howarth and P. C. Jupp (eds), *Contemporary Issues in the Sociology of Death, Dying and Disposal* (Basingstoke, 1996); P. C. Jupp and G. Howarth (eds), *The Changing Face of Death: Historical Accounts of Death and Disposal* (Basingstoke, 1997); D. Field, J. Hockey and N. Small (eds), *Death, Gender and Ethnicity* (1997); M. Cox (ed.), *Grave Concerns: Death and Burial in England, 1700–1850* (York, 1998).

21 N. Llewellyn, *The Art of Death: Visual Culture in the English Death Ritual c. 1500– c. 1800* (1991); J. Litten, *The English Way of Death: The Common Funeral since 1450* (1991). Other collections based on or accompanying exhibitions include: A. Sumner (ed.), *Death, Passion and Politics* (1995); G. Waterfield (ed.), *Soane and Death: The Tombs and Monuments of Sir John Soane* (1996); D. Petherbridge and L. Jordanova, *The Quick and the Dead: Artists and Anatomy* (1997); A. Werner (ed.), *London Bodies: The Changing Shape of Londoners from Prehistoric Times to the Present Day* (1998).

From remote times to the Bronze Age: *c*. 500,000 BC to *c*. 600 BC

When did 'death' begin? This curious question, as old as the origins of thought itself, is central to how we define ourselves as human.[1] Answers to the puzzle have often been phrased as myths of human origin. Versions of genesis stories explain how death was a price paid by the first humans for the receipt of earthly benefits ranging from the earliest farmed crops to the institution of marriage.[2]

The place of death and the dead in the world-view of prehistoric societies is only indirectly knowable today because we have no written accounts or observations to draw upon. Archaeology as a study has developed partly in response to this problem. Some understanding of the physical circumstances of 'ancient' death can be achieved through laboratory study of human remains,[3] while excavations and scientific analyses can identify methods used for the disposal of dead bodies.

However, archaeological research should also seek to identify the cultural traditions behind early mortuary rituals, as well as possible attitudes to death and the dead in prehistoric societies. This needs an informed perspective on preindustrial mortuary practice, and archaeologists have studied anthropological descriptions of communities in recent times to gain these insights.

Current approaches to the study of death in prehistory reflect contrasting theories.[4] Some favour an evolutionary approach in which increasing levels of social complexity are traced. Changing social forms are inferred from the kinds of object placed in graves, or the energy used in digging them.[5]

In Britain since the mid-1980s other ideas have developed. One approach is to identify patterns in archaeological remains that can be interpreted so as to suggest the operation of symbolic and ideological codes.[6] Another emphasises how human intentions and social relations create the historical reality of prehistoric funerary ritual, and how archaeologists should aim to write narratives from this silent 'discourse'.[7]

In the parts of the British Isles that have become 'England', the earliest traces of dead people have now been dated to about 500,000 years ago. Evidence for formal burial is much more recent, and generalisations about burial practices are only possible from around six thousand years ago. While death is attested from before this time, therefore, the emphasis in this chapter is upon a period of just over three thousand years. This spans 150 generations of inhabitants of the central, southern and eastern areas of 'mainland' Britain, and a complex distribution of peoples across the area concerned.

Knowledge of this historical terrain is uneven and is skewed geographically by accidents of preservation, retrieval and research emphasis. This explains why there is so much evidence from the chalklands of central southern England, for instance. Here accessibility, good preservation conditions, traditions of field activity and recent economic development are among the biasing factors. New discoveries elsewhere, therefore, can prompt substantial rethinking of former impressions. This is particularly so because hardly any detailed quantitative studies of excavated remains relating to prehistoric death and burial have so far been carried out.

The time from which generalisation is possible is around 4000 BC, when there appear the first traces of human activity that have survived as features of the modern landscape. Some, including 'long barrows', are still visible. Others, like the earliest earthwork enclosures, are traceable only with effort. These sites signal the 'Neolithic' period, a 'new' stone age in Britain, as elsewhere in the world, featuring pottery and polished stone axes and the local adoption of 'farming'.

In the third millennium BC 'ceremonial' activity occurred on a grander scale. During this later Neolithic period elaborate monuments were built. Ostentatious display in burial ritual marked the succeeding early Bronze Age, and continued into the middle of the second millennium BC. By the start of the next millennium, however, very different traditions had emerged. The creation of fields and the building of more permanent settlements perhaps also implies new attitudes to death.[8]

Elements first of a 'traditional' understanding of death are identified in this chapter, underlining the great diversity of belief and action that has been recorded through a century of anthropological study and comparison. Any conception of death before six thousand years ago is inevitably 'remote'. Only a scan of the meagre evidence from so many thousands of years of cultural richness and diversity is possible here. Accordingly, reference is widened to continental Europe to hint at patterns in death practices.

In contrast, later centuries have left a wealth of traces, including complex mortuary structures [1].[9] In narrative sequence, therefore, but also in recent archaeological thought, the death practices of Neolithic Britain are 'ancestral'. The part of the chapter dealing with the fourth and third millennia surveys some of the diversity and complexity of practices to which the investigated remains bear testimony.

Contemporary with archaic Greece, often dramatically staged with exotic artefacts, and with martial overtones, Bronze Age death is arguably 'heroic'. There had been some celebration of prominent people at their burial in earlier centuries. However, in the second millennium BC

1] The primary mortuary structure at Wayland's Smithy, Ashbury, Oxfordshire. Bones are stacked centrally on paving in the chamber. Successive corpses were inserted beyond this to decay. Sorted bones then placed on to the nearer paving were probably removed altogether from the site. Pits held posts that supported the timber roof.

this became more pronounced despite the fact that burial itself, most frequently of cremated remains, became more general to the population as a whole.

'Traditional' death: socio-cultural perspectives

Among the Bara of Madagascar, the bones of dead relatives are placed in wooden caskets, and stored in stone tombs. The bones of all the male ancestors are grouped to the north of the tomb. At the south end of each tomb, by the door, are grouped the bones of the women born into the male lineage that owns the tomb. In the women's casket, an individual's bones are stored with those of her sister, her father's sister, her brother's daughter, and those of their young children. These childrens' skeletons formally belong to the tomb of their father, but are given as a kinship 'gift' into the mother's paternal tomb.[10]

Each of these burial caskets is said to contain the bones of ten or so individuals. The location and contents of caskets within a communal tomb serve here to 'map' the kinship and descent of the living. The burial, decay and reburial of human remains is believed to change them into ancestral matter. In the reburial ceremonies the decayed corpses are reclothed by 'strong birds' (more powerful kin). A sombre atmosphere pervades, as ox horns – symbols of intense vitality and fertility – are brought into the presence of the ancestors inside the tomb chamber. Such gravity contrasts with the vigour and apparent chaos of the initial burial ceremonies.

Relocation of bones, the building of tombs with chambers, and the practice of excarnation (the defleshing of corpses before the collection and burial of the bones) present interesting parallels between such Malagasy and some Neolithic British mortuary processes. Could this indicate similar attitudes to the veneration of ancestors?[11] While simple equations between widely differing traditional societies are questionable, it is possible to isolate some common factors.

For instance, many peoples for whom kinship is a positive resource regard the dead as continuing to exist in some way. Venerated in death, the ancestors legitimate the authority of elders among the living. A ritualised 'translation' of the dead into ancestors involves processes common to all ritual. These feature stages of separation, then of liminality (a state of suspension and transition) and then of reintegration.[12] In death rituals both the living and the dead undergo such a series of transformations. For this reason, rather than any practical need for the defleshing of the corpse, there occur extended mortuary rites and 'second burial'. The resolution sought in these death ceremonies is between actual and 'social' death. Death is both denied and reinforced by controlled passage of the individual out of the web of social ties and obligations.[13]

Nor in traditional societies can actual bodily death and funeral practices be divorced from broader ideas about transition that may involve symbolic death and rebirth. An example is initiation rites. In chiefship investiture rites in southern Nigeria, a man may temporarily be buried alive and then awoken to symbolic rebirth. This 'death', and the investiture ceremony itself, are ultimately re-enacted in the burial of the chief after his actual death. A metaphor of burial as planting and the myth of death exchanged for food are symbolically invoked in these ceremonies and in the artefacts associated with them.[14] In Asia, Buddhist monks dress in a robe that symbolises the assumption of a state of chastity. This robe is nonetheless made from the saffron-coloured cloth used more widely for a shroud, while the sandals that the monk also wears are those put on the feet of corpses.[15]

Dead bodies may in some societies be regarded as volatile, and their status considered unsatisfactory and in need of resolution. The Dowayo of Cameroon view a fresh corpse as undesirably 'wet', requiring ritual treatment to reach the preferred state of 'dryness', just as the 'wet' uncircumcised penis is said to become 'dry' through circumcision.[16] In such societies, the fleshed corpse is associated with the world of the living, and its continuation in that state is seen as polluting. The process of defleshing not only releases the spirit of the individual, but the dry bones are conceptually clean. They are also associated with fertility and contain an ancestral essence that itself sustains tradition.

Symbols of transition are important because they contribute to the patterns found in archaeological remains. This is, for instance, the case where death provides an opportunity for making material exchanges to cement new social ties. In Assam and parts of Melanesia, for instance, there are parallels between gifts at marriage and at death. These gifts both bring into effect and also then reflect changes in the status of individual women in relation to one another and the wider society.[17]

Besides insights into the transitional nature of mortuary rites, ethnography reveals the enormous variety of specific practices concerned with the disposal of corpses. They may, for instance, be burned or buried, with or without animal or human sacrifice, preserved or stored or eaten, exposed or dismembered for carrion, or a mixture of any of these. Societies may reveal their central preoccupations through their death practices, whether these are with gender-based roles, or competitive gift exchange, or fears of (and predilections towards) poisoning.

Changes in the culture of a society are underscored in mortuary practices. The people who became known as 'Plains Indians' had, at the time of European contact, only practised a mobile life style for a few generations. The Mandan people of Nebraska for example replicated in death rituals the traditions associated with their former static earth lodges. This they did through placing warrior skulls in circular settings in the open prairie. The deliberate reference to buffalo evident in such sites perhaps reflected their greater dependency on these animals as a food source.[18]

The way that the human body is conceptualised in social relationships is central to differences in attitudes to it at death. The dead body is entirely subject to the living. It provides an important symbolic field for the negotiation of the social order. There exists an inherent tension here. This is between deliberate commemoration of the past role of the deceased person, and signalling through the treatment of their corpse the status of their surviving kin. This can affect the place of disposal, the formality of the ceremony, the dressing of the corpse and the inclusion of gifts or sacrifices.

Finally, a further note of caution. There is a tendency in 'commonsense' archaeological reconstructions to suggest that all past humans were 'people like us'. Many cultural differences may be viewed simply as 'variations on a theme', but we should not underestimate how sometimes subtle differences in practice can mask huge contrasts in worldview. The cultural landscapes of Neolithic and Bronze Age Britain would not be familiar to us today. Some of the rites connected with sacrifice, propitiation, ritualised warfare or initiation (to name but a few practices) would seem to us bizarre indeed, even were we to have had an anthropological training. We must therefore beware of imposing the cultural constructs and vocabularies of the modern world on the exotic worlds and, specifically, on the death practices of these early societies.

'Remote' death: hints and traces before 4000 BC

In 1994, at the Lower Palaeolithic site at Boxgrove in Sussex, were found the earliest securely dated remains of ancestral humans in Britain.[19]

2] Boxgrove, Sussex: handaxes and flakes found below a male tibia, on the former interglacial coastal plain (inset: the male tibia fragment). The shin bone and a tooth are from people ancestral both to modern and to Neanderthal-type humans living over 500,000 years ago. Large-scale tool use and extensive foraging are also represented at Boxgrove.

These traces comprised a tooth, and part of a shin bone from a large male hominid. They were located in a landscape that existed in a period between glaciations. [2].[20] The plain by an ancient cliff at Boxgrove had been used as a hunting area and bones from a variety of animals were also found in the excavations. They included horse and woolly rhinocerous and some bore cut marks from the flint tools. These objects had been rapidly sealed by deposits dated to around 500,000 years ago. With the less securely dated skull fragments from the Swanscombe gravels in Kent, the Boxgrove bones are the first vestiges of these distant peoples.

Remains of more recent Neanderthal-type individuals have been found during excavations in caves at Pont Newydd, Denbighshire. These traces date from *c.* 225,000 BC. A tooth was from an adult probably in his or her mid-twenties, and an upper jaw fragment belonged to an eight-year-old child. Bones of wild horse and bear bore cut marks, showing that they had been butchered locally.[21]

The experience of death as an event recognised by whole communities, however, is as yet only known from *c.* 100,000 BC, and not from Britain. Burials of people of Neanderthal type at Shanidar cave in Iraq seem in some cases to have been deliberate inhumations (that is, burials of complete fleshed corpses) with red ochre and other offerings.

Human remains have for some while been known from caves in the limestone regions of England, in particular from Devon, the Mendips and Derbyshire. These bone finds have been taken to indicate deliberate burial of anatomically modern humans from early times. Until recently, their apparent association with the bones of animals of the last Ice Age and before has been the sole means of dating them. In Europe, there have been finds of burials of the period 30,000–25,000 years ago. These have been found in pits, as at Kostenki on the river Don in Russia, or in caves, as at Cueva Morin in Spain.

Enhanced radiocarbon techniques have now provided the first direct dating of individual inhumations from British sites. So far, in the late 1990s, the earliest material reliably dated by this means is a single human jaw bone dated to *c.* 28,950 BC from a nineteenth-century excavation at Kent's Cavern at Torquay in Devon.[22] Also dating to just before the last Ice Age was the red-ochre-covered burial from Paviland in Gower, discovered in 1823. This is the earliest recorded formal inhumation in Britain, now dated *c.* 24,380 BC. Besides the red ochre scattered around and over the body, the young man of around twenty-five years was accompanied by grave goods that included walrus-ivory bracelets and rods. A group of perforated seashells was found by his thigh.

This Paviland find is remarkably similar to contemporary burials in continental Europe, like those from the site of Dolni Vestonice in the Czech Republic. These were also buried with ivory ornaments and were covered in red ochre. Such a covering is frequently encountered, and it has been suggested that it represents 'life blood'. At the Grimaldi caves of the Italian Riviera such burials also had batons and perforated seashells, apparently used as head-dresses. One ochre-covered burial at the very end of the Ice Age from St Germain-la-Rivière in France was even found within a stone chamber.[23]

The late glacial recolonisation of Britain is represented by the flint artefacts and other traces of people who hunted wild horses and red deer. At Gough's Cave, Cheddar, cut marks on human bones dated to *c.* 12,100 BC show that corpses were deliberately skinned and the insides removed before being dismembered and the remains placed around the sides of the cave. While ritual consumption of some soft tissue cannot be ruled out, the practices are thought to represent early examples of multi-stage burial practices.[24]

From post-glacial times, Mesolithic period burials are also, so far, rare in Britain. Fragments of human bone have been found in shell middens, and bones from caves in the Mendips and Derbyshire are also of Mesolithic date. As yet there have been no discoveries in Britain like those from Scandinavia or Brittany. These have included both extended inhumations, as at Skateholm in Sweden and Bogebakken, Denmark, and crouched burials, as at Teviec and Hoedic in Brittany. The red ochre, perforated shells and ivory items with these burials echo earlier practices. Antlers of reindeer or red deer are common to Scandinavian and Breton burials, and the burial from the coastal midden at Teviec was surrounded by stone slabs.[25]

At Old Parkbury, St Albans, a burial in a wooden container has been excavated. Inside a hollow log-coffin was placed a wooden box and another container. These were then set alight, but were not completely burned. The date of *c.* 4700 BC obtained from the newer timbers locates the event at the point of transition into the Neolithic period. The use of a wooden box for an inhumation prefigures in a vivid way the practices of the succeeding millennium.

'Ancestral' death: Neolithic societies, 4000–2000 BC

Today, the enduring image of Neolithic death is of the great long bar-rows of the British Isles that survive as vivid features of the landscape. Excavations within, beneath and around such mounds have revealed a complex history of activity that had often happened before they developed into massive monuments. The mounds served a variety of purposes, and although bones were placed in and removed from them, not all rites that occurred at them necessarily involved burials.

While barrows were not exclusively used for burial, neither were human bones placed only within such structures. Rather, there was a wide-ranging and complex 'location' of the dead, often in token deposits, in the landscape. Human bone was for instance often intentionally placed with other material such as stone axe fragments, broken pottery and animal bones in 'causewayed enclosures' constructed on hilltops and by rivers. These sites had arcs of separated lengths of ditch, defin-ing a circular or oval (and sometimes large) area. Many sites had mul-tiple rings of these ditch lengths, which often had been cut, back-filled soon after deliberate deposits had been put in them, and then recut and again refilled.

An awareness by prehistorians of the quantities of human bone sometimes present at causewayed enclosures has been slow to develop, despite observation of this phenomenon at Whitehawk Camp and else-where in Sussex back in the 1930s. In the main enclosure at Hambledon Hill in Dorset, and dating to *c.* 3600 BC, the remains of around seventy people were found in the 20 per cent of the ditch excavated. Overall, 'Sixty percent of the very large quantity of fragmented bone pertains to young children and no sexual bias (in favour of males) is apparent in the record'.[26] This was taken to imply that the site had been used for excarnation. Most striking were the skulls placed, and sometimes reset, facing along the ditch bottoms [3].[27] Similar groups of bones have been found at Windmill Hill near Avebury in Wiltshire, Etton near Peterborough and Offham in Sussex.

Burials of the earlier and middle Neolithic period are also found in caves. Rarely have survival conditions in such places enabled reconstruction of the original placing of burials as at Church Dale, Derbyshire. Here, the grouping of mixed bones in a stone box and the laying out of skeletons of adults and children echo similar treatments in long barrows [4].[28] Were tombs, therefore, 'artificial caves'? In fact, the opposite can be argued, with use of caves representing a 'domestication' of remote and mysterious locations.[29]

At Cissbury in Sussex, the bones of a young woman were found in the fill of a flint mine shaft that also contained pieces of a fine pottery bowl of an early type.[30] Such shafts had been dug to quarry flint nodules, but any opening of the earth to this extent appears to have required 'marking' with deposits of human remains. This was sometimes also the case with smaller pits dug in numbers in the landscapes of Neolithic Britain and very often these were also filled in both rapidly and deliberately. Dispersed bone fragments also occur in the ditches of 'long mortuary enclosures' and of

right 3] A skull placed in the base of a length of ditch *c.* 3500 BC, at Hambledon Hill, Dorset. Skulls and long-bones were apparently often removed from long barrow chambers and used in ceremonies elsewhere. Some enclosures, like this one, might also have been places for exposure and defleshing of corpses.

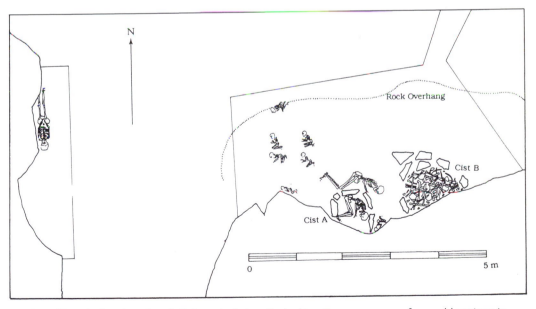

4] Plan of burials found in Church Dale rock shelter, Derbyshire. Caves were one of several locations in the landscape in which it was appropriate in the Neolithic period to inter human remains. Church Dale provides a rare example where built structures accompanied inhumation burials, replicating the forms of barrow chambers.

'cursus monuments'. These are extended linear constructions with parallel sides and few entrances. Their purpose is unknown, but may have involved processions as part of mortuary rituals.

In later times human bones were also found inside the dwelling houses. Post settings, bedding trenches, hearths, paved areas and compartments that indicate living structures occupied over extended periods of time are, however, rare during the Neolithic period.[31] Instead, the structures that have been found appear ephemeral, fitting better with an image of Neolithic peoples as mobile. It is odd, however, that traces interpreted as domestic in character have been found underneath later barrows. An alternative explanation for these features, and the piles of knapped flint found near them, is that they derive from earlier mortuary rites and simple structures. Such rites may have included feasting and the interment of the single bodies sometimes found beneath monuments with mortuary associations, as at the Windmill Hill causewayed enclosure.

The earliest complex structures built to hold the remains of the dead are essentially large wooden boxes. These occur widely, range from 2 to 10 metres long, and are set lengthways in a trench or between small elongated mounds. The rectangular box or chamber had a wooden post placed at each end. Where it has been possible to establish such detail, each side of the chamber and sometimes the floor itself was made up of longitudinal wooden planking. So too was the roof, sometimes supported by a smaller post halfway along its length. It might seem reasonable, given that these boxes had posts, 'walls', 'floors' and roofs, to think of them as 'houses for the dead'. Examples in southern England include the first phase of Wayland's Smithy on the Berkshire Downs [1], and the structure beneath the Whiteleaf barrow in the Chilterns. In the north, examples are Whitwell Quarry in the Peak District, and Willerby Wold and Kemp Howe in Yorkshire.

Human remains are often found stacked in one part of the chamber, with another area devoid of bones. This was the case at Foulmire Fen, Haddenham, in Cambridgeshire, where parts of a box-chamber made from massive planks of oak survived charring. The bones of five people were found at one end, which had an earth floor and was separated from the timber-floored front area by an upright slab of wood.[32] If the chambers were store houses for bones, however, they saw withdrawals as well as deposits. The empty areas of the chambers may have been points of exit rather than entry. Analysis of skeletal parts at Wayland's Smithy suggests that whole bodies were initially interred there, and indeed one was found apart from the bone stack at the north end of the chamber.

Within the structure at Fussell's Lodge on Salisbury Plain, many of the smaller bones were missing. This was perhaps because a different place was used for primary defleshing of the corpses. Bones of adults predominate among all such burial groups, but the numbers of people whose remains were stored at any one time in the chambers appear to have been small. Two adjacent structures were found at Whitwell Quarry, incorporated in a later stone cairn. The smaller box contained the remains of one female, while the other contained a group deposit.[33]

From an early stage, the mortuary chambers were often the focus for carefully sited wooden posts. Most frequently, as at Haddenham, this involved the creation of a facade structure of some kind. Elsewhere, there were more intricate 'focusing devices' comprising pairings of posts narrowing towards the facade, as at Wayland's Smithy. They reached greater elaboration at Yorkshire sites such as Kemp Howe, Kilham, and Street House [5].[34] At Nutbane in Hampshire and Worbarrow in Dorset, the chambers were enclosed from the outset by rectangular post-set enclosures with complex entrances.[35] Ditches and quarries around or along the long sides were another common feature of these early mortuary structures.

The period of use of wooden chambers was often brought to an end by deliberate firing. At Haddenham, the timber structure was carefully dismantled, slowly burned and buried under an earthen mound 50 metres long and 16 wide. At Fussell's Lodge the chamber was filled, and a pit was cut into this deposit. This was then sealed by turf, and another human bone deposit was inserted, this time with potsherds, worked flints and three cow's feet. Finally, a small mound capped by flint nodules was built covering all these deposits.

The primary container at Fussell's Lodge was at one stage set within an enclosure defined by timber posts like those at Nutbane and Worbarrow. It was 50 metres long and was later used as the framework for the building of a massive cairn framed by side ditches. Before the middle of the fourth millennium, such larger mounded structures began to predominate, and many more of them were built with stone components. Chambers placed integrally within the stone structures were used in a similar way to the earlier timber containers.

At Hazleton North in the Gloucestershire Cotswolds, a completely excavated barrow is one of a pair sited only 100 metres apart. It was constructed in a single episode, and was roughly rectangular in shape. The mound was built using stone rubble from adjacent quarries, and was contained within drystone walls. Its wider western end had projecting 'horns', defining a forecourt area. Stone-lined chambers that occupied only a fraction of the mounded area were set midway along each long side, with entrances that could be walled up.[36]

As such, the Hazleton North barrow shared features with hundreds of other mounds built in earth or in stone across Britain in the fourth millennium. The most frequent orientation was, however, towards the east. The Cotswolds has a particularly high concentration of these tombs, some of which reached massive proportions [6].[37]

Chambers were often built with access from the centre of the forecourt. Here, rites could be enacted that perhaps concerned communication with and propitiation of the spirits of the departed [7].[38] An association between feasting and death is well documented in ethnography. Rites

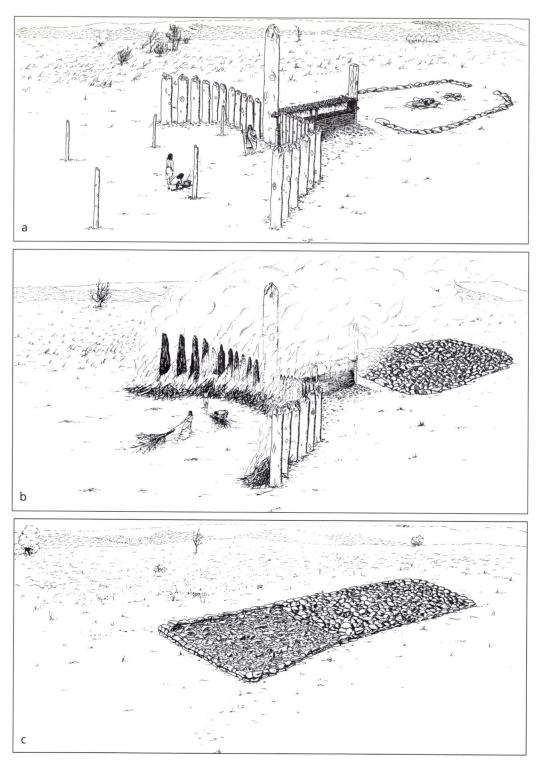

5] Street House mortuary structure, Cleveland: (a) as originally constructed; (b) as later fired, and (c) closed as a stone cairn. The chamber, roofed and walled in timber, the facade and the forecourt, are typical of the earliest mortuary structures. Dramatic acts of closure and monumental cairns lent the sites an ancestral finality and permanence.

6] The long barrow at Belas Knap, Gloucestershire. Partial reconstruction has restored the scale and impact of the mound as originally built. Here the forecourt had a mock entrance only, and chambers were located in the long sides, as at Hazleton nearby. Its prominent Cotswolds ridge-top setting is also apparent.

right 7] Central facade entrance into the passage and chambers of Stoney Littleton long barrow, Somerset. A prominent limestone slab announces a built entrance, as elsewhere including drystone walling. The western jamb features a slab set intentionally to give prominence to a fossil ammonite, perhaps, as in some traditional societies, used to symbolise eternity.

of transition, incorporation and commemoration included the consumption of animals and other foodstuffs, and the votive destruction of objects. Areas of burning, and pits and deposits containing food remains and pottery, often occur both in barrow forecourts and in their flanking ditches.

At Hazleton, the earlier interments in the chambers had been rearranged, with skulls and long-bones stacked against the side walls. A skeleton was found near the entrance to the north chamber, placed on top of a flexed burial. Ashes from a cremated body had then been sprinkled over these corpses. This shows the variety of rite that could occur, and mirrors a cremation scattered over burials at West Kennett in Wiltshire. Skulls and long-bones were also underrepresented at West Kennett, suggesting again use in rites elsewhere. The importance of access to chambers, and of limiting such access, is clear at sites such as Windmill Tump, Rodmarton, also in Gloucestershire. Here, steps leading into one chamber and a blocked 'port-hole' for another indicate an anticipated passage of bones to and from the tomb.[39] Different arrangements of chambers may moreover have represented different traditions of access and expression of social relations.[40]

The question has often been asked as to why, in the fourth millennium, such investment was made in the building of these tombs. One answer offered is that they served as territorial markers. This is too simple. They may have arisen as a means of stating ancestral links monumentally, and may also reflect a growing intricacy and formality of oral traditions. These might include traditions of descent, or of belief, or of social obligations marked by duties of labour.[41]

The burial already mentioned that was inserted last into the northern chamber at Hazleton North was found, unusually for such tombs, with 'grave goods' [plate 1].[42] These were curious gifts for the dead, since one was an incompletely used flint core, to the right of the corpse, and the other, a hammerstone placed by the left hand. It may be that there was a deliberate association intended here, and already indicated by a frequent coincidence of piles of knapped flint and mortuary sites, between flint-knapping and death. Could not the burial of an adult but not elderly man 'in the act' of knapping itself have constituted a metaphor for death in the midst of life? Such a notion is reinforced by the fact that the nodule itself was only half-knapped.[43]

Another frequent association in the burial of human remains by Neolithic communities is between human and cattle bones. The 'bundles' in causewayed-enclosure ditches involved deliberate selections and associations of body-parts 'representing' people and cows. At some barrows cattle bones replaced human bones as the cardinal deposits, as at Beckhampton Road in Wiltshire, a late monument. At other sites, cow heads and hooves were matched by human skulls and long-bones in symbolic correspondence.

In some writings about Neolithic death the interment of the bones of groups of people has been contrasted with individual burials.[44] The latter were once thought to have coincided with a change from long to round barrows in the Bronze Age. We now know that round barrows were constructed throughout the Neolithic period, and that they did not just cover individual burials. A dramatic example of the contrary was the discovery of the bones of between 28 and 44 people within a boat-shaped chamber underneath The Soldier's Grave round barrow at Frocester in Gloucestershire.[45] Moreover, both inhumation and cremation took place beneath round barrows, as at Whiteleaf in the Chilterns, and in the cemeteries under barrows and within circular ditched enclosures at Dorchester-on-Thames.

Placing of the dead in separate but successive pits and graves in such mounds, as at Duggleby Howe in Yorkshire, may represent a dynastic sequence. Burial of the corpses of younger men in the fill of the grave pits of elders at this site and others could itself have been used to symbolise generational succession.[46] Several individual burials with fine grave goods and under oval mounds early in the third millennium were of men, while individual burials under round barrows were often women.

An even more difficult problem than why long barrows with their massive proportions, side ditches and elaborate forecourts were built is why they went out of use. The Hazleton sequence showed that this could happen at an early point in time. Well before the end of the fourth millennium, many chambers had been carefully blocked and facades closed off. Could this have represented a conceptual and physical distancing of the ancestors and collective burial from the living? That this happened at an early stage in some areas has also been taken to mean that the importance of monumental forms, and of a particular view of the ancestors as a source of legitimacy for land tenure, declined rapidly.[47]

There is therefore some room for debate over how long it was before new monumental forms emerged as a focus for ritual activity. Most recognisable among these new forms are those that have been termed 'henge monuments', and appropriately Stonehenge is among the places where the earliest stages in their development have been traced. These were circular or oval enclosures defined by banks that stood outside, but mirrored, the arc of ditches from which their material was dug. The crucial definition was of a central area within which activities could be focused. This may have been associated with the elaboration of processions to the focal area, for which timber avenues were sometimes built.

Such sites developed in parallel with enclosed cremation cemeteries like those at Fordington Farm in Dorset. However, the central areas of the larger sites contained structures with elaborate circular or oval settings of concentric rings of posts. While the ditches remained areas for interment of bones or ashes, increasingly such deposits were integrated with the timber structures, as at Overton Down and Woodhenge in Wiltshire.

In some cases cremation burials and inhumations occurred after the dismantling of the timber structures. At Stonehenge (a variant form of such sites) a ring of posts had been removed, and mortuary deposits placed among soil filling the holes. At Maumbury in Dorset, still more complex events unfolded [8].[48] Use of later Neolithic enclosures for such elaborate ritual represents a link with the earlier practices that took place within the ditches of causewayed enclosures.

The above account has hardly touched upon the causes of death among Neolithic people. This is in part because when people die through ageing or by sudden systemic illness it is nearly always impossible to detect the cause from their skeletons. We do know, however, that many Neolithic individuals, and particularly males, suffered from knocks and injuries which broke bones that successfully

8] Maumbury Rings, Dorset: H. St George Gray's excavations of late Neolithic ritual shafts. Two series of deposits filled these 12-metre deep shafts within the henge. The lower contained pottery, with bones of domestic cattle and pigs. The upper 4 metres included human bones, red deer antlers and bones, and much struck flint.

healed. Equally, many suffered considerable degenerative disease, such as osteoarthritis. The weakening caused by damage and disease, and doubtless by periodic malnutrition, must have accounted for substantial numbers of 'premature' deaths from viral infections such as the case of poliomyelitis recorded from a skeleton at Cissbury, Sussex.[49]

The dead were not only 'placed' in the landscape as dead bodies or excarnated bones. Some people died traumatically and were left where they were killed. An example is that of a young adult male apparently shot with an arrow in the back while carrying an infant, coincidentally with signs of attack and destruction by fire, at the Stepleton enclosure on Hambledon Hill.[50] One category not so far represented in the British evidence is that of sacrificial deaths, such as those of Neolithic date from Sigersdal in Sweden. Nonetheless, the practice of trephination, which involved the cutting out of a hole across the skull of a living person, was not necessarily a hapless attempt at brain surgery as sometimes supposed.

A vivid image of death in the later Neolithic period, certainly from around 2500 BC, is provided by flexed burials accompanied by a distinctive pottery beaker as the single or principal object buried with the corpse. The suddenness of the appearance of such beakers has led to the idea that a major influx of immigrants occurred, appropriately named the 'Beaker People'. Migration was certainly a factor, and some beakers are found in areas away from earlier monuments. Elsewhere, there was in contrast a deliberate location of burials with beakers in close association with earlier burials and monuments. While such placings could be read as 'legitimation' of an intrusive element, they could equally have signified a pattern of continuing reference.[51]

Among the more elaborate burials, wooden mortuary chambers have been found, as at Fordington Farm in Dorset, and Hemp Knoll, Wiltshire. However, stone chambers similar to the earlier long barrows made a reappearance, especially in the north and west, in a strangely altered form as a stone-lined box interred below ground, and sealed following interment. Moreover, these boxes often contained burials of selected bones, and of the products of cremation, together with beakers, or one or other of a limited range of other items. Continuity of symbolic practices is certainly therefore attested. This is underlined by the presence in some graves of cattle parts, and the activity of flint knapping on and around the barrows.

'Heroic' death: life and lineage in the Bronze Age

The presence of steps within grave pits, traces of wooden biers and coffins, and evidence for furs and hides, give an impression of the ceremony with which early Bronze Age funerals were sometimes conducted. As in the Neolithic period, feasting and offerings often accompanied funeral rites. At Irthlingborough in Northamptonshire, another wooden chamber contained a richly adorned Beaker burial. Stones had been piled on top of the chamber, and over this were stacked cow bones and the skulls of at least 184 young cattle.

Many such burials appear to have emphasised a male-oriented concern with the representation of warfare (in weaponry), with alcohol (drinking vessels) and with bodily ornamentation that was echoed across contemporary Europe. In England, this was first noticeable in the male Beaker graves that contained not only the beaker itself but also quivers of arrows with finely worked flint arrowheads, stone wristguards, hair and clothing ornaments, and (by the start of the second millennium) also copper and bronze daggers in fine sheaths [9].[52]

Martial associations became more pronounced in the richer graves through time, culminating in the so-called 'Wessex' grave series of c. 2000–1600 BC. Batons with perforated carved-stone 'mace-heads', larger-bladed and finer bronze daggers with richly worked handles and pommels, and gold sheetwork on wood formers attached to clothing, were added to the display repertoire [10].[53] Slightly later,

9] Beaker grave group from a cist burial beneath a round barrow: Driffield, Yorkshire. The body, wrapped in a linen shroud, had two amber buttons near its neck. The stone wristguard with gold-capped rivets was found on the right forearm. The copper dagger was behind the back and the beaker behind the legs.

pins, oval-shaped razors and bone and metal tweezers appear in such 'display' graves. In a grave at Winterslow in Wiltshire, human eyebrow-shavings were found. Such materials indicate a concern to celebrate in death an ethic of warrior beauty in life that we know best from 'Homeric' literature. The elaborate dressing of the richer burials is mirrored in the complex arrangement of the burial location, as at the famous Bush Barrow site near Stonehenge [10] and [plate 2].[54]

Such an ethic, then, transcended mere demonstration of wealth and 'power', but represented also ideals of conduct.[55] Handled cups in exotic materials such as shale, gold and amber perhaps made reference back to beakers, just as the stone baton heads echoed the finely polished and shaped axeheads of the third millennium. The presence of tiny pottery 'accessory cups' in burials reflects a more general miniaturisation of items (except daggers and clothing) included as grave goods in these display burials. Exactly why this occurred needs to receive closer attention from prehistorians.

Nor was such display limited to male burials and martial themes. Not all such burials are securely identified as those of men, and some of the larger barrows had female burials at their centre.[56] Among the most vivid expressions of dress display are the jet and amber multiple strand necklaces with spacer-plates from several elaborate burials of women.

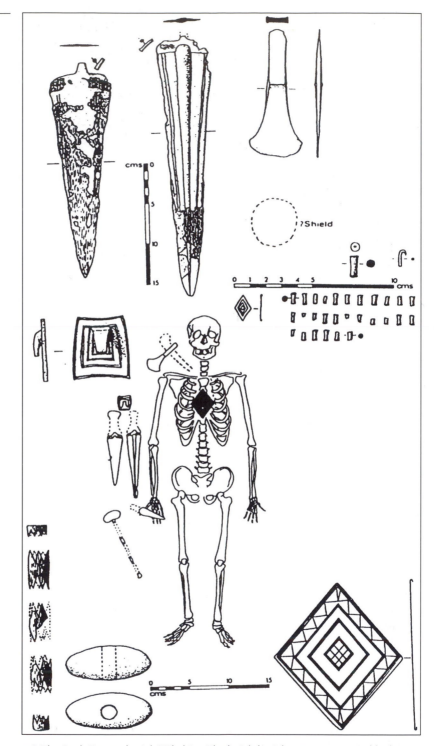

10] The Bush Barrow burial, Wiltshire. The lavish burial was accompanied by bronze and copper daggers (with elaborate pommels and in leather sheaths), a bronze axe, and three gold plaques. The 'shield' was more likely a leather helmet; the stone mace-head and bone mounts more probably represented two leadership staffs.

Cremation and the burial of cremated remains became more common from the start of the second millennium. The act of cremation may itself have been an occasion for display. At Bromfield in Shropshire and Lockington in Derbyshire, the pyre was located in the same spot as the subsequent barrow. Finds of badly damaged bronzework and other objects near the sites of pyres suggest that much material wealth could have been destroyed in the process.[57]

An association of heroic life and death with especially powerful places could also have figured in Bronze Age mortuary activity. Besides the prominent siting of burial mounds, the deposition also occurs of single cremations in rock faces, as at the Dewerstone, Dartmoor, where a small late Bronze Age urn was wedged in a crevice of a granite crag. Such locations featured wide views, and this practice is echoed in the borderlands of Wales, where an urn with cremation was placed within a spine of rock at Fan-y-Big, near the crest of the Brecon Beacons.[58]

Despite the prominence of warriors and heroes in elaborate funerary display, the societies in question also had more subtle concerns. For instance, it seems that viewing of the corpse itself in a mortuary house or on a bier was an important element in some of these rituals. Beaker burial may have followed specific codes that enabled particular identities to be understood during the mortuary rites.[59] Choices about inclusion or exclusion of different objects in the grave may have been dictated by strategies for the negotiation of social statuses.[60] They might alternatively indicate belief in a destination for the dead, beyond life and in a higher-order 'paradise' of idealised social relations. In such a situation, the 'seeing' of included objects need not have been a human one.

Simpler flexed inhumations placed in small pits or stone cists represented a more standard 'formula' for burials in the earlier second millennium. Due to the greater numbers of the formally buried and cremated dead excavated, views on demography and pathology have been expressed more confidently for this than for other periods. Given the number of finds of bones from caves and other places in the landscape, however, the formal burials are unlikely to be representative of the numbers of deaths.

Studies of grave orientation, positioning of bodies, their gender and artefact associations can nonetheless produce significant insights. An example is an analysis of 636 Yorkshire burials with either Beakers or Food Vessels (a later style of urn that was often a container for ashes). It was the norm in Beaker graves for males to be placed with their heads to the east, on their left sides. Females had heads placed westwards and were laid on their right sides. In over 80 per cent of Beaker graves, the corpses therefore faced southwards. Interestingly, however, the richer and more complex ones contradicted this norm. Among Food Vessel burials up to half of the total faced north, while later graves containing developed daggers followed the general Beaker pattern, facing southwards.[61] Such positionings contrast markedly with those in Wessex, where males were most often placed with heads to the north, and females to the south, with equal numbers of each gender facing either east or west.

Beaker burials in many cases formed a nucleus for later burials that developed sequentially upwards or outwards from them. Indeed, from around 2500 BC, for the next thousand years, the digging of a burial pit, or the laying out of a flat inhumation, seems often to have been the founding event that initiated long sequences of interments and cremation deposits.

Circular ditches dug with such burials at their centre served to highlight such a focus, as did circles of wooden stakes or poles. There followed the piling of upcast earth over the burials, the stacking of turves, and the laying of clay, chalk, flint or stone cappings. The mounds then provided the site for the digging of pits for further deposits of cremated ashes. Such barrows are sometimes found to have been enlarged or redefined by repeated digging of encircling ditches. These may have been cut in rapid succession, recalling traditions of the Serer people of Senegal, where successive age grades (generations of men initiated into adulthood) dug ditches at the same burial site to pile earth over each interment.[62]

Contrasting patterns for the accumulation of burials from 'founding' mortuary deposits also occurred. At Barrow Hills near Abingdon, Oxfordshire, an arc of Beaker burials was carefully transected by a line of cremation pits containing Collared Urns, while a linear sequence of barrows was constructed north-eastwards along a ridge away from this early series. This 'attraction' of later burials to earlier ones is also demonstrated at Ewanrigg, Cumbria, where a central cremation cist was surrounded by a circle of later cremations.[63] How the location of such burials was marked is not known, since only a small proportion was apparently covered by barrows.

Linearity and grouping in these round-barrow cemeteries provide potentially significant implications for descent among long-localised communities. The observation of sequences of interment and building can reveal traditions of practice. In Yorkshire, the orientation of a 'founder' burial could determine that of subsequent ones, contrary to later norms for burial orientation.[64]

A series of interments in barrows at Net Down and Rolleston Down near Shrewton in Wiltshire may embody oral traditions concerning lines of descent expressed through the cumulative formation of cemeteries.[65] Here a memorised 'code' seems to have operated, both in burial rite and in styles of construction of barrows in rows. A commemorated status for older males was also contrasted with a more anonymous one for associated burial of youths, a practice that echoes Neolithic shaft burials.

As the second millennium BC progressed, a shift became evident to more permanent settlements, with compounds containing groups of circular huts. This was accompanied by the construction of boundaries that defined field-like enclosures and in some areas divided up large tracts of land. At the same time urn-cremation cemeteries appeared alongside settlements. There are indications that unurned cremations also continued, with deposition in bags or other organic containers inserted into shallow pits.

The urn cemeteries occurred mostly without mounds to mark their presence. The urns were interred in pits, and were either inverted or placed the 'right' way up. The earliest cemeteries of this kind often contained elaborate and sometimes large vessels reminiscent of late Neolithic styles of pottery. However, by *c*. 1400 BC these had given way to plainer types.[66] Individual pots of these later types have often been found to have been poorly fired, suggesting that they were made hurriedly and in less than ideal conditions, purposely to act as containers for burial deposits.

The pits found at these sometimes extensive cremation cemeteries were often clustered in groups, as at Ardleigh in Essex, Coneygre Farm, Nottinghamshire, and Pasture Lodge Farm in Lincolnshire. These clusters – again often featuring a 'central' burial – were first interpreted as representing different peoples, and more recently have been seen as reflecting kin groups. However, the complexity of the pattern of burials, that sometimes include small deposits also of unburnt bone, hints that complicated mortuary selection may have been enacted.

The close inter-relation of houses and cemeteries appears to be a novel feature of the middle Bronze Age. The best-known sites are those such as Itford Hill in Sussex and South Lodge, Rushmore, Dorset. Excavations at the latter site, and at Down Farm in the vicinity, have shown how sequences of burial established an 'axis' that determined the placing of subsequent burials. Settlement may have gravitated towards earlier burial grounds representing an established 'ancestral' presence in the landscape.[67] The proximity of enclosed settlement 'compounds' to such cemeteries is certainly a marked feature of this period, with intervals of less than 100 metres between them.

The idea that burial was by this time regarded as something integral with the community is reinforced by such discoveries as that of a house with burial inserted into its central hearth at Trethellan Farm, Newquay, in Cornwall. The choice of location for this burial in a house central to a group of four such houses underlines its focal nature [11].[68] It is as if the house itself was regarded as a 'living' entity, a view consonant with ethnography. If so, the closing act for another such house at a settlement site near St Columb Major could be especially significant. A spear apparently thrown into its ashes might have constituted the ritualised 'killing' of the house itself.[69]

Moreover, it has also been proposed that the 'dialogue' between burial and settlements was represented symbolically. One idea is that urns were inverted in pits containing cremation deposits because such circular 'roofed structures' represented the containment of the ashes of the dead within a symbolic 'home',[70] an idea further explored in Chapter 3 (see p. 81). If this seems far-fetched, less so are links noted

11] Trethellan Farm, Newquay, Cornwall: Reconstruction by Rosemary Robertson of House 2222. A growing association is noticeable between settlements and death in the Bronze Age. This is dramatically illustrated in the burial of a young adult male beneath the central hearth of this structure at the core of the settlement.

between houses and contemporary circular mortuary enclosures (the ditched areas of barrows and flat burial grounds). In each case, there is a tendency for entrances to be facing southwards, and for ritual activity to be focused by the entrance area. Indeed, metalwork finds more normally buried actually with the deceased have in several instances been located buried in that part of a building or settlement enclosure 'facing' the nearby cemetery.[71]

After 1000 BC, urn cemeteries began to fall out of use. For several centuries, until inhumation cemeteries became common again towards the later Iron Age, there is an absence of any formal burial rite. It may be that the deposition of many bodies followed the same route as that of prestige metalwork, being placed in watery locations. This could be borne out by the many finds of human skulls close to finds of metalwork that have been discovered in the Thames and other rivers.[72]

The association of human bone with deposits specifically of weaponry in hoards parallels the rare finds of burials with spearheads lodged

12] Later Bronze Age male burial with a bronze spearhead found embedded in its spine: West Littleton Down, Tormarton, Gloucestershire. Warfare in the later Bronze Age is attested by defensive enclosures, and by direct evidence of violent death. The remains of two young men with spinal and pelvic wounds were found interred here.

in them, indicating the prevalence of warfare, and the continuing existence of a warrior ethos. An example is the two skeletons found hastily buried at Tormarton, Gloucestershire, one of which has a spearhead in its vertebrae [12].[73]

A more frequent occurrence, however, is of finds of individual bones in settlements. Here, they occur most often in 'liminal' locations, near entrances and in boundary ditches.[74] This coincides with a trend towards better defined and often defended settlements, for the first time since the early Neolithic period. Display is also likely to have been important at such settlements. This is reflected in the finds of human skulls in locations close to entrances as at Breedon-on-the-Hill in Leicestershire: perhaps indicating that human heads had been mounted on the gateways.

Death before the Iron Age

It can be questioned whether there really was a dramatic change in the third millennium from a focus on the collectivity of the ancestors to individual leaders. While the ownership of 'ancestral matter' implies reference collectively to 'the ancestors', specific people are also often recognised for their ancestral role in lineage succession. Prehistorians have envisaged a shift away from an active deployment of 'ancestral' legitimation after the Neolithic. However, this may be simply because they have treated as stark alternatives two contrasting attitudes to ancestors that may have varied in relative significance in different societies at different times in their histories.

Convenient though this may be in narrative terms, therefore, I believe that a model of such evolutionary change masks more than it reveals. What was more likely at any one time was a diversity of thought about death and the ancestors, and indeed the holding of mutually contradictory views by the same people, in different contexts. That is to say, at any given point, the dead could have comprised 'ancestors' as a collectivity, individual ancestors ('heroes', or 'heroines', gift-givers, dynasts) and recent relatives.

The existence of individual graves in areas such as the Yorkshire Wolds and the Thames valley, where contemporary 'collective' tombs were also in use, appears to emphasise such plurality of concepts. It might be observed, too, that the dead also included enemies, and any potentially disruptive or inconvenient community members that the living might rather have forgotten. They were deliberately not housed or commemorated, but their existence was sometimes just as influential in the consciousness of their descendants.

We have seen that a more radical distinction may perhaps be drawn between an era of physical separation of the dead from the realm of the living and one in which they existed integrally together, a theme which recurs in several later chapters of this book. This is thought to have happened not at the divide between the Neolithic and the Bronze Age, but rather during the middle Bronze Age, perhaps between *c.* 1400 and 1200 BC, when the landscape underwent considerable redefinition, and settlements and field systems made a widespread appearance. The main problem with accepting the reality of such a dramatic change at present is the uncertainty that continues over the location of residence in earlier periods.

Again, a concern with 'housing' the dead appears to characterise some attitudes to death throughout these millennia, albeit with contrasting emphases. A more subtle series of contrasts appear to be those between formal burial places and the inclusion of part-deposits of human remains in a wide variety of places in the landscape. Rather than an ancestral connection concerned with land tenure, this may accord more with active linkage to the divine presences that permeated the land.

Meanwhile, some specific practices may reflect consistently held beliefs. One such practice noted severally here is the flint-knapping that seems to have been associated with mortuary activity. Another may be the way that both cattle and hide preparation are invoked in mortuary rites.[75] Such circumstances merit further archaeological study in the future.

As with many of the transitions we have considered above, that between the 'Bronze Age' and a succeeding 'Iron' one can have had little perceptible lived reality across the generations concerned. Exceptions will have existed where the use of iron by migrating peoples coincided with other innovative cultural practices. Bronze continued in

plate 1] The so-called 'flint-knapper burial' in the north entrance at Hazleton North long cairn, Gloucestershire. Three radiocarbon dates from the thigh bones of this 30–45 year old man point to a year close to 3620 BC as the time of his death. This probably coincided with the final use of the structure.

plate 2] Reconstructed ceremonies at the primary burial at Bush Barrow on Salisbury Plain near Stonehenge, *c*. 1600 BC. The corpse was laid on the ground surface, on its back. The circle of wooden stakes is documented from many such sites, while the cattle sacrifices are attested at barrows such as Irthlingborough, Northamptonshire.

use, and probably for a wider variety of objects than it had been before. It has also been noted that excarnation makes a reappearance in early Iron Age death rituals, and flexed inhumations may also indicate some continuity of practice.[76]

This raises questions relevant to all predocumentary societies, concerning memory and tradition. The prehistoric practices traceable archaeologically may have served to reinforce oral literature and prevalent myths. How then did traditions concerning death and burial ever change? If the past existed as a resource, it was one that could be represented differently according to transformations in social or political circumstances and under different cultural influences.

The degree of 'unbrokenness' of tradition is perhaps less important here than the realisation of connectedness of people with place, through burial in the landscape, across up to three millennia. In the areas of Britain not substantially resettled in the first millennium AD, the landscape was very closely 'peopled', with traditional namings of landscape features. Embedded within these namings were remembered histories of relations between resident communities. To illustrate this point, I have chosen to end the chapter with a poem. This is one of a small number of *Englynion y Beddau*, literally 'The Stanzas of the Graves', that found their way, however altered in form, into the written records of medieval Wales from oral traditions of unknown antiquity.[77] They represent a recording of the associations that accumulated around the ubiquitous burial mounds of the Welsh hills. No doubt these links were replayed and sometimes transformed. What is especially interesting about this one is the remembered, or attributed, lineage of Cynon.

Bet gur gwaud urtin in uchel tytin.
  inifel gwelitin.
  bet Kynon mab clytno idin.

(The grave of a man
  of high renown
  lies on a lofty height
  in low
  last repose,
  the grave of Cynon
  the son of Clydno Eiddin.)[78]

Notes

In all references, place of publication is London unless otherwise stated. I wish to record my thanks to John Barrett, Andrew Chamberlain and Julian Thomas for their comments on the content of this chapter.
1 R. Leakey, *The Origin of Humankind* (1994), pp. 153–4.
2 For example, for Africa, H. Abrahamsson, *The Origins of Death: Studies in African Mythology*, Studia Ethnographica Upsaliensia 3 (Uppsala, 1951).
3 Papers in A. Boddington, A. N. Garland and R. C. Janaway (eds), *Death, Decay and Reconstruction: Approaches to Archaeology and Forensic Science* (Manchester, 1987), consider aspects of such study. See also A. Chamberlain, *Human Remains*

(1994), and C. Roberts and K. Manchester, *The Archaeology of Disease*, 2nd edn (Stroud, 1995).

4 See J. Chapman, 'The living, the dead and the ancestors: time, life-cycles and the mortuary domain in later European prehistory', in J. Davies (ed.), *Ritual and Remembrance: Responses to Death in Human Societies* (Sheffield, 1994), pp. 40–85.

5 Recent examples are: T. Earle, *How Chiefs Come to Power* (Stanford, 1997): see especially pp. 158–69; and P. K. Wason, *The Archaeology of Rank* (Cambridge, 1994): see pp. 67–71, where the author lists seventeen ways in which he claims relative rank can be gauged from mortuary evidence.

6 For example, M. Shanks and C. Tilley, 'Ideology, symbolic power and ritual communication: a reinterpretation of Neolithic mortuary practices', in I. Hodder (ed.), *Symbolic and Structural Archaeology* (Cambridge, 1982), pp. 129–54.

7 A perspective elaborated in J. Barrett, *Fragments from Antiquity: An Archaeology of Social Life in Britain, 2900–1200 BC* (Oxford, 1994).

8 Recent accounts of these transitions, from differing perspectives, include: M. Parker Pearson, *Bronze Age Britain* (1993); C. Gosden, *Social Being and Time* (Oxford, 1994); and R. Bradley, *The Significance of Monuments: On the Shaping of Human Experience in Neolithic and Bronze Age Europe* (1998).

9 An account of the Wayland's Smithy excavation was published in A. Whittle et al., 'Wayland's Smithy, Oxfordshire: excavations at the Neolithic tomb in 1962–63 by R. J. C. Atkinson and S. Piggott', *Proceedings of the Prehistoric Society*, 57: 2 (1991), 61–101.

10 R. Huntington, 'Death and the social order: Bara funeral customs (Madagascar)', *African Studies*, 32: 2 (1973), 65–84.

11 As suggested in, for example, Shanks and Tilley, 'Ideology, symbolic power and ritual communication'.

12 These processes were evident in Robert Hertz's 1907 ethnography of double burial and formulated by Arnold Van Gennep in 1909. See R. Hertz, 'A contribution to the study of the collective representation of death', in R. Needham and C. Needham, *Death and the Right Hand* (New York, 1960); and A. Van Gennep, *The Rites of Passage*, trans. M. B. Vizedom and G. L. Caffee (1960).

13 Described by Van Gennep, *Rites of Passage*.

14 See K. Ray, 'Material metaphor, social interaction and historical reconstructions: exploring patterns of association and symbolism in the Igbo Uwu corpus', in I. Hodder (ed.), *The Archaeology of Contextual Meanings* (Cambridge, 1987), pp. 66–77.

15 N. Barley, *Dancing on the Grave: Encounters with Death* (1995).

16 N. Barley, 'The Dowayo dance of death', in S. C. Humphreys and H. King (eds), *Mortality and Immortality: The Anthropology and Archaeology of Death* (New York, 1981), pp. 149–60.

17 P. Metcalf and R. Huntington (eds), *Celebrations of Death: The Anthropology of Mortuary Ritual*, 2nd edn (Cambridge, 1991), p. 13.

18 From George Caitlin, *North American Indians*, ed. P. Matthiessen (1989), p. 85.

19 M. Pitts and M. Roberts, *Fairweather Eden* (1995).

20 See N. Barton, *Stone Age Britain* (1997), pp. 51–70.

21 C. B. Stringer, 'The British fossil hominid record', in S. N. Colcutt (ed.), *The Palaeolithic of Britain and Its Nearest Neighbours: Recent Trends* (Sheffield, 1986), pp. 59–61.

22 I am grateful to M. Bishop of Torquay Natural History Society Museum for this information; see also R. E. M. Hedges, R. A. Housley, I. A. Law and C. R. Bronk, 'Radiocarbon dates from the Oxford AMS system: *Archaeometry* Datelist 9', *Archaeometry*, 31: 2 (1989), 207–34.

23 See Barton, *Stone Age Britain*, for Dolni Vestonice and other European sites.

24 N. Barton, 'The lateglacial colonisation of Britain', in J. Hunter and I. Ralston (eds), *The Archaeology of Britain* (1999), pp. 13–24.

25 This evidence is summarised most recently in Bradley, *The Significance of Monuments*, pp. 22–30.

26 As vividly described in R. J. Mercer, 'Hambledon Hill, Dorset, England', in C. Burgess et al. (eds), *Enclosures and Defences in the Neolithic of Western Europe*,

(British Archaeological Reports, International Series 403, Oxford, 1988), pp. 89–109.

27 T. Darvill, *Prehistoric Britain* (1987), p. 62, Fig. 29. Some of the bones have been found on microscopic examination by J. McKinley to bear cut-marks, suggesting that 'assisted excarnation' had been practised. See R. Mercer and F. Healey, *Hambledon Hill, Dorset. Excavation and Survey of a Neolithic Monument Complex and its Landscape, 1974–86*, English Heritage Archaeological Monograph (forthcoming).

28 J. Thomas, *Time, Culture and Identity: An Interpretive Archaeology* (1996), pp. 174–5.

29 The Ebbsfleet ceramic associations at Church Cave reinforce such a view: *ibid.*, p. 177.

30 As noted in E. C. Curwen, *The Archaeology of Sussex* (1954), pp. 109–11.

31 Varied views on the existence and form of Neolithic dwellings are given in the contributions to T. Darvill and J. Thomas, *Neolithic Houses in Northwest Europe and Beyond*, Oxbow Monograph 57 (Oxford, 1996).

32 This account is drawn from P. Shand and I. Hodder, 'Haddenham', *Current Archaeology*, 118 (1990), 339–42.

33 For Fussell's Lodge, see P. Ashbee, 'Fussell's Lodge long barrow excavations, 1957', *Archaeologia*, 100 (1966), 1–80. For Whitwell, J. Hedges *et al.*, 'Radiocarbon dates from the Oxford AMS System: Archaeometry Datelist 18', *Archaeometry*, 36 (1994), 337–74.

34 From B. Vyner, 'The excavation of a Neolithic cairn at Street House, Loftus, Cleveland', *Proceedings of the Prehistoric Society*, 50 (1994), 151–95; middle reconstruction courtesy of Blaise Vyner, 1999.

35 For comparative plans and sequences of these and other examples, see I. Kinnes, *Non-Megalithic Long Barrows and Allied Structures in the British Neolithic*, British Museum Occasional Publication 52 (1992).

36 A. Saville, *Hazleton North, Gloucestershire, 1979–82: The Excavation of a Neolithic Long Cairn of the Cotswold–Severn Group*, Historic Buildings and Monuments Commission for England, Archaeological Report 13 (1990).

37 See T. C. Darvill, *The Megalithic Chambered Tombs of the Cotswold – Severn Region* (Highworth, 1982).

38 As at Stoney Littleton, Somerset. See M. Sharp, *A Land of Gods and Giants* (1989), pp. 46–7.

39 Early photographs showing these features revealed by excavation can be found in G. Clark, *Prehistoric England* (1941), plates 85 and 86.

40 J. Thomas, 'The social significance of Cotswold–Severn burial rites', *Man*, n.s., 23 (1988), 540–59.

41 Chapman, 'The living, the dead and the ancestors', pp. 44–5.

42 See Saville, *Hazleton North, Gloucestershire*, p. 25.

43 The idea for the latter 'reinforcement' I owe to Andrew Chamberlain.

44 Both as a contrast within that period and with succeeding ones; as in Darvill, *Prehistoric Britain*; Parker Pearson, *Bronze Age Britain*; and Barrett, *Fragments from Antiquity*. Views nonetheless differ as to the significance of the contrast, and the reasons for it.

45 For 'The Soldier's Grave' barrow, see T. Darvill, *Prehistoric Gloucestershire* (Gloucester, 1987), p. 74.

46 For a vivid account of this sequence, see A. Burl, *Rites of the Gods* (1981), p. 143. See also, I. T. Kinnes, T. Schadla-Hall, P. Chadwick and P. Dean, 'Duggleby Howe reconsidered', *Archaeological Journal*, 140 (1983), 83–108.

47 See, for example, I. J. Thorpe and C. Richards, 'The decline of ritual authority and the introduction of beakers into Britain', in R. Bradley and J. Gardiner (eds), *Neolithic Studies: A Review of Some Current Research*, British Archaeological Reports 133 (Oxford, 1984), pp. 67–84. Barrett, *Fragments from Antiquity*, pp. 61–7, sees the contrast arising more from differences in the manipulation of genealogy at different times.

48 See Fig. 8 for details. An original photograph indicates, with its included wooden ladder, something of the enormity of the shafts.

49 Noted in Roberts and Manchester, *The Archaeology of Disease*.

50 Found in the debris of the fired rampart. See Mercer, 'Hambledon Hill'. In the course of the recent publication project, the skeleton of a second young man has been found with a spinal injury also caused by an arrow wound. Moreover, many of the leaf-shaped arrowheads found in long barrows have broken tips, and it is therefore likely that some of them entered these contexts embedded in bodies.

51 A contrary view is outlined in J. Thomas, *Rethinking the Neolithic* (Cambridge, 1991). There, Beakers are seen to have been used specifically to disrupt accustomed codes of practice (see pp. 129–38).

52 For example, the grave assemblage from Driffield. See D. V. Clarke, T. G. Cowie and A. Foxon, *Symbols of Power at the Time of Stonehenge* (Edinburgh, 1985), Fig. 4.15, p. 93.

53 Items from the Bush Barrow burial, Normanton Down, Wiltshire, were reassembled to their projected original positions of entombment in a drawing from C. B. Burgess, *The Age of Stonehenge* (1980), Fig. 3.4.

54 The cover illustration, Parker Pearson, *Bronze Age Britain*, reproduced here, provides a reconstruction of events here.

55 P. Traherne, 'The warrior's beauty: the masculine body and self-identity in Bronze-Age Europe', *Journal of European Archaeology*, 3:1 (1995), 105–44.

56 A fact first noted by P. Ashbee in his *The Bronze Age Barrow in Britain* (1960), pp. 170–1.

57 The potential information from pyre sites and cremation debris that finds its way into burial deposits is discussed in J. McKinley, 'Bronze Age "barrows" and funerary rules and rituals of cremation', *Proceedings of the Prehistoric Society*, 63 (1997), 129–45.

58 Dewerstone vessel: Crow's Buttress, Dewerstone, Meavy, Devon (SX541639). Plymouth Museum cat. 60.13.2; see also, J. Barber in *Reports and Transactions of the Devonshire Association*, 92 (1960), 78–9. Fan-y-Big cremation vessel: C. S. Briggs, W. J. Britnell, and A. Gibson, 'Two cordoned urns from Fan-y-Big, Brecon Beacons, Powys', *Proceedings of the Prehistoric Society*, 56 (1990), 173–8.

59 While at the same time the paraphernalia associated with it 'would become an axis for the symbolic integration of the key productive and reproductive practices of the community'. J. Thomas, 'Reading the body: Beaker funerary practice in Britain', in P. Garwood *et al.* (eds) *Sacred and Profane* (Oxford, 1991), pp. 33–42.

60 Barrett, *Fragments from Antiquity*, pp. 63–5.

61 See A. Tuckwell, 'Patterns of burial orientation in the round barrows of East Yorkshire', *Bulletin of the Institute of Archaeology, University of London*, 12 (1975), 95–123.

62 This tradition was recorded by Professor Alain Gallay of the University of Geneva during an excavation project in 1980 (personal communication, 1981).

63 Ewanrigg: R. H. Bewley, I. H. Congworth, S. Browne, J. P. Huntley and G. Varndell, 'Excavation of a Bronze Age cemetery at Ewanrigg, Marypert, Cumbria', *Proceedings of the Prehistoric Society*, 58 (1992), 325–54.

64 Tuckwell, 'Patterns of burial orientation'.

65 A possibility explored in K. Mizoguchi, 'A historigraphy of a linear barrow cemetery', *Archaeological Review from Cambridge*, 11:1 (1992), 39–49. A detailed description recaptures something of the texture and variety of the original rituals: C. Green and S. Rollo-Smith, 'The excavation of eighteen round barrows near Shrewton, Wiltshire', *Proceedings of the Prehistoric Society*, 50 (1984), 255–318. Ashbee, in *The Bronze Age Barrow*, envisaged the items buried in the individual graves of such cemeteries as reflecting the changing fortunes of the kingroup through time (p. 174).

66 A process described in Burgess, *The Age of Stonehenge*, pp. 80–98.

67 Barrett, *Fragments from Antiquity*, pp. 145–51.

68 J. A. Nowakowski, 'Trethellan Farm, Newquay: excavation of a lowland Bronze Age settlement and Iron Age cemetery', *Cornish Archaeology*, 30 (1991): reprint p. 46; Fig. 18.

69 The excavator, Jacky Nowakowski, interpreted the discovery of the spearhead as representing a deliberate symbolic termination of the use of the structure. See also Chapman, 'The living, the dead and the ancestors', pp. 53 ff., for a parallel example of the 'killing' of Koros-period houses in Hungary.
70 C. Lynn, 'House-urns in Ireland?', *Ulster Journal of Archaeology*, 56 (1993), 70–7.
71 Bradley, *The Significance of Monuments*.
72 See R. Bradley and K. Gordon, 'Human skulls from the River Thames, their dating and significance', *Antiquity*, 62 (1988), 503–9.
73 Darvill, *Prehistoric Britain*, p. 129, Fig. 74.
74 Documented in J. Brück, 'A place for the dead: the role of human remains in late Bronze Age Britain', *Proceedings of the Prehistoric Society*, 61 (1995), 245–77.
75 See M. E. Robertson-Mackay, 'A "head and hooves" burial beneath a round barrow', *Proceedings of the Prehistoric Society*, 46 (1980), 123–76, for an initial discussion of this association.
76 A view developed by G. Carr and C. Knusel, in A. Gwilt and C. Haselgrove (eds), *Reconstructing Iron Age Societies*, Oxbow Monographs 71 (Oxford, 1997).
77 M. Stephens (ed.), *The Oxford Companion to the Literature of Wales* (Oxford, 1986), p. 179.
78 The medieval Welsh is reproduced here as Diplomatic text, that is, as a direct transliteration from the original. The text is that of a transcription by J. Gwenogvryn Evans and G. Jones in an edition of 1899. The translation reproduced here is from M. Pennar, *The Black Book of Carmarthen* (Lampeter, 1989), pp. 100–3.

Select bibliography

Barrett, J., *Fragments from Antiquity: An Archaeology of Social Life in Britain, 2900–1200 BC*, Oxford, 1994.
——, Bradley, R., and Green, M., *Landscape, Monuments and Society: The Prehistory of Cranborne Chase*, Cambridge, 1991.
Barton, N., *Stone Age Britain*, 1997.
Boddington, A., Garland, A. N., and Janaway, R. C. (eds), *Death, Decay and Reconstruction: Approaches to Archaeology and Forensic Science*, Manchester, 1987.
Bradley, R., *The Significance of Monuments: On the Shaping of Human Experience in Neolithic and Bronze Age Europe*, 1998.
Burgess, C., *The Age of Stonehenge*, 1980.
Chapman, J., 'The living, the dead and the ancestors: time, life-cycles and the mortuary domain in later European prehistory', in J. Davies (ed.), *Ritual and Remembrance: Responses to Death in Human Societies*, Sheffield, 1994, pp. 40–85.
Green, C., and Rollo-Smith, S., 'The excavation of eighteen round barrows near Shrewton, Wiltshire', *Proceedings of the Prehistoric Society*, 50 (1984), 255–318.
Kinnes, I., *Non-Megalithic Long Barrows and Allied Structures in the British Neolithic*, British Museum Occasional Paper 52, 1992.
Metcalf, P., and Huntington, R. (eds), *Celebrations of Death: The Anthropology of Mortuary Ritual*, 2nd edn, Cambridge, 1991.
Parker Pearson, M., *Bronze Age Britain*, 1993.
Saville, A., *Hazleton North, Gloucestershire, 1979–82: The Excavation of a Neolithic Long Cairn of the Cotswold–Severn Group*, Historic Buildings and Monuments Commission for England, Archaeological Report 13, 1990.
Thomas, J., 'Reading the body: Beaker funerary practice in Britain', in P. Garwood, D. Jennings, R. Skeates and J. Toms (eds), *Sacred and Profane*, Oxford University Committee for Archaeology Monograph 32, Oxford, 1991, pp. 33–42.
——*Understanding the Neolithic: A Revised Second Edition of Rethinking the Neolithic*, Cambridge, 1999.

The Iron and Roman Ages:
c. 600 BC to AD 400

British or Roman?

Who the first inhabitants of Britain were, whether natives or immigrants, is open to question: one must remember we are dealing with barbarians. But their physical characteristics vary, and the variation is suggestive. The reddish hair and large limbs of the Caledonians proclaim a German origin; the swarthy faces of the Silures, the tendency of their hair to curl, and the fact that Spain lies opposite, all lead one to believe that Spaniards crossed in ancient times and occupied that part of the country.[1]

Tacitus, writing at the end of the first century AD, on the subject of Roman involvement in the province named Britannia, tried to characterise the inhabitants of the island. He noted differences in physical characteristics; it was difficult to define the average Briton. Tacitus explained aspects such as variation in hair colour and stature in terms of invasion; the different regions of Britain had seen influxes of people from various parts of the continent. We may doubt the veracity of Tacitus' claims, and in fairness he admits both to uncertainty about who first occupied the island and to the impact on physical characteristics of alternative factors such as climate. The degree to which invasion or population movements affected Britain during the first millennium BC still remains unclear. Britain's island status, however, in itself is not a reason for doubting mobility. The Iron Age was not a period of isolation from the rest of Europe. Cultural similarities between mainland Europe and Britain suggest, if not population movements, at the very least contact and interaction. It is the extent and nature of that interaction which it is difficult to reconstruct, although we can say that it was not uniform across the British isles; southern England, for example, was more open to influences from Gaul and the south than was the north of England. So any attempt to generalise or to provide a simple description of the quintessential Englishmen of the Iron Age is thwarted.

If the invasions of the first millennium BC remain speculative, the invasion of Britain by Rome in the first century AD is well documented. It is no more straightforward, however, to define and characterise the

Briton of the Roman age than of the Iron Age. The extent of native interaction with Rome is difficult to gauge; it may have differed dramatically by region, economic status and time. There are also difficulties in defining the term Roman. Many of the troops who arrived in Britain in AD 43 and thereafter were not from Rome or even Italy. The army was recruited from across the empire and although all were united behind the standards of Rome their experiences of and interpretations of being Roman may have varied enormously. What it was to be a Roman in Britain could be as subjective and individualised as what it was to be a Briton. And such variety must have affected death as much as life.

The missing dead: Iron Age cemeteries

Paradoxically, despite the substantial evidence for the lives of the people of the pre-Roman British Isles, there is little evidence as to how they died.[2] There is a general absence of known Iron Age burial sites although comparatively recent scholarship has led to the identification of certain regional burial trends. Nevertheless the evidence still remains relatively limited especially when compared to continental Iron Age communities. This raises questions as to how the dead of the Iron Age were disposed of in Britain especially during the early and middle years of the period.

For the first part of the first millennium BC the evidence is at its most minimal and the identification of recurrent or distinctive burial practices is almost impossible. A few limited observations about burial rites can be made although we have to be wary of asserting these to be the normal patterns of behaviour across the island. Cremation rites are reasonably well attested from the seventh to the fifth centuries BC although definitive and close dating often remains problematic. The ashes, occasionally placed in urns, were buried in cemeteries which sometimes developed at sites of older barrows. Some of these cremations were also placed under barrows although these were generally much smaller than those of the Bronze Age. Cemeteries of small groups of barrows have been found at, for example, Ampleforth Moor in Yorkshire.[3] Other isolated barrow burials have been found across the south of England. By the fifth century BC some distinctive inhumation burial forms were emerging. The trend towards inhumation is best represented by the cist burials of south-west England and the Arras culture burials in Yorkshire (see pp. 43–5). In many areas of Britain, however, little evidence for careful and organised disposal of the dead exists for any period of the Iron Age.

One common discovery which may be indicative of opportune use of available space for burial rather than the utilisation of specifically prepared graves is the burial of bodies and isolated bones at settlement sites, in places such as storage pits, ditches and postholes (see Chapter I).[4] At Maiden Castle in Dorset, for example, a crouched female burial

13] Pit burial from Maiden Castle, Dorset. The female body was placed, in a crouched position, in an abandoned storage pit during the middle Iron Age.

was discovered in an abandoned storage pit [13]. It is possible that such settlement-based burials fulfilled some sort of ritual purpose. This explanation appears particularly suited to those human remains which have been discovered deliberately placed beneath buildings and ramparts.[5] But such site-based interments can account for only a minority of the population and some areas produce no traces of human remains at all.[6] How the dead bodies of the majority of the population were disposed of remains a mystery. Explanations can be suggested but it is difficult to find detailed corroborating evidence. The discovery of arms and weapons in rivers has led to the suggestion that some cremated remains of the earlier years of the Iron Age may have been scattered on water accompanied by the equipment and accoutrements of the dead (see Chapter 1).[7] Another possible explanation, which could account for the low occurrence of human remains and the lack of cemeteries, particularly in the south-east of England, is that the bodies of the dead were exposed.[8] Direct evidence for this is unlikely to survive but the theory would explain the unearthing of isolated human bones (see Chapter 1). Skull fragments, in particular, are common discoveries and may have been retained for ritual purposes after exposure or received special treatment as did the isolated skull buried at Danebury [14].[9]

The low level of burial remains from Iron Age Britain leaves a gap in our knowledge since how people treat their dead can reveal a good deal about living society. Skeletal remains are indicative of how people died, the state of their diet and health; how the corpse is treated may suggest religious beliefs or reveal further aspects of the rituals associated with death.[10] Cemetery populations can also provide a means for accessing social structure. Varied burial rites may indicate or reflect the

14] Skull burial from Danebury, Hants. The skull appears to have received special treatment by being buried separately. The fate of the rest of the body is unknown.

social hierarchy or divisions based on age, gender and status (see Chapter 1).[11] Yet to state what it is difficult or problematic to achieve with the evidence from Iron Age Britain creates perhaps an unnecessarily negative picture. For the Iron Age it is still possible to identify certain significant features within the British burial record, not least of which are regional and chronological variations. The inhabitants of Iron Age Britain were not a homogenous mass, across space and time. Nor were their burials.

Cists, carts and warriors

One of the most striking archaeological finds of the Iron Age in Britain is the group of burials centred on Arras in Yorkshire and hence known as the Arras culture. These burials, dating from the fourth to the first centuries BC, illustrate well the important role that mortuary evidence can play, since the graves are among the few surviving traces of the Iron Age community in this part of the country. A significant feature of the burials of the Arras culture was the construction of earth mounds over north-oriented crouched inhumation burials. Some of these small barrows were clustered together to form substantial cemeteries. At Wetwang Slack, Burton Fleming and Danes Graves there are several hundred graves and barrows. The majority of the barrows were surrounded by circular ditches but in some cemeteries distinctive rectangular ditches were employed.[12] In general few grave goods are associated with these graves but in several cases exceptional grave assemblages have been found. These rich inhumation burials included the remains

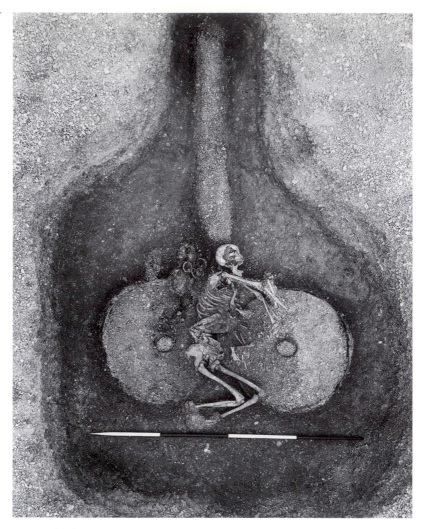

15] Burial 2 from Wetwang Slack. The grave included the remains of wheels from a cart. Behind the head and shoulders of the skeleton were found an iron pin, a mirror, two horse bits and a bronze case with a chain attached. Pork bones were also located in the grave.

of cart wheels and horses' harnesses.[13] The so-called 'King's barrow' at Arras covered a circular grave pit in which had been placed a single inhumation and the bodies of two horses. The wheels of a cart had been removed and were placed against each of the horses while the various pieces of the harness had been placed in the western half of the grave. Two pig's heads had been positioned close to the head of the corpse.[14] In 1984 three cart burials were discovered at Wetwang Slack. The second of these burials [15] included not only the wheels of the cart and the horse's harness but also a mirror, a decorated bronze box and pork bones.[15] Cart burials are unusual elsewhere in Britain although several graves provide evidence for the inclusion of horses within the grave. At Mildenhall, Suffolk, the remains of an inhumed body was found with a sword, axe and a gold torc and flanked by the skeletons of two horses, although no cart fittings were found.[16] The significance of the distinctive cart burials and rectangular enclosures centred on the Arras area remains unclear. Parallels are found on the continent and it seems probable that the rite spread from there to Yorkshire. The mechanism of diffusion, however, is not known. Was there a large movement of people from one area to another; or was a small but influential group involved; or did the details of the rites reach Yorkshire through other means such as trade or a mobile elite?[17]

Another distinctive burial rite also associated with inhumation is the occurrence of cist burials. Such inhumations, which involved the placing of human remains in stone lined cists, have been found in the north and west of England but are more widespread in the south-west. Substantial cemeteries are known from Devon and Cornwall although unfortunately their excavation during the nineteenth century led to inadequate recording of cemetery layout and organisation. General features can, however, still be noted. The bodies, in a crouched position, were placed in graves lined with stone slabs. Sometimes the graves appear to have been arranged in rows. Grave goods mainly consisted of items of personal ornament and were not particularly rich which in itself may suggest a degree of stability and continuity for the communities represented.[18] This impression is reinforced by the chronological distribution. Although precise dating for the cist cemeteries is problematic they appear to have originated from as early as the fourth century BC and to have continued in use to the first century BC.[19] All these features are well illustrated by the cist cemetery at Harlyn Bay, Cornwall. Excavations at the beginning of the twentieth century revealed more than 130 individual inhumations in a cemetery located on a gentle valley slope little more than 200 metres from the present sea shore [16]. The majority of the bodies were placed in graves lined and covered with flat slabs of slate. The excavation records and plans are limited but it appears that the graves were arranged in rows with the heads of the bodies oriented to the north.[20]

The cist burials of the south-west and the northern graves of the Arras culture represent the most comprehensive evidence for the cemeteries of the Iron Age. Towards the end of the period, however, some rich individual burials took place which were not confined to one geographical area. Distinctive among these are male inhumations accompanied by swords and weapons which are sometimes termed 'warrior graves'. These mainly date to the first century BC. At Owlesbury in Hampshire a body was interred with a long iron sword in a sheath and a spear which had been broken in two, while the remains of a bronze boss suggest that the body may have originally been covered by a shield [17].[21] A few rich graves containing mirrors, beads and other ornaments have been interpreted as a high-status female equivalent to the warrior graves.[22]

45

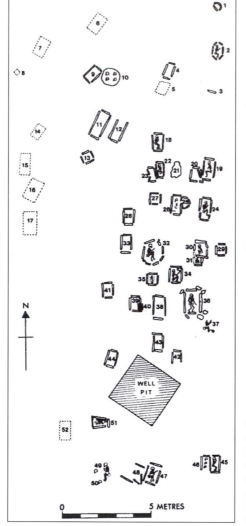

left 16] Harlyn Bay cist cemetery, Cornwall. Plan of burials excavated in 1900. The majority of bodies were placed in graves lined and covered with slabs of slate. Further excavations in the period 1901–5 revealed a total of over 130 individual inhumations.

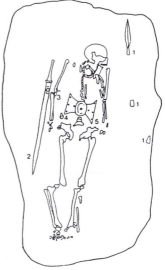

17] 'Warrior' grave from Owlesbury, Hampshire. The body was interred with a broken spear (1); a long iron sword in a sheath (2); bronze rings from a sword belt (3); a silver-bronze belt hook (4), and a bronze shield boss (5).

Cist, cart and warrior graves, however unusual or isolated their discovery, reveal that in some respects Iron Age Britain does provide a wealth of burial evidence. The difficulty for the archaeologist is how to relate this evidence to the wider picture. What do these rites reveal about both Iron Age British communities and Britain's interaction with the continent? Are the distinctive rites indicative of population movements, emulation and competition or increasing levels of social organisation and differentiation? One thing is clear. Whatever the source and reasons for their adoption, the rites were modified and adapted to meet local requirements, taking on their own colour and significance. A key feature is the repeated burial of bodies in a crouched position with the head to the north; this trait unites inhumation burials across England and appears to be unique to the island.[23]

Death, religion and the afterlife in the Iron Age

In the search to categorise graves and find inter-relationships between Iron Age communities there is a danger of overlooking the emotional, spiritual and religious elements of death. On the other hand, religion can all too easily become a catch-all explanation for aspects of funerary ritual which otherwise cannot be fully understood. It is tempting, for example, to relate changes in burial rites, such as a shift from cremating to inhuming the corpse, to changes in religious belief. But such a connection is almost impossible to prove. The truth is that the graves themselves directly tell us little about how the Iron Age inhabitants reacted or coped with the fact of their own mortality; or what they felt occurred to the individual after death; or any changes in such beliefs across time. Many graves contained grave goods such as jewellery or weapons or what appear to be offerings to the dead such as joints of meat. This is suggestive of some basic belief in an afterlife, the deceased's need for certain objects and even the affection of the survivors. But we know little about what dictated the choice of items included and their full significance to both the deceased and the survivors.[24] We should also note that the inclusion of precious items in the grave would have had more impact upon the living than the dead. The placement of the grave goods may have served to articulate not only the status of the deceased but also the status of the survivors as the international comparisons in Chapter 1 suggest.

Literary evidence, admittedly much of it Roman in origin and date, does attribute a belief in an afterlife to Iron Age populations. Julius Caesar, for example, suggests that the Druids believed that the soul did not die but passed to another body.[25] Much attention focuses on the Druids, experts in religious ritual. Julius Caesar argued that Druidic religion originated in Britain.[26] Yet the surviving accounts of both its practices and practitioners provide generalised accounts of the Druids and thus it is hard to judge geographic specificity in much of what is said and its applicability to the Britain of the late Iron Age. Besides it was often the more extreme elements of native practices which captured the attention of ancient commentators. Graphic accounts of human sacrifice, for example, were designed to shock the reader and to emphasise the sophistication of Roman society compared to the barbaric practices of her neighbours.[27] The belief that such practices occurred in Britain is suggested by Tacitus' account of the Roman battle for Anglesey (known as Mona).

> Suetonius [the Roman commander] garrisoned the conquered island. The graves devoted to Mona's barbarous superstitions he demolished. For it was their religion to drench their altars in the blood of prisoners and consult their gods by means of human entrails.[28]

It is tempting to dismiss the report by Tacitus as little more than an exaggerated view. The discoveries at Lindow Moss in the 1980s brought, however, new life and significance to such stories. The well-preserved

18] Lindow Man. The well-preserved body was found in a peat bog at Lindow Moss. The exact cause of death and precise dating remain disputed.

body of Lindow man was discovered in a peat bog [18]. He appeared to be the victim of a ritual sacrifice which had occurred in the years immediately before or immediately after the Roman invasion.[29] After a last meal which had contained the pollen of mistletoe[30] – a plant sacred to the Druids – he had been 'triple killed' by garrotting, bludgeoning and the slitting of his throat.[31] Lindow man captured the popular imagination – he literally gave a face to the Iron Age and provided insights into fascinating aspects of ritual behaviour. The interpretation is not without controversy. The dating of the body has proved difficult. Radiocarbon dating suggests a range of c. 300 BC to AD 400 but it is possible that the body may be substantially later.[32] The sacrifice theory is also disputed; the practicalities of executing and burying a body in a bog have been raised and it is possible that the body's injuries occurred postmortem. Maybe Lindow man met his death by accidentally falling into the bog.[33] If his injuries are accepted as the cause of death Lindow man may have been a victim of a mugging or a random killing rather than of an organised sacrifice. The debate continues over whether, as one author has put it, Lindow man fell or was pushed.

An age of transition?

In many areas of Britain inhumation may have remained the basic method of burial up to the time of the Roman invasion. For the immediate pre-Roman period there is some evidence of greater organisation of burials within defined cemetery areas. In Dorset the local tribe which had previously disposed of its dead in a seemingly invisible fashion began to inhume its dead in defined cemeteries.[34] At Maiden Castle, for example, a series of inhumation burials was found to the south of the main entrance gate which appears to represent a section of a well-ordered burial ground. A second major burial ground was found close to the eastern entrance and involved the shallow graves of thirty-eight adults. Sword cuts and other injuries to the skeletons [19] suggest

19] Iron sword head in a backbone, Maiden Castle, Dorset. Thirty-eight shallow graves were found to the east of the main entrance. Many of the skeletons had injuries of a violent nature which has led to the suggestion that the graves may contain the victims of a possible Roman attack.

that the dead may have been victims of the Roman attack and capture of Maiden Castle in AD 44. Despite these circumstances the bodies were still buried with a degree of care and according to local funerary customs.[35]

The development of defined cemeteries was most marked in the south-east where there was also a shift towards cremation from the mid-first century BC. The cremated remains were often placed in pottery vessels and buried in clearly demarcated cemetery areas. The quantity and quality of the grave goods placed with the dead varied greatly, suggesting that the graves were being used to articulate social differences. In Essex and Hertfordshire a series of very rich graves has been excavated which included large quantities of amphorae or jars for wine storage and imported Roman goods. A particularly striking example was discovered at Welwyn Garden City in a small cemetery of about a dozen graves. The cremated remains were those of a man aged about thirty-five who had been wearing a bear skin. The grave also included five wine amphorae, a bronze Campanian pan, a silver cup of Italian origin, coloured-glass gaming beads and an iron object which may have been the boss of a shield [20].[36] The introduction of cremation cemeteries to the south-east could be interpreted as indicative of an influx of population since parallel cemeteries are found on the continent. The inclusion of objects of Italian origin in the graves, however, is telling. Julius Caesar's temporary invasions of southern England during the mid-first century BC underlined the proximity and might of the Roman presence. The first century BC was a time of transition for the south-east in particular; settlements were growing, coinage was adopted and trade was increasing. The move to cremation may have been part of this package of change which preceded the Roman invasion even if the influences

20] Grave from Welwyn Garden City (reconstructed). The grave contained five wine amphorae and numerous other vessels including a bronze Campanian pan and a silver cup of Italian origin. Coloured-glass gaming beads and an iron object which may have been the boss of a shield were also present. The cremated remains were those of a man. Among the preserved bones was a paw and finger of a brown bear, suggesting that the deceased had been wearing a bear skin.

were derived from neighbouring provinces rather than directly from Rome and Italy.[37]

In those areas of Britain where cremation and burial in a defined cemetery area were already the norm, the impact on mortuary customs of the Roman invasion of AD 43 was not great. At the King Harry Lane cemetery at Verulamium (St Albans), for example, the excavated graves have been dated from AD 1–60. Roman objects were present in graves both before and after the conquest and the Roman arrival brought no immediate change to the burial rites.[38] Although in some areas, especially rural ones, the inhumation of the dead may have continued to be the standard practice, during the first century AD the cremation rite did become more widespread in Britain.[39] The question is whether this process was as a result of or was accelerated by the Roman presence, specifically through the role of the army and colonists.[40] Did cremation become a symbol of conquest utilised only by those who were outsiders in the province or those who assimilated to Roman ways? And if so for how long did such a distinction persist? Or was cremation adopted by all regardless of background?

On one level the diffusion of the cremation rite could be seen as part of the Roman package which went with the toga, baths and Latin. The

Romano-British cremation cemeteries which developed in association with Roman colonies and settlements shared certain features. The cemeteries were extra-mural and often focused on major roads. At these cemeteries the corpse was cremated on a pyre and the remaining bones were gathered and placed most often in a pottery vessel although glass and wooden containers could be used.[41] The container was buried and the grave might be furnished with additional items such as pottery, lamps and personal ornaments.[42] Yet in describing such cemeteries as Roman it needs to be remembered that cremation, the urned burial of cremated remains and the provision of grave goods had been practised in some parts of England before the advent of the Romans and may have spread with or without their agency. Sharp distinctions between native practices on the one hand and Roman ones on the other may not be sustainable.

The overall impact of the Roman presence upon both the life and the death of the Britons is hard to gauge, as mapping the spread of cremation and exploring its underlying significance illustrates. Death and burial become related to wider questions concerning the adoption of Roman cultural practices by native populations. Did the inhabitants begin to dispose of their dead according to Roman religious customs; did they employ Roman-style funerals and methods of commemoration? The answer to such questions is obscured by several factors. The evidence may be substantial compared to the Iron Age but it must represent only a small proportion of the burial population for the Roman period. In addition the geographic distribution of this evidence is uneven since the majority of the graves are located in the south-east; there is also a marked urban over rural bias; and a chronological concentration of excavated cemeteries in the fourth century AD, that is to say in the late rather than the early Roman period.[43] Above all, to know what changed with the Roman arrival requires accurate knowledge of what preceded it, when details of native pre-Roman beliefs and practices are at best patchy. Further we would need to define what the Roman way of death entailed. Herein lies one of the greatest difficulties – the empire was so diverse and people's experiences of and interpretation of Rome so varied that it is almost impossible to provide a definitive account of Roman funerary customs.

Roman tombstones

One possible gauge of the potential Romanisation of British death practices is the tombstone. The marking of graves during the Iron Age had not been uncommon. Barrows or mounds of earth provided a visually striking indication of a grave site. The construction of barrows persisted after the invasion, especially in the south of England where they were used to mark rich cremation graves.[44] In the Roman context these mounds may, however, have gained a new significance. On the one hand the mounds could be interpreted as a native tradition but on the

21] Mausoleum of Augustus, Rome. The circular ruin planted with trees was originally dressed in limestone and surmounted by an earth mound. It was constructed by the first Roman emperor, Augustus, who died AD 14.

other the appearance of the mounds resembled tomb types which were fashionable in Rome among the elite during the first century AD. Note, for example, the mausoleum of the emperor Augustus which was a substantial round structure modelled on the Etruscan tumulus [21]. Thus the reaction to the British mounds may have differed; to the native population the mounds may have suggested that the elite were maintaining indigenous practices while to the Roman conquerors it may have appeared that the elite were emulating Roman traditions.[45]

No such ambiguity, at least in terms of appearance, surrounded the creation of stone funerary monuments inscribed with Latin epitaphs. The Romans, themselves, did not invent the tombstone; in design and format Roman tombstones owed much to Greek and Etruscan antecedents. But nevertheless, for the western provinces of the Roman empire, the introduction of stone monuments with distinctive Latin epitaphs coincided with the arrival of Roman influence. These monuments varied in style and shape and were decorated with sculptural themes which reflected the eclectic nature of Roman culture.[46] Many of the surviving Romano-British tombstones are stelae. These are blocks of stone taller than they are wide which resemble modern headstones. A fine example is the tombstone set up in Colchester to the centurion Marcus Favonius Facilis during the early years of the Roman presence [plate 3]. The Latin epitaph was complemented by a detailed full-figure portrait of the deceased. As a Roman symbol tombstones such as this, and the extent of their adoption by the native population, are often viewed as a gauge of the penetration of Roman culture and the acceptance of Roman customs.

There are several hundred tombstones of Roman date surviving from Britain. In comparison to other provinces this number is not great. Many individual settlements of the German provinces, for example, produce as many tombstones as survive from the whole of Britain.[47] The low occurrence of tombstones within Britain has been interpreted as an indication that the Britons remained un-Romanised although the frequently poor quality of British stone and the vagaries of survival have also been noted.[48] It does seem that tombstone production never really caught on in Britain but this in itself may not be an indicator that the natives were un-Romanised. The fact that few stone memorials were associated with the elite – a group who would be expected to be most familiar with Roman culture – suggests that tombstones may simply have had little significance to the populace, Romanised or not. Intriguingly the surviving tombstones are mainly of those who can in some respects be classed as outsiders. The earliest examples were associated with the army. Soldiers, recruited from across the empire, arrived in Britain during the first century AD. The tombstones they set up and were commemorated by celebrated both the Roman and military identity of the dead and thus contrasted their status and skills with those of the native population. The tombstone of Marcus Favonius Facilis illustrates this well [**plate 3**]. Another fine example survives from Cirencester, which was erected to an auxiliary cavalryman during the first century AD [**22**]. The detailed relief carving shows the horseman about to spear a prostrate barbarian beneath the horse's feet.[49] The Latin epitaph is full of standard military details on the career of the dead man, Dannicus, such as his unit and his years of service. It is notable that Dannicus was a member of a German tribe and his single name suggests that he was not a Roman citizen; it was standard military practice to recruit auxiliary units from the provinces. The tombstone with its Latin epitaph and military decor lays claim to Roman identity when Dannicus was neither Italian nor a Roman citizen. Ironically not so long ago Dannicus or his immediate ancestors may have been the enemy beneath the horse's feet.[50]

Many of the tombstones which survive from Roman Britain stress this sense of mixed or confused identity. Those commemorated and their commemorators are using the tombstones as a symbol of Roman identity but in the process they reveal that this identity is uncertain and might have been questioned or challenged by others. A striking example is the tombstone which commemorates Regina at South Shields [**23**].[51] The picture portrays Regina as a dignified and well-to-do Roman matron. The epitaph, however, captures her mixed status. Regina was a former slave and her husband and former owner was from Palmyra (in present-day Syria) and did not hold Roman citizenship. The sculptural image echoes these diverse influences since elements of the design are reminiscent of tombstones found in Palmyra and the Regina tombstone may even have been carved by a Palmyrene.[52] The epitaph concludes not in Latin but in Palmyrene. This highly unusual bilingual inscription

22] Tombstone of Dannicus, Cirencester. The sculpture depicts a horseman with a spear riding down a fallen barbarian. The epitaph reads: 'Dannicus a horseman of the Cavalry Regiment Indiana of the troop of Albanus, served 16 years a tribesman of Rauricus [a German tribe], lies here. Fulvius Natalis and Flavius Bitucus set this up according to the will.'

right 23] Tombstone of Regina, South Shields. The sculpture depicts a seated female figure with a distaff and spindle in her lap. At her left side is a wool basket and with her right hand she opens a jewellery box. The epitaph reads: 'To the spirits of the departed Regina. Barates of Palmyra set this up to his freedwoman [a former slave] and wife, a Catuvellaunian by tribe, aged thirty. [In Palmyrene beneath] Regina, the freedwoman of Barate, alas.'

stresses the complex status of Regina who was a British slave who married her Palmyrene master and was commemorated by a Roman-style tombstone which was perhaps executed by a Palmyrene hand. Roman customs could clearly exist alongside British and even Palmyrene ones!

The general lack of British tombstones does not necessarily suggest a rejection of Roman ways, rather that the specific form had little relevance. Tombstones were often associated with those who were in some ways different from the mass of the population, such as soldiers and foreigners, and the tombstones communicated this sense of difference. The majority of the population probably felt secure in their identities;

they knew who and what they were and where they belonged; what we cannot know is whether they regarded themselves as British, Roman or neither.

Cremation to inhumation

During the second century AD a gradual but nevertheless dramatic change in burial rites pervaded the Roman empire.[53] Inhumation replaced cremation as the normal method of disposing of the dead. The change is well attested in Britain. At the Trentholme Drive cemetery at York, for example, the earliest burials, dating to the early second century AD, were cremations. Inhumation appeared by the mid-second century and dominated by the late third century.[54] In the intervening period the two rites co-existed. This shift would seem to emphasise that Britain was indeed part of the wider empire in terms of its burial traditions and that even in the far reaches of the kingdom changes were felt. Yet why this change occurred and where it emanated from is poorly understood. The traditional explanation that the shift to inhumation was caused by altering religious beliefs including the spread of Christianity, which placed new emphasis on the afterlife and resurrection, is now felt to be inadequate. There are obvious flaws in this theory, in particular the fact that the ancients themselves did not associate the change with religion, that many sarcophagi had little religious symbolism in their decor and that cremation was not incompatible with the majority of the new beliefs.[55] The vagaries of fashion were probably more influential than any deep-rooted religious associations. The reasons for the change, whether religion, philosophy or fashion, are less important than the fact that the change spread. Communities across the empire emulated what was happening elsewhere and took up the new form of disposing of the dead. Inhumation united the empire at a time when it was coming under increasing threat and on the point of disintegration.[56]

The shift to inhumation affected both the appearance and organisation of the cemetery. Bodies were placed on their backs in an extended position. This contrasted with the native British tradition of crouched inhumation (see p. 46) which may have persisted in some areas until this time. This is not to say that all British inhumation cemeteries were now the same. At York the Trentholme Drive cemetery was characterised by the cutting of inhumation graves into earlier burials. By contrast at other York cemeteries the inhumations were cut in an orderly fashion which respected earlier burials.[57] How is this difference to be explained? Could it indicate variations in attitudes to death and the dead or the operation of differing funerary rituals? Or does it suggest that within the community of Roman York differing social groups, however these were defined, were using different cemeteries?

Within inhumation cemeteries many bodies were buried in wooden coffins although often all that now survives of these containers are a few nails. At Trentholme Drive, York, for example, 2,300 nails were

24] Sarcophagus of Flavius Bellator, York. The lid and front of the sarcophagus survive. It contained a skeleton and a gold ring. The epitaph reads: 'To the spirits of the departed Flavius Bellator a decurion of the colony of York who lived 28 years . . .' (Thereafter the inscription is damaged.)

found, suggesting that many of the inhumations had originally been coffined.[58] Lead containers which could be decorated with simple designs were also widely used although these may have been originally protected by outer wooden shells.[59] Stone sarcophagi were employed at some Roman settlements. A sarcophagus weighing more than 2 tonnes which had been hollowed out of a single block of stone was excavated at Trentholme Drive.[60] Other sarcophagi, especially those which were inscribed or decorated, may have been left on the ground, possibly within mausolea. Sarcophagi would have been expensive items and those inscribed with Latin epitaphs often record people of wealth and status such as the decurion or town councillor, Flavius Bellator, from York [24].[61] Romano-British sarcophagi were not, however, richly decorated with relief sculpture depicting, for example, mythological scenes of the kind which were commonplace elsewhere in the empire.

The rite of inhumation is less destructive than cremation and thus inhumed remains provide more scope for skeletal analysis and demographic assertions. It is rare, however, for large numbers of bodies to be excavated from one site and, even when this is the case, relating the data to a living population is problematic. At Trentholme Drive, York, the remains of more than 400 bodies, most of which had been inhumed, were excavated. An unexplained high ratio of male to female remains suggests, however, that the cemetery as excavated does not represent a cross-section of the populace. It would be misleading to use the available data to assert, for example, average age at death for the living population. Nevertheless the studies of the remains are suggestive of general aspects of the life and health of the people buried. At Trentholme Drive it was possible to identify individuals who had suffered from arthritis, which was common in the over-thirties, or who had suffered broken limbs.[62] In most cases it is not possible to detect the actual cause of death. At the late Roman cemetery at Poundbury, Dorset, however, the discovery of a female skeleton interred with the skeleton of a full-term foetus suggests death in childbirth.[63] Skeletal variations may also indicate ethnic origins and techniques to measure the lead levels in bones have also been employed to establish region of origin. This method identified as Greek the remains of a young man buried at Poundbury.[64]

Death, religion and the afterlife in the Roman period

Religious change has been dismissed as the underlying motive behind the shift from cremation to inhumation. Indeed in many respects it is difficult to relate Roman burial practices to religion. There is little in the surviving tombstones, for example, whether in their images or in their language, which suggests religious affiliation or strong belief. The emphasis most often falls on the status achieved in life rather than contemplation of what lay beyond the grave. Many epitaphs do begin with the invocation to *Dis Manibus* which, roughly translated, means 'to the spirits of the dead'. But it remains unclear as to what was meant by these 'spirits'. The oft repeated formula may have been employed with scant regard for its meaning just as contemporary epitaphs so often begin with 'In loving memory' regardless of whether the expression is appropriate or not. Death to the Romans often appears to have been viewed as a practical problem rather than a spiritual one. Death was a potential cause of pollution from which the living had to be protected.[65] The law was employed to separate the living and the dead; cemeteries had to be situated outside towns and settlements; the dead had to be disposed of both decently and effectively; and those employed to handle the corpse, undertakers and body collectors, were isolated from others.[66] But pollution can be spiritual as well as physical and often it is impossible to separate the two. Undertakers may have been regarded as untouchable not just because they might be harbingers of disease but also because they were seen in some ways as spiritually dangerous.

Roman beliefs about the fate of the soul and the afterlife are difficult to characterise simply or succinctly. The options available ranged from well-developed beliefs about the nature of the world hereafter to the complete annihilation of the soul or spirit.[67] Intellectual explorations and discussions survive but these often represent an elite and public perspective and thus tell us little about what the majority of the population may or may not have believed or how such beliefs may have changed across time. Customs apparent from both literature and the archaeological record suggest, however, that the belief in an afterlife, even if vaguely conceived, could be active. At the deathbed, custom demanded that a relative kiss the deceased to capture the soul; the provision of grave goods and offering of wine and food at the grave suggest that the dead were regarded as needing sustenance; festivals were held annually to placate the spirits of the dead; tombs could take on the appearance of houses and be referred to as homes for the dead.[68]

25] Libation grave, Caerleon. The lead canister, containing the cremated remains of the deceased, was placed in a grave lined with slabs of slate. A lead libation pipe connected the grave to the ground surface.

There is a danger, however, when drawing upon diverse sources, of creating a composite picture which may never actually have been true of any specific time or place. It has to be acknowledged that throughout the empire there were considerable variations in funerary customs and beliefs about the afterlife, depending on local traditions. In England there may also have been differences between regions which originated in localised Iron Age customs. The survival of native religion and belief systems may have been all-important. Roman religion was itself fairly flexible and many pre-Roman gods of Britain were simply assimilated with Roman ones; the goddess Sulis associated with the hot springs of Bath, for example, was identified with the Roman goddess Minerva.[69] A dialogue between Roman and native cultures may often have existed and the resulting customs and beliefs were hybrids rather than either simply Roman or native. Indeed things might be given a Roman veneer but this did not necessarily mean that underlying beliefs had changed.

In terms of physical burial evidence a high degree of unity appears to have developed between Britain and the empire although it is difficult to infer ritual actions and associated beliefs from this material. Evidence suggests, for example, that Romano-British graves could have been tended and that offerings were made to the dead. At Caerleon in South Wales a cremation grave was excavated complete with a lead pipe which connected the ashes to the ground surface [25]. This pipe has been interpreted as a libation tube down which offerings of wine could be poured. Parallels for such libation tubes can be found in the cemeteries of Rome and Italy.[70] Many Romano-British graves also contained grave goods – lamps, jewellery, coins, and glass and pottery vessels.[71] As with the Iron Age equivalents, the full meaning and value of these items often remains unclear but similar grave goods are found throughout the provinces of the empire. Coins provide a good illustration of a standardised type of grave good and the difficulties of interpreting its significance. Coins are found in Romano-British cremation and inhumation graves, often being placed in or near the mouth within inhumations. On one level the presence of the coins suggests an active adherence to the widespread 'Roman' custom of providing the dead with the ferryman's fare to enter the Underworld. On another level it has to be acknowledged that such gestures can become customary with little questioning of their actual meaning. It is also possible that the significance of the action might not only become obscured across time but also gain new meanings and associations.[72]

In contrast to physical features such as grave goods and libation tubes many aspects of Roman funerary ritual are not apparent in Britain.

There are no recorded deathbed scenes or visits to the grave; there is no direct evidence for the existence of undertakers or details of funeral ceremonies. We may assert that these things happened or existed but to infer the exact nature of Romano-British beliefs in the afterlife or to describe what happened at a Romano-British funeral would involve a high degree of speculation.

Just as there are aspects which tie Romano-British funerary beliefs and customs to those found elsewhere, there is evidence which also distances them. There were some unique burial rites found in Britain which may have resulted from localised beliefs. One of these is the occurrence of decapitated corpses in the south of England. At the Lankhills cemetery, Winchester, for example, seven skeletons were found with skulls and upper vertebrae located near the legs or feet.[73] At least some of the known decapitated corpses probably represent victims of violent death whether due to battles or punishment for crimes. But some of the corpses may have been decapitated postmortem. Several explanations have been postulated which focus on beliefs concerning the afterlife and the fate of the soul. Perhaps the severing of the head would prevent the dead haunting the living, or would somehow help or alternatively prevent the deceased from reaching the afterlife, or perhaps the skull itself became imbued with special powers.[74] Similar problems of interpretation surround the presence of hobnails from footwear in some inhumation graves. This rite was focused on rural settlements and was most common during the fourth century AD. The hobnailed shoes were often worn by the deceased or were sometimes just placed in the grave. The rite may have mirrored a fashion in this particular type of footwear but an association with some sort of religious belief, such as the person's need for shoes in the afterlife, seems likely.[75]

The advent of Christianity

It is sometimes difficult to reconstruct religious beliefs from material remains. But can the process work the other way; can we identify known religious beliefs in the material record? Christianity was a major religious movement of the late empire, but did it have an impact upon how the dead were buried and commemorated? A handful of graves has been found with evidence which is highly suggestive of Christian faith. At York, for example, two graves with plaques inscribed with Christian phrases have been found. At Poundbury finds include a lead coffin inscribed with a Christian inscription and a coin with the *chi-rho* symbol while the walls of a mausoleum were painted with possibly Christian symbols.[76] However, these examples remain rare.

Indirect evidence has also been employed to identify possible Christian cemeteries. It was believed that Christ would reappear in the east at the end of time and thus graves oriented on an east–west alignment may be suggestive of Christian beliefs. The Christian renunciation of earthly goods has been associated with the absence of grave goods and furnishings in many burials. The Christian belief in the resurrection of the body has also led to the suggestion that the use of gypsum and lime in burials may have been intended to protect or preserve the corpses of believers.[77] Features such as these lie behind the overall identification of some late Roman cemeteries, such as that excavated at Poundbury, as cemeteries serving Christian communities.[78] Such interpretations are not, however, without problems. An east–west alignment of graves, a decline in the use of grave goods, and the use of lime and gypsum appear to be fairly typical features of most late Roman cemeteries and thus not automatically indicative of the Christian faith.[79] It seems that pagans and Christians were buried in similar ways in comparable cemeteries and that Romano-British Christians did not use distinctive procedures in the burial context which would reveal their religious adherence. Or at the very least that features which may have marked Christians from pagans have not, in general, survived in the archaeological record. Distinctions of faith did not produce distinctions in death. Instead, the fourth century AD, a time when the end of Roman rule was approaching, saw in the ordered inhumation cemetery the closest the island had come in a thousand years to being united by a common burial rite.[80]

Notes

In all references, place of publication is London unless otherwise stated.
1 Tacitus, *The Agricola*, 11. trans. H. Mattingly (1948).
2 G. Wait, *Ritual and Religion in Iron Age Britain*, British Archaeological Report 149: 1 (Oxford, 1985).
3 G. J. Wainwright and I. H. Longworth, 'The excavation of a group of round barrows on Ampleforth Moor, Yorkshire', *Yorkshire Archaeological Journal*, 62 (1969), 283–94; B. Cunliffe, *Iron Age Communities in Britain: An Account of England, Scotland and Wales from the Seventh Century BC until the Roman Conquest*, 3rd edn (1991), pp. 498–9.
4 R. Whimster, *Burial Practices in Iron Age Britain: A Discussion and Gazetteer of the Evidence c. 700 BC–AD 43*, British Archaeological Report 90: 1 (Oxford, 1981), pp. 5–16; C. E. Wilson, 'Burials within settlements in southern Britain during the Pre-Roman Iron Age', *Institute of Archaeology Bulletin*, 18 (1981), 127–69; for the occurrence of pit burials and isolated bone fragments at Danebury, see B. Cunliffe and C. Poole, *Danebury: An Iron Age Hill Fort in Hampshire*, vol. V, *The Excavations 1979–1988: The Finds*, Council for British Archaeology Research Report 73 (1991), pp. 418–25.
5 Whimster, *Burial Practices*, pp. 29–31.
6 For the possibility that site-based Iron Age graves represent an outcast or deviant minority, see Wait, *Ritual and Religion*, pp. 119–20, 240.
7 Cunliffe, *Iron Age Communities*, p. 499. For skulls found in the River Thames, some of which may date to the Iron Age, see R. Bradley and K. Gordon, 'Human skulls from the River Thames, their dating and significance', *Antiquity*, 62 (1988), 503–9.
8 G. Carr and C. Knüsel, 'The ritual framework of excarnation as the mortuary practice of the early and middle Iron Ages of central southern Britain', in A. Gwilt and C. Haslegrove, *Reconstructing Iron Age Societies: New Approaches to the British Iron Age*, Oxbow Monographs 71 (Oxford, 1997), pp. 167–73.

9 Bradley and Gordon, 'Human skulls from the River Thames'.

10 For the study of skeletal remains, see D. R. Brothwell, *Digging up Bones: The Excavation, Treatment and Study of Human Skeletal Remains* (Oxford, 1981); for observations on inferences to be drawn from burial studies, see V. G. Childe, 'Directional changes in funerary practices during 50,000 years', *Man*, 3 (1945), 13–19.

11 See, for example, the papers collected in R. Chapman, I. Kinnes and K. Randsborg (eds), *The Archaeology of Death* (Cambridge, 1981).

12 I. M. Stead, *The Arras Culture* (York, 1979), pp. 29–35; Whimster, *Burial Practices*, p. 113.

13 Stead, *Arras Culture*, pp. 20–9; I. M. Stead, *Iron Age Cemeteries in East Yorkshire* (1991), pp. 29–33.

14 Stead, *Arras Culture*, p. 22.

15 J. Dent, 'Three cart burials from Wetwang, Yorkshire', *Antiquity*, 59 (1985), 85–92.

16 Cunliffe, *Iron Age Communities*, pp. 504–5.

17 For exploration of possible theories, see Stead, *Arras Culture*, pp. 92–3; Stead, *Iron Age Cemeteries*, p. 84.

18 Childe, 'Directional changes', 17.

19 Whimster, *Burial Practices*, pp. 62–4.

20 *Ibid.*, p. 72.

21 *Ibid.*, p. 134.

22 *Ibid.*, pp. 144–5.

23 *Ibid.*, p. 194.

24 For the difficulties of interpreting grave goods and the beliefs behind them, see H. R. Ellis, *The Road to Hel: A Study of the Conception of the Dead in Old Norse Literature* (Westport, Conn., 1968).

25 For a summary of the literary evidence concerning Celtic beliefs in the afterlife, see Wait, *Ritual and Religion*, pp. 205–6.

26 Caesar, *Gallic Wars*, VI, 14.

27 Diodurus Siculus, V, 32, 6; Strabo, IV, iv, 5; Caesar, *Gallic Wars*, VI, 16, 4–5. For a summary of these sources, see Wait, *Ritual and Religion*, pp. 206–7.

28 Tacitus, *Annals*, 14.30, trans. M. Grant (1987).

29 M. Stead, J. B. Bourke and D. Brothwell (eds), *Lindow Man: The Body in the Bog* (1986), p. 177; R. C. Turner, 'The Lindow Man phenomenon: ancient and modern', in R. C. Turner and R. G. Scaife (eds), *Bog Bodies: New Discoveries and New Perspectives* (1995), pp. 168–82.

30 A. Ross, 'Lindow Man and the Celtic tradition', in Stead, Bourke and Brothwell (eds), *Lindow Man*, pp. 167–8; Turner, 'The Lindow Man phenomenon', p. 192.

31 J. R. Magilton, 'Lindow Man: the Celtic tradition and beyond', in Turner and Scaife, *Bog Bodies*, pp. 183–7.

32 C. S. Briggs, 'Did they fall or were they pushed? Some unresolved questions about Bog Bodies', in Turner and Scaife, *Bog Bodies*, p. 172.

33 *Ibid.*

34 Whimster, *Burial Practices*, p. 42.

35 R. E. M. Wheeler, *Maiden Castle, Dorset*, Reports of the Research Committee of the Society of Antiquaries of London (Oxford, 1943); Whimster, *Burial Practices*, p. 40.

36 I. M. Stead, 'La Tène III burial from Welwyn Garden City', *Archaeologia*, 101 (1967), 1–62; J. Collis, *The European Iron Age* (1984), p. 172. For similar graves from east Hampshire, see M. Millet, 'An early Roman burial tradition in central southern England', *Oxford Journal of Archaeology*, 6 (1987), 63–8.

37 S. Esmonde Cleary, 'Town and country in Roman Britain', in S. Bassett, *Death in Towns: Urban Responses to the Dying and the Dead, 100–1600* (Leicester, 1992), p. 32. For general observations about the impact of invasion and trade upon grave goods and funerary monuments, see Childe, 'Directional changes', 17–18.

38 I. M. Stead and V. Rigby, *Verulamium: The King Harry Lane Site*, English Heritage Archaeological Report 12 (1989). Note that the Roman presence did ultimately impact upon the cemetery through the construction of a road which cut through

its heart. For continuity in cemetery use, see also E. W. Black, 'Romano-British burial customs and religious beliefs in South East England', *Archaeological Journal*, 143 (1986), 201–39.

39 For the continuity of inhumation, see R. Philpott, *Burial Practices in Roman Britain: A Survey of Grave Treatment and Furnishing AD 43–410*, British Archaeological Report 219 (Oxford, 1991), pp. 57, 222.

40 For descriptions of cremation graves of Roman date, see *ibid.*, pp. 8–52.

41 For a brief comparison between Romano-British cremation graves and those of neighbouring provinces, see R. F. J. Jones, 'Cultural change in Roman Britain', in R. F. J. Jones (ed.), *Britain in the Roman Period: Recent Trends* (Sheffield, 1991), pp. 116–17.

42 The disposal of infants differed according to the normative rite. The bodies were generally inhumed and often buried in houses and buildings: Philpott, *Burial Practices in Roman Britain*, pp. 97–102.

43 *Ibid.*, p. 2. For the urban over rural bias and the dates of excavated cemeteries see Esmonde Cleary, 'Town and country in Roman Britain', p. 28. Jones summed up the situation thus: 'we cannot therefore pretend that the evidence we do have is representative of the province's population as a whole' (Jones, 'Cultural change', p. 117).

44 R. F. Jessup, 'Barrows and walled cemeteries in Roman Britain', *Journal of the British Archaeological Association*, 22 (1959), 1–32; R. G. Collingwood and I. Richmond, *The Archaeology of Roman Britain*, 2nd edn (1969), pp. 169–71.

45 J. Foster, *The Lexden Tumulus: A Re-appraisal of an Iron Age Burial from Colchester*, British Archaeological Report 156 (Oxford, 1986), pp. 190–8.

46 For the various types of Roman funerary memorial and their decor, see J. M. C. Toynbee, *Death and Burial in the Roman World* (1971, reprinted 1996); S. Walker, *Memorials to the Roman Dead* (1985).

47 V. M. Hope, 'Words and pictures: the interpretation of Romano-British tombstones', *Britannia*, 28 (1997), 245–58.

48 For assessments of densities of tombstones, specifically inscribed examples, see M. Biró, 'The inscriptions of Roman Britain', *Acta Archaeologica Scientiarum Hungaricae*, 27 (1975), 13–58; A Cepas, *The North of Britannia and the Northwest of Hispania: An Epigraphic Comparison*, British Archaeological Report International Series 470 (1989); J. C. Mann, 'Epigraphic consciousness', *Journal of Roman Studies*, 75 (1985), 206.

49 R. G. Collingwood and P. R. Wright, *The Roman Inscriptions of Britain*, vol. I (Stroud, 1965, rev. edn 1995), no. 108; M. Henig, *Roman Sculpture from the Cotswold Region: With Devon and Cornwall, Corpus Signorum Imperii Romani*, Great Britain, vol. 1.7 (Oxford, 1993), no. 138.

50 Hope, 'Words and pictures'.

51 Collingwood and Wright, *Roman Inscriptions*, no. 1065; E. J. Phillips, *Corbridge, Hadrian's Wall east of the North Tyne, Corpus Signorum Imperii Romani*, Great Britain, vol. 1.1 (Oxford, 1977), no. 247.

52 D. Smith, 'A Palmyrene sculptor at South Shields', *Archaeologia Aeliana*, 37 (1959), 203–11.

53 The change has been described as 'the biggest single event in ancient burial' by I. Morris, *Death-Ritual and Social Structure in Classical Antiquity* (Cambridge, 1992), p. 31.

54 L. P. Wenham, *The Romano-British Cemetery at Trentholme Drive, York*, Ministry of Public Buildings and Works Archaeological Report 5 (1968).

55 A. D. Nock, 'Cremation and burial in the Roman Empire', *Harvard Theological Review*, 25 (1932), 321–59, reprinted in A. D. Nock, *Essays on Religion and the Ancient World* (Oxford, 1972), pp. 277–307.

56 Morris, *Death-Ritual*, p. 68.

57 R. F. J. Jones, 'The cemeteries of Roman York', in P. V. Addyman and V. E. Black (eds), *Archaeological Papers from York presented to M. W. Barley* (York, 1984), pp. 15–19.

58 Wenham, *The Romano-British Cemetery*, p. 39. For evidence of coffins at Lankhills cemetery, Winchester, including drawings of coffin nails, see M. Biddle, *The*

Roman Cemetery at Lankhills, Winchester Studies 3, *Pre-Roman and Roman Winchester*, part II (Oxford, 1979), pp. 332–41.

59 H. Toller, *Roman Lead Coffins and Ossuaria in Britain*, British Archaeological Report 38 (1977).

60 Wenham, *The Romano-British Cemetery*, pp. 40–1.

61 Collingwood and Wright, *Roman Inscriptions*, no. 674; S. Rinaldi Tufi, *Yorkshire, Corpus Signorum Imperii Romani*, Great Britain, vol. 1.3 (Oxford, 1983), no. 62.

62 R. Warwick, 'The skeletal remains', in Wenham, *The Romano-British Cemetery*, pp. 113–74.

63 T. Molleson, 'Mortality patterns in the Romano-British cemetery at Poundbury Camp, near Dorchester', in Bassett, *Death in Towns*, p. 53.

64 *Ibid.*, p. 46. For a survey of the use of grave contents and grave alignments to argue the presence of intrusive foreign groups, see R. Baldwin, 'Intrusive burial groups in the late Roman cemetery at Lankhills, Winchester – a reassessment of the evidence', *Oxford Journal of Archaeology*, 4 (1985), 93–104.

65 Compare M. Douglas, *Purity and Danger: An Analysis of Concepts of Pollution and Taboo* (1966).

66 For legislation controlling burial, see O. F. Robinson, *Ancient Rome: City Planning and Administration* (1992), pp. 124–6. For restrictions on undertakers, see J. Gardner, *Being a Roman Citizen* (1993), pp. 130–4; J. Bodel, 'Graveyards and groves: a study of the Lex Lucerina', *American Journal of Ancient History*, 11 (1986).

67 F. Cumont, *Afterlife in Roman Paganism* (New Haven, 1922); Toynbee, *Death and Burial*, pp. 33–9.

68 For a summary of funerary traditions, based on diverse sources, see Toynbee, *Death and Burial*, pp. 43–55, 61–4; Walker, *Memorials to the Roman Dead*, pp. 9–13.

69 For similarities between Roman and Celtic religion, see J. Macdonald, 'Pagan religions and burial practices in Roman Britain', in R. Reece (ed.), *Burial in the Roman World*, Council for British Archaeology Research Report 22 (1977), pp. 35–8.

70 Toynbee, *Death and Burial*, pp. 51–2. For further examples of libation tubes, see Philpott, *Burial Practices in Roman Britain*, p. 28.

71 For categories of items discovered, see *ibid.*. For grave goods found in the southeast and attempts to interpret their religious significance, see Black, 'Romano-British burial customs', 220–5.

72 Philpott, *Burial Practices in Roman Britain*, pp. 208–16.

73 Biddle, *The Roman Cemetery at Lankhills*, p. 342.

74 *Ibid.*, pp. 84–5; M. Harman, T. I. Molleson and J. L. Price, 'Burials, bodies and beheadings in Romano-British and Anglo-Saxon cemeteries', *Bulletin of the British Museum (N. Hist.) Geol.*, 35 (1981), 145–88.

75 Philpott, *Burial Practices in Roman Britain*, pp. 165–75.

76 C. S. Green, 'The cemetery of a Romano-British community at Poundbury, Dorchester, Dorset', in S. M. Pearce (ed.), *The Early Church in Western Britain and Ireland*, British Archaeological Report 102 (1982), p. 73.

77 C. S. Green, 'The significance of plaster burials for the recognition of Christian cemeteries', in Reece (ed.), *Burial in the Roman World*, pp. 46–53.

78 Green, 'The cemetery of a Romano-British community', 61–76.

79 P. Rahtz, 'Late Roman cemeteries and beyond', in Reece (ed.), *Burial in the Roman World*, p. 54; Green, 'The significance of plaster burials'.

80 Esmonde Cleary, 'Town and country in Roman Britain', p. 34.

Select bibliography

Cunliffe, B., *Iron Age Communities in Britain: An Account of England, Scotland and Wales from the Seventh Century BC until the Roman Conquest*, 3rd edn, 1991.

Esmonde Cleary, S., 'Town and country in Roman Britain', in S. Bassett (ed.), *Death in Towns: Urban Responses to the Dying and the Dead, 100–1600*, Leicester, 1992.

Morris, I., *Death-Ritual and Social Structure in Classical Antiquity*, Cambridge, 1992.

Philpott, R., *Burial Practices in Roman Britain: A Survey of Grave Treatment and Furnishing AD 43–410*, British Archaeological Report 219, Oxford, 1991.

Reece, R. (ed.), *Burial in the Roman World*, Council for British Archaeology Research Report 22, 1977.

Stead, I. M., *The Arras Culture*, York, 1979.

—— *Iron Age Cemeteries in East Yorkshire*, 1991.

——, Bourke, J. B., and Brothwell, D. (eds), *Lindow Man: The Body in the Bog*, 1986.

Toynbee, J. M. C., *Death and Burial in the Roman World*, 1971, reprinted 1996.

Turner, R. C., and Scaife, R. G. (eds), *Bog Bodies: New Discoveries and New Perspectives*, 1995.

Wait, G., *Ritual and Religion in Iron Age Britain*, British Archaeological Report 149: 1, Oxford, 1985.

Walker, S., *Memorials to the Roman Dead*, 1985.

Whimster, R., *Burial Practices in Iron Age Britain: A Discussion and Gazetteer of the Evidence c. 700 BC–AD 43*, British Archaeological Report 90: 1, Oxford, 1981.

Pagans and Christians: 400–1150

This chapter, covering seven and a half centuries, charts changing attitudes and practices regarding death and burial in the context of early medieval migration and invasion, and the movement from paganism to Christianity. After the collapse of Roman power in the early fifth century, the immigration of Anglo-Saxon settlers from northern Europe resulted in the formation of a number of tribal units, some of which, like Kent, Wessex and Northumbria, later became kingdoms. Following missions from Rome and Ireland from the late sixth century onwards, the Anglo-Saxon kingdoms were gradually converted to Christianity. The next invasions were those by the Vikings from the ninth century; these Scandinavian settlers, too, were converted to Christianity. The final invasion was the Norman Conquest in 1066; this time the conquerors were themselves already Christian. Each wave of migration and invasion brought with it new beliefs and cultural practices, of which some replaced and others mingled with the existing native traditions.

The chapter is divided into two sections. The first section describes the pagan practices of the early Saxons and the Vikings, an area of research which relies primarily on archaeology. The second section discusses the evidence for Anglo-Saxon and Anglo-Scandinavian Christian beliefs and practices, for which there is archaeological, historical and literary evidence.

Pagan Saxons and Vikings

Archaeology provides the main source of evidence for events during and after the collapse of Roman authority in Britain in the early fifth century. We are thus dependent on chance and the circumstances of both deposition and excavation and it is impossible to paint a comprehensive picture. There is an almost total lack of evidence about the burial practices of the post-Roman British communities living to the west and north of a line from Exeter to Lindisfarne from the fifth to the eighth centuries, a problem already raised in regard to the burial rites of Iron Age communities (Chapter 2, pp. 41–3). It is of course possible to

dispose of the dead in ways which leave no physical remains: bodies may be left in the open to be eaten by animals, they may be hung up in trees, or they may be cremated and then the ashes scattered: we cannot tell which, if any, of these means was employed. Only when the first Christian churches and graveyards are founded, from the seventh century onwards, does evidence slowly reappear. East and south of this Exeter–Lindisfarne line, however, in the Anglo-Saxon areas, the archaeological evidence is much more plentiful and many thousands of burials have been discovered.[1] Despite the scale of this database, fifth- and sixth-century cemeteries are, to a great extent, still a mystery. Only one pagan Anglo-Saxon cemetery, Spong Hill in Norfolk, has been entirely excavated; many were dug in the nineteenth century and poorly recorded: if this huge body of data is ever to be fully understood, many more, and more thorough, studies will be needed.

26] Excavated ship at Sutton Hoo in 1939. The ship contained the greatest collection of Anglo-Saxon material ever discovered. Traditionally thought to be the burial of King Redwald, the actual identity of the person remains a mystery.

INHUMATION AND CREMATION

A typical fifth- to sixth-century Anglo-Saxon cemetery contains a mixture of burial practices. Approximately half of all inhumations were buried with grave goods; these graves are the ones most often discussed but it should not be forgotten that many people went unadorned to their burial. The high-status dead could be accompanied by weapons, clothes and jewellery, tools and food. In exceptional cases, they might be buried with horses [plate 4], or interred in ships [26]. Grave goods were probably only included in the graves of higher-status individuals, but we cannot know whether that status derived from military prowess, wealth, religious function or ancestry. Grave goods are gender-related: women may be buried with brooches, beads and weaving tools; men with weapons, ranging from a knife or spear in the poorer graves to shields and swords in the richer ones. There are also regional differences which show up most clearly in women's jewellery and may represent ethnic affiliation.

Pagan Anglo-Saxons also practised cremation; cremation is more common north of the Thames, and inhumation south of it, although both forms of disposal may be found in the same cemetery. The ashes were either buried directly in the ground, or placed in a pot [27] and then buried. A different range of grave goods is found in cremation urns, as is discussed below.

plate 3] Tombstone of the centurion Marcus Favonius Facilis, Colchester. The sculpture shows a soldier in military dress holding the *vitis* (vine stick) which was the symbol of office of the centurion. The epitaph reads: 'Marcus Favonius Facilis, son of Marcus of the Pollia voting tribe, centurion of the Twentieth Legion, lies here. The freed slaves Verecundus and Novicius set this up.'

plate 4] Warrior and horse excavated at RAF Lakenheath, Suffolk. The burial also contained a bucket, sword and horse harness. Horse burials are very rare in England and may point to influence from the continent where they are more common.

The archaeological evidence from these cemeteries falls into three categories: the body, the grave and the objects placed in the grave, each of these categories informing us about different aspects of the burial. The body can reveal details about the individual and her or his health. Broken bones are often obvious, especially when they have healed badly. Other identifiable features of the individual's pathology may include cut marks, bones pitted by disease and dental problems. DNA analysis can show family groupings through the female line within a cemetery.[2] Skeletons are hard to date precisely: measuring the Carbon 14 within bones is the commonest way to date a skeleton but it is an imprecise science. In the Anglo-Saxon era the margin of error could be several hundred years, and it is thus impossible to tell the relative ages of bodies found together.[3] Analysis of traces of metals and chemicals in teeth is revealing more information about where

27] A typical cremation urn from Spong Hill, Norfolk. Cremation urns contain the ashes of the dead who had been cremated on a funeral pyre. The urns often contain miniature items such as tweezers. The symbols on the urns have still not been properly deciphered.

people lived. By comparing the levels of lead with patterns from specific areas, it may be possible to deduce where someone had been born and raised. In terms of early Anglo-Saxon burials, this might determine whether someone had come from the continental homelands of the Angles, Saxons or Jutes, or had been born in England (see Chapter 2, p. 57).

The position of the body in the grave may also be informative. The normal position of the body in fifth- and sixth-century cemeteries is supine and extended, arms by the sides with legs straight or slightly flexed. There are minor variations to this pattern, such as the hands across the pelvis, or across the waist, but the meaning of these various positions, if any, is obscure. Two other types of burial have led to more speculation. The first is the crouched burial, where the body is curled up, with the knees almost to the chin. This position is also found in Iron Age and Roman burials (Chapter 2) and may represent Romano-British tradition continuing within the Anglo-Saxon population. At Norton, in Cleveland, almost half the skeletons in the Anglo-Saxon cemetery were crouched, perhaps indicating different populations buried there.[4] In general, however, it is impossible to say whether a particular burial is that of an Anglo-Saxon or a Briton.

The second unusual type is the face-down, or prone, burial. This position is so rare that occurrences have been seen as punishment burials for criminals or 'evil' people, the theory being that if they tried to dig themselves out, they would only bury themselves more deeply. At Sewerby in Yorkshire a younger woman was buried in a deep grave, with an older woman on top of her facing downwards, with a stone placed in the middle of her back.[5] The meaning of this burial may never be conclusively proved, but it has been suggested that the older woman may have been held responsible for the death of the younger, and executed as a punishment.

The structure and alignment of the grave itself can reveal elements of social organisation and belief. The commonest alignment is east–west; this can be either Christian or pagan, but, as east–west is the Christian norm, a north–south alignment is often assumed to be a pagan burial. Various attempts have been made to determine if the east–west graves were aligned on the rising or setting sun, but there are too many complicating factors: there is no reason why the graves should have been dug at any particular time of the day or the year, and features, such as buildings, within the cemetery are more likely to dictate the alignment of graves.[6]

There was a wide range of different grave structures, both above and under the ground. Cemeteries dug into chalk, such as St Peter's, Broadstairs, Kent, preserve evidence for sockets or ledges around the sides of graves. These were for boards or planks which were either placed down the sides or across the top, though their significance is unknown. Above ground, graves often had visible distinguishing features such as structures or mounds, which are identifiable archaeologically by post holes or ring ditches. The cemeteries were designed to be noticeable: the most famous Anglo-Saxon mound cemetery is the group of high-status burials at Sutton Hoo in Suffolk, where the mounds are located on the false crest of a hill. They dominate the skyline from the river in an assertive re-creation of the landscape typical of the location of Saxon burial mounds, perhaps announcing ownership of the land.[7]

The positioning of cemeteries is also interesting in other ways. Many Anglo-Saxon sites, such as Norton in Cleveland, incorporate earlier Bronze Age burial mounds, perhaps in an attempt to identify the new landowner as part of an older tradition.[8] Another common, but enigmatic, feature is the positioning of Anglo-Saxon burials on parish boundaries. This has long been recognised, but we cannot be sure whether the burials were placed on existing boundaries, or whether later people laying out new boundaries used the cemeteries as a landmark. Boundaries were also later used for the burial of criminals and those executed, so that they were as far from the settlements as possible.[9] Given the common understanding of death as a liminal state (see Chapter 1, p. 14), these burials may have been an acknowledgement of the dead as hovering on the edges of the society of the living.[10]

Grave goods are the third component of the burial. They range from the most basic, such as stones, to highly prestigious objects like those buried at Sutton Hoo, although it is not uncommon to find swords, spears, brooches or other objects buried with the body in much less ostentatious graves. While the object's function is often obvious, its meaning is debatable. Such artefacts may have been buried for the use of the dead person, or as a showy gesture by the mourners, or to indicate ethnicity, rank or social function. These are questions which have no concrete answers, and the problems are the same for all societies where no adequate historical records survive to explain the beliefs behind the actions (Chapters 1 and 2).

Grave goods have also been studied to see if they can tell us about the age and sex of the person buried, or her or his ancestral descent, wealth, social status, ethnic identity, religious beliefs or political allegiance. The acknowledgement of this complex web of meanings has resulted in criticism of simplistic approaches. One study of two small inhumation cemeteries in Suffolk came to the conclusion that although the grave goods certainly represented something, there were so many potential meanings and possibilities that it would be almost impossible to decipher their total message.[11] An attempt to rank different objects in terms of importance was made by assessing the amount of time required to make them, but the problem with this approach is that it looks at only one understanding of value, ignoring the age of the object, its rarity, its place of origin, the circumstances of its acquisition and its symbolic importance.[12]

Work undertaken on the study of cremation urns and their contents has revealed that the tallest pots are often those of adult males, and that women's pots were taller than children's. Even such a relatively straightforward conclusion was only arrived at by a painstaking measurement and statistical analysis of hundreds of urns.[13] Once a conclusion has been arrived at, other elements can be included: gaming pieces and glass vessels seem to be particularly associated with tall urns and probably indicate the burial of a high-status male. The cremation urns are usually highly decorated with designs made by different pottery 'stamps', including swastikas, circles, dots, and complex symbols in semi-circles, circles and squares [27]. The meaning of these is mostly lost and it is very rare that designs reveal beliefs or obvious meaning, though a pot from Spong Hill does have the runic letters 'TIW', an Anglo-Saxon god, and the swastika pattern may be connected with the pagan god Thunor.

CHANGING BURIAL PRACTICES: ROMANO-BRITISH TO ANGLO-SAXON

From the body, the grave and the grave goods, the broad chronological outline of burial trends has been established. At the end of the Roman period the predominant method of burial was by inhumation (Chapter 2, pp. 55–7) in large cemeteries, several of which have been excavated: Poundbury, Dorset, with 1,450 excavated burials, Cannington, Somerset, with 542 burials, Cirencester, Gloucestershire, with 453, and Lankhills, Hampshire, with 451. The burials within these cemeteries were carefully laid out in rows and new burials did not intercut former ones. This indicates that old graves were respected and marked in some way and that there was management of these burial grounds.

The end of Roman authority and the arrival of the Anglo-Saxons are visible in the archaeological records. It had been Roman policy to recruit peoples from across the empire and the late Roman army included Franks, Goths and Saxons. One sign of Roman office was a distinctive belt fitting and some belts have been discovered in cemeteries also containing grave goods of Germanic style. One such belt was discovered in a male grave in Dyke Hills, Oxfordshire, and nearby was a woman's grave with Germanic style brooches in it, which has led to the suggestion that the belt belonged to an Anglo-Saxon working as a Roman official.[14] An alternative explanation is that the cemetery continued in use from the Roman to the Anglo-Saxon period.

However, it should not be assumed that Roman objects in graves necessarily show the Romano-British population intermingling with Anglo-Saxon newcomers, as the Anglo-Saxons were adept at finding Roman objects on Roman sites and using them for their own purposes. Writing in the early eighth century, Bede describes an occasion when the community at Ely wanted to honour St Ethelthryth, their former abbess, with a better coffin sixteen years after her death and unearthed a Roman sarcophagus for her in Grantchester, a former Roman settlement.[15]

Some Roman customs continued, such as the crouched burials, but the Roman custom of placing of a coin in the mouth of a corpse stopped almost as soon as Roman authority came to an end.[16] In a few cases, cemeteries which had been Roman in origin continued in use long after the end of Roman rule. Cannington, Somerset, was used from the end of the Roman period into the seventh or eighth century, and the cemetery at Wasperton in Warwickshire has what appear to be Roman and Anglo-Saxon burials. The Roman burials are distinguished by their hobnail boots and typical metal fittings, whilst the Anglo-Saxon graves have been identified both by their grave goods and the revived practice of cremation by the Anglo-Saxons (see Chapter 2).[17]

The Anglo-Saxons had cremated their dead in their homelands in northern Germany, Denmark and Netherlands: the best preserved cemetery from these areas is at Liebenau in Saxony. In one case a cremation urn found at Wehden, Lower Saxony, is so similar in style and design to one found at Markshall cemetery in Norfolk that it is thought the same potter made both [28].[18] However, we cannot tell whether it was made in Norfolk or carried with the new settlers.

Cremation is a much more labour-intensive option than burial. A pyre was constructed over the fully dressed and supine body. After the cremation the burnt bones and ashes were deposited in a cremation urn, or more rarely a cloth bag or bronze bowl, and buried. Not all the bones were put in the urn, and sometimes an urn contains more than one individual. Small objects were commonly placed in the urn, in particular toilet implements such as tweezers, razors and combs. These are of particular interest because they are miniature versions of the real objects, probably made especially for the cremation urn and the burial.[19]

Cremation cemeteries range in size from a few urns to the large folk cemeteries containing hundreds or thousands of burials, the most famous and thoroughly excavated of which is Spong Hill in Norfolk, which was used for 150–200 years. It contained both inhumation and cremation burials; archaeological excavation revealed 2,284 individuals and the total cemetery population was probably around 2,700. This suggests a population of fifty to a hundred families. The cemetery probably served not only the adjacent and unexcavated settlement but a region as well, estimated to extend from five to ten miles around the site.

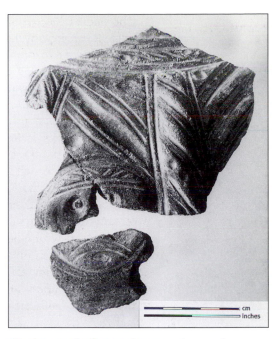

28] The use of a face on this cremation urn from Markshall, Norfolk, is very unusual, but can be matched by a similar urn from Wehden, Lower Saxony. This has led to speculation that they were made by the same potter.

From the fifth to the seventh century, the archaeological record reveals a shift from the relatively uniform folk cemeteries to an increasing concentration upon the very high-status princely burials. This change has been associated with the development of the newly forming Anglo-Saxon kingdoms: whereas in the fifth and sixth centuries burials were probably community-based, in the seventh century the new kingdoms elevated individuals and families, an elevation mirrored in their burials.[20]

This pattern appears in East Anglia. By the beginning of the seventh century the folk cemeteries, such as Spong Hill, are in decline and being replaced by smaller cemeteries displaying a large variation in burial practice, with more wealth being concentrated in fewer graves. The burial ground at Snape in Suffolk is one such cemetery and may be the intermediate stage between the folk cemetery of the fifth and sixth centuries and the richer burials of the seventh century, particularly those nearby at Sutton Hoo. The cemetery at Snape is a mixture of cremations and inhumations with a wide range of burial practices: burial in a boat, a wooden chamber over a grave, charred timber in the grave and bodies in different positions. This eclecticism may reflect the religious beliefs of a pagan society: people who worshipped different gods were buried in different ways.[21] By the later seventh century the emphasis was on a few high-status burials, which dominate the burial record by the quantity of artefacts they contain. The most dramatic example is Mound 1 at Sutton Hoo, containing the richest Anglo-Saxon burial yet found.[22] No body was discovered, probably because of the acidic soil, but the grave goods included gold and silver ware, clothes, weapons, coins, musical instruments and food, all buried within a magnificent ship, the outline of which remained preserved in the soil

[26]. There is no precise way to identify the person buried there, but it is often argued that it was the burial of Redwald, King of the East Angles, who died *c*. 620.[23]

These burials often leave an impression of high drama and elaborate ritual. Excavations at RAF Lakenheath in Suffolk uncovered a sixth-century Anglo-Saxon cemetery, in which one large grave contained the body of a man, accompanied by a complete horse in harness, with a bucket of food by its head [**plate 4**]. Another horse burial has been discovered at Sutton Hoo where the horse was buried beside a man in a separate grave under Mound 17. Other than these two examples, horse burials are exceptionally rare in England, but they are more common on the continent; they may show that the Lakenheath and Sutton Hoo communities had strong continental links.[24]

By the eighth century the pattern of burials had changed again: the high-status burials disappear, to be replaced by more uniform and simple graves, unfurnished and increasingly found associated with churches. These burials and the causes of change will be dealt with in more detail in the second half of this chapter.

THE VIKINGS

In the ninth century the arrival of new pagan invaders and settlers, the Vikings, is briefly marked by a new phase of burials with grave goods. From the late eighth until the eleventh century the Vikings' raids and settlement dominate the history of England, but there is sparse evidence for distinctive burial practices. There are only twenty-five pagan Viking sites in England whereas on the Isle of Man alone there are over forty. With so little evidence, it is hard to say what normal practice was. Nor is it possible to describe Viking belief in an afterlife with any confidence, though odd glimpses remain in contemporary Scandinavian poetry, such as the descriptions of the fighting dead in Valhalla.[25]

Two of the most remarkable sites yet discovered, Ingleby and Repton, lie within 4 kilometres of each other in Derbyshire but reveal very different ways of disposal of the Viking dead. Ingleby is the only known Viking cremation site in England. Some of Ingleby's sixty mounds contained cremations of men and women, as well as of cattle, sheep and goats. Other mounds were empty and may have simply been memorials to the dead.[26]

At Repton a group of remarkable Viking inhumation burials was found. The Viking army spent the winter of 873–74 at Repton, and the burials were found within their camp. Some were individual graves, excavated at the east end of the later church; the most elaborate of these contained a man who had died from sword wounds and had been buried with his weapons and a pendant in the shape of Thor's hammer. There was also a mass grave containing at least 249 individuals [29]. Of these, 80 per cent were males aged from 15 to 45: these may have been the Viking army, and the 20 per cent of bones identifiable as female may have been those of camp followers.[27] A problem arises,

29] The charnel pit at Repton. The charnel pit contained at least 249 individuals. The bones are probably the remains of the Viking army but the presence of some women, and the lack of sword cuts, may mean that people died in an epidemic rather than in battle.

however, as there was very little evidence of the injury to the bones that might be expected with battle injuries. One possible explanation is that they may have been the victims of plague rather than battle. Plague was a common occurrence throughout the centuries and a particularly devastating one decimated Europe in the seventh century.[28]

Ingleby and Repton are exceptions; elsewhere in England information about Viking burial practice comes from individual graves and piecemeal evidence. The reasons for this are threefold. First, many Vikings, whatever their religious persuasion, may have been buried in unexcavated churchyards which, as we shall see with Christian Saxons, present particular problems when it comes to excavation. This theory is endorsed by the occasional finds of Viking weapons in churchyards, especially in the north and north-east: swords and cloak pins have been discovered in Cumbria, belt fittings at Carlisle Cathedral, and weapons at Kildale and Wensley in Yorkshire. Second, many Vikings were swiftly converted to Christianity, thus becoming archaeologically indistinguishable from their Saxon neighbours: Oda, whose Danish father was a

30] Hogback tombstones from Brompton, North Yorkshire. These charming and mysterious carvings were probably gravestones covering a tomb. They are predominantly found in areas of Norse settlement in Great Britain, although they do not occur in Scandinavia.

first-generation immigrant and presumably pagan, became Archbishop of Canterbury in 941.[29] Third, there may never have been very many Vikings in the first place.

In adopting Christianity, the Vikings also took some Anglo-Saxon traditions and developed them. The Anglo-Saxon monastic tradition of carved gravestones was adopted by secular Viking landowners, becoming much more widespread in the process. Particularly distinctive are the hogback tombs [**30**], which depict the roof of a house, often shingled, with bears or other beasts clasping the gable ends. The distribution pattern indicates that they are a fusion of Viking and Saxon culture, for they are found in the Viking-controlled parts of England and Scotland, but not where the Vikings heavily settled in Ireland or the Isle of Man. None has been found in definite association with a burial, but they are located in churches and are assumed to be gravestones, perhaps assimilating Christian imagery of the grave as a shrine to Viking animal cults.[30]

This process of fusion and adaptation is also evident at York, where a collection of tombstones showing Viking influence was discovered near and under the site of the present Minster, though it should be noted that the site of the early medieval cathedral is unknown. The Viking nature of the burials is reinforced by the discovery of a body interred in part of a boat.[31] Boat burials are found in the Isle of Man and the Scottish isles as well as in Scandinavia.[32] Boat burials may reflect pagan beliefs, as at Sutton Hoo, but it would be extraordinary for the York burial, very probably associated with the Minster, to have been that of a practising pagan: we may assume his soul to have found a Christian harbour.

Christian practices

It is now necessary to go back in time and follow the Christian rather than the pagan thread. During the years from *c.* 600 onwards, the practices associated with death and burial in England took the shape that is still considered to be some kind of norm. The crucial elements of change result from the ever-growing involvement of the Church in both the place and the process of burial. From the end of the sixth century, Irish and Roman missionaries were working at the Anglo-Saxons courts, building churches, creating new and desirable places for burial and disseminating Christian concepts of the afterlife. Monastic centres introduced new ideals of death based on the conduct of the saints and ultimately of Christ himself; their cemeteries set a new model, with their inscribed gravestones and unfurnished graves.[33] From the ninth and tenth centuries, a spreading network of parish churches meant that more and more people had a local churchyard in which they could be buried and a local priest to commit them to the ground; by the eleventh century unfurnished churchyard burial had become the norm.[34] From 954, England north and south of the Humber was united under one monarch for the first time; this and the contemporary revival of Benedictine monasticism meant that practices were increasingly unified throughout the kingdom. Thus, the overall impression is one of regional variation and complexity giving way to simpler and more uniform practices. There were, however, many exceptions, most notably in the areas under Viking rule from the mid-ninth to the mid-tenth centuries, already considered in the first half of this chapter, and in the ways in which criminals' bodies were treated. It is also interesting to ask how Anglo-Saxon Christianity differed in its expression from continental practice, and how that difference is expressed in death-related behaviour.

This impression may well be distorted by the nature of the sources: the earlier period is dominated by archaeological material, the latter by documentary sources such as law codes, wills, guild statutes, poetry and sermons, which uphold an ideal rather than describe a real practice. Archaeological evidence for burial in the Christian Saxon period is elusive for the good reason that their graves form the bottom layer of parish graveyards still in use, while their churches have often disappeared with Norman and later rebuilding. This necessary reliance on written sources also means that the evidence for the later period is overwhelmingly biased in favour of the male elites of royalty, aristocracy and Church.

This difference in the nature of the sources should not lead us to stress change over continuity, however. Although the richly furnished inhumation and cremation graves of the pre-Christian and converting (and back-sliding?) Anglo-Saxons had given way, by the late seventh and early eighth centuries, to a much more austere form of burial, it should be emphasised that depositing grave goods was not in conflict with the practice of Christianity. The Christian Franks across the Channel were buried with as much wealth and elaboration as their pagan Saxon cousins and there is little convincing evidence for any specifically Christian burial practice.[35] Nonetheless, there may be an indirect correlation between the changing religious ideology and mortuary behaviour: Christianity provided kings with a literate and sophisticated clerical bureaucracy which permitted them to tax their people in new ways, and thus the wealth that had once gone into the grave may now have been diverted into death duties.

CHURCH AND STATE

One of the features of the later Anglo-Saxon period is the ever-closer identification between Church and state, with archbishops, like Wulfstan of York, involved in the writing of law codes, and kings, like Alfred of Wessex, turning to the Bible to discover a model of a just monarch. This was in part an attempt to create an ever-stronger sense of community, with the population defined as both English and Christian for the first time. In burial practice, we can see what it meant both to be part of, and to be excluded from, that community.

One way of demonstrating allegiance to a community is by paying taxes: by the late Saxon period there are two forms of taxation associated with death: *heriot* and *sawlscot*, both of which illuminate changing attitudes and practices. *Heriot* was a fee paid in kind to the king. Bishop Theodred, who died around 951, left the king 'two hundred marks of red gold, and two silver cups and four horses, the best that I have, and two swords, the best that I have, and four shields and four spears' in addition to a considerable amount of land.[36] Every item quoted in this list, including the horses, can be paralleled in the grave goods deposited under the mounds at Sutton Hoo over three hundred years earlier.

Sawlscot, on the other hand, was a fee payable to the Church, specifically to the establishment in which one intended to be buried. Thus the Church now had a financial incentive to interest itself in the burials of all Christians, whereas earlier it had only extended the privilege of church burial to those who were either professional religious or people, such as kings, too important to refuse. By the beginning of the tenth century it was common for the wealthiest members of society to found, refound or lavishly endow ecclesiastical centres, with the specific intention of using them as mausolea. Ælfgifu, a member of the royal family who died *c*. 975, states in her will that 'she grants to the Old Minster [Winchester], where she intends her body to be buried, the estate at Risborough just as it stands'.[37] The Church's involvement in burial came late, however, and seems to be as much the result of lay pressure as of decisions made by the Church hierarchy.[38] The Church's continued monopoly of burial rites and space through the centuries is a theme which reappears in many of the later chapters in this book.

As well as developing a monopoly on burial, the Church also had the last word on the afterlife. However, this is no simple statement: ideas about Christian eschatology were still fluid at this point. Purgatory was not established as doctrine by the Papacy until the late twelfth century, and as a result there were rival geographies of the afterlife.[39] Similarly, canonisation, the Church's response to its most valued dead, was still a local affair rather than a matter for the Papacy. At this period, the institutions, both material and ideological, which came to be taken for granted in the Middle Ages and to some extent were dismantled at the Reformation, were only beginning to take shape.

ST CUTHBERT

An object which encapsulates many of these ideas is the coffin of St Cuthbert (c. 634–687), Bishop of Lindisfarne in Northumbria [31]. Born within a decade of the building of Mound 1 at Sutton Hoo, Cuthbert was one of the most attractive and influential figures in the early Church in England. We know about his death and burial in 687 and the later adventures of his corpse from a variety of sources: an anonymous *Life* written by a Lindisfarne monk; Bede's *Ecclesiastical History of the English People* and *Life of St Cuthbert*; the Norman monk Reginald of Durham, and the wide range of artefacts associated with the body. A discussion of St Cuthbert's death and burial reflects many of the most important topics connected with the Christian Anglo-Saxon understanding of the good death and the holy body.

According to Bede, Cuthbert foresaw the approach of his death and modestly begged his monks to bury him at his island hermitage on Inner Farne but gave way to their plea that they should be allowed to inter him in the church on Lindisfarne. Eleven years later they exhumed him and discovered his corpse was incorrupt, whereupon they gave it new clothes and reburied it in a tomb above ground level.[40] Viking raids drove the monks of Lindisfarne to Chester-le-Street in 857 and on to Durham in 995, carrying Cuthbert's body with them. When the present Durham cathedral was completed in 1104 he was moved into it, his body then being examined and found again incorrupt. Although the tomb was despoiled at the Reformation, Cuthbert was secretly reburied in a grave which was examined in 1827. His body was contained in a carved wooden coffin and accompanied by a gold and garnet pectoral cross, an ivory comb, a silver-covered portable altar, and a range of silks and embroidered vestments.[41]

The saga of Cuthbert's death and burials is illuminating in a number of ways. Both the anonymous *Life* and Bede's *Lives* were written for an audience who had known Cuthbert; they demonstrate the rapidity with which a holy man could officially become a saint, in those days of the ascendancy of the local in Church affairs. It was not until the twelfth century that canonisation became a Papal monopoly, and it is clear,

31] Coffin of St Cuthbert. The wooden coffin, probably made for St Cuthbert's reburial in 698, is incised with stylised images of Christ, the Virgin, the Apostles, Archangels and Evangelists. It was almost certainly designed as a literal and spiritual protection for the saint's body, rather than to be seen by human eyes.

from the vast number of Anglo-Saxon saints who were only honoured in the place where they had lived, that people felt a great need for a more personal figure to whom they could pray. Saints straddled the chasm between earth and Heaven, their bodies and possessions venerated as relics, and provided their followers with the reassurance that the saint was not really dead but present and able to perform miracles and to intercede for them.

Cuthbert's first posthumous miracle was his failure to decay: this quality of incorruptibility becomes a feature of Anglo-Saxon saints' *Lives* and is part of a widespread belief that death and decay were a punishment for Adam and Eve's Fall. The processes of decay almost always represent sin when they are discussed in Old English literature and, conversely, for a body to remain wholesome means that its inhabitant was a person of special virtue. Thus in the most extreme example, when St Edmund's head, removed from its body by marauding Vikings, is replaced on his neck, the two join together with only a thin line round the throat to show what had happened:

> Also the wounds, which the heathen had inflicted on his body with their frequent shots, were healed through the grace of the heavenly God. And he lies so uncorrupted until the present day, awaiting resurrection and the eternal glory. His body, which lies undecayed, tells us that he lived here in the world chastely and went to Christ with a stainless life.[42]

Perhaps as a result of this belief in the sanctity of the intact body, the bodies of Anglo-Saxon saints were not normally broken up and disseminated to a number of ecclesiastical centres as became the practice in later centuries.[43]

When opened in the nineteenth century, Cuthbert's coffin was found to be full of rich objects. Some of these grave goods were almost certainly his personal possessions, such as the pectoral cross, that symbol of episcopal authority. Others, such as the Byzantine silks and the gold-embroidered vestments, were later gifts to the shrine. Cuthbert's burial clearly demonstrates that the practice of depositing grave goods was still acceptable after the advent of Christianity, although the practice may have been restricted to the graves of a few very special people, and it may have meant something wholly different in 698 from its significance in the fifth and sixth centuries.

The coffin was probably made for his second burial in 698. Every side except the base is thinly incised with iconic figures, showing Christ surrounded by the four Evangelists, seven archangels, the twelve apostles and, at the foot, the Virgin and Child. The choice of images and their arrangement have been shown to have close affiliations with intercessory prayers, while Christ and the Evangelists occur in a context of judgement in Revelation 4:7, and the coffin should be seen as an embodiment of prayer literally embracing the precious corpse. In a unique reference to grave goods, the anonymous *Life of St Cuthbert* of *c.* 700 describes the dead man as being 'dressed in his priestly robes, wearing his shoes in readiness to meet Christ'.[44] The whole burial was designed as a means of assisting the bishop's soul to Heaven.[45]

THE AFTERLIFE

This leads us on to ask what Christian Anglo-Saxons believed would happen to them at death. However, there is no precise answer: as noted above, Christian eschatology was not to be codified until the late twelfth century (see Chapter 4). Nonetheless, it had been acknowledged from the early days of the Church that the binary opposition of Heaven and Hell was insufficient, few people being outright saints or sinners; and writers such as Augustine, the fifth-century Bishop of Hippo, had explored concepts of intermediate destinations where the soul was purified.[46] Furthermore, biblical justification for the idea that one can

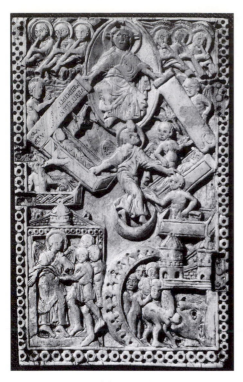

ameliorate the condition of the dead encouraged the living to work on their behalf.[47] In addition, the Bible is ambiguous as to whether one is judged at the moment of individual death or collectively at the end of time. Thus in the grey areas between Heaven and Hell, between death and Doomsday, there was plenty of scope for theory.

Certainly, as we can see from Cuthbert's coffin, there was a belief that the actions of the living assisted the dead, just as the intercessions of the saints aided the living. The dead were not seen as absent but in a vigorous reciprocal relationship with those still alive.[48] Bede's *Ecclesiastical History* of 731 includes the Vision of Drycthelm, which describes scenes of both suffering and happy souls, explicitly defined as being in neither Heaven nor Hell; Drycthelm's spiritual guide tells him:

32] Ivory carving of the Last Judgement. This English carving, *c.* 800, is the earliest surviving representation of the Second Coming and the Resurrection of the Dead in Western Art. It shows Christ in a mandorla (an oval shape signifying holiness) and the dead rising to meet Him, while angels blow their trumpets. It may have come from a book cover.

> The valley that you saw, with its horrible burning flames and icy cold, is the place where souls are tried and punished who have delayed to confess and amend their wicked ways, and who at last had recourse to penitence at the hour of their death, and so depart this life. Because they confessed and were penitent, although only at death, they will all be admitted into the Kingdom of Heaven at the Day of Judgment. But many are helped by the prayers, alms, and fasting of the living, and especially by the offering of Masses, and are therefore set free before the Day of Judgment.[49]

Another of Bede's visionaries, Fursey, carried a burn scar which he claimed he had received from the flames 'that burn away sinful desires',[50] a very tangible reminder of the afterlife.

These intermediary destinations, however, figure nowhere in the art of the period. An ivory carving of the Last Judgement [32] shows a strictly bipartite division of the dead into saved and damned, with an angel on Christ's right welcoming the clothed and righteous souls into the courts of Heaven, while the naked bodies of sinners are engulfed to his left by the mouth of Hell. This ivory of *c.* 800 is the first surviving fully realised depiction of the Last Judgement in Western art,[51] though presumably not the first such image to have existed. The iconography is loosely based on Revelation 20, showing the division of souls at the bottom, the raising of the dead in the middle plane and Christ in Majesty at the top. The dead are shown either recumbent in their coffins, immobilised by their shrouds, or climbing out of the tombs, carrying their shrouds in one hand: there is no suggestion that they have done anything other than rest while waiting for judgement. Here, their souls are represented by birds, an ancient image of the soul but also one that brings to mind Bede's famous parable, put into the mouth of a Northumbrian nobleman at the court of King Edwin, *c.* 627:

> Your Majesty, when we compare the present life of man on earth with that time of which we have no knowledge, it seems to me like the swift flight of a single sparrow through the banqueting-hall where you are sitting at dinner on a winter's day with your thanes and counsellors. In the midst there is a comforting fire to warm the hall; outside, the storms of winter rain or snow are raging. This sparrow flies swiftly in through one door of the hall, and out through another. While he is inside, he is safe from the winter storms; but after a few moments of comfort, he vanishes from sight into the wintry world from which he came. Even so, man appears on earth for a little while; but of what went before this life or of what follows, we know nothing. Therefore, if this new teaching has brought any more certain knowledge, it seems only right that we should follow it.[52]

The importance of the story lies in its claim that Christianity offered a greater guarantee of life after death than the pagan beliefs. The image of the soul inhabiting the body as if it were a hall or house is elemental to the Anglo-Saxon understanding of the body/soul relationship, apparent in the very word *banhus* (bone house), meaning 'body', and echoed in the house-shaped reliquaries for the bones of the saints and the Viking-period hogback stones with their tiled roofs [30].

Prayers for salvation were seen as a form of insurance against the events of Doomsday. From early on, monasteries had exchanged lists of monks' names so that the communities could engage in reciprocal prayers. Bede, from the monastery at Jarrow, wrote the *Life of Cuthbert* for the monks of Lindisfarne, and in return he was added to the register at Lindisfarne.[53] These lists of names developed into the institution of the *Liber Vitae*, or Book of Life: a register of dead monks for whom their living brethren could pray and thus speed to Heaven. One such book is the New Minster *Liber Vitae* of *c.* 1040, produced in Winchester, which has an illustration of the Last Judgement, covering two pages [33]. One striking thing about the picture is that the Last Judgement is being watched by two figures, one of whom is identifiable as Abbot Ælfgar. The other, an unnamed monk, may be giving Ælfgar a guided tour of Doomsday just as Drycthelm was guided by 'a handsome man in a shining robe'. Again, in the New Minster *Liber Vitae*, we see a bipartite division, a choice between Heaven above and Hell below, with St Peter and a devil in the middle section wrestling over the souls. This image reinforces the impression that the Anglo-Saxons emphasised the final and general Judgement over the interim fate of the soul;[54] even a scholar like Ælfric of Cerne, who was much clearer on the subject than most of his contemporaries, preached on the general more than the individual judgement.[55]

In both the ivory carving and the New Minster *Liber Vitae*, the blessed are clothed and some of the damned, at least, are naked. The differences between types of the blessed are indicated by their carrying books

33] New Minster *Liber Vitae*. A *Liber Vitae* lists the names of the dead so that the living may pray for them. This example of *c.* 1040 shows St Peter challenging the devil for a soul in the central scene. Above are the courts of Heaven, below the mouth of Hell.

or martyr's palms, but the nakedness of the damned emphasises their humiliation: they are placed beyond the bounds of normal human society, in which identity and rank are displayed through dress and accessories. This exclusion was represented in the legal penalties as well as in the religious images of the time, reflecting the identification of crime and sin.

JUDICIAL DEATH

Only one Anglo-Saxon manuscript [**plate 5**] includes a representation of execution by hanging. This manuscript[56] is an illustrated adaptation into Old English of the first six books of the Old Testament and this illustration represents not an Anglo-Saxon court but Pharaoh and his counsellors. It is risky to assume that Anglo-Saxon artists were using the habits of their own day to illustrate biblical events, and many manuscripts were close copies of earlier and foreign exemplars. This manuscript, however, like the Bayeux Tapestry, closely reflects contemporary practice,[57] and the gallows, with its pair of posts and the running noose, should be an accurate reflection of the execution scenes mentioned in works such as Ælfric's *Life of St Edmund*, when Bishop Theodred, whose will we looked at above, orders that thieves 'all be hanged on a high gallows'.[58] The idea of the gallows as the normal means of judicial killing comes in the poem *The Dream of the Rood*, when the Cross describes itself as a *gealgan*, gallows-tree.[59]

The traditional punishment for harming or killing other people had been through a complex system of fines called *wergild* (man-money), but from the end of the seventh century the death penalty first appears in English law codes. It seems to be possible to identify the bodies of executed criminals in Saxon cemeteries by the ways that these bodies had been treated or mutilated. It has been argued that while in the pagan Saxon period the bodies of the executed are buried with their kin in the folk cemeteries, by the seventh and eighth centuries they are treated differently, buried separately as if their punishment has not ended with death. At the cemetery at Sutton Hoo bodies were found so eroded by the acid soil that only casts of them remain. There were thirty-nine of these burials in two separate groups, one on the eastern edge of the cemetery and the other surrounding Mound 5, a cremation burial of the late sixth to early seventh century. Analysis of these satellite burials produced dates from the seventh through to the eleventh centuries. Many of these burials were disfigured in some way, lying face down, apparently with hands fastened behind their backs, or missing their heads. Burial 28 was kneeling, with the top of its head missing; Burial 48 had its head removed and placed below its knee.[60] Since the Christian ideal was to be buried *ad sanctos*, with the saints, these burials, which are far from unique, may represent an inversion of that, the punishment of being buried *ad paganos*, with the heathen. By the end of the eleventh century, however, the victims of capital punishment were being buried in hospital cemeteries, perhaps because the change of elites at the Conquest had broken the link with the past which had kept the Saxons returning to pagan burial sites.[61]

The image of the judicial death on the gallows is transformed, however, in the poem mentioned above, *The Dream of the Rood*. This is an account of a vision of the Crucifixion, partly narrated by a dreamer and partly by the Cross itself. The Cross describes itself as being 'set up on a hill': this is the hill of Calvary from the Gospel narrative but it may have brought to mind the image of the gallows set on a burial mound, and, as noted, the Old English word used for the Cross is *gealga*, the ancestor of the modern *gallows*. In the poem, however, the Cross is changed from an instrument of torture and murder to the means of salvation. The death of Christ is far and away the commonest death represented in Anglo-Saxon art, illustrated here by an ivory carving, now set in a later continental enamelled cross [34]. The theme of Christ's death transcending and transforming the human experience of death is explored widely in Old English poetry and prose.

The funeral of King Edward from the Bayeux Tapestry [35] draws together many of the themes discussed above. The scene of the sombre procession of a royal body to Westminster Abbey is deceptively familiar, but its very familiarity should not blind us to the fact that King Edward's burial stands at the beginning of this tradition. Edward had refounded Westminster Abbey with the specific intention of being buried there. He had a lavish funeral paid for out of the royal purse.[62] Edward's death is described, not only in the Tapestry but also in a contemporary biography and the *Anglo-Saxon Chronicle,* as exemplary; he is a model king, borne splendidly to his grave, and a model Christian, going meekly to his maker. Within a century of his death he was canonised. This image stresses the public nature of royal funerals, both in that it was a great spectacle at the time and also in that it was worthy of commemoration in the Tapestry, carrying the image to a wider audience. We learn from it that, at the grandest funerals at least, the shrouded corpse was on display, carried on an elaborate bier, accompanied by the ringing of bells and a cortège including men with books, possibly choristers.

34] Ivory crucifixion. This is only one of many surviving Crucifixion images from Anglo-Saxon England, though most of them are drawings rather than carvings. This little ivory may have been an object for the private devotion of a wealthy person. The enamelled Cross is later than the ivory.

35] Bayeux Tapestry: funeral of Edward the Confessor. King Edward's death and burial in 1066 were commemorated within fifteen years of the event in the embroidery commissioned by William the Conqueror's half-brother, Odo of Bayeux. The image gives an idea of how a grand eleventh-century funeral would have looked.

The Bayeux Tapestry, however, is no objective record of the events it depicts, but a highly political document, produced, within a generation of the Conquest, by English craftspeople for a new Norman overlord.[63] The designer chose to place Edward's funeral centrally in the Tapestry and give it great weight, both in the amount of space it takes up and by its layout. The funeral procession moves from right to left, against the flow, as it were, of the narrative, forcing the reader to slow down to concentrate. This sense of dislocation is intensified by the paradoxical way in which Edward is first shown alive and enthroned, then dead on his bier, thirdly alive though dying and lastly in the process of being shrouded. The prominence given to the funeral reflects the role of Edward's death as the catalyst for the Tapestry's plot: without it there could have been no Norman Conquest.

This image is unique: the only depicted funeral of an historical individual from the whole of the Anglo-Saxon period. It functions as propaganda, putting it in a different category from the other surviving representations of death and dying. It is categorically different even from most of the other images of corpses in the Tapestry itself, where the dismembered bodies of Norman and English soldiers litter the margins as a kind of decorative motif. The only comparable images are the bloody deaths of Harold and his brothers towards the end of the Tapestry. The contrast is sharply drawn between the stately death, the ritual-embedded funeral, of the true king and the painful, undignified end of Harold, whom the Tapestry presents as a usurper.

Thus, the image of Edward's death has more in common with burials such as Sutton Hoo than is first apparent. It has been said of the ship burial at Sutton Hoo that 'Mound I [is] not to be construed as some mindless custom, the helpless betrayal of a fossilised social system, but the artificial contrivance of a creative mind; not so much an assemblage of finds, as a statement or a text, composed of carefully selected symbols'.[64] The Bayeux Tapestry needs to be read with the same *caveat*.

THE NORMAN CONQUEST

In 1066, Anglo-Saxon England came to an abrupt and violent end; over the next century England saw new royal and aristocratic elites, a new Church hierarchy, a new language and a different kind of architecture. One thing that does not appear to have changed significantly, however, is burial practice. Whereas seventh- and eighth-century burial often consisted of nothing more than a shallow grave containing a shrouded body, burial practices became more complex again from the ninth century. However, the variety of grave constructions remained similar throughout the later period, another complicating factor in the archaeology of the period as it is impossible to date these graves with any precision either side of 1066. Typically, they are aligned west–east, unfurnished, with the body wrapped in nothing more than a shroud. The bodies are often placed in coffins, which sometimes were purpose-made, although at other times they were containers such as chests or even part of a boat.[65] The construction of the grave is often elaborate, mortared or lined with stone and tile as at the church of St Nicholas Shambles, London.[66] Graves are frequently found lined with charcoal: examples have been excavated at Worcester, Hereford, Exeter, Winchester, Oxford, Shrewsbury, Lincoln and York; many bodies are accompanied by 'pillow-stones' either side of the head, keeping it in position. These graves are most often found in the vicinity of cathedrals and may represent the burials of high-ranking Church men and women: a common theme in all this complexity is a concern for the preservation of the body, perhaps an intuitive response to the idea that disease, death and decay are the punishment for sin, and therefore an intact body, like those of Cuthbert, Edmund, Edward and so many other Anglo-Saxon saints, has a better chance of salvation.

Anglo-Saxon cathedrals do not survive, nor do we have many pre-Conquest parish churches, so it is hard to say precisely when changes began to occur in the design of tombstones. It seems that over the course of the century after 1066, a new form of tombstone came into being for the first time since the Roman period (see Chapter 2), one which bore the effigy of the deceased person. Among the earliest of these is the tomb of Abbot Gilbert Crispin of Westminster (d. 1117 or 1118), whose tomb although much worn clearly shows the figure of an abbot in low relief. This was probably intended to attract the attention of the passer-by and invoke their prayer for the dead person's soul, and marks the beginning of a tradition of portrait tomb sculpture which has continued, for some people at least, down to the present day.

Another area which felt the effect of the Conquest was the choice of burial place for the wealthy. As the Anglo-Saxons had, the Norman landowners founded churches and granted land to existing ones, though often giving lands in England to religious houses in Normandy.[67] While many of the first generation of settlers chose to be buried in Normandy, it is notable that the second generation more often chose England as their waiting place for judgement.[68]

However, the century immediately after the Norman Conquest shows no great change where death and burial are concerned, either in practice or in attitude, perhaps because the religion and the culture of the conquerors were close to those conquered. The next great institutional change came in the late twelfth century, with the establishment of the doctrine of Purgatory and the centralisation of the Church under Rome.

Notes

In all references, place of publication is London unless otherwise stated.

1 A. Meaney, *A Gazetteer of Early Anglo-Saxon Burial Sites* (1964).

2 W. D. Klemperer, 'The study of burials at Hulton Abbey', in *Death and Burial: Pre-printed Papers of a Conference on Medieval Archaeology in Europe*, York, 21–24 September 1992, 4, pp. 85–91.

3 T. W. Potter and R. D. Andrews, 'Excavation and survey at St Patrick's Chapel and St Peter's Church, Heysham, Lancashire 1977–8', *The Antiquaries Journal*, 74 (1994), 53–134, esp. 93.

4 S. Sherlock and M. Welch, *An Anglo-Saxon Cemetery at Norton, Cleveland*, Council for British Archaeology Research Report 82 (1992), p. 103.

5 S. M. Hirst, *An Anglo-Saxon Inhumation Cemetery at Sewerby, East Yorkshire*, York University Archaeological Publications (York, 1985), p. 4.

6 G. Kendall, 'A study of grave orientation in several Roman and post-Roman cemeteries from southern Britain', *Archaeological Journal*, 139 (1982), 101–23; P. Rahtz, 'Grave orientation', *Archaeological Journal*, 135 (1978), 1–14.

7 C. Hill, 'The archaeology of Anglo-Saxon England in the pagan period: a review', *Anglo-Saxon England*, 8 (Cambridge, 1979), 297–329, 310; and for Sutton Hoo specifically, M. Carver, *Sutton Hoo: Burial Ground of Kings?* (1998), p. 166.

8 A. Ellison, 'The potential for prehistoric research', *Bulletin of the Sutton Hoo Research Committee*, 4 (1986), 41.

9 A. Reynolds, 'The definition and ideology of Anglo-Saxon execution sites and cemeteries', in G. De Boe and F. Verhaeghe (eds), *Death and Burial in Medieval Europe: Papers of the 'Medieval Europe Brugge 1997' Conference*, vol. II (1997), 33–41, and 'Executions and hard Anglo-Saxon justice', *British Archaeology*, 31 (1998), 8–9.

10 V. Turner, *Ritual Process: Structure and Anti-Structure* (Harmondsworth, 1969).

11 E. Pader, *Symbolism, Social Relations and Interpretation of Mortuary Remains: British Archaeological Reports*, International Series 130 (Oxford, 1982), p. 200.

12 C. Arnold, 'Wealth and social structure: a matter of life and death', in P. Rahtz, T. Dickinson and L. Watts (eds), *Anglo-Saxon Cemeteries 1979*, British Archaeological Reports, British Series 82 (Oxford, 1980), pp. 81–142; H. Härke, 'Changing symbols in a changing society: the Anglo-Saxon weapon burial rite in the seventh century', in M. Carver (ed.), *The Age of Sutton Hoo* (Woodbridge, 1992), pp. 149–66.

13 J. D. Richards, *The Significance of Form and Decoration of Anglo-Saxon Cremation Urns*, British Archaeological Reports 166 (Oxford, 1987).

14 M. Welch, *Anglo-Saxon England* (1992), pp. 100–2.

15 Bede, *A History of the English Church and People* (hereafter *HE*), ed. L. Sherley-Price (Harmondsworth, 1955), I:19, pp. 239–40.

16 R. White, *Roman and Celtic Objects from Anglo-Saxon Graves*, British Archaeological Reports, British Series 191 (Oxford, 1988).

17 Welch, *Anglo-Saxon England*, pp. 104–7.

18 J. Campbell, *The Anglo-Saxons* (Oxford, 1982), p. 30.

19 G. Putnam, 'Spong Hill cremations', *Anglo-Saxon Cemeteries 1979*, pp. 217–19.

20 N. Higham, *Rome, Britain and the Anglo-Saxons* (1992), pp. 229–30.

21 W. Filmer-Sankey, 'Snape Anglo-Saxon cemetery: the current state of knowledge', in Carver (ed.), *The Age of Sutton Hoo*, pp. 39–51.

22 R. Bruce-Mitford, *The Sutton Hoo Ship Burial*, vol. I (1975), p. 457.

23 Although Bede gives no precise date for Redwald, he probably died in the mid-620s (*HE*, II:15). The coins found in Mound 1 indicate a date of deposition between 622 and 629.

24 A. Morgan, 'One man and his (Saxon) horse', *History Today*, 48:1 (1998), 35.

25 G. Jones, *A History of the Vikings* (Oxford, 1968), p. 240. The greatest sources for Viking mythology were written down in the thirteenth century. For a description of Viking mythology, see H. R. Ellis-Davidson, *Gods and Myths of Northern Europe* (Harmondsworth, 1990).

26 M. Posnansky, 'The Pagan-Danish barrow cemetery at Heath Wood, Ingleby', *Derbyshire Archaeological Journal*, 76 (1956), 40–56.

27 M. Biddle and B. Kjølbye-Biddle, 'Repton and the Vikings', *Antiquity*, 62 (1992), 36–51.

28 J. R. Maddicot, 'Plague in seventh century England', *Past and Present*, 156 (1997), 7–54.

29 R. Fletcher, *The Conversion of Europe from Paganism to Christianity 371–1386* (1997), p. 393.

30 R. H. Bailey, *Viking Age Sculpture* (1980), pp. 85–100; P. Jones and N. Pennick, *A History of Pagan Europe* (1995), pp. 132–3. One exception may be the hogback tomb found in 1800 during grave digging at St Peter's, Heysham: although no

body was reported, the discovery of a very corroded Viking spear probably indicates a Viking-style burial. See Potter and Andrews, 'Excavation and survey'.

31 J. Lang, *Continuity and Innovation in Anglo-Saxon Sculpture: A Study in the Metropolitan School at York*, British Archaeological Reports 49 (Oxford, 1978), pp. 145–55; B. Kjølbye-Biddle, *Excavations at York Minster*, vol. I, part 2: *The Finds*, ed. M. Carver (1995), pp. 500–5.

32 M. Dalland, 'Scar: a Viking age boat burial', *Current Archaeology*, 131 (1992), 475–7; J. D. Richards, *Viking Age England* (1991), p. 115.

33 D. O'Sullivan and R. Young, *Lindisfarne* (1995), p. 47.

34 D. Bullough, 'Burial, community and belief in the early medieval West', in P. Wormald, D. Bullough and R. Collins (eds), *Ideal and Reality in Frankish and Anglo-Saxon Society: Studies presented to J. M. Wallace-Hadrill* (Oxford, 1983), pp. 177–201.

35 E. James, *The Franks* (Oxford, 1988), pp. 139 ff.

36 D. Whitelock, *Anglo-Saxon Wills* (Cambridge, 1930), p. 3.

37 *Ibid.*, p. 21.

38 Bullough, 'Burial, community and belief', p. 186.

39 J. Le Goff, *The Birth of Purgatory* (Chicago, 1981), p. 1.

40 Bede, *HE*, IV:29–30, pp. 263–7.

41 C. F. Battiscombe (ed.), *The Relics of St Cuthbert* (Oxford, 1956).

42 Ælfric, *Passion of St Edmund*, in K. Crossley-Holland, *The Anglo-Saxon World* (Oxford, 1984), pp. 228–33.

43 For the trade in relics, see P. J. Geary, *Furta Sacra: Thefts of Relics in the Central Middle Ages* (Princeton, N.J., 1978).

44 Bede, *Two Lives of Saint Cuthbert*, ed. B. Colgrave (Oxford, 1940), IV:13, p. 130.

45 H. Mayr-Harting, *The Coming of Christianity to Anglo-Saxon England*, 3rd edn (1991), p. 190.

46 See for example Augustine, *City of God*, ed. and trans. H. Bettenson, (Harmondsworth, 1984), XXI:19, pp. 989–90.

47 The crux passage occurs in the Second Book of the Maccabees 12:41–6.

48 P. J. Geary, *Living with the Dead in the Middle Ages* (New York, 1994), p. 2.

49 Bede, *HE*, V:12, pp. 292–3.

50 *Ibid.*, III:19, p. 172.

51 C. R. Dodwell, *Anglo-Saxon Art: A New Perspective* (Manchester, 1982), p. 88.

52 Bede, *HE*, II:13, p. 127.

53 Mayr-Harting, *The Coming of Christianity*, p. 166.

54 M. Gatch, *Preaching and Theology in Anglo-Saxon England: Ælfric and Wulfstan* (Toronto, 1977).

55 Ælfric, *Homilies of Ælfric: A Supplementary Collection*, ed. J. C. Pope, 2 vols, Early English Texts Society 259–60 (1967–68); *The Homilies of the Anglo-Saxon Church: The First Part, containing the Sermones Catholici or Homilies of Ælfric*, ed. B. Thorpe, 2 vols (1844–46).

56 British Library Cotton Claudius B.Iv.

57 Dodwell, *Anglo-Saxon Art*, pp. 171–2.

58 G. I. Needham, *Lives of Three English Saints* (New York, 1966), p. 55.

59 *The Dream of the Rood*, line 40, in *A Choice of Anglo-Saxon Verse*, ed. R. Hamer (1970), p. 163.

60 M. Carver, *Sutton Hoo Research Committee Bulletins 1983–1993* (Woodbridge, 1993), and Carver, *Sutton Hoo: Burial Ground of Kings?*, esp. pp. 137–53.

61 Reynolds, 'Definition and ideology'.

62 F. Barlow, *Vita Eadwardi regis qui requiescit apud Westmonasterium* (*The Life of King Edward who rests at Westminster*) (Oxford, 1992), p. 81.

63 D. J. Bernstein, *The Mystery of the Bayeux Tapestry* (1986), pp. 37 ff.

64 M. Carver, 'The Anglo-Saxon cemetery at Sutton Hoo: an interim report', in Carver (ed.), *The Age of Sutton Hoo*, p. 350.

65 D. Philips, and B. Heywood, *Excavations at York Minster*, vol. I: *From Roman Fortress to Norman Cathedral*, part 2: *The finds* (York, 1995), pp. 502–5.

66 M. Carver, *Underneath English Towns: Interpreting Urban Archaeology* (1987), p. 95.

67 A. Williams, *The English and the Norman Conquest* (Woodbridge, 1995), p. 210.
68 B. Golding, 'Anglo-Norman knightly burials', *Medieval Knighthood (Proceedings of the Strawberry Hill Conference)*, vol. I (Woodbridge, 1986), 35–48.

Select bibliography

Bailey, R. H., *Viking Age Sculpture*, 1980.

Battiscombe, C. F. (ed.), *The Relics of St Cuthbert*, Oxford, 1956.

Bede, *A History of the English Church and People*, ed. L. Sherley-Price, Harmondsworth, 1955.

Binski, P. *Medieval Death: Ritual and Representation*, 1996.

Bruce-Mitford, R., *The Sutton Hoo Ship Burial*, 1975.

Campbell, J., *The Anglo-Saxons*, Oxford, 1982.

Carver, M. O. H. (ed.), *The Age of Sutton Hoo: The Seventh Century in North-Western Europe*, Woodbridge, 1992.

Le Goff, J., *The Birth of Purgatory*, Chicago, 1981.

Morris, R., *Churches in the Landscape*, 1989.

Rahtz, P., Dickinson, T., and Watts, L. (eds), *Anglo-Saxon Cemeteries 1979*, British Archaeological Reports, British Series 82, Oxford, 1980.

Reynolds, A., 'The definition and ideology of Anglo-Saxon execution sites and cemeteries', in G. De Boe and F. Verhaeghe (eds), *Death and Burial in Medieval Europe: Papers of the 'Medieval Europe Brugge 1997' Conference*, vol. II, 1997.

Richards, J. D., *Viking Age England*, 1991.

Welch, M., *Anglo-Saxon England*, 1992.

Whitelock, D., *Anglo-Saxon Wills*, Cambridge, 1930.

4 · Rosemary Horrox

Purgatory, prayer and plague: 1150–1380

In the twelfth century the culture of western Europe was transformed. It is a transformation which had many dimensions – so many, that historians now see the period as a renaissance rivalling 'The Renaissance' in significance. Central authority claimed a growing jurisdiction over local power structures, while beliefs and systems became increasingly defined. Custom, to put it rather simplistically, was beginning to give way to law. The shift can be clearly seen in the efforts of Rome to define and establish acceptable belief throughout western Christendom. The centralising authority of the Papacy was not new, and nor were the beliefs being promulgated, but the reality of the shift is reflected in the ease with which historians have talked of 'the teaching of the Church' in these centuries as if it were a synonym for belief. In fact, as historians have become increasingly aware, knowing what the Church taught is not evidence that the teaching was being absorbed. If one looks closely at the behaviour and attitudes of the laity, it rapidly becomes apparent that required belief at times co-existed uneasily with actual belief, and nowhere is this more true than in the case of ideas about death and the afterlife.

In theological terms, the twelfth century saw the beginnings of the formalisation of the concept of Purgatory: a halfway stage between earth and Heaven, where the sinful but repentant soul could, through purgatorial or cleansing punishment, complete the process of making satisfaction for sin and so be rendered fit for Heaven. The doctrine was promulgated in this developed form at the second Council of Lyons in 1274, but it took time to percolate through all social levels, and there is reason to think that the process was not complete until well into the fourteenth century.[1] But although dissemination may have been slow, it was steady. The doctrine of Purgatory, and particularly the belief that the punishment of the soul could be lightened by the prayers of the living, was a theological success story, and its wide acceptance constituted a significant shift in thinking about death, and about the relationship of the living and the dead.

If the twelfth-century renaissance defines the beginning of the period covered in this chapter, demographic disaster defines its end.

The fourteenth century saw the reversal of the steady population growth which had characterised earlier centuries. Twelfth- and thirteenth-century England displayed many of the characteristics of a rising population, including a fall in real wage levels, major land reclamation and a marked rise in the value of land. Many modern commentators have regarded the turn of the thirteenth and fourteenth centuries as the point at which demand began to outstrip resources, with a consequent reduction in living standards among the mass of the population and a greater vulnerability to disease. Some historians have argued that this in itself was sufficient to halt population growth, through reduced fertility and increased mortality. But the real villain of the piece in the first part of the century was a major famine, which affected all of northern Europe and brought mortality of at least 10 per cent (and perhaps nearer 15 per cent) in England. The famine's immediate cause was a series of bad harvests in 1315–17 caused by a run of cold wet summers, although the high mortality levels suggest that this disaster had hit a population which was dangerously near the margin of subsistence.

Although the death rate was dramatic, it is unlikely that the famine initiated a long-term population decline. Such evidence as there is suggests that the population began to recover once the run of bad harvests was over. But the impact of the famine was in any case eclipsed a generation later by the arrival of epidemic plague – the Black Death – in Europe. The disease, bubonic plague and its variants, reached the south coast of England in the summer of 1348 and it was not until December 1349 that the archbishop of Canterbury felt able to refer to the plague as something which was safely in the past.[2] In fact, the disease had become endemic, and there were further outbreaks in 1361 and 1369, with regular recurrences thereafter. These later outbreaks did not rival the virulence of the first, which had killed almost half the population, but by attacking predominantly adolescents and children they blocked any population recovery for at least a century.

Causes of death

Apart from the fourteenth-century famine and plague it is almost impossible to generalise about causes of death in these centuries. Contemporary writers, even when describing the death of an eminent individual, rarely offer any sort of diagnosis. This reflects their perception of illness. Where modern doctors and most laymen see disease as an identifiable entity (such as tuberculosis or smallpox), their medieval predecessors thought primarily in terms of symptoms (such as fever or palsy) which needed to be relieved. The modern concept of a 'terminal illness' was therefore barely present, but doctors and their patients did recognise the approach of death, and the warning symptoms were frequently listed:

Wanne mine eyhen misten	(When my eye mists
and mine heren sissen	and my hearing fails
and mi nose koldet	and my nose goes cold
and mi tunge ffoldet	and my tongue curls back
and mi rude slaket	and my face falls in
and mine lippes blaken	and my lips blacken
and mi muth grennet	and my mouth gapes
and mi spotel rennet	and my spittle runs
and min her riset	and my hair stands on end
and min herte griset	and my heart trembles
and mine honden biuien	and my hands shake
and mine ffet stiuien[3]	and my feet go stiff)

Other writers drew attention to a sharpening of the nose, panting breath, chattering teeth and a rattling in the throat.[4] Such lists served a moralising as well as a medical purpose, encouraging the sinner to think on his ultimate fate and to recognise the approach of death in time to make proper spiritual preparation. The stanza quoted above concludes, warningly, 'All too late, all too late / When the bier is at the gate'.

None of the symptoms listed is an infallible sign of death and although contemporaries were aware of the importance of checking for respiration, mistakes could occur. Medieval miracle stories regularly feature the recovery of people thought to be dead, like the toddler Roger who fell into the castle ditch at Conway and was the subject of a coroner's inquest before he revived. One of the recorders of Becket's miracles observed that recoveries from death after two or three days were not uncommon in England.[5] Perhaps just because such recoveries were invariably explained as miraculous interventions rather than errors of diagnosis, there seems to have been little anxiety about premature burial, even though there was usually only a short space of time between (presumed) death and funeral.

If the medical definitions of death were, to modern eyes, rather vague, contemporaries were alert to differences in the *type* of death, including the distinction between natural and unnatural death, and the division of the latter into accidental death or murder. Such distinctions were the concern of coroners: the county officials appointed from 1194 to watch the king's interests at a local level. The Crown had a double interest in sudden death. Homicide was a felony, and as such was usually reserved to the royal courts. The first duty of the coroner's jury was thus to decide the cause of death. That of Henry Colburn of Barford, Bedfordshire, in August 1266 was a clear case of homicide. He had failed to return after going out for a drink one evening, and his mother found his body the next morning with seven knife wounds to the heart and stomach, four wounds to the head made with a pickaxe and further wounds to the throat, chin and head. By contrast, the death of Nicholas Mandeville of Watford, Northamptonshire, in June 1301 was ascribed by the jurors to a stroke of paralysis as he slept, not to the slight wound he had received three days earlier when he had been playing quoits and had been struck on the head by his brother's quoit. In cases of homicide or misadventure the object which had caused death was forfeit to the Crown and it was accordingly the responsibility of the jury to value such objects. When a beggar-woman was found with her throat cut at Buckby, Northamptonshire, in 1321, her male companion who was assumed to have committed the murder could not be traced, but the knife was duly valued at 1d.[6]

Memento mori

Important as the differentiation of natural and unnatural death might be for legal process, the crucial distinction in spiritual terms was between the good and the bad death. The two types of categorisation often, in fact, overlapped, since an unnatural death was more likely to be one for which proper preparation had not been made, so compromising the salvation of the individual concerned. The medieval Church was insistent that, to avoid this danger, individuals should live as though each day might be their last: fulfilling the necessary religious observances, including the performance of good works, and, above all, ensuring as far as possible that they were in a state of grace. They should eschew sin and make spiritual reparation, through contrition and penance, for any wrongs committed.

Preachers and moralists saw the contemplation of death as a valuable part of this preparatory process. Thinking on death in general, and the bodily dissolution which would accompany one's own death in particular, would inculcate humility and put worldly glory in its proper perspective. As an early-fourteenth-century Franciscan preacher expressed it:

> Nothing is more abhorrent than [a] corpse: it is not left in the house lest his family die; it is not thrown into the water lest it become polluted; it is not hung in the air lest it become tainted; but it is thrown in a ditch like deadly poison so that it may not be seen any further, it is surrounded with earth so that its stench may not rise, it is firmly trodden down so that it may not rise again but stay, earth in earth.[7]

Other than in illustrations of the fourth horseman of the Apocalypse, who is usually shown simply as a crowned human figure [**plate 8**], Death itself was hardly ever personified in this period, although there is a rare and powerful exception in the bestiary produced *c.* 1270–90 and now in Westminster Abbey [**plate 6**]. It was the Dead whom men were urged to visualise. The most dramatic of these visual confrontations was the popular story of the three living and the three dead, in which three men out hunting meet three dead men, who tell them 'what you are, we were, and what we are, you will be'. The theme was probably introduced into England in the thirteenth century through the poems of Baudoiun de Conde and others, and in the course of the fourteenth century became a popular subject of manuscript illumination and wall painting throughout England.[8] In the pictorial versions, the three men are often shown as kings and, influenced perhaps by the

36] St Guthlac's soul being taken to God. The saint's soul is shown as a small naked figure issuing from his mouth into the hands of an angel. A second angel is poised to take up the soul in a cloth, compare also [44] and [45].

iconography of the three Magi, as representatives of the three ages of man: youth, prime of life and age. One of the earliest, if not the earliest, English illustrations of the story is in the de Lisle Psalter [**plate 7**], where the kings' horrified comments and the responses of the dead run:

Ich am afert	(I am afraid
Ich wes wel fair	I was well fair
Lo whet ich se	Lo what I see
Such scheltou be	Such shalt thou be
Me thinketh hit beth develes thre	I think these be devils three
For godes love be wer by me	For God's love be warned by me)

The animated corpses of this story are one hint that in western Europe at this time the death of the body was not seen – as Christian teaching required – as something which occurred at the moment when the soul left the body. The orthodox version of events dominates the religious iconography of the period, with the moment of death shown by the departure of the soul, represented as a little naked figure, from the mouth of the dying person [36].[9] But an alternative tradition gives the body a continuing postmortem life of its own, and this version even surfaces occasionally in the Church's own teaching. A thirteenth-century English collection of *exempla* illustrates the value of prayers for the dead with the story of a Gascon priest who was in the habit of sprinkling the graves in his churchyard with holy water while praying for the souls of the dead. One day the bodies of the dead arose from their graves, holding out cupped hands for the holy water. Once they had received it they went back to sleep.[10]

The belief that corpses retained some form of life – at least until the flesh had rotted off the bones – can often be glimpsed in medieval literature. It is present, for instance, in Walter Map's story of a shoe-maker of Constantinople who had sexual intercourse with his dead wife in her tomb and engendered a Medusa-like head whose gaze killed anyone looking upon it. One form of story-telling where it is rarely made so explicit is in ghost stories. Most of the surviving tales were produced under the aegis of the Church and present ghosts not as corpses but as souls returning from Purgatory to advise or seek help from the living – their visitation unsettling perhaps, but beneficial. There can be little doubt, however, that an alternative interpretation of ghosts existed. A group of Yorkshire ghost stories written down in *c.* 1400 conforms to the clerical stereotype of an appearance motivated by the need for spiritual help, but the revenants are material (they can be held) and they terrify observers. Evidence of fear, in fact, can be the clearest indication of belief in the restless dead. In the second half of the twelfth century a penitential refers to rituals being performed at funerals 'lest the dead take vengeance'.[11]

Good and bad deaths

If Christians had prepared themselves for death during their lifetimes, even an unexpected death (*mors improvisa*) was not necessarily to be feared. But in practice the expectation was that, for lay people at least, intensive preparation would not begin until death was at hand: hence the value of recognising approaching death in good time, and the anxiety attached to a sudden death. The Church, echoing the Psalmist, regarded knowledge of how long one had to live as a spiritual blessing, and it was taken as evidence of sanctity that an individual had shown foreknowledge of their exact time of death.[12]

As ever in discussing medieval attitudes to death, the Church's views on what was desirable are better documented than how people actually behaved. But there are indications that not everyone wanted to be warned of their approaching death. At least one medieval doctor went on record as saying that patients should not be given bad news about their condition. Even warning the family was to be avoided unless there was no possible doubt about the prognosis. Doctors seem also to have ignored the ruling of the fourth Lateran Council in 1215 that a patient should make confession to a priest before commencing treatment – presumably on the grounds that patients would think that they had been given up for lost already.[13] Preachers addressed this unwillingness to make sickbed confessions with a vehemence which suggests that it was widespread. Among the *exempla* they used to make their point was the story attributed to Bede of a sick knight who postponed confession until he should be well again and was disembowelled by two demons wielding ploughshares, who then carried him off to Hell.[14] Even those patients who accepted the wisdom of regular confession, like William Marshal, whose long dying, like his life, is presented by his biographer as a model for the Christian knight, might still find it hard to confront their own mortality. The sharpness of Marshal's rejection of the suggestion that the robes made ready for his retainers' summer livery should be sold and the money used in alms surely owes something to an unwillingness to accept that he would not be alive at Whitsuntide, when such robes were usually distributed.[15]

Even if acceptance of one's own death proved harder than the Church thought desirable, the perception of a good death as a prepared death does seem to have been fairly generally shared. Warning of the end meant that earthly business could be brought to a tidy conclusion, and most medieval wills were made, or at least revised, on the deathbed. It also allowed the dying person to make their peace with God through the last rites. The priest would be summoned when it was thought that death was near, and priests with the cure of souls were forbidden to sleep outside their parish or even to go far from the church at night, so that they could be easily found if needed. It is clear that the dying or their families often resisted sending for the priest until the last minute, seeing it as an admission that death was inevitable. The Church responded by urging priests to instruct parishioners that the sacrament of extreme unction could be repeated and that if recipients of the last rites subsequently recovered there was nothing to stop them returning to their normal life style. There was a widespread popular belief that such people had been severed from ordinary life, and must observe a penitential life style for the rest of their days, abstaining from meat and from sexual intercourse.[16]

The last rites generally had three components. The priest would hear the individual's confession and grant absolution. Then followed the anointing: the sacrament of extreme unction. The priest used his right thumb to make the sign of the cross in holy oil on the eyes, ears, nostrils, mouth, hands, feet and back of the dying person, seeking God's pardon for the sins committed through each part of the body. Finally, the patient would receive the consecrated wafer which the priest had brought with him, known in the context of the last rites as the viaticum (provisions for a journey). But this was only to be administered if the patient was aware of what was happening, that is, was not mad or drunk, and was able to swallow the wafer without risk of vomiting it back.[17]

After the last rites the dying waited for death, often with a crucifix held or placed before their eyes. As the moment of death approached,

37] The deathbed of Llewelyn of Wales, with his sons Griffin and David. Although a highly standardised representation it reflects the assumption that family members would be present at the deathbed. Both the sons are depicted in a restrained attitude of grief.

doors and windows would be opened so that the soul would not be hindered in making its escape.[18] In monastic communities, the dying religious would be lifted from the bed and placed on ashes on the ground as a demonstration of the humbling of the body in death. Some laymen adopted the practice as a dramatic assertion of penitence, among them Henry II's son Henry, the Young King, who died in rebellion against his father. Other lay people were sufficiently attracted by the spiritual benefits of a monastic deathbed to enter an order late in life, sometimes at the point of death.[19]

Deathbeds were public occasions. Family and friends were expected to be present, taking turns to watch for the changes which warned that death was close [37]. Neighbours and acquaintances would be alerted by the summoning of the priest to perform the last rites, his passage through the streets with the Host marked by the ringing of a handbell.[20] For contemporaries, perhaps the most shocking thing about the Black Death was that fear of contagion led people to abandon the sick, leaving

97

them to die alone, like animals.[21] The human condition demanded a companioned death.

In spiritual terms, not all these elements of a good death were equally important. If for some reason the last sacraments could not be provided, faith would suffice. Even confession to a priest was not essential, as the bishop of Bath and Wells reminded his flock at the height of the first plague outbreak. Confession to a lay man, even to a lay woman, would be sufficient in an emergency.[22] The crucial element was contrition for sins committed and a desire to make reparation, since penance which had been willed could be completed in Purgatory. That might be achieved even if death caught one unawares and, although only God could know whether an individual had indeed repented, the dead were normally given the benefit of the doubt. The office for the dead in the Sarum Missal accordingly included a collect to be used in the exequies of one overtaken by sudden death:

> Almighty and merciful God, in whose power rest all the conditions of human life, absolve, we beseech thee, the soul of thy servant from all his sins; that he may not lose by a sudden death the fruits of that repentance which his soul desired.[23]

Contemporary writers thus avoided making outright claims that an individual was damned. Instead, they signalled the possibility by ascribing a bad death to the person concerned: a death, that is, which had struck when the individual, whether through passion or despair, was in no state of mind to be thinking of salvation. The circumstances of such deaths were often presented as grotesque or undignified, as in Matthew Paris's account of the boozy prior of Thetford, disembowelled in a drunken quarrel.[24] But the most extreme form of the bad death, and the one generally thought to preclude hope of salvation, was suicide. This was the most profound of sins – the ultimate rejection of divine grace – and the overwhelming sinfulness of suicide eclipsed any perception of it as a crime, although the confiscation of a suicide's possessions to the Crown does carry the implication that self-murder, like treason, was a sort of superfelony. Unless the verdict could be softened by an assumption of madness the suicide was refused burial in consecrated ground. In spite of the spiritual penalties, suicide was not uncommon in the Middle Ages. But although contemporaries speak of self-killing in general as if it were a familiar option, their reference to *specific* deaths which might have been suicides tend to be more guarded and ambiguous.[25]

Preparation of the body

In most cases, the preparation of the body for burial was a relatively straightforward matter and followed immediately upon death. The naked body would be washed in warm water and then shrouded, usually in a linen sheet. In England it was the practice to cover the face. Styles of shrouding varied, to judge by contemporary illustrations, but the cloth was usually drawn closely round the body, with the ends tucked in to

plate 5] Execution scene. This scene from an illustrated translation of part of the Old Testament purports to show Pharaoh sitting in judgement and ordering an execution. In fact, the details of dress and custom are based on contemporary Anglo-Saxon practice.

plate 6] Death comes for a young man. Death's face has been largely erased, but he is a less threatening figure than the animated corpses shown in such contexts in the fifteenth century and is not holding a weapon. The young man appears to welcome his appearance.

plate 7] The Three Living and the Three Dead. One of the earliest English representations of the story. The kings are shown as much of an age and the corpses are all in a similar state of decomposition. Later versions often have the kings representing the three ages of man and the dead showing the progressive stages of decay.

plate 8] The Fourth Horseman of the Apocalypse: Death with Hell following after. The usual representation of Hell mouth has here been set on feet, with a devil riding aloft. Death is a haloed figure almost indistinguishable from the Evangelist on the left. Above them is the Lamb with the book of seven seals, four of which have been opened (Revelation 6.7–8).

give a smooth surface. The practice of rolling the corpse in the shroud and tying or knotting the edges in bunches at head and feet seems to have come into use in the course of the fourteenth century, and the illustration of the dead coming out of their tombs in the Holkham Bible Picture Book, which dates from the second quarter of the century, includes a single example among the various styles of shroud [38]. Some illustrations show the shroud hugging the body so tightly that it must have been taped or sewn in place, which would have made the body easier to handle in a coffinless burial. Where a coffin was to be used, the shrouding may have been done more loosely, although the very loose shrouds and bare heads shown in representations of the raising of the dead were intended to show the newly resurrected freed from their constricting grave clothes.

For the elite, the postmortem preparation of the body might be considerably more elaborate, sometimes for reasons of display but more commonly because a longer time was likely to elapse between death and interment. Two methods could be used to allow the body to be kept unburied. If the object of the exercise was simply to allow easy transport over a long distance, the body would be disembowelled, dismembered and boiled, to separate the flesh from the bones. The flesh and entrails would be buried at the place of death and the bones transported to the preferred burial site. This was the usual way of dealing with important casualties of military campaigns, such as Sir John Marmaduke, who died in Scotland early in the fourteenth century and was boiled up on his executors' orders for transport back to Durham.[26] It was, however, a drastic deconstruction of the body and where a long journey was not involved, embalming was generally preferred. Embalming was in any case essential when the body was to be displayed during the obsequies, which was the case at royal and elite ecclesiastical funerals until at least the end of the thirteenth century.

Medieval embalming entailed opening the body from throat to groin, removing the viscera and cleansing the body cavity with vinegar before packing it with salt and spices.[27] This would have had only a limited preservative effect, but the body was then wrapped closely in cerecloth: strips of fine linen cloth (or even silk) soaked in molten wax. If the wrapping was sufficiently fine (and in the case of Edward I even the thumbs and fingers were individually wrapped) the body could then be dressed: kings in their coronation regalia, with replica insignia; prelates in their mass vestments.[28] In the case of female corpses, modesty may have demanded that the task was undertaken by women. The body of Edward I's queen, Eleanor, who died at Harby, Nottinghamshire, in 1290, was taken to the Gilbertine house of St Catherine's just south of Lincoln where it could be prepared by the lay sisters of the hospital for its journey to London.

38] The dead emerge from their tombs at the end of the world. They are in the process of freeing themselves from their shrouds, and are shown with their faces uncovered, although English practice was to cover the face for burial. Various styles of shrouding are suggested, including the practice of rolling the corpse in a sheet tied at head and feet, which is the method usually illustrated in later shroud brasses.

39] The heart monument of Bishop Aymer de Valence (d. 1260) in Winchester Cathedral. A rare survival of the once-common practice of marking the separate burial of the heart or viscera. It is possible that some small monuments traditionally claimed to be the tombs of children are in fact heart monuments. The bishop is shown half-length, holding his heart between his hands.

The evisceration of the body, whether as a prelude to boiling or embalming, allowed the division of the body between various sites. The burial of the entrails near the place of death was initially, and largely remained, a matter of practical hygiene, although they would be buried in consecrated ground and sometimes, as in the case of the viscera of Abbot William de Trumpington of St Albans (d. 1235), given their own monument.[29] But by the end of the twelfth century it was becoming common among the elite to request the separate burial of the heart at a place dear to them. Before William de Mandeville died in Normandy in 1189 he wished his body to be taken back to Walden, Essex, for burial, but when he was assured that this would be too difficult given the stormy seas he reluctantly compromised on his heart being carried to Walden and his body buried at the nearby abbey of Mortemer. For Richard I, ten years later, separate heart burial was no longer simply a matter of convenience but a way of maintaining links with more than one favoured place. His body travelled to Fontevrault for burial but he willed his heart to Rouen. In the thirteenth century such sentimental, rather than practical, division of the body became commonplace among the elite. William Beauchamp (d. 1276) wanted his heart to be buried wherever his wife was buried. Edward I (d. 1307) asked for his bones and flesh to be separated: the bones to be carried with the English army against Scotland until the Scots were vanquished and his heart to be taken to the Holy Land. In fact his wishes were ignored and his body embalmed and buried at Westminster, but many individuals (including Edward's father Henry III) did secure separate heart burial [39].[30]

This desire to apportion the body between favoured places was no doubt partly a means of soliciting prayers from more than one religious foundation, but it also seems to be another indication that the corpse was expected to retain some awareness after death.[31] At the least it implies that human identity after death was taken to reside in the body as well as the soul; an attitude which, it has recently been argued, was within this period bringing about a greater theological emphasis on the bodily resurrection. This is likely to be one area – the formulation of the doctrine of Purgatory has been seen as another – where theologians were taking up existing popular assumptions. The equation of identity with body might seem to put a premium on keeping the body intact, and the Church did indeed feel it necessary to give assurance that limbs devoured by wild animals, or whole bodies eaten by cannibals, would be restored to their rightful owners at the Last Judgement. But what was causing anxiety here was the fate of body parts after they had passed through a digestive system. The value attached in this period to the possession of relics – which led to the wholesale dismemberment of saintly bodies to supply the demand – makes it clear that contemporaries had no problems with the idea that surviving body parts could be reassembled for resurrection, however scattered they had become.[32]

The respect accorded to relics reveals a conviction that the saint was in some sense present wherever pieces of his or her body survived. Viewed from this perspective, division of a body between burial sites might be taken to imply not merely the body's continuing sense of self, but a multiplication of that selfhood. Although in the twelfth and thirteenth centuries the clerical as well as the lay elite of northern Europe embraced the division of their bodies with enthusiasm, neither implication was orthodox, and in 1299 Pope Boniface VIII outlawed the practice. On 27 September he issued the bull *Detestande feritatis* which required that in future bodies were to be buried immediately and intact, under pain of excommunication.[33] If this meant that the body could not be buried in the desired place, it could be exhumed and moved once it had returned to ashes, that is, decomposed naturally – a process conventionally assumed to take a year. In England, the bull may have contributed to the marked decline in separate heart burials over the next fifty years, but it did nothing to stop the practice of preparing bodies for transport over a distance.

Funeral and burial

Once the body had been made ready it could be taken for burial in consecrated ground. Where burial was taking place locally the assumption was that it would take place soon after death, even on the following day. Until then, the body would usually be kept at home, watched over by family and friends and with lights burning around it. This watching – the wake – was regarded with suspicion by the Church, and confessors were encouraged to ask penitents about their behaviour on such occasions. What was feared is revealed by the thirteenth-century regulations of the Palmers' Guild of Ludlow:

> If any man wishes, as is customary, to keep night-watches with the dead, this is permissible, on condition that he does not venture to summon up ghosts, make rude jokes about the body or its reputation, or play other indecent games [*ludos inhonestos*].[34]

If the funeral was taking place locally, the body would be carried to burial, accompanied by family and friends and preceded by clergy

40] Hares officiating at the funeral procession of a hound. Dogs carry the bier, covered in a pall. A hare in priestly vestments asperges the coffin, while an acolyte censes it. Three hares carry tapers and a cross, and the procession is led by a bell ringer. Only the triumphant hare, perched on top of the bier and blowing a trumpet, breaks with convention.

bearing a processional cross and candles [40]. Where the deceased had been a member of a guild there might be an opportunity for additional pageantry, with a guild banner leading the procession and fellow members marching in their guild livery.[35] Sometimes the body would be carried in a wooden box or coffin. More usually the shrouded body was placed on a bier: a wooden stretcher with feet to keep it clear of the ground when set down. A wooden or metal frame, called the hearse – in contrast to the twentieth-century use of the word – would generally be set over the body and a pall draped over that, forming a kind of tent to hide the corpse from view. Parishes were expected to have their own hearse and pall which could be lent out for funerals. The bier would normally be carried by men of similar social status to the deceased – it was regarded as improper for females to act as bearers.[36] Another of the shocking departures from custom during the Black Death was the need to hire people to carry the body (or for the immediate family to have to cope alone) rather than having friends and relations do it.[37]

If the body had to be taken a significant distance it would be enclosed in something more substantial than a shroud. Ox hide was favoured in the twelfth century. Earl Geoffrey de Mandeville, who died at Chester in 1167, was disembowelled and then wrapped in leather before being closed in a box for the journey to Essex. In such cases the body was transported by cart for most of the way, but respect demanded that at journey's end the body was again taken up by bearers. The importance attached to shouldering the body is powerfully conveyed by the funeral of St Hugh of Lincoln (d. 1200). When, after a journey of six days, the bishop's cortège reached the foot of the hill on which his cathedral stood, the king and magnates of England took up the body for the final procession.[38]

The liturgy for the dead consisted of a Requiem mass preceded by the office of the dead: vespers on the evening before the funeral (known as *Placebo*, from the opening word of the antiphon), and lauds and matins (*Dirige*) on the following morning. By the fourteenth century, and probably earlier, the belief that the bodies of lay people should remain outside the church during the exequies had eroded, and it seems to have been accepted that even non-elite bodies should be present at least for the mass itself, unless there was any risk of pollution by blood leaking from the body, which would necessitate the church's reconsecration. During the exequies the bier would be surrounded by candles held by mourners or mounted on the hearse. Light played a central role in the liturgy – the opening words of the Requiem mass were 'Rest eternal grant them, Lord, and light perpetual shine on them' – and the importance attached to providing lights at even humble funerals is suggested by the tradition in some churches of breaking up the paschal candle after Trinity Sunday each year to supply lights for poor people's funerals.[39]

The bodies of the elite were set down in the centre of the chancel, feet towards the high altar, but it is not clear that ordinary men and women, who had not enjoyed access to the chancel during life, were granted it at their funerals and it is possible that their bodies remained in the nave. The body was censed at key points during the mass, but it was not the focus of events and it was ritually the sign that the mass was over and the burial service about to commence when the priest, now divested of the cope he had worn during the mass, came to stand at the head of the corpse.[40] The procession then re-formed and moved off towards the grave.

The place of burial reflected the status of the deceased. The elite generally favoured burial within a religious house, and the right to such a burial was a recognised return for their benefactions. Burial within the parish church was usually also reserved for members of locally important families, with their precise status further signalled by the proximity of their resting place to the high altar or to the tombs of saints. Indeed some medieval bishops made it a formal requirement that only patrons and their families could be buried inside the church. The resort to regulation reflects the growing demand for intramural burial: a demand which clergy found it hard to resist, particularly when the request was coupled with an offer of endowment. A survey of wills from the diocese of Salisbury reveals that while 65 per cent of testators before 1399 anticipated burial in the churchyard, in the fifteenth century 61 per cent asked for burial within the church.[41] This increase probably owes most to considerations of status, but it may also indicate a growing awareness that a grave inside the church was more likely to retain its identity than one in the increasingly crowded churchyard.

Burial indoors naturally demanded some care in the enclosing of the corpse. High-status burials used a stone sarcophagus, either carved from a single block of fairly soft stone (such as sandstone or limestone) or made up of slabs. Such receptacles were not easily come by, and the chronicler's emphasis that Geoffrey de Mandeville (d. 1167) was buried in a sarcophagus which had never before held a body hints at the practice of recycling them.[42] The sarcophagus was usually placed just below the floor level, with its stone lid flush with or just proud of the paving stones, although sometimes it was built into a monument above ground. In either case, secure sealing was essential, with the lid thoroughly mortared in place. The tomb of Archbishop Geoffrey de Ludham of York (d. 1265) had a lead lining inside the limestone coffin to give a good seal.[43] For those buried inside the church but without a stone sarcophagus, deeper burial was desirable. Sir Hugh Hastings (d. 1347) of Elsing, Norfolk, was buried in a wooden coffin about 1.3 metres below floor level, in a brick-lined shaft capped with a Purbeck marble grave slab.[44]

Most lay people would be buried in the churchyard, usually uncoffined. Even where a coffin had been used for transporting the corpse, it would not necessarily be interred with it. To be buried in a coffin was thus generally a sign of status, although it may on occasion have been dictated by the state of the corpse. During the Black Death European cities for which sanitary regulations survive insisted on coffined burial, the lid sealed to prevent the egress of corrupt air.[45] The favoured coffin wood, and the one used in Hugh Hastings' coffin, was elm, because of its water-resistance, with the planks held together with wooden pegs or with iron corner pieces and nails; the latter often the only archaeological evidence of coffin burial.

The priest would have marked the grave site before the obsequies by sprinkling it with holy water and making a cross in the earth. The grave was then dug after the Requiem mass in the presence of the cortège, which helps to explain why medieval graves are normally much shallower than their modern counterparts, often less than a metre deep [41]. Hence the insistence on keeping animals, especially rooting animals like pigs, out of cemeteries lest they dug up bodies. Although this might seem to imply a rather casual attitude to disposal, it is clear that graves were marked and respected, with new ones carefully placed relative to existing burials of a similar date. This was, of course, only possible while there was still room for new graves. Ultimately some sites had to be reused, with any bones turned up in the process removed to a charnel.[46] In theological terms there was nothing against this, so long as the bones were treated with respect, since the bodies would be safely reassembled at the Last Judgement and until then were surplus to spiritual requirements. But given the prevalent belief that bodies and body parts retained some sense of identity, individuals valued the possession of their own graves, and the absence of recorded anxieties about the disturbance of graves is more likely to be because such disturbance was uncommon than because people were untroubled by it; a reading supported by the lack of references to charnels in England much before the fifteenth century.

41] The burial of Joshua, showing the characteristically shallow burial of a shrouded but uncoffined body. The gravediggers have turned up a skull from an earlier burial. Such stray bones were generally removed to charnel houses.

This sense of the grave as a private space explains why the necessity of mass burials during the Black Death horrified observers. Contemporary chronicles give dramatic accounts of bodies flung huggermugger into pits. In fact, the plague pit excavated in London's Smithfield reveals that bodies were carefully placed, with due regard to their correct orientation with the head to the west.[47] It seems to have been the mere fact that the burials allowed no personal or social differentiation which shocked contemporaries, coupled with the unpleasantness of large numbers of decomposing corpses covered by only a skin of soil as the pits were filled. The contemporary Rochester chronicler commented that people could hardly bear to pass a graveyard because of the stench.[48]

Mourning and memorialisation

Just as the deathbed was a public occasion, so people hoped to be well escorted to the grave. Religious fraternities had always concerned themselves with providing a good send-off for their members, even to the extent of paying for an honourable funeral for those members who could not afford one. Part of that concern was that the funeral should be well attended, and this desire seems to have intensified after the Black Death, when the proliferation of guilds and their emphasis on funeral arrangements surely owes something to a reaction against the impersonal and truncated exequies of the plague years. The Norwich tailors' guild, for instance, established in 1350, expected all the brothers and sisters to attend the dirge, mass and burial of a dead member who died locally and sent representatives to funerals within 7 miles of the city. This was partly to demonstrate guild solidarity, but it also reflects the value attached to prayers at the funeral, and the guild duly made provision for prayers to be said locally for any member who died too far away for any attendance at the funeral to be feasible.[49]

Little is known about behaviour at funerals, but it seems that expressions of grief which would be acceptable in private were considered a breach of decorum at the funeral itself. Accounts of miraculous revivals from death sometimes include descriptions of friends and neighbours wailing around the corpse, and although the lamentation serves an obvious dramatic purpose – heightening the tension before the moment of resurrection – it was important that such stories should seem credible to their audience. When it came to the funeral, however, the prevailing attitude, at least in clerical circles, was that excessive emotionalism should be discouraged since it implied a lack of confidence in salvation and an undue emphasis on the things of this world. When the king of Scotland was so overcome at the funeral of St Hugh 'that he could not approach the coffin, but remained behind weeping bitterly' the chronicler comments that 'if his sorrow had been less intense he would have realised that he had more cause for rejoicing'.[50] The account is not unsympathetic, but there is a clear implication that the king's grief was misplaced.

42] The burial of Judas Maccabaeus. The shrouded body is placed in a tomb while mourners look on. The placing of one or both hands against the cheeks is the conventional sign of grief in this period.

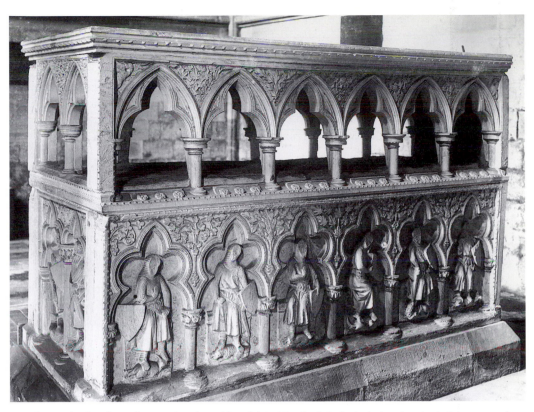

43] The tomb of Bishop Thomas Cantilupe (d. 1282) in Hereford Cathedral, showing the knights around the tomb chest. Their shields would probably once have identified them as the bishop's kinsmen or associates. They wear armour rather than mourning robes, but their posture leaves no doubt that they are there as mourners. The top of the chest originally carried a brass of the bishop, of which only the indent now remains.

Clearly grief was expressed in public, but throughout this period illustrations of funerals strongly suggest that emotional decorum remained the goal, however intense the underlying sense of loss. The iconographic representation of grief in the twelfth century is characterised by restrained gestures but an unmistakable emotional intensity [42]. The mourners who begin to appear around the sides of tomb chests from the end of the thirteenth century convey the same message, and their usual appellation of 'weepers' is misleading. The fourteen knights around the tomb chest of Thomas Cantilupe in Hereford Cathedral (1287) are mournful rather than grief-stricken [43], and the figures on the tombs of Edmund Crouchback and his wife in Westminster Abbey (1295–1300) have been characterised as 'a composed courtly entourage'.[51] Such figures became more dolorous, although no more abandoned in gesture, in the course of the fourteenth century as the practice grew of showing them in voluminous hooded mourning gowns, as, for instance, on the Harrington tomb of the 1340s in Cartmel Priory church. Wearing black had been a feature of elite funerals from at least the late thirteenth century. In 1281 the executors of Cecily Talmache paid for black gowns for her funeral, and since they were furred, albeit not lavishly, they were probably provided for elite mourners – distinguishing them from the poor candle-bearers clad in white. By the fourteenth century, however, it was usual to put the poor into black, and the provision of such gowns is a common element in contemporary wills. In 1346, for instance, Hugh Tunstead, the rector of Catton, Yorkshire, stipulated that four poor men (whom he named) should stand about his corpse holding torches, wearing black gowns with hoods.[52]

Once the funeral was over the mourners would return to the dead person's home for a meal. In 1345 John Woodhouse, the rector of Sutton on Derwent, Yorkshire, left money to lay on food and drink after the funeral for his friends and others.[53] It is likely that among the elite the funeral dinner replaced the wake as the main social element in the burial process, with the watching over the corpse before burial taking the form of a religious exercise, as the Church wished. After the meal, the mourners would disperse, although where there were the resources to pay for further liturgical commemorations of the dead, some at least might reassemble for the month's mind (a repetition of the mass for the dead thirty days after death) or the obit (a mass performed on the anniversary of the death).

Such prayers were, for most people, the main public expression of remembrance. Churchyard graves might be marked and the location of individual burials remembered for a time, so that, for example, in 1342 Christiana the widow of John Rous was able to stipulate that she wished to be buried beside her husband in the churchyard of St Peter, York.[54] But the provision of stones or monuments identifying the deceased was almost entirely restricted to elite intramural burials. Here the earliest forms of memorial were the carved slabs sealing stone coffins, from which developed more elaborate carved stones placed above the grave. By the late thirteenth century the practice of setting brass images or inscriptions into the stone had begun, although the earliest surviving examples date from *c.* 1310–15. Funeral monuments incorporating effigies were even rarer, but by the late thirteenth century had become established as the appropriate form of commemoration for the eminent, so much so that effigies might sometimes be made for individuals long dead.[55] Brasses and effigies in this period were never portraits. They identified the deceased through conventional attributes as a knight or widow and so on, and in that sense deal with the ideal rather than the individual. But they did commemorate the living person, and the view of some authors that the images were intended to show the resurrected rather than the earthly body can be discounted. The iconographic convention at this time was to show the resurrected loosely robed in their shrouds, the trappings of their worldly life, upon which funerary monuments set such emphasis, set aside for ever.

For the elite, churches could become an open book of family history. The apse of Tewkesbury Abbey church was colonised by the Despensers, with the dynastic message of their tombs further developed in commemorative stained glass, while parts of Norton Priory were paved with Dutton coffin slabs and heraldic tiles.[56] The less wealthy increasingly sought their own, more modest, memorialisation. This was most simply achieved through a gift to the church which would earn their inclusion on the bede roll: the list of benefactors read to the congregation on Sundays. Those with the necessary resources might provide the church with an object of liturgical use which would keep their memory green, like Joan de Walkington who gave her parish church a cope and new missal, to be used as long as they would last.[57]

The afterlife

Such bequests had a double motive. The donors wished to be remembered, but they also, increasingly, wished to be prayed for, to facilitate their passage through what was becoming the most central part of the spiritual landscape: Purgatory. Prayers for the dead were not new. Well before this period prayers for the faithful departed had been a regular part of religious observance, and benefactors and patrons had sought to be remembered in the prayers of monastic communities – a burden which ultimately became so heavy that in the mid-twelfth century Cluny abandoned the individual commemoration of every monk and benefactor lest, in Peter the Venerable's phrase, 'the dead drove out the living'. Cistercian houses followed in the 1270s, replacing all individual anniversaries with twelve general commemorations.[58]

The burgeoning demand for postmortem prayers was a facet of the formalisation of Purgatory.[59] Purgatory allowed the completion of penance which had been willed, but not completed, during life. Unlike Hell, the permanent abode of unrepentant sinners, Purgatory was a place of temporary suffering, entry to which guaranteed ultimate salvation. The belief in an intermediate state which was neither Heaven nor Hell can already be seen in the writings of the Church Fathers, but it was formalised and elaborated, in part in response to popular belief, from the twelfth century onwards. Much the most potent aspect of that process was the emphasis placed on the belief (again, not itself new) that the length of time which individuals suffered in Purgatory was dictated not only by their own actions in life, but by the actions of others on their behalf after their death. Thirteenth-century preachers encouraged their congregations to pay the spiritual debts of the dead with stories of the grateful dead appearing to announce to friends or family who had taken action on their behalf that their suffering was now at an end.[60]

Some of these stories imply the taking over of a specific penitential obligation, and the Londoner Geoffrey Godard (d. 1274) may have been thinking in these terms when he charged his executors to find someone to undertake the pilgrimage to the Holy Land on his behalf.[61] Usually, however, it was a matter of saying prayers for the general health of the dead person's soul. As understanding of Purgatory spread, individuals increasingly tried to make provision for this before their death. The retreat of the religious orders from the provision of individual commemorations meant that people looked instead to their parish church and endowed prayers there for themselves and others, either in perpetuity or for a defined period. Predictably, the clergy themselves seem to have been in the vanguard of this development. An early example is provided by William the rector of Buckland (d. 1235) who left his land to his nephew Robert for the endowment of various liturgical and charitable observances, including a mass for his soul each year on the anniversary of his death. But by the later thirteenth century lay people were also endowing masses – or, as it is technically known, founding chantries. In 1273 Walter de Kingston, poulterer in the royal household, endowed a chantry in the London church of St Mary Aldermanchurch for three years after his death.[62] In the case of perpetual chantries, and where resources allowed, a chapel might be created by partitioning off the church's internal space or even building an extension, as at North Moreton, Berkshire, where the Stapleton chantry chapel was added to the south side of the chancel in *c.* 1300.

Some commentators have seen this development as the privatisation of religion, with the individual buying the prayers necessary for personal salvation. In one respect, acceptance of Purgatory did turn the spotlight on the individual, who now faced a personal judgement at the point of death to decide the soul's immediate destination. That judgement took the form of a spiritual audit in which sins were balanced against good deeds. This was often imagined as a literal weighing of the soul – a process which, in popular accounts at least, was not without some cheating by the saints. On his visit to the other world in October 1206, the Essex farmer Thurkill watched St Peter win a soul by throwing a holy water sprinkler into the scales with such force that the weights on the other side fell out and landed on the devil's foot,[63] and a popular late-medieval image was of the Virgin Mary weighing down the scales with her rosary (see Chapter 5, pp. 128–9).

Individual Christians were increasingly encouraged to anticipate the audit by developing an awareness of their own behaviour and motivation. The requirement of annual confession placed upon every Christian by the fourth Lateran Council in 1215 was a crucial step in the process of self-examination. But self-help was not enough. The development of the doctrine of Purgatory was, more importantly, making a statement about the community of the living and the dead. Prayers for the dead brought living and dead very close together. It was surely no coincidence that when two monks drew up an agreement that the first to die would appear to the other, they envisaged being able to do so either on the night after death, the thirtieth night or the anniversary – precisely the times when prayers for the dead would have been most concentrated.[64] Preachers stressed the extent to which the dead were reliant on the living, illustrating the point with stories of suffering souls returning from Purgatory to remind family and friends of their obligations. Less often the subject of *exempla*, but clearly present in contemporary thinking, was the belief that the obligation was reciprocal, and that the dead who had achieved salvation were in a position to intercede for the living. As Edward III expressed it, seeking consolation for the death of his daughter Joan in the 1348 plague: 'We give thanks to [God] that one of our own family, free of all stain ... has been sent ahead to heaven to reign among the choirs of virgins, where she can gladly intercede for our offences before God himself.'[65]

As Edward's letter makes clear, Purgatory was not the only destination open to the souls of the dead. But beyond Purgatory the picture fragments, partly because the idea that the soul was immediately dispatched somewhere upon death sat rather uneasily with the older tradition that the dead would sleep until the Last Judgement and then be assigned to Heaven or Hell for eternity. The two versions could be reconciled by emphasising that what happened before the Last Judgement happened to the soul alone, which would not be reunited with its body until the general resurrection which would immediately precede that judgement, but illogicalities and contradictions remained. There was general agreement that the irredeemable would go straight to the torments of Hell, mainly because there was nowhere else for them to go. Heaven, however, was more problematic. Although the saints were assuredly there, not everyone agreed that the souls of the righteous would join them before the Last Judgement. Instead, many commentators felt that virtuous or purified souls would go to Abraham's Bosom (Luke 16:22): a place of rest and happiness which was, nevertheless, not Heaven itself. The collect used in the Sarum ritual on the day of burial prayed that the soul 'be laid on the bosom of thy patriarch Abraham; that, when the day of recognition shall arrive, he may be raised up, at thy bidding, among the saints and thy elect'.[66]

Abraham's Bosom is usually shown very literally in English art of this period as a napkin full of souls held against the breast of a patriarchal figure by two angels, although sometimes the treatment is more allusive, with an angel – often St Michael, the conductor of souls – carrying a soul in a napkin [**44** and **45**]. Similarly Heaven tends to be represented by an assembly of the blessed rather than evoked as a place. Even in images of the Last Judgement, where the judged are being led off to their final home, it is rare to catch a glimpse inside the gates of Heaven. Artists spread themselves more enthusiastically on representations of Hell, traditionally shown as a gaping, bestial mouth [**46** and **plate 8**] although even here the emphasis is more often on the contortions of the damned [**46**]. This does not mean that Heaven and Hell were not envisaged as places, but rather that what happened to the souls there was theologically more important than questions of geography. The result, however, was a rather static perception of the next world, which seems to have been at odds with popular thinking, which emphasised rather the journey of the soul through a series of experiences.

One consequence of this idea of a linear progress was that popular visions of the afterlife, such as that of Thurkill, saw Hell, Purgatory and

44] Abraham's Bosom; the apex of the ogee arch of the Percy tomb in Beverley Minster, mid-fourteenth century. Two angels hold the soul between them in a cloth above the patriarch's lap. Iconographically there is often nothing to distinguish Abraham from God the Father in such images.

right 45] Probable tomb of Bishop Nigel of Ely: St Michael carrying a soul to God. As usual, the soul is held in a cloth between the angel's hands. The saint's image has been defaced.

Heaven as adjoining regions, between which movement was possible, rather than as separate states. The implication was often that Purgatory is a temporary stay in Hell, a view with which some theologians would have agreed, so that the three conditions in effect form a continuum. This is dramatically captured in the famous early-thirteenth-century wall painting at Chaldon, Surrey, which has a great ladder running up the centre of the image from which souls tumble into Hell or up which they ascend from Purgatory towards Heaven [47].

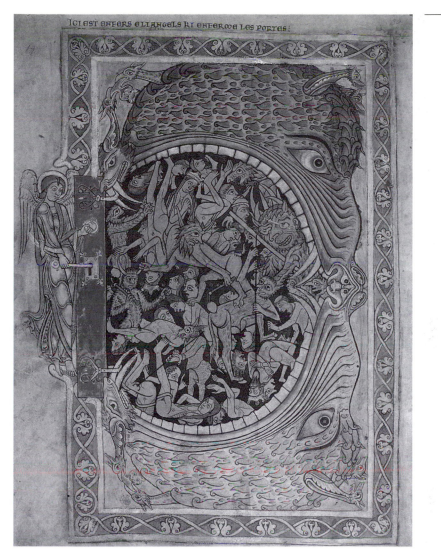

ICI EST ENFERS ELI ANGELS KI ENFERME LES PORTES:

46] The angel locking the gates of Hell after the Last Judgement, when souls are assigned for eternity to Heaven or Hell. Hell mouth in medieval art is almost invariably, as here, shown as a gaping bestial jaw. The damned, several of whom are tonsured or crowned, are being subjected to a variety of punishments.

The popular view of the next world also insisted on a much more direct link between individual action and its due punishment than the generalised suffering to be found in the Church's teaching. The undated Lyke Wake Dirge embodies this in its description of Whinny Muir: a landscape of vicious thorns where those who have given stockings and shoes by way of charity are allowed to pull them on to protect their legs. Accounts of the next world often allowed retributive imagination full rein. Thurkill, for instance, watched a famous judge being force-fed red hot gold coins.[67]

113

47] The next world. The top panels show the weighing of souls (left) and the harrowing of Hell (right); below is Hell. Linking the two levels is a ladder with souls ascending towards Heaven or tumbling off into Hell.

The end of the world?

Although belief in Purgatory shifted the pastoral emphasis towards preparation for an individual judgement at death, this did not eclipse the importance attached to Christ's second coming in judgement. Contemporaries, indeed, were fascinated by the events which would precede and hence signal the Last Judgement, and when the Black Death arrived in Europe they were swift to locate it within the context of this apocalyptic narrative. Plague and Death, after all, were two of the four Horsemen of St John's Apocalypse (Revelation 6) and the fourteenth century had already experienced the ravages of the other two riders: famine and war [**plate 8**]. In England, the Rochester chronicler interpreted the demand of workers for higher payment as evidence that Gog and Magog had been loosed from Hell and the reign of Antichrist was at hand, and rumours reached East Anglia that Antichrist had already been born.[68]

But the world did not end, and moralists were soon grumbling that mankind had not learnt its lesson but, after the terror-induced good behaviour of the plague years, had returned to its old, sinful, ways. This insistence that nothing had changed sits oddly with more recent views of the plague as a major turning point in history, but culturally the moralists had a point. Traumatic as the Black Death undoubtedly was, it is very hard to point to changes in attitude which were a direct consequence of it.

Representations of death are a case in point. Many historians have felt that the death of almost half the population in eighteen months 'must' have brought a change in the way that death itself was perceived, and have pointed to the fascination with the macabre which manifests itself in the late Middle Ages as evidence of a society which had become obsessed with death and corruption. But the chronology of this development warns against too glib an association with the plague. As representations of the three living and the three dead reveal, there was a lively sense of the macabre before the plague. Conversely, the 'classic' representations of the macabre in funerary art, the development of shroud brasses and the representation of cadavers in *transi* tombs, do not develop until significantly after the plague (see Chapter 5). The representation of Death as an armed, attacking corpse also seems, in England at least, to postdate the plague by a considerable margin.

This apparent time lag is not restricted to the cultural field. Socially and economically, too, the full impact of demographic collapse was held at bay for a generation. It was in the 1370s that the social temperature began to rise significantly, and in 1381 that rebellion boiled over in the so-called 'Peasants' Revolt'. It looks very much as if the survivors of the 1348–49 plague, far from being radicalised by their experience, wanted to turn the clock back and take refuge in traditional assumptions, and that it was left to the inheritors of the post-plague world to begin seeing things in new ways.

Notes

In all references, place of publication is London unless otherwise stated.

1 P. Binski, *Medieval Death: Ritual and Representation* (1996), p. 186.
2 R. Horrox (ed.), *The Black Death* (Manchester, 1994), pp. 118–19.
3 C. Brown (ed.), *English Lyrics of the XIIIth Century* (Oxford, 1932), no. 71.
4 S. Wenzel (ed.), *Fasciculus Morum: A Fourteenth-Century Preacher's Handbook* (1989), pp. 719–21. See also F. S. Paxton, 'Signa mortifera: death and prognostication in early medieval monastic medicine', *Bulletin of the History of Medicine*, 67 (1993), 631–60.
5 R. C. Finucane, *Miracles and Pilgrims: Popular Beliefs in Medieval England* (1977), p. 74.
6 C. Gross (ed.), *Select Cases from the Coroners' Rolls, AD 1265–1413*, Selden Society IX (1896), pp. 3–4, 68–9, 74. For the coroner, see R. F. Hunnisett, *The Medieval Coroner* (Cambridge, 1961).
7 Wenzel, *Fasciculus Morum*, p. 99.
8 E. Carleton Williams, 'Mural paintings of the three living and the three dead in England', *Journal of the British Archaeological Association*, 3rd series, 7 (1942), 31–40.
9 Compare the medieval belief that the guilty soul of Judas could not pass his lips, which had kissed Christ, and had to burst out of his guts instead.
10 J. T. Welter (ed.), *Le Speculum Laicorum: edition d'une collection d'exempla composée en Angleterre a la fin du XIIIe siècle* (Paris, 1914), pp. 36–7; P. Tristram, 'Strange images of death', *Leeds Studies in English*, n.s., 14 (1983), 196–211.
11 Walter Map, *De Nugis Curialium*, ed. M. R. James, rev. C. N. L. Brooke and R. A. B. Mynours (Oxford, 1994), pp. 364–6; A. J. Grant, 'Twelve medieval

ghost stories', *Yorkshire Archaeological Journal*, 27 (1924), 363–75, discussed further in Chapter 5; C. Platt, *The Parish Churches of Medieval England* (1981), p. 49, quoting the penitential of Bartholomew, bishop of Exeter (1161–84).

12 Psalm 39:4: 'Lord, make me to know my end and the number of my days, so that I may know what I am lacking.' For examples of saintly foreknowledge, see D. Crouch, 'The culture of death in the Anglo-Norman world', in C. Warren Hollister (ed.), *Anglo-Norman Political Culture and the Twelfth-Century Renaissance* (Woodbridge, 1997), pp. 158–9.

13 M. R. McVaugh, 'Bedside manners in the Middle Ages', *Bulletin of the History of Medicine*, 71 (1997), 201–23.

14 Wenzel, *Fasciculus Morum*, pp. 489–91.

15 D. Crouch, *William Marshal: Court, Career and Chivalry in the Angevin Empire* (1990), p. 194.

16 F. M. Powicke and C. R. Cheney (eds), *Councils and Synods*, vol. II, part I: AD 1205–1313 (Oxford, 1964), pp. 90–1, 305–6, 596.

17 *Manuale et processionale ad usum insignis Ecclesiae Eboracensis*, Surtees Society 63 (1875), pp. 50–4; 48*–52*. There is a brief paraphrase in D. Rock, *The Church of Our Fathers*, ed. G. W. Hart and W. H. Frere, 4 vols (1903), II, pp. 369–70.

18 S. Painter, *William Marshal, Knight-Errant, Baron, and Regent of England* (Toronto, 1982), p. 288.

19 Crouch, *William Marshal*, p. 49; C. Holdsworth, *The Piper and the Tune: Medieval Patrons and Monks* (Reading, 1991), pp. 12–13.

20 Platt, *Parish Churches*, p. 28.

21 Horrox (ed.), *Black Death*, pp. 22–3, 30–2, 43–4.

22 *Ibid.*, pp. 271–2.

23 F. E. Warren (trans.), *The Sarum Missal*, 2 vols (1913), II, p. 189.

24 R. Vaughan (ed.), *The Illustrated Chronicles of Matthew Paris* (Stroud, 1993), pp. 72–3; C. Daniell, *Death and Burial in Medieval England 1066–1550* (1997), pp. 71–8.

25 A. Murray, *Suicide in the Middle Ages*, vol. I: *The Violent against Themselves* (Oxford, 1998). I am extremely grateful to the author and publisher for allowing me access to a proof copy before publication.

26 J. Raine (ed.), *Wills and Inventories illustrative of the History . . . etc of the Northern Counties of England*, Surtees Society 2 (1835), pp. 16–17.

27 C. A. Bradford, *Heart Burial* (1933), pp. 23–4.

28 E. Hallam, 'Royal burial and the cult of kingship in France and England, 1060–1330', *Journal of Medieval History*, 8 (1982), 359–80. Examples of clothed burials include: J. Ayloffe, 'An account of the body of king Edward the first, as it appeared on opening his tomb in the year 1774', *Archaeologia*, 3 (1775), 376–413; F. T. Havergal, *Fasti Herefordenses* (Edinburgh, 1869), pp. 197–9.

29 Bradford, *Heart Burial*, pp. 23–4.

30 W. Dugdale, *Monasticon Anglicanum*, 6 vols (1817–30), IV, pp. 144–5; B. Golding, 'Burials and benefactions: an aspect of monastic patronage in thirteenth-century England', in W. M. Ormrod (ed.), *England in the Thirteenth Century* (Grantham, 1985), pp. 66–9; Hallam, 'Royal burial', 364; E. A. R. Brown, 'Death and the human body in the later Middle Ages: the legislation of Boniface VII on the division of the corpse', *Viator*, 12 (1981), 230.

31 K. Park, 'The life of the corpse: division and dissection in late medieval Europe', *Journal of the History of Medicine*, 50 (1995), 111–32.

32 C. Walker Bynum, *The Resurrection of the Body in Western Christianity, 200–1336* (New York, 1995).

33 Brown, 'Death and the human body', 221–2.

34 L. Toulmin Smith (ed.), *English Gilds*, Early English Text Society, original series, 40 (1870), p. 194, n. (my translation). For the *ludos inhonestos* compare the question to be asked by fifteenth-century confessors: 'Are you in the habit of making plays at corpse-wakes?': E. Peacock (ed.), *Instructions for Parish Priests by John Myrc*, Early English Text Society, original series, 31 (rev. 1902), p. 42.

35 Toulmin Smith, *English Gilds*, p. 178.

36 G. Rowell, *The Liturgy of Christian Burial* (1977), pp. 65–6.

37 Horrox (ed.), *Black Death*, pp. 23, 31, 44, 70.
38 Dugdale, *Monasticon*, IV, p. 143; D. M. Owen, *Church and Society in Medieval Lincolnshire* (Lincoln, 1971), p. 40
39 Rock, *The Church of our Fathers*, p. 379.
40 *Manuale ad usum Eboracensis*, p. 80*. Details of the liturgy are taken from *ibid.*, pp. 60–102, 60*–85*. There is a brief description in A. S. Duncan-Jones, 'The burial of the dead', in W. K. L. Clarke (ed.), *Liturgy and Worship* (1932), p. 621.
41 Daniell, *Death and Burial*, pp. 96–7; A. D. Brown, *Popular Piety in Late Medieval England: The Diocese of Salisbury 1250–1550* (Oxford, 1995), p. 93, n.
42 Dugdale, *Monasticon*, IV, p. 143.
43 H. G. Ramm, 'The tombs of Archbishops Walter de Grey (1216–55) and Godfrey de Ludham (1258–65) in York Minster and their contents', *Archaeologia*, 103 (1971), 131.
44 B. Hooper *et al.*, 'The grave of Sir Hugh de Hastyngs, Elsing', *Norfolk Archaeology*, 39 (1984), 88.
45 Horrox (ed.), *Black Death*, pp. 52, 196.
46 Duncan-Jones, 'The burial of the dead', p. 621; M. Harman and B. Wilson, 'A medieval graveyard beside Faringdon Road, Abingdon', *Oxoniensia*, 46 (1981), 56; G. Stroud and R. L. Kemp, 'The cemeteries of St Andrew, Fishergate', *The Archaeology of York*, 12:2 (1993), 139; Daniell, *Death and Burial*, pp. 110–11, 146–7.
47 Horrox (ed.), *Black Death*, pp. 33, 64–5, 70, 81, 267; D. Hawkins, 'The Black Death and the new London cemeteries of 1348', *Antiquity*, 64 (1990), 637–42.
48 Horrox (ed.), *Black Death*, p. 70.
49 Toulmin Smith, *English Gilds*, pp. 35–6.
50 Crouch, 'The culture of death', p. 178; Owen, *Church and Society*, p. 40.
51 P. Binski, *Westminster Abbey and the Plantagenets* (New Haven, 1995), p. 115.
52 J. Cullum, *The History and Antiquities of Hawsted and Hardwick in the County of Suffolk* (1813), p. 11; *Testamenta Eboracensia* (hereafter *Test. Ebor.*), I, Surtees Society 4 (1836), no. XIV.
53 *Test. Ebor.*, I, no. XII.
54 *Ibid.*, no. VI.
55 H. Colvin, *Architecture and the After-Life* (New Haven, 1991), p. 138.
56 J. P. Greene, *Norton Priory* (Cambridge, 1989), pp. 12–14, 124–8.
57 *Test. Ebor.*, I, no. XIII.
58 Colvin, *Architecture and the After-Life*, pp. 152–3.
59 J. Le Goff, *The Birth of Purgatory* (Aldershot, 1984); B. P. McGuire, 'Purgatory, the communion of saints, and medieval change', *Viator*, 20 (1989), 61–84; M. McLaughlin, *Consorting with Saints: Prayer for the Dead in Early Medieval France* (Ithaca, N.Y., 1994).
60 Welter (ed.), *Speculum Laicorum*, p. 38.
61 R. R. Sharpe, *Calendar of Wills proved and enrolled in the Court of Husting, London, AD 1258–AD 1688*, 2 vols (1889–90), I, pp. 17–18.
62 Brown, *Popular Piety*, p. 93; Sharpe, *Wills*, p. 15.
63 P. G. Schmidt, 'The vision of Thurkill', *Journal of the Warburg and Courtauld Institutes*, 41 (1978), 53.
64 C. J. Holdsworth, 'Eleven visions connected with the Cistercian monastery of Stratford Langthorne', *Citeaux: Commentarii Cisterciensis*, 13 (1962), 198.
65 Horrox (ed.), *Black Death*, p. 250.
66 Warren (trans.), *Sarum Missal*, p. 182.
67 Schmidt, 'Thurkill', 54.
68 Horrox (ed.), *Black Death*, pp. 73, 98–100, 154–5.

Select bibliography

Binski, P., *Medieval Death: Ritual and Representation*, 1996.
Boase, T. S. R., *Death in the Middle Ages: Mortality, Judgement and Remembrance*, 1972.

Brown, E. A. R., 'Death and the human body in the later Middle Ages: the legislation of Boniface VII on the division of the corpse', *Viator*, 12 (1981), 221–70.

Bynum, C. Walker, *The Resurrection of the Body in Western Christianity, 200–1336*, New York, 1995.

Carpenter, D., 'The burial of King Henry III, the *Regalia* and royal ideology', in Carpenter (ed.), *The Reign of Henry III*, 1996.

Coales, J. (ed.), *The Earliest English Brasses: Patronage, Style and Workshops, 1270–1350*, 1987.

Daniell, C., *Death and Burial in Medieval England 1066–1550*, 1997.

Golding, B., 'Burials and benefactions: an aspect of monastic patronage in thirteenth-century England', in W. M. Ormrod (ed.), *England in the Thirteenth Century*, Grantham, 1985.

Le Goff, J., *The Birth of Purgatory*, Aldershot, 1984.

McGuire, B. P., 'Purgatory, the communion of saints, and medieval change', *Viator*, 20 (1989), 61–84.

Murray, A., *Suicide in the Middle Ages*, vol. I: *The Violent against Themselves*, Oxford, 1998.

Park, K., 'The life of the corpse: division and dissection in late medieval Europe', *Journal of the History of Medicine*, 50 (1995), 111–32.

Schmitt, J.-C., *Ghosts in the Middle Ages: The Living and the Dead in Medieval Society*, Chicago, 1998.

5 · Philip Morgan

Of worms and war: 1380–1558

New death for old

For those seduced by clear outlines rather than complex detail, the later Middle Ages has always seemed to have firm chronological and cultural boundaries. At the outset, the great and fearful mortality of the Black Death of 1348–49 may have killed between a third and a half of the population, producing a greater sensitisation to death, and suggesting explanations for the apparent morbidity of much of fifteenth-century visual and literary culture.[1] The cadaver tomb of Sir Roger Rockley (d. 1534) at Worsborough, Yorkshire, is a typical example, with the knight in life, as if in prayer on his bier, with the cadaver in its winding sheet below [48]. In this and countless other examples there has always seemed

48] The timber tomb of Sir Roger Rockley (d. 1534) in the parish church at Worsborough. A typical cadaver tomb of the late Middle Ages showing the dead person in life, and with a corpse below. Viewers were offered a stark warning of the perils of a sinful life in a worm-eaten body, but also the hope of resurrection to an eternal life.

to be both an emphasis upon the grim physical reality of death and the fearful warning that death and reckoning comes to all. 'Lade, helpe! Ihesu, merce! *Timor mortis conturbat me.*'[2] 'The fear of death terrifies me.' The fear was hardly new but had been transformed by the experience of the Black Death, the new death of the late Middle Ages.

The view owes much to an influential opening line, written by Johan Huizinga in the shadow of another great mortality during the First World War, though from the safety of his mother-in-law's attic. In the dust-jacket hyperbole of 1919 he observed that 'no other epoch has laid so much stress as the expiring Middle Ages on the thought of death'.[3] At the close, in what remained a strikingly homogeneous culture, in which attitudes to death mirrored those of Christian theology and practice, the Reformation witnessed a sustained assault on the Catholic culture of death. Of the second revision of the Prayer Book in 1552, which recast the theology of the funeral service, Eamon Duffy has written that 'the boundaries of human community have been redrawn'.[4] Although the detail will soften the extravagance of both claims, the further limits of these two centuries remain significant.

The fact of mass death in the mid-fourteenth century is incontrovertible; indeed recent estimates have tended to move the levels of mortality to the higher parts of the traditional range, in many cases to around 50 per cent of local populations.[5] Recovery was slow; rural populations stabilised at little more than half of their pre-plague levels, towns shrank. From the 1430s to the 1460s England experienced a series of economic recessions. Yet, what seems self-evident, that death on such a scale should have brought in its wake profound social and economic changes, has long been the territory of historical debate. The naive proposition that mass death inevitably initiates immediate and revolutionary change has been undermined by studies of both the mid-fourteenth-century plague and that of the years between 664 and c. 687.[6] In what would be the second crisis of the European Middle Ages, the English economy and society, it is argued, were already vulnerable following the famines and economic upheavals of the early fourteenth century, a victim of much longer trends in the European economy. The effects of demographic collapse are seen as slow to manifest themselves, either in labour relations, or in the straitened powers of lordship, or in changing standards of living. In Chapter 4, Rosemary Horrox has likewise already pointed to the evident dislocation between the outbreak of the plague and the representational changes which have traditionally been associated with it. The story is less simple than once it seemed.

Rather, elements of the old world persisted with diminishing force into the later fourteenth century, even as new *mentalités* emerged in the fifteenth. For Archbishop Henry Chichele it was evidently death in war which engaged his spirit. His foundation at All Souls in Oxford was directed towards those 'who had drunk the cup of bitter death' in the continuing Anglo-French wars. His earlier architectural patronage at Canterbury has been said to represent 'the generation – if one may be excused a flagrant anachronism – of the "first war", the *bellum de Agincourt*'.[7] Important though war had been, it was rather two further trends which gave a distinctive edge to late medieval perceptions of death. If nothing else, the Black Death had inaugurated a lengthy period of recurrent epidemic disease and demographic fragility. The English population seems to have stabilised around 1450 but did not begin to grow strongly until the mid-sixteenth century; outbreaks of plague grew less frequent and narrower in their geographical impact after 1479, but continued to be a major cause of mortality throughout the sixteenth century and beyond. Those who supported the several communities of the dead to whom we shall shortly turn were fewer in number and more vulnerable to sudden death. Since sin was widely considered to be the principal cause of untimely death, and since plague carried with it the implicit notion of moral as well as physical decay, little wonder that new

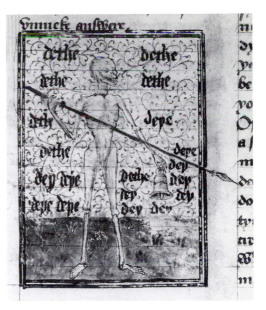

49] A small drawing illustrates John Lydgate's poem, *Death's Warning*. 'My dredefull spere that ys full sharpe ygrounde, Doth yow now, lo, here thys manace, Armour ys noon that may withstande hys wounde.' In the later Middle Ages death, it was widely feared, would attack its victims.

attitudes to death arose. In striking fashion, the illustration to John Lydgate's *Death's Warning to the World* now shows death as a grinning and armed attacker [49]. Nearly a century later Henry Williams, vicar of Stanford on Avon, Northamptonshire, in his will of 5 April 1500, instructed his executors to provide a similar image in the glass of the parish church where he was to be buried. It shows him at prayer being shot by the figure of death kneeling in a coffin [50].[8]

The fate of individual communities throughout the century can be observed clearly in the evidence from two monastic houses, Westminster Abbey and Christ Church Priory in Canterbury, in which death rates were at least 30 per 1,000 over the years between 1410 and 1509, and 40 per 1,000 over the period 1460–1509. The life expectancy of monks in these two communities fell between 1430 and 1485. At Westminster in 1479 the mortality rate reached 150 per 1,000 during what seems to have been a national outbreak of plague.[9] In probably the same epidemic, the churchwardens of the tiny Staffordshire parish of Adbaston received fees and bequests at the burials of at least twenty-two people, of whom twelve were children from only three families.[10] How communities great and small, so embattled, came to terms with a militant death, and what actions and responses were available to them is the theme of much that follows and has left its traces even in the modern world.

Amongst the saints a number came to be perceived as 'auxiliary' or helper saints, invoked on specific occasions to provide help or guidance,

50] Henry Williams, vicar of Stanford on Avon, commissioned his own portraits in 1500 in the glazing of the church, 'I wyll that the glasse windowes in the chancell with ymagery that was thereyn before allso with my ymage knelyng in ytt and the ymage of deth shotyng at me, another wyndowe before Saynt John with ymagery in ytt now with my image knelyng in ytt and deth shoting at me theys to be done in smalle quarells of as gode glasse as can be goten.'

most frequently during serious illness or in fear of untimely death. In the 'Life of Saint Christopher' the saint had escaped sudden and violent death on two separate occasions, announcing to his persecutor that he would not die that day but the next. No one who saw the likeness of Saint Christopher, it was argued, would die that day, and his image proved one of the most popular in the fifteenth century, in churches often painted on a wall facing the door to afford passers-by the saint's protection at a passing glance. Despite papal demotion in 1969, the fossil remains of his late-medieval cult survive in the modern invocations of motorists and the anachronism of often secular baptismal gifts of 'St Christophers'.[11] Written charms were also popular. Robert Reynes of Acle copied the so-called 'Charlemagne prayer', originally seen as a protection against death in battle, but which here reassured its copyist that 'Whosover carries this writing with him need have no fear of any enemy, sudden death, fire, water, poison, prison, thunder, lightning, fevers nor any other wicked evil'.[12]

Aside from natural causes, sudden death also visited those engaged in war and those who suffered execution. Neither cause was unique to this period but it is important to consider their impact, not least because it has frequently been argued that medieval society in some way grew inured to brutal execution, and conversely that the Wars of the Roses

51] A medieval war memorial, the chantry college on the battlefield at Shrewsbury, founded in 1406 to pray for the souls of the king and other benefactors, and those whose bodies lay on the adjacent field. The battlefield had thus been turned into a consecrated enclosure. The image of King Henry IV is placed in the gable of the east end, watching over the corpses of those he had vanquished and towards the homes from which most had marched in July 1403.

between 1452 and 1497 occupied no more than two and a half years of active fighting, were fought by small armies and had a minimal disruptive effect on society.[13] That said, it is also evident that the monuments to mass death in the fifteenth century were invariably those connected with death in war, from Henry IV's memorial chapel at Battlefield near Shrewsbury built *c*. 1406 [51] to the battlefield chantry at Dadlington near Bosworth, for which funds were still being collected in 1511.[14]

Possibly the most fatal of fifteenth-century battles had taken place at Towton, Yorkshire, on Palm Sunday 1461. Contemporary estimates of the number of dead varied wildly between 9,000 and 30,000 and, like Shrewsbury and Bosworth, it too attracted the foundation of a chantry chapel. Edward IV sought seven-year indulgences on behalf of the 'innumerable concourse of the faithful' who came to pray for the souls of the dead. The emotional intensity of prayers of intercession for the numerous victims of divine judgement on human affairs seems to have been shared at other battle sites and, importantly, to have endured. Patronage at Towton continued under Richard III and in 1486 the church was said to be a 'splendid chapel expensively and imposingly erected from new foundations', with only the roof and glazing waiting completion.[15] In most cases battlefields remained contested political landscapes; memorial chapels invariably stood on the site of the graves of the vanquished and served to appropriate their memory to the interests of the victors.

52] *The Martyrdom of St Erasmus*, 1474, painted by a Flemish artist working in England. The saint's gruesome death, his intestines removed by a windlass, is being viewed by the painting's donor, John Holingborne, a monk at Canterbury Cathedral and former fellow of Canterbury College, Oxford. Was it perhaps a votive picture commissioned after recovery from an abdominal complaint?

Execution by one of several gruesome methods was also the price of political and religious opposition. The index entry under 'punishment', with sub-headings for the varieties of judicial execution, occupies a whole column in the standard book on the law of treason.[16] Of the popular impact of the routine display of the body parts belonging to those hung, drawn and quartered the evidence is limited, but for the most part the exposure and ill-treatment of traitors' corpses drew little criticism. The kindness of the woman who combed Owen Tudor's hair, washed away the blood from his head and set burning candles around him, following his execution after the battle of Mortimer's Cross in 1461, suggested rather to contemporaries that she was mentally unbalanced.[17] Henry VI, who ordered the removal of a corpse from Cripplegate, explaining that he would not 'have any man so cruelly handled for my sake', was equally unusual and the action fitted him for sanctity, so willing was he to undergo physical ill-treatment whilst remaining unwilling to inflict it upon others.[18]

That the mutilation of the flesh of saints might have a redemptive quality makes it perilous to 'read' the many images of suffering and martyred saints, whose tortured and mutilated bodies on painted screens and images received the stares and prayers of congregations, much less those in which donors appear almost as voyeurs of violent and painful death [52]. There is some evidence that politics was more brutal at the close of the fifteenth century, in the hands of a run of 'serial killers', than it had been.[19] Thomas More worried that Lord Hastings, executed with indecent haste in June 1483, was forced to take 'a priest at random and made a short shrift'.[20] Political elites appear to have given little consideration as to the restraints which might govern how they inflicted death. At the same time there was a considerable literature on how to prepare for one's own death.

The craft of dying

Death in the Middle Ages invariably had a social context, just as life was essentially gregarious. For most, the idea of solitude was one reserved to those who exhibited extraordinary piety in the life of a hermit or anchorite. The deathbed was likely to be a busy and noisy place, even if for once the dying got to occupy the bed alone; it was open not merely to the immediate family but to other solidarities of which the dying person was a member. Margery Kempe, of whose loud and tearful devotions in the street most townspeople of King's Lynn disapproved, was regularly invited to the deathbeds of her neighbours; 'though they loved not her weeping nor her crying in her life-time, they desired that she should when they were dying, and so she did'.[21]

The parish was itself a kind of fraternity, its activities recorded in the accounts of its churchwardens. At the onset of serious, possibly fatal illness the sacrament was brought to the sick, often in a pyx reserved for the purpose, at the head of a ritualised procession with candles and bells [53]. In King's Lynn townspeople knelt in the streets as the procession passed.[22] After death most parishioners were admitted to the burial ground of the parish church, carried there in a parish coffin on a parish bier, their shrouded corpse awaiting the priest on a coffin table beneath the lichgate. Popular fears of burial in unconsecrated ground remained widespread and admission at this earthly gate was seen as being as necessary as that to which St Peter was keeper. Inside the church, community education, following a seemingly international curriculum, was organised by the churchwardens, even if the ultimate responsibility for the theology lay elsewhere. Death itself was everywhere, whether in the burgeoning display of funerary monuments or in the decoration of surfaces which so clearly pleased and engaged the English mind in the Middle Ages.

A notable addition to the repertoire in the fifteenth century, with a peak in popularity in the early sixteenth century, was the depiction of the Dance of Death or *Danse Macabre*. A series of people, generally from all social ranks, are shown as skeletons or putrefying corpses leading their living selves towards the grave. English examples derive from the famous version painted in St Paul's churchyard in London in 1430. This was decorated with John Lydgate's translation of French verses which he found accompanying the original model at the churchyard of the Holy Innocents in Paris shortly after 1425.[23] In many parishes the dance, in England also known as the 'Dance of Paul's', was

53] The pyx at Warkleigh church in Devon constructed from re-used painted panels, probably those which enclosed a small alabaster altarpiece for domestic use in the late fifteenth century. It has been argued that the reconstruction took place during the reign of Queen Mary, the church having been stripped of its own hanging pyx in 1552.

painted on canvas and hung up in the church at Easter, as at St Edmund's in Salisbury in 1490 when William Joynour was paid 10s 2d for the painting work.[24] That in the great town church at Newark-on-Trent was painted on the outside screen of the Markham chantry in the 1520s [54].

It is difficult to know quite how we should take these images. Did Chaucer's audience laugh at the word 'fart'? It is a question of the same weight. How did those who saw these schemes read them? It has been suggested that parishioners were unimpressed by cadaver tombs, that they guffawed at 'the fiction of the proud being humble' and chortled 'at the wealthy being worm eaten', preferring the vulgar but life-affirming cult of saints.[25] If the dance of death merely affirmed what all knew and believed it would have lacked authority. Rather, it must have argued that death was indeed the leveller of all, and sought to confront the aspirations of those whose rising position in fifteenth-century society challenged the social order. There is certainly more than a hint of the dance of death as state-inspired art when we consider the famous series designed by Hans Holbein in 1526, but not

54] A fragment of the Dance of Death from the screen of the Markham chantry in the parish church at Newark-on-Trent. A wealthy townsman, his hand on a bulging purse, is mocked by the image of his own recently dead self with the stomach cavity emptied of its internal organs and bearing a carnation, a flower which symbolised human flesh.

right 55] The sin of impatience from a continental version of the *ars moriendi*. The dying man, surrounded by family and friends, yields to one of the devilish temptations which beset the deathbed, kicking away a man who proffers advice on patience and overturning a table set for a meal. A model housewife or servant rescues a plate of chicken but a gleeful devil announces his victory.

published until he was in England in 1538, where in one scene death comes to a cardinal in the act of selling indulgences to a pilgrim.[26] The cult of death in the fifteenth and early sixteenth centuries, as we shall see, was far from homogeneous.

The homiletic tone of depictions of the dance of death, as of the cadaver tombs of the great, is likewise repeated in the Church's teaching on the way in which people might prepare for death. Much of this was to be found in the manuals for clergy like John Mirk's, which were compiled, mostly for the assistance of unbeneficed clergy, in the fourteenth and fifteenth centuries.[27] Increasingly, however, the responsibility to prepare for death was felt to be shared by the whole community, members of which might be directed to texts like the *ars moriendi*, 'the craft of dying' [55]. The practical advice here concerned the hours before the priest arrived with the sacrament. Interestingly such texts thus implicitly recognised the failings of the local church in not always providing a suitable support for the dying, and were addressed to what was described as a shrinking audience of those who planned for death.

Most people, it was argued, felt that they would live for ever, a 'folly from the hope to live long'.

William Caxton's printed version of 1491 and the slightly earlier *Arte and Crafte to know well to dye* (1490) were therefore meant to be distance-learning packs, not only for those who were dying but for those who might organise the deathbeds of their family and neighbours.[28] Most contain three discrete elements, the first on doctrines which informed the relationship between death and salvation, the second on the condition and preparedness of the dying person's soul and the third on practical measures for managing the deathbed. The emphasis upon religious orthodoxy, 'do you believe all the principal articles of Holy Church?', reveals a narrowing horizon of official teaching. There were those, increasingly classed as heretics and labelled as Lollards, whose preparations were of a different quality. These are therefore manuals on how people ought to die, not necessarily revealing of how they did die.

Nevertheless, people did admire good deaths. Clearly, Agnes Paston approved of the manner of Sir John Heveningham's albeit sudden death in July 1453. Her letter to her son, John I, describes a death which might have come from a manual; as a letter from a mother to her son, it was no doubt meant to be read as such.

> On Tuesday Sir John Heveningham went to his church and heard three masses, came home again merrier than usual, and said to his wife that he would go say a short prayer in his garden and then he would dine; and straightway he felt a fainting in his legs and 'sighed' down. This was at nine o'clock, and he was dead before noon.[29]

The dying person was to be warned against the five temptations at the hour of death – loss of faith, despair, impatience, vainglory and avarice – asked a series of questions which allowed a process of self-examination, and counselled to adopt a pattern of behaviour, based on Christ's own death, which would prepare him for a good death. The tone is reassuring and hopeful, 'to die well is to die gladly', emphasising the efficacy of interior signs over external display. It is better that the dying man 'cry from the deepness of his heart and not from his voice'. Those about the deathbed are warned not to give hope of recovery, or to distract by talk of family, friends and worldly possessions; they are encouraged to say prayers when the dying person is unable to say them for themselves, and to read 'histories and devout orisons' of which their friend had been especially fond.

Continental block-book illustrations [55] show the deathbed beset by devils and demons as family and friends encourage the dying person with the aid of prayers and images, notably those associated with the passion of Christ. English examples are less common, but at the Commandery in Worcester, now a museum of civil-war killing, the dying room of the former medieval hospital of St Wulfstan preserves much of its fifteenth-century iconographic scheme which can be read in the same fashion as recommended in the *ars moriendi* [plate 9]. Carried into the room, the dying man would first have seen St Michael weighing souls and a large figure of St Mary using her rosary to weigh down the scales. A much smaller figure of the devil appears to the left. To the left of the main panel is St Gudwal, a Cornish saint with a local Worcestershire cult and reputation for healing, and to the right, St Etheldreda whose corpse after death was found to have been healed of its tumours. From the bed facing the wall, the dying poor man saw the martyrdom of St Erasmus, flanked by St Roch, saints for abdominal pain and plague, with St Peter carrying the golden keys to Heaven to the right. Beneath was a second panel showing the martyrdom of St Thomas Becket, for afflictions of the head. The most important paintings were, however, reserved for the ceiling on which is depicted the Trinity, with the prayers 'Jesu merci' and 'Lady helpe' and the instruments of Christ's passion.[30]

Whilst we may marvel at the theological battery brought to bear upon the treatment of the dying man's soul, it is worth remembering that the message of texts like the *ars moriendi*, as of the Commandery scheme, was essentially hopeful. Despite physical and spiritual afflictions, the soul triumphs, often with the aid of the cross. The passion and the detail of Christ's physical suffering were an important part of religious devotion in the fourteenth and fifteenth centuries. The beatific smile on the body resurrected at the touch of the true cross from the cycle of glass in Ashton-under-Lyne church [**plate 10**] is as important as the apparent morbidity of the cadaver tomb or the dance of death.[31] There is a large question here, to which we shall return; whether death was approached hopefully or fearfully.

Communities of the dead

Whilst texts like the *ars moriendi* are characteristic of the later Middle Ages, they derived from but did not entirely replace earlier diagnostic visions of death which married both medical and moralising purposes. Such 'signs of death' texts were described in the previous chapter (see pp. 91–2) but continued to be copied in ever larger numbers into commonplace books in the fifteenth century. Robert Reynes the churchreeve of Acle, a man whose role and prominence in the community may have given him a more than passing and practical interest in the business of dying, copied one in the 1470s.[32] The reader was offered a diagnostic forecast as to whether a sick man might live or die, and an admonition counselling the sinner to repent and prepare for his death. Death was still seen both as a physical and as a moral state.[33] But it was also a transitional state. Where for Reynes's contemporaries did the boundary between life and death lie, and what prominence was afforded the dead amongst the living?

Medieval society included within its ranks a number of groups who, in various guises, were said to be dead to the world. Chief amongst these were the members of religious orders who underwent a form of ritual death before admission, those who had been excommunicated and those social ranks to whom the concept of civil death extended. It remained possible to absolve people from the sentence of excommunication following their actual death.[34] The ranks of the living were similarly delineated since the deaths of pagans, Jews, suicides and unbaptised children were regarded as qualitatively distinct from those of Christians. Death came to all but it came differently. Perhaps the most important group of walking dead were lepers, although the disease was in retreat during the later Middle Ages. The very word 'death', Latin *mors*, was held to derive from *morsus*, a 'bite'; those whose putrid flesh bore witness to the encounter with the jaws of death were thus already dead. In the Rite of Sarum, the order for the seclusion of lepers involved a mock funeral mass before the leper was led outside and earth thrown at his or her feet.[35] The presence in the world of souls already in Purgatory had long given opportunities for the visible exercise of humility. Margery Kempe's long-suffering confessor warned her that if she really wished to seek out lepers that 'she should kiss no men, but that as she would kiss anyway, she should kiss only women'.[36]

Humility was a quality rare amongst lawyers. In 1400 Adam Usk boasted that he had successfully obtained costs against the sureties of John Montagu, earl of Salisbury, for the latter's non-appearance at a judicial combat with Thomas, lord Morley, in April of that year. The defence, that Salisbury had been dead since January, was not accepted.[37] Trials of corpses were, indeed, not uncommon and illustrate graphically one of the ways in which the dead did not quite leave the world.

It seems also that the signs of approaching death were regularly misread in the Middle Ages, a lack of precision which had an important impact upon burial practice, an interval of one or more days being left between death and burial.[38] Recovery after extreme unction had been administered created interesting problems for theologians as they struggled to legislate on popular perceptions of the different quality of those who had stood at the brink of death.[39] More prosaically, survivors caught a glimpse of their likely earthly reputation, as did the unfortunate Sir Geoffrey Mascy who recovered from a seemingly fatal illness in the winter of 1455–56. He had time to complain, in a second will, that his family had 'slandered and noised in the country' about him and observed that his brother's bastard daughter was a strumpet.[40] Not everyone, it would appear, was prepared to go quietly.

Others not merely teetered at the threshold of death but seemingly returned from the other side. Miracles were perhaps less common in the later Middle Ages than they had been, but the raising of the dead still had something of a routine character to it. Amongst the allegedly proven miracles attributed to Henry VI between 1481 and 1500 many concerned the intervention of the 'saint' (Henry VIII abandoned the attempt to pursue the canonisation in 1528) following the death of drowned children, including a stiff and cold grandson in a mill trough in Westwell, Kent, an ice-cold girl in a well in Staplehurst, Kent, and

plate 9] The dying room at the Commandery, Worcester. Here the dying man was counselled to contemplate the means of his own salvation amidst the examples of the saints whose bodily suffering mirrored his own.

plate 10] The popularity of St Helen in the later Middle Ages rested largely on her role in the rediscovery of the True Cross. In this image, the Empress's archaeological team, having been faced by three crosses, test the True Cross on a shrouded corpse. The smile encapsulates the essential optimism of the late Middle Ages.

plate 11] *The Unton Memorial Picture* by an unknown artist, *c.* 1596. Commissioned by his widow Dorothy, the painting tells the story of Sir Henry Unton's life, from cradle to grave. Scenes include his deathbed and magnificent funeral procession. His portrait is flanked by figures of Death and Fame.

a seven-year-old girl who had lain at the bottom of a fish pond in Rye, Sussex, for over an hour. The sceptical reader may cough here, but must also explain the resurrection of one-year-old Anne, crushed 'as flat as a pancake' under the wheels of a carelessly driven dung cart at Minster-in-Thanet, Kent.[41] A regular traffic back and forth across the bridge between life and death was taken for granted.

Equally impressive was the possibility of contact with those firmly dead but now in Purgatory. Visions and revelations of Purgatory, a genre later exploited by Dante, appear in the twelfth century, as in an Eynsham monk's stark delineation, later printed in the 1480s. English vernacular accounts of pilgrimages to Station Island in Lough Derg, Donegal, believed to be a cave entrance to Purgatory revealed to Saint Patrick, survive from the mid-fourteenth century. The popularity of such visions and pilgrimage accounts in the fifteenth century is a distinctive aspect of late-medieval piety and a feature of an expanding world of individual religious experience.[42] In a less-well-known example, the 1492 *Vision in a Trance,* a Congleton draper, John Newton, 'visited' Purgatory during a three-day plague fever and was able to meet his recently dead wife and children.[43] Such religious experiences, once restricted to the saints, now knew few boundaries of social rank. Significantly, it seems also that political elites, not merely the sick, or the dying, pilgrims and dreamers, felt threatened by the insecure boundaries between the living and the dead.

A compelling case, for example, can be made for the proposition that ghosts played an important role in English politics between the years 1397 and 1403. Certainly both Richard II and his usurper, Henry Bolingbroke, took stern action against reported sightings of their murdered opponents. Richard had ordered the reburial of the earl of Arundel's corpse following rumours that the head and torso had been reunited, but continued to have bad dreams, and finally recruited a bodyguard which would protect him against the ghost.[44] Political ghosts were, of course, to continue to have a role in fifteenth-century politics, though they are far from being a uniquely English phenomenon. Medieval Europe was roamed by Perkin Warbecks and Lambert Simnels, impostor kings and princes, whose ghostly resurrections afforded legitimacy to political opposition. That they were taken seriously now seems barely credible and they are often elided in political narratives as more fit for studies of religion, as if piety were always a matter of cognitive dissonance with the real world.

More generally, medieval ghosts seem to have played an important role in policing the blurred boundary between life and death, often counselling or threatening family and friends from beyond the grave and, finally, aiding in the complete separation of the dead as they pleaded for intercession on their behalf from the living. The twelve ghost stories assembled by a monk of Byland, Yorkshire, sometime after 1399, collected recent and local testimony, notably in the vicinity of Ampleforth, and probably for use as exemplars. The ghosts appear in several forms beyond the human, as thorn bushes, horses and other animals. In one, a man burdened by sacks of beans after his horse is lamed, is aided by the ghost of a Rievaulx mercer who helps to carry them across a stream in return for masses for his soul. In another, the ghost of Robert, son of Robert de Boltby de Kilburn, buried in Kilburn churchyard, appeared to the young men of the township who met there to talk and drink. The intended audience is less the family than the neighbourhood, and the purpose of the exemplar in each case is to encourage intercession for the excommunicate and other unquiet souls.[45]

Late-medieval religion, as has been often observed, was frequently the living in the service of the dead. The rise of Purgatory and the ensuing social and religious significance of intercession on behalf of those held there had created enormous bonds of obligation between the living and the dead. In many respects the living must have felt beleaguered. Thus far, however, we have looked principally at admonitory and homiletic writing, based no doubt upon real experiences but offered as models of right practice. How did real practice sustain such burdens? We should remember that in the Byland ghost stories the point is not that the ghost appears in the churchyard, which is what the preacher wishes us to hear, but that the youth of Kilburn cared so little about the dead that they were happy to use the burial ground for loose talk and heavy drinking. Indeed, the catalogue of what the English were prepared to do in churchyards and cemeteries – the list of what they were not prepared to do is shorter – is probably as good a commentary on popular attitudes to death as any.

Individuals might look to purchase indulgences and masses to ease the passage of their souls through Purgatory, or even establish a perpetual chantry specifically for the purpose. But we need first to assess the terms on which people engaged in the process of intercession on behalf of others, either family or, as the monk of Byland might have advised, neighbours.

The most common form of neighbourly intercession was provided by the parish fraternity or guild, one of the most common of local associations which often operated as a kind of communal chantry, providing burial and prayers for deceased members.[46] The ordinances of c. 1400 for the Guild of St Mary and St John the Baptist in Lichfield, Staffordshire, the latter always a popular guild saint given the importance attached to feasts as part of the social activities for the living members, established that the names of new brothers and sisters of the guild should be inscribed in a membership register with their gifts and fees and that, when they died, the entry would be annotated with the date of their death so that they might be held in perpetual memory. The register does indeed continue until the enrolment of the last eleven members in 1546–47, the year in which chantries were suppressed, but the requirement to annotate the register with the obituaries of deceased members was not fulfilled.[47] In Dunstable, Bedfordshire, William Grene, who became master of the guild of St John the Baptist for the second time in 1522, and presented the guild with an ostentatiously decorated new register, had the membership list for his first period of office from 1506 to 1508 copied into the new volume but felt no responsibility for the members in the intervening years.[48] Often, guild members seem to have retained their individuality at the moment of joining, during their membership and perhaps for a time after their death, but weight of numbers drove further commemoration into a subsumed collective identity in which prayers were directed on behalf of all dead members.

The responsibility of the living for the dead, but more particularly for the recently dead, is emphasised, too, in a unique record which lists some 50,000 names in the archdeaconry of Stafford in 1532–33 and which has been tentatively explained as a fabric confraternity for Lichfield Cathedral connected with the guild of St Chad. The recipients of spiritual benefits, arranged in family groupings, include deceased wives and children, a few dead husbands, grandchildren, brothers and sisters and parents.[49] But there is no indication that the concerns of Staffordshire guild members extended to what Mormons today might describe as the unity of the historical family, only to the living and the recently dead kinship group. Here is a pragmatic rationalisation of the burden of the dead, operated as a kind of nine-year moving average, older souls joining the ranks of All Souls at one end, as the passing of years added new members at the other. There were clear physical limits to the community of the dead in much the same way that once the principle of interment in consecrated ground had been established in the tenth century, graves were reused, cemeteries levelled and ossuaries filled.[50]

There were exceptions, of course, in the devotion to institutional patrons and founders, but genealogy seems always to have been a secular and civil programme, the dead in the service of the living, supporting the claims and aspirations of contemporary families rather than the needs of their ancestors. Sir Thomas Erpingham's lost east window in the Augustinian friary in Norwich of 1419, 'in memory of all those lords, barons, bannerets and knights who have died without male heirs in Norfolk and Suffolk' is surely to be read in this way.[51] More characteristic of the attitudes of individuals to the spiritual welfare of the historic family is the way in which family obits were added to liturgical calendars. That belonging to the Legh family of Lyme, Cheshire, commenced between 1422 and 1439, and continued until 1541 (1635, if one counts a last recusant Legh), is characteristic [56]. The obits of five generations, their wives and sons, but no daughters, are recorded; and they are joined by a dean of Warrington, the chantry priest at Winwick and the stepson of the original patron. Of the family already dead at the time the missal was commissioned, including the Peter Legh executed by Henry Bolingbroke at Chester in 1399, there is no sign. Lady Joan Legh presumably felt that her father should have looked out for himself.[52]

56] An addition to the private missal of the Legh family of Lyme records the death of Mabel, daughter of James Croft and wife of Peter Legh esquire, who died in Dalton in Lonsdale, 8 July 1475. The feast of the translation of St Thomas Becket was later erased in accordance with a royal proclamation of 1538.

Death, the individual and memory

The ways in which individuals did shift for themselves are to be viewed largely through the evidence of wills and memorials, each indicative of that bossiness beyond the grave which accumulates to manufacture old countries and traditional cultures.

The funeral was an occasion for the first massive updraught of prayers of intercession, its arrangements choreographed by executors, and the body often camouflaged by a screen of the poor and the humble (see Chapter 4, pp. 101 ff.). We inevitably know more about the funerals of the wealthy. They seem rarely to have planned them to express other than sure and certain hope, sweetly wrapped in platitudes of unworthiness. In the justly famous illustrations which Gerard Horenbolte added to the mortuary roll of John Islip, Abbot of Westminster (d. 1532), the Abbot's hearse is shown as if battering the high altar of the abbey like a siege tower [57]. Little wonder that his adopted name in the monastic community, John 'Patience', never stuck.[53] Such people, secure in the theology of deathbed rituals, did not expect to be much troubled by Purgatory.

The process is neatly illustrated in the death plan of the chronicler, lawyer and disappointed churchman, Adam Usk, whose will of January 1429 is couched in conventional terms, 'fearing that the hazards of death are soon to befall me'. Earlier, in his chronicle, he had recorded that, 'anticipating my own death, I have already left to the church of

57] The funeral hearse of Abbot John Islip in Westminster Abbey, 1532. The central structure bore several hundred candles and a valance of cloth with the abbot's name. Mourners carrying torches walk behind the coffin within a timber enclosure whilst poor men, bought in for the occasion, stand or kneel beyond an outer rail.

Usk, my birthplace, my own memorial'. Amongst other things these comprised a set of vestments and copes embroidered with Usk's arms, 'commending myself thereby to the intercession of those who pray there'. Usk had also experimented with his epitaph, first in Latin, the prominent ecclesiastical teacher 'laid for worms', yet 'here he lies in peace, may he live henceforward in peace without end'; and finally in Welsh, 'May a home in heaven be your's, good sir. Behold! A Solomon of wisdom, Adam Usk, is sleeping here.'[54] That the sleep would be peaceful is assumed. Usk's was not a pragmatism born of unbelief, a charge frequently levelled at prominent churchmen by later writers.

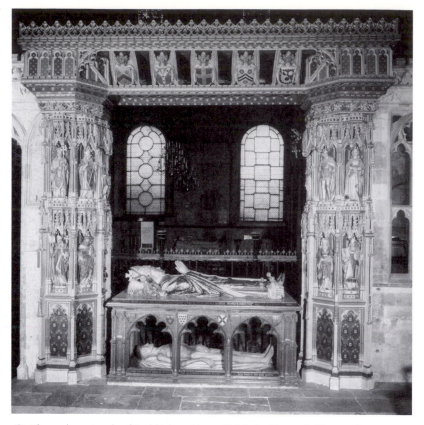

58] The cadaver tomb of Archbishop Henry Chichele (d. 1443). The tomb was completed and in position for at least seventeen years before receiving the corpse for which it was intended, offering a complex sermon in stone on the living archbishop's views on the significance of his own and others' deaths.

Rather, sensitisation to mortality and the reality of bodily decay which had followed the Black Death had been assimilated without replacing either hope or smugness with a morbid fear of death.

Hopefulness is emphasised too by the memorial to Archbishop Henry Chichele, the headmaster of the English Church in the first half of the fifteenth century. It is an apparently straightforward cadaver tomb on the north side of the choir in Canterbury Cathedral, the living or sleeping archbishop in his finery above, with a naked decaying corpse below [58]. Inscriptions address both the pilgrim passing along the aisle, monks leaving the choir and the archbishop's successor sitting on the archiepiscopal throne; 'I was born a poor man: and was afterwards raised to be Primate here. Now I am cast down: and turned into food for worms.' However, other texts and imagery, the ensemble depicting the heavenly kingdom, moderate the apparently fearful message of the corpse into a hopeful theology of resurrection. The cry 'Emanuel, Emanuel' is inscribed at head and feet, and Christ appears on the pier facing the archbishop, as if anticipating the triumphal words of the Office of

59] The Wakeman cenotaph in Tewkesbury Abbey. On this unusual example of the cadaver tomb, the corpse is shown covered by several vermin, including a toad, a mouse and a serpent, each allegories of the sins which beset the dead, which are in turn driven away by prayer and by the sacrifice of Christ's Passion, the symbols of which appear on the screen beneath the effigy.

the Dead, 'on the last day I shall rise from the earth. And in my flesh I shall see my saviour.'[55] English cadaver tombs were always more restrained than in the rest of Europe, and even on one of the more gruesome examples, the 'Wakeman cenotaph' at Tewkesbury Abbey, with its five kinds of 'vermin' consuming the decaying corpse, the message remains essentially optimistic [59].[56]

However the individual met his death, the postmortem fate of his corpse and the design of his memory was frequently in the hands of others. Testators dotted their wills with gifts of vestments, books and lights in order to associate their names and souls with the continuing intercession which occupied the ritual life of the church. In 1394 Sir William Mainwaring left a relic of the true cross to the church at Acton, Cheshire, in which he had already commissioned his tomb; others left livestock to parochial herds, and libraries to the parochial chapel.[57] The intent was the same: ritual as power, artfully communicated. The challenge of intercession beyond the rituals associated with the first year after death was met by the chantry movement, the provision of masses for an individual or nominated group of souls such as the membership of a guild. At its simplest, the individual might provide sufficient income to pay a temporary chaplain for a fixed period of time; the more elaborate provisions established perpetual chantries within existing churches or colleges of priests. Whilst the principal focus of the chantry remained the celebration of masses for the soul of the founder, other roles might be included so that many were founded as schools, almshouses and hospitals.[58]

Statutes circulated, often acting as models for each other and throwing into sharper focus the particular concerns of founders. All were touchingly concerned that any lack of moral integrity in their earthly memorial should not contaminate the prayers of intercession. The statutes of the college at Bunbury, Cheshire, founded in 1387 by the veteran soldier, Sir Hugh Calveley, in honour of St George, 'special protector of the English', to support a master, six priests, two clerks and two choristers, laid down severe prescriptions as to the quality of the priests, their behaviour and dress. Women, however decent, were not allowed within the precinct; dice, chess and ball games were prohibited; initially no stranger was permitted at table so that 'the opportunity for distraction is nipped in the bud'.[59] The twelve men in reduced circumstances who staffed Archbishop's Chichele's almshouse were to be 'clean men of their bodies, without blotches, blains or boils' and were to go to their friends to be nursed when they had a contagious disease, presumably to ensure that sympathy for their demise did not detract from prayers for the founder.[60] Not all foundations were successful. Some were stillborn, others failed after a few years, many were amalgamated with other small and poorly funded chantries. Yet the greater part of initial clerical career opportunity and most newly created benefices in the Church in the later Middle Ages derived from this source.

The difficulties of securing the establishment of chantries after death were notorious, for they remained institutions in the world, draining the resources of the living family and determining its structures. John Paston I was famously responsible for the non-foundation of two such, one for his father William Paston in Norwich Cathedral after 1444 and the other for his patron, Sir John Fastolf, in Caister after 1459.[61] Many, not merely those without heirs, looked to establish the boundaries of their memorials before death.

Such is the case with Archbishop Henry Chichele (d. 1443) whose tomb in Canterbury was in place before 1426, whose college at All Souls, Oxford, was in construction from 1438, and whose foundations (properly speaking several were refoundations) in his birthplace at Higham Ferrers, the college, almshouse and grammar school, had commenced in 1422.[62] Like All Souls, part of the 'gradual take-over of a declining town by an expanding university', the proliferation of memorial institutions in Higham Ferrers, accompanied by the archbishop's image, transformed it into a new town, a virtual Chicheleville [60].[63]

However, just as the deathbed was often a communal event, so too was the funeral and the memorial. The relationship between living and

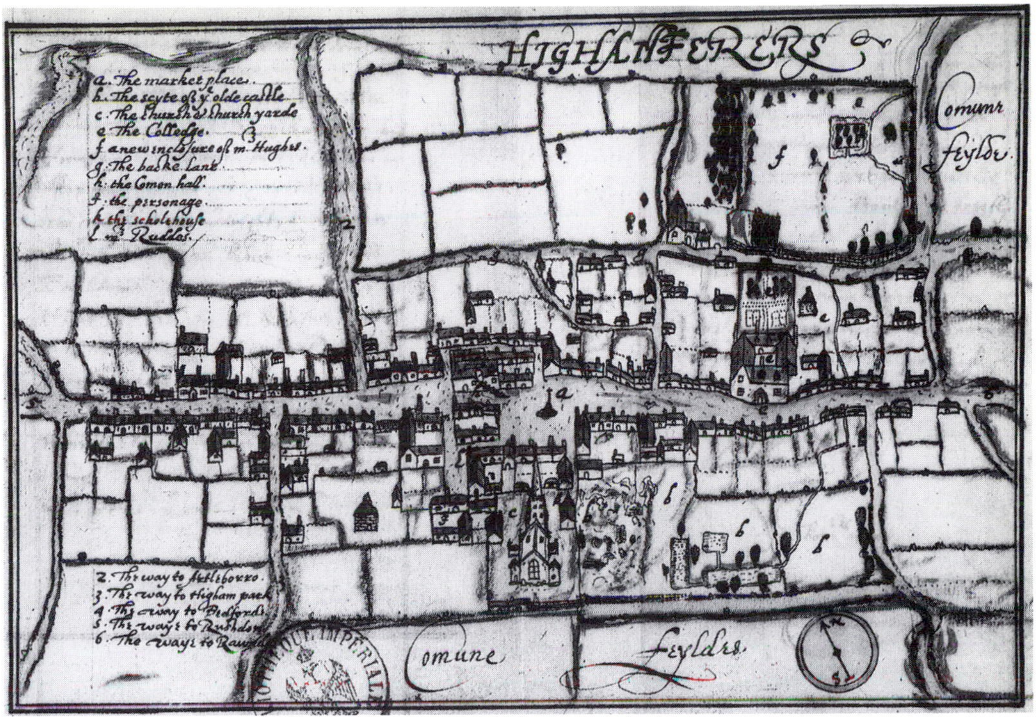
HIGHAMFERRERS
a. The market place.
b. The scyte of ye olde castle
c. The Church & Church yarde
e The Colledge.
f a new inclosure of m. Hughes.
g. The backe lane
h. the Comon hall.
the personage
the scholehouse
2. The way to Ketleborro.
3. The way to Higham park
4. The way to Bedforde
Comune Feyldes
Comune Feylde.

60] 'Chicheleville'. Of the several identitites of Higham Ferrers in the Middle Ages, the Anglo-Saxon *burh*, the Anglo-Norman castle-borough, the small market town, it is the memorial landscape of Archbishop Chichele, including the college, almshouse and grammar school, which survives, both in Norden's survey of 1591 and as the visible heritage of the modern town.

dead was ever a reciprocal one. The funeral was also a political occasion, wrapped in piety. It drew the kinship group, the lordship, the local community and the neighbourhood with the prospect of at least a good meal and the expectation of the reaffirmation of their solidarity. Invitations were circulated, at least for the greater funerals. The Prior of Worcester received summonses to accompany the body of Queen Anne of Bohemia from Sheen to Westminster, and that of Constance of Castile, John of Gaunt's wife, to Leicester, both in 1394, duly enrolling both in the Worcester *Liber Albus* together with his apology for absence from the latter.[64]

The funeral feast might be the occasion for an ostentatious display. In 1466 John Paston I's famous £230 funeral, perhaps four times the going rate, was surely meant to announce the completion of the family's social elevation. That two windows in the church had to be removed to clear the smoke from the number of torches lit during the *dirige* speaks clearly of the vulgarity of the occasion.[65] The reburial of Richard, duke of York, at Fotheringay in 1476, sixteen years after his death at the battle of Wakefield, with its 1,500 place settings, was probably worse still but then commentators have been kinder to kings.[66]

A powerful counter-current of burial practice, in which testators requested modest interments, is a mirror of the humility of the cadaver tomb. 'Anon as I be dead thud me in the earth', as Sir Thomas Latimer put it. Both Philip Berney (d. 1453) and his father John (d. 1440) specified that they were to have no funerals.[67] Others were seemingly careless as to the place of burial and, after bequeathing their souls, disposed of their corpses 'wherever it will have pleased God'. John Reve, a glover of Beccles, abjuring his heresy in the chapel of the Bishop's palace in Norwich on 18 April 1430, confessed 'Also that I have held, believed and affirmed that it is as great merit, reward and profit to all Christ's people to be buried in middens, meadows or in the wild fields as it is to be buried in churches or churchyards'.[68] Such wishes were common amongst churchmen without heirs, merchants and pilgrims, but also amongst a minority of laypeople for whom personal piety or family tradition weighed heavily. Some were associated with reforming beliefs known as Lollardy, amongst which strict injunctions against funeral pomp seem to have been characteristic.[69] Their modest and anonymous funerals represented a socially corrosive individualism in the face of the more common and gregarious gatherings.

The vast majority of testators not only nominated their burial place but sought to embellish it. The rebuilding of churches was increasingly the responsibility of lords, leading citizens and other notables who impressed their own imagery on the architecture and colonised much of the space as a private necropolis. They fastened box-like chantry chapels to the outsides of churches, filled the interior with their images and ringed existing fabric with parapets bearing their arms. In stained glass they commissioned portraits of themselves as if in prayer. At Ashton-under-Lyne, Lancashire, the great east window containing a cycle of the life of St Helen, erected around 1500, included four generations of Ashetons and two rectors, both also Ashetons. That such imagery, no less than that of the cadaver tomb, has been seen as a memorial, not to the fragility of human existence but to the continuing authority of lordship, the Church and the state, is hardly surprising. If for most people medieval Christianity was promissory, a Macmillanesque future perfect 'you will never have had it so good', that the rich would get their comeuppance must have seemed hardly likely in the surroundings of English religion in the later Middle Ages. For them death in all its horrors had been tamed.

Place-loyalty amongst the dead, even amongst those, like merchants and soldiers, who in their wills often anticipated death at a distance, is notable. Often, then, corpses were returned home, like that of Sir Thomas Morley who had died in Calais on 24 September 1416. Henry V and the Emperor Sigismund attended a funeral mass in the chapel of St George, and the body, embalmed, was returned to Norfolk for final burial in the Augustinian friary in Norwich, the household chaplain accompanying it on the journey on the sterncastle of the ship, two candles burning around the corpse.[70] Incredibly, bodies were also occasionally exhumed for return home many years after original burial elsewhere. John, lord Talbot, killed at Castillon in 1453, was not returned to Whitchurch, Shropshire, for over half a century, but forensic dentistry confirms that the skeleton, briefly exhumed in 1874, was indeed his.[71] That the long-dead might seem so instrumental to the authority of the lineage makes the assault of the English state upon the cult of the dead in the mid-sixteenth century seem all the more remarkable.

The state and death

Recent accounts of changes introduced during the English Reformation tend to embody an unfolding chronological narrative, in which the concept of power is central and the state, as the focus of that power, generated both agents and victims. A summary of the state's ambition for a reformed death suggests a sudden and cathartic transformation. In 1538, amongst the injunctions directed towards the clergy, Thomas Cromwell established the keeping of parish registers and with it a virtually national system of registration of burials. At the time it was widely rumoured to be a prelude to taxation.[72] The cult of saints was swept away [56]. Prayers for the dead initially survived, but the existence of Purgatory was denied; in 1536 it was said of the dead that 'the place where there be, the name thereof, and the kinds of pain there, be to us uncertain by scripture'. Denial of Purgatory had earlier been a feature of John Wyclif's thought and was often asserted by those tried as Lollards in the fifteenth century, but such beliefs were then not widely held. Now the state proffered it as official theology. Between 1545 and 1547 the chantries were dissolved, condemned as expressions of 'blindness and ignorance'. In the two revisions of the Prayer Book, first in 1549 and then more decisively in 1552, the order for burial no longer elicited intercession or imagined a community of the living and the dead.[73] Physical death was to become final and the funeral to serve only as solace for the living.

Whether religion in the fifteenth century was homogeneous and broadly consensual, and the power of the state relatively thin, are both questionable. Neither can have seemed the case for those towards whom were directed both the 1401 statute on the burning of heretics and Archbishop Arundel's constitutions on the governing of the English Church in 1407 (Henry VIII was not the first king to attempt to pre-scribe the practice of the English Church). The involvement of heralds in the funerals of the nobility and greater gentry from the 1460s must also have suggested that the state and its agents were prepared to involve themselves even in the secular elements of funeral ritual.[74] Yet there was something remarkable about the legislative unity and intensity of the mid-sixteenth century, especially of Edwardian changes to the theology and practice of death between 1547 and 1552. Whether such changes reflected or even immediately effected a transformation in popular attitudes and practice is the subject of some debate amongst historians who have sought to comprehend the making of the English Reformation.[75]

How vital or hollow was popular subscription to the rituals, notably those associated with Purgatory and prayers for the dead, in the first half of the sixteenth century? It has been argued that the practice of prayers for the dead was already in decline by 1543, witnessed an indifferent revival under Mary and ended abruptly thereafter.[76] Chantry foundations, it is claimed, were declining in number. With what approval did they embrace reformed protestant theology? Many aspects of medieval practice, not least funeral wakes and the general precept that a sinful life posed terrible dangers in death, continued.[77] The 1552 Prayer Book, which had removed all prayers of commendation of the soul in favour of simple committal of the body, was abandoned in Mary's reign. That which was restored in 1559 at least included prayers for the repose of the souls of the dead. Even reformers envisaged a certain busyness around the deathbed. The ringing of bells, seen by many, probably rightly, as pagan in origin, seems to have survived throughout the period, with the passing bell and three short peals, at the time of death, and before and after the funeral, prescribed in 1561 by the Bishops' *Interpretations* of the 1559 Prayer Book.[78] Local studies reveal a diversity of distinctive regional and chronological responses. The English Reformation stands in relation to many of the changes in the culture of death in much the same fashion as did the Black Death.

What may have secured the final disappearence of the dead from the community of the living was less changes in theology and liturgy, and more the destruction of the institutions and personnel which had sustained, in however vigorous a fashion, the industry of prayers for the dead. The dissolution of the chantries had first been planned in 1545 but postponed by Henry VIII's death; it was renewed in December 1547 and justified on religious grounds, chantries condemned as the product of 'devising and phantasing vain opinions of Purgatury'. Yet it is difficult to disagree with the judgement that this was merely 'the enrichment of the rich at the expense of the rest of the community'.[79] Deprived of financial resources, local communities throughout England could never revive or rebuild them, no matter what their own attitudes to Purgatory and the efficacy of prayers for the dead. A vast army of chaplains who had manned the chantries disappeared, like John Whitby, chaplain and newly appointed bailiff of the depopulated township of Misterton, Leicestershire, in the 1550s, whose careful accounts and stewardship, not of lost souls but of the local rabbits, are bound in the redundant folios of medieval service books and homiletic writing.[80]

With suitable irony, the grandest chantry of them all, that of the king in St George's Chapel, Windsor, survived and was fattened to become one of the wealthiest foundations in the country, prayers for its dead being said with a carefully reformed liturgy. Earlier in 1537, Lord Stafford had rescued the tombs of his ancestors from Stone priory, briefly reinstalling them in the Augustinian friary in Stafford. This too was dissolved in 1538 and the tombs abandoned.[81] An equally significant moment occurred in April 1549 when Edward, duke of Somerset, one of the architects of the Edwardian reforms, ordered the demolition of the pardon cloister on the north side of St Paul's cathedral, famous for its tombs, monuments and depiction of the *danse macabre*, and employed the now 'found materials' to build his new house on the Strand.[82] The dead, it seemed, must shift for themselves.

Notes

In all references, place of publication is London unless otherwise stated.

1 C. Platt, *King Death: The Black Death and Its Aftermath in Late Medieval England* (1996), provides a good introduction.

2 The thoughts are entirely conventional in the fifteenth century; their expression in this form belongs to the poet John Audley, *The Poems of John Audelay*, ed. E. Keats Whiting, Early English Text Society 184 (1931), p. 211.

3 J. Huizinga, *The Waning of the Middle Ages: A Study of the Forms of Life, Thought, and Art in France and the Netherlands in the Fourteenth and Fifteenth Centuries* (Harmondsworth, 1955), p. 134. The original and longer Dutch edition was first published in Haarlem in 1919, now translated as *The Autumn of the Middle Ages* (Chicago, 1996).

4 E. Duffy, *The Stripping of the Altars: Traditional Religion in England 1400–1580* (New Haven, 1992), pp. 301–37, 475.

5 J. Hatcher, 'England in the aftermath of the Black Death', *Past and Present*, 144 (1994), 9.

6 J. R. Maddicott, 'Plague in seventh-century England', *Past and Present*, 156 (1997), 45–6.

7 E. F. Jacob, *Henry Chichele* (1967), pp. 97–9.

8 R. Marks, 'Henry Williams and his "Ymage of deth" roundel at Stanford on Avon, Northamptonshire', *The Antiquaries Journal*, 54 (1974), 272–4. A lost inscription records Williams's death the following year.

9 J. Hatcher, 'Mortality in the fifteenth century: some new evidence', *Economic History Review*, 39 (1986), 19–38; B. Harvey, *Living and Dying in England, 1100–1540: The Monastic Experience* (Oxford, 1993), pp. 124, 128, 138.

10 Stafford, William Salt Library, Salt MS M64.

11 H. C. Whaite, *St Christopher in English Mediæval Wallpainting* (1929); A. Masseron, *Saint Christophe, patron des automobilistes* (1933), cited by D. H. Farmer, *The Oxford Dictionary of Saints* (Oxford, 1978), p. 79.

12 *The Commonplace Book of Robert Reynes of Acle: An Edition of Tanner MS 407*, ed. C. Louis, Garland Medieval Texts 1 (1980), pp. 245–50.

13 A. J. Pollard, 'Introduction: society, politics and the Wars of the Roses', in Pollard (ed.), *The Wars of the Roses* (1995), p. 1.

14 *Victoria County History (Shropshire)*, 2 (1973), pp. 128–31; Peter J. Foss, *The Field of Redemore: The Battle of Bosworth, 1485* (Leeds, 1990), pp. 23–4.

15 *Calendar of Entries in the Papal Registers*, 12 (1902), p. 623; *The Register of Thomas Rotherham*, ed. E. Barker, Canterbury and York Society 69 (1976), no. 1741. I am grateful to Moira Habberjam for her transcript of the latter entry.

16 J. G. Bellamy, *The Law of Treason in England in the Later Middle Ages* (Cambridge, 1970), p. 261.

17 *Historical Collections of a Citizen of London in the Fifteenth Century*, ed. J. Gairdner, Camden Society (1876), p. 211.

18 *Henry VI: A Reprint of John Blacman's Memoir*, ed. M. R. James (Cambridge, 1919), pp. 17–19, 39–41.

19 *The Politics of Fifteenth-Century England: John Vale's Book*, ed. M. L. Kekewich et al. (Stroud, 1995), p. 49. The characterisation of Richard Neville, earl of

Warwick, is Professor Colin Richmond's, repeated in his, 'Richard III, Richard Nixon and the brutality of fifteenth-century politics: a discussion', in S. D. Michalove and A. Compton Reeves (eds), *Estrangement, Enterprise and Education* (Stroud, 1998), pp. 89–106.

20 Sir Thomas More, *The History of King Richard III* (1965), p. 71.

21 *The Book of Margery Kempe*, ed. S. B. Meech and H. E. Allen, Early English Text Society 212 (1940), pp. 172–3.

22 M. Rubin, *Corpus Christi: The Eucharist in Late Medieval Culture* (Cambridge, 1991), pp. 77–82; C. Daniell, *Death and Burial in Medieval England 1066–1550* (1997), pp. 34–5.

23 Huizinga, *The Waning of the Middle Ages*, pp. 139–44; J. M. Clark, *The Dance of Death in the Middle Ages and the Renaissance* (Glasgow, 1950); E. Carleton Williams, 'The Dance of Death in painting and sculpture in the Middle Ages', *Journal of the British Archaeological Association*, 3rd series, 1 (1937), 230–8.

24 J. H. Bettey, *The English Parish Church and the Local Community* (1985), p. 12.

25 C. Richmond, 'The visual culture of fifteenth-century England', in Pollard (ed.), *The Wars of the Roses*, pp. 195–6.

26 D. Howarth, *Images of Rule: Art and Politics in the English Renaissance, 1485–1649* (1997), pp. 217–24.

27 *John Mirk's Instructions for Parish Priests*, ed. G. Kristensson (Lund, 1974).

28 M. Aston, 'Death', in R. Horrox (ed.), *Fifteenth-Century Attitudes: Perceptions of Society in Late Medieval England* (Cambridge, 1994), pp. 208–11.

29 *Paston Letters and Papers of the Fifteenth Century*, ed. N. Davis (Oxford, 1971), no. 26. John Paston's wife Margaret's letter on the same topic omits the homiletic tone, *ibid.*, no. 147.

30 Richmond, 'The visual culture of fifteenth-century England', p. 194; E. M. Moore, 'Wall-paintings recently discovered in Worcestershire', *Archaeologia*, 88 (1938), 281–4.

31 H. Reddish, 'The St Helen window at Ashton-under-Lyne: a reconstruction', *The Journal of Stained Glass*, 18 (1986–87), 150–61.

32 *The Commonplace Book of Robert Reynes of Acle: An Edition of Tanner MS 407*, ed. C. Louis, Garland Medieval Texts 1 (1980), pp. 245–50.

33 R. H. Robbins, 'Signs of death in Middle English', *Mediaeval Studies*, 32 (1970), 288–93.

34 *John Lydford's Book*, ed. D. M. Owen, *Devon and Cornwall Record Society*, n.s., 20 (1975), p. 133.

35 R. C. Finucane, 'Sacred corpse, profane carrion: social ideals and death rituals in the later Middle Ages', in J. Whaley (ed.), *Mirrors of Mortality: Studies in the Social History of Death* (1981), p. 55; Daniell, *Death and Burial in Medieval England*, Appendix, pp. 203–5; C. W. Bynum, *The Resurrection of the Body in Western Christianity, 200–1336* (New York, 1995), p. 148.

36 *The Book of Margery Kempe*, pp. 176–7.

37 *The Chronicle of Adam Usk, 1377–1421*, ed. C. Given-Wilson (Oxford, 1997), xxxvii–xxxviii, epitaph, pp. 96–7, Montagu case; 'Morley *vs.* Montagu (1399): a case in the Court of Chivalry', in M. H. Keen and M. Warner (eds), *Camden Miscellany*, 34 (1997), pp. 145–95.

38 Daniell, *Death and Burial in Medieval England*, pp. 48–9.

39 Finucane, 'Sacred corpse, profane carrion', pp. 41–2.

40 Warrington Public Library, Mascy of Tatton Deeds, MS 372.

41 P. Grosjean, *Henrici VI Angliae regis miracula postuma, ex codice Musei Britannici Regio 13 C VIII*, Subsidia Hagiographica 22 (Brussels, 1935).

42 *St Patrick's Purgatory*, ed. R. Easting, Early English Text Society 298 (1991); Edward Arber, *The Revelation of the Monk of Evesham* [sic], (1901); G. R. Keiser, 'The progress of Purgatory: visions of the afterlife in late middle English literature', *Analecta Cartusiana*, 117 (1987), 72–100.

43 D. Marsh, 'Humphrey Newton of Newton and Pownall (1466–1536): a gentleman of Cheshire and his commonplace book', unpublished Ph.D. thesis, Keele University (1995), pp. 311–17.

44 P. Morgan, 'Henry IV and the shadow of Richard II', in R. Archer (ed.), *Crown, Government and People in the Fifteenth Century* (Stroud, 1995), pp. 3–4.

45 J.-C. Schmitt, *Les Revenants: les vivants et les morts dans la société médiévale* (Paris, 1994), pp. 168–71; M. R. James, 'Twelve medieval ghost-stories', *English Historical Review*, 37 (1922), 413–21.

46 R. N. Swanson, *Church and Society in Late Medieval England* (Oxford, 1989), pp. 280–4; V. Bainbridge, *Gilds in the Medieval Countryside: Social and Religious Change in Cambridgeshire, c. 1350–1558* (Woodbridge, 1996).

47 A. G. Rosser, 'The Guild of St Mary and St John the Baptist, Lichfield: Ordinances of the late fourteenth century', *Collections for a History of Staffordshire*, 4th series, 13 (1988), p. 23; and 'The town and guild of Lichfield in the late Middle Ages', *South Staffordshire Archaeological and Historical Society Transactions*, 27 (1985–86), 39–47.

48 R. Marks, 'Two illuminated guild registers from Bedfordshire', in M. P. Brown and S. McKendrick (eds), *Illuminating the Book: Makers and Interpreters: Essays in Honour of Janet Backhouse* (1998), pp. 121–41.

49 *A List of Families in the Archdeaconry of Stafford 1532–3*, ed. A. J. Kettle, *Collections for a History of Staffordshire*, 4th series, 8 (1976), xvi–xix.

50 W. Rodwell, *The Archaeology of the English Church: The Study of Historic Churches and Churchyards* (1981), pp. 131–61; Daniell, *Death and Burial in Medieval England*, pp. 145–74.

51 F. Blomefield, *An Essay Towards a Topographical History of the County of Norfolk* (1775), II, pp. 548–50.

52 The National Trust, Lyme Park, missal. Sarum calendar fos 1r–6v.

53 Harvey, *Living and Dying in England*, p. 75; *The Obituary Roll of John Islip, Abbot of Westminster, 1500–1532*, ed. W. H. St John Hope, *Vetusta Monumenta*, 7 (1906).

54 *The Chronicle of Adam of Usk*, pp. xxxvii–viii, xliii–iv, 118–19, 272; J. Morris-Jones, 'Adam of Usk's epitaph', *Y Cymmrodor*, 31 (1921), 112–34.

55 P. Collinson, N. Ramsay and M. Sparks (eds), *A History of Canterbury Cathedral* (Oxford, 1995), pp. 476–80.

56 P. M. King, 'The iconography of the "Wakeman Cenotaph" in Tewkesbury Abbey', *Transactions of the Bristol and Gloucestershire Archaeological Society*, 103 (1985), 141–8.

57 John Rylands University Library, Manchester, Mainwaring Deed 173; C. Richmond, 'The English gentry and religion c. 1500', in C. Harper-Bill (ed.), *Religious Belief and Ecclesiastical Careers in Late Medieval England* (Woodbridge, 1991), pp. 121–6, discussing a London gentleman with Cheshire origins, Geoffrey Downes.

58 Swanson, *Church and Society in Late Medieval England*, pp. 45–50.

59 Lichfield Joint Diocesan Record Office, B/A/1/6, Register of Richard Scrope, ff. 116v–120r. I am grateful to Nigel Coulton for a transcript and translation of these statutes.

60 *Victoria County History (Northamptonshire)*, 2 (1906), p. 178.

61 C. Richmond, *The Paston Family in the Fifteenth Century: The First Phase* (Cambridge, 1990), p. 175.

62 Jacob, *Henry Chichele*, pp. 78–99.

63 H. M. Colvin and J. S. G. Simmons, *All Souls: An Oxford College and Its Buildings* (Oxford, 1989), p. 2; M. Beresford, *History on the Ground* (1957), pp. 153–79.

64 Worcester Cathedral Library, MS A 5, *The Liber Albus*, f. 374r–v.

65 C. Richmond, *The Paston Family in the Fifteenth Century: Fastolf's Will* (Cambridge, 1996), pp. 154–5.

66 A. F. Sutton and L. Visser-Fuchs, with P. W. Hammond, *The Reburial of Richard Duke of York 21–30 July 1476* (1996).

67 Richmond, *The Paston Family in the Fifteenth Century: The First Phase*, pp. 154–7.

68 *Heresy Trials in the Diocese of Norwich, 1428–31*, ed. N. P. Tanner, Camden Society, 4th series, 20 (1977), p. 112.

69 K. B. McFarlane, *Lancastrian Kings and Lollard Knights* (Oxford, 1972), p. 210.

70 Staffordshire Record Office, D641/3/R/1/2. Morley is discussed in C. Richmond, 'Thomas Lord Morley (d. 1416) and the Morleys of Hingham', *Norfolk Archaeology*,

39, part 1 (1984), 1–12. I am grateful to Professor Richmond for the gift of his unpublished edition of the roll.

71 A. J. Pollard, *John Talbot and the War in France 1427–1453* (1983), p. 138.

72 G. R. Elton, *Policy and Police: The Enforcement of the Reformation in the Age of Thomas Cromwell* (Cambridge, 1972), pp. 254, 259–60.

73 *The Statutes of the Realm*, Record Commission (1810–28), 4, pp. 24–33; Duffy, *The Stripping of the Altars*, pp. 454 ff.; Gittings, *Death, Burial and the Individual*, pp. 39–59.

74 C. Gittings, 'Urban funerals', in S. Bassett (ed.), *Death in Towns: Urban Responses to the Dying and the Dead, 100–1600* (Leicester, 1992), pp. 178–9.

75 N. Tyacke, 'Introduction: re-thinking the "English Reformation"', in Tyacke, *England's Long Reformation 1500–1800* (1998), pp. 1–32.

76 R. Whiting, *Local Responses to the English Reformation* (1998), pp. 71–7.

77 Gittings, *Death, Burial and the Individual*, pp. 235–9.

78 E. Cardwell, *Documentary Annals of the Reformed Church of England*, 2 vols (Oxford, 1844), I, p. 238.

79 A. Kreider, *English Chantries: The Road to Dissolution* (Cambridge, 1979); W. G. Hoskins, *The Age of Plunder* (1976), p. xii.

80 Staffordshire Record Office, D(W)1734/4/1/6; 11.

81 *Victoria County History (Staffordshire)*, 3 (1970), p. 246.

82 *Vertue Note Books*, Walpole Society 18 (Oxford, 1930), p. 37.

Select bibliography

Aston, M., 'Death', in R. Horrox (ed.), *Fifteenth-Century Attitudes: Perceptions of Society in Late Medieval England*, Cambridge, 1994.

Binski, P., *Medieval Death: Ritual and Representation*, 1996.

Burgess, C., 'A service for the dead: the form and function of the Anniversary in Late Medieval Bristol', in *Transactions of the Bristol & Gloucestershire Archaeological Society*, 105 (1987), 183–211.

Cohen, K. Rogers, *Metamorphosis of a Death Symbol: The Transi Tomb in the Late Middle Ages and the Renaissance*, Berkeley, Cal., 1973.

Cressy, D., *Birth, Marriage and Death*, Oxford, 1997.

Daniell, C., *Death and Burial in Medieval England, 1066–1550*, 1997.

Davies, R., 'Religious sensibility', in C. Given-Wilson (ed.), *An Illustrated History of Late Medieval England*, Manchester, 1996.

Duffy, E., *The Stripping of the Altars: Traditional Religion in England 1400–1580*, New Haven, 1992.

Finucane, R. C., 'Sacred corpse, profane carrion: social ideals and death rituals in the later middle ages', in J. Whaley (ed.), *Mirrors of Mortality: Studies in the Social History of Death*, 1981.

Gittings, C., *Death, Burial and the Individual in Early Modern England*, 1984.

Harvey, B., *Living and Dying in England, 1100–1540: The Monastic Experience*, Oxford, 1993.

Huizinga, J., *The Autumn of the Middle Ages*, Chicago, 1996.

Platt, C., *King Death: The Black Death and Its Aftermath in Late Medieval England*, 1996.

Richmond, C., 'The visual culture of fifteenth-century England', in *The Wars of the Roses*, ed. A. J. Pollard, 1995.

6 · Clare Gittings

Sacred and secular: 1558–1660

In 1635 Sir Thomas Aston commissioned an unusual family portrait [61]. He stands in black, his hand resting on a skull which surmounts a black-draped, empty cradle, inscribed in Latin 'Who sows in flesh will reap bones'. Beside him, in a bed with black curtains, lies the dead body of his wife, Magdalene. His young son Thomas holds a surveying instrument shaped like a cross, which records the death of his elder brother aged three and three-quarters; young Thomas was himself to die two years later. Further emblems of mortality include the half-withered garland around the coat of arms and the unstrung lute.

This mingling of sacred and secular imagery of mortality is characteristic of the time, reflecting the doctrinal changes at the Reformation. The scaling down of the funeral service and the ban on religious imagery helped promote the secular aspects of death in both rituals and images. During the period from 1558 to 1660 there was a growing secularisation of death, together with important shifts in emphasis within both the religious and social spheres. At the foot of the bed in the Aston picture sits a woman with her head resting on her hand in a gesture of melancholy. Is this a mourning relative or is it, as has been suggested, Magdalene grieving for her dead baby and for herself?[1]

Demography and the causes of death

Sadly, the Aston family's experience of mortality was not uncommon in early modern England. Birth and death were inextricably linked. In one London parish early in Elizabeth's reign, almost one-third of all baptised babies were buried within a year. Nor were infants the only victims; around 2.5 per cent of childbirths resulted in the mother's death.[2] In the later sixteenth and early seventeenth centuries life expectancy at birth was actually remarkably high, sometimes even exceeding forty years. Indeed, from the mid-1560s to the mid-1580s, mortality was lower than it would be again until after 1815, mainly because there were few epidemics. The seventeenth century, however, saw life expectancy considerably shorten.[3] The Civil War was in part responsible for this fall. Sir Thomas Aston himself was one of its casualties, dying aged

147

forty-five of infected wounds, attempting to escape from the Parliamentarians in 1645 after the siege of Chester. Many more non-combatants died from epidemics, probably of typhus, spread by the troops and fanned by the social dislocation and famine attendant on the war.[4]

The most spectacular of all Civil War deaths was, of course, that of the King himself on the scaffold outside the Banqueting House in Whitehall on 30 January 1649 [62]; the identity of his two masked executioners remains uncertain to this day. Charles, in his last speech, declared, 'I am the martyr of the people', adding the final word 'Remember'. Although the German artist who made this engraving was not present at the scene, he gives a sense of the crowd's responses, some people pointing, others weeping or fainting at the sight. One witness recorded that, at the instant of the blow 'there was such a

61] *Sir Thomas Aston at the Deathbed of his Wife*, by John Souch, commemorating the death of Magdalene Aston in childbirth in 1635. Many emblems of mortality appear in the painting, including the skull and the black-draped cradle, while the various inscriptions reflect on the inevitability of death.

62] *Execution of Charles I*, 30 January 1649. With the King on the scaffold in Whitehall are Bishop Juxon, two Parliamentarian colonels and two anonymous executioners. In the three roundels above, Charles is flanked by his opponents, Fairfax and Cromwell.

groan by the thousands then present, as I never heard before, and desire I may never hear again'.[5] Prints such as this, showing cherubs descending with a laurel wreath, were part of an extensive martyrology which rapidly grew up around the dead King. It took a wide range of forms from paintings to jewellery and helped keep Royalist sympathies alive until the Restoration in 1660.

Hanging was far more common than beheading. Despite what is popularly believed, hanging was the usual punishment for witchcraft; only those 'witches' convicted of murdering their husbands or masters were actually burned.[6] At some executions the punishment even continued after death, with vengeance taken on the corpse. High treason was thought to merit particularly gruesome revenge, as explained by the judge passing sentence, in 1615, on John Owen, who had said it was lawful to kill the King:

> he shall be drawn to execution . . . as he is not fit to walk upon the earth: 2. His privy members cut off . . . which shows that his issue is disinherited with the corruption of blood . . . 3. His bowels burned because in them he hatched the treason: 4. Beheaded: 5. Dismembered.[7]

Surgeons were allowed a small number of the corpses of executed murderers each year for anatomy. These occasionally appear in the parish registers of London churches; in February 1615 at St Martin's, Ludgate, 'was buried an anatomy from the College of Physicians'.[8]

Even the far lesser crime of debt might be pursued after death. A case in the church courts in Essex in 1598 reported how Thomas Bett 'did go into the grave made for the body of Edward Godfrie and there did arrest the body with very unseemly, unrelevant and intemperate speech'.[9] Those who fell foul of the church courts and were excommunicated also had their bodies punished after death, by the denial of Christian burial. They were often laid to rest 'without the bounds of the churchyard . . . in the limits and meres of the parish'. Suicides were accorded a particularly 'infamous and reproachful . . . burial',[10] as the parish register of Pleasley, Derbyshire, recorded in 1573:

> Tho[mas] Maule f[oun]d hanging on a tree by the wayside after a drunken fit April 3. Coroner's inquest in the church porch April 5. Same night at midnight buried at the highest crossroads with a stake in him, many people from Mansfield.

Sometimes the suicide was buried on the north side of the churchyard, an area considered inauspicious and generally shunned. At Drypole, Yorkshire, in 1597, 'Anne Ruter a singlewoman drowned herself and was buried the 4th day of July on the north side of the church'.[11]

Perhaps the least dignified disposal of dead bodies was that accorded to stillborn babies who died before baptism. They were often treated as less than human. A seventeenth-century midwives' oath had to contain the instruction that 'you yourself shall see [a stillborn] buried in such a secret place as neither any hog, dog nor any other beast may come unto it . . . [nor] any such child . . . be cast into the lanes or any other inconvenient place'.[12]

For many people in early modern England, the plague was like a sentence of execution. Between 60 and 80 per cent of all who caught it died, about half of them within eight days of infection.[13] Not all the worst epidemics which swept the country, however, were bubonic plague itself. The sharpest mortality crisis between 1485 and 1665 came around the start of Elizabeth I's reign. This was the 'sweating sickness' of 1557–59, probably an influenza epidemic, which caused a fall of about 6 per cent in England's population. Despite this, plague remained the most feared of all epidemic diseases, although its identification was sometimes unsure.[14]

Given the speed and ferocity of the disease, it is surprising how tenaciously the rituals of decent burial were maintained during plague time. An infected house would be sealed, imprisoning all inhabitants within, and marked with a cross, but a plague victim's corpse would often still be carried to burial by friends and neighbours, in spite of regulations to halt the spread of infection. A woodcut of 1641 contrasts 'London's charity' towards plague victims with 'the country's cruelty' [63]. In the scene depicting London, the body is coffined, covered with a black pall and followed to the churchyard by a throng of people carrying sprigs of rosemary, the men dressed in mourning cloaks. By contrast, in the country, the dead are merely dragged to a large pit and

63] Woodcut from the title page of *London's Lamentation*, of 1641, a work of propaganda contrasting the burials of plague victims in country and metropolis. The male mourners in London wear hats and cloaks and carry sprigs of rosemary, while the body is coffined and covered with a pall.

thrown in. While such images resulted from the existing tensions between town and country being exacerbated by the scourge of plague, there were certainly times when there was simply no one left to bury the rural dead. At Malpas, Cheshire, in 1625:

> Richard Dawson being sick of the plague and perceiving he must die at that time, arose out of his bed and made his grave . . . and went and laid down in the said grave . . . and so departed out of this world; this he did because he was . . . heavier than his . . . nephew and another wench were able to bury.[15]

The omnipresence of death in England in the period 1558 to 1660 finds expression in the secular emblems of *memento mori*, most commonly a skull or skeleton, which abound in the visual imagery of the period [**61**, **64**, **70**, and **plate 11**]. The skeleton with dart and hourglass is frequently used to personify death itself, in the Unton picture issuing the command 'memento mori' ('remember death'). A particularly revealing memento mori image is the Judd marriage of 1560 [**64**]. Its theme is the transitory nature of all human existence, compared with eternity. It combines marriage with death, not in the literal sense of death in childbirth, but as linked rites of passage. The couple affirm their marriage vows on a skull while the man points to a corpse. Above is the motto:

The word of God
Hath knit us twain
And death shall us
Divide again

– while beneath are the words, 'Live to die and die to live eternally'.

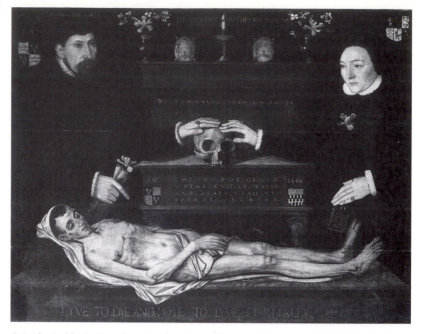

64] *The Judd Marriage Portrait*, dated 1560, by an unknown artist. An enigmatic painting combining images of marital union with those of bodily decay, the couple confirm their wedding vows on a skull. Marriage and death are shown as similarly transient mortal rites of passage, when compared with eternity.

Doctrine and belief

One looks in vain, however, for representations of the afterlife, such as those found both in earlier and later centuries (see Chapters 3–5 and 8–9). The prohibition against all religious images had been a key feature of reform in Edward VI's reign, although temporarily reversed during the time of Mary I. In Elizabethan England it prevented visualisations of Protestant bliss. The nearest equivalent is the secular figure of Fame, looking confusingly like an angel, descending with her trumpet to crown the deceased with laurels. Fame can be seen greeting Sir Henry Unton and also surmounting the funeral chariot of the earl of Essex [**68** and **plate 11**]. In the top left corner of Unton's picture the River of Life runs out into the Sea of Eternity in the moonlight.

Although the doctrine of Purgatory had been abolished at the Reformation, there was a degree of uncertainty surrounding both the geography and the chronology of the Protestant hereafter. Did the virtuous soul at death go straight to Heaven, and if so, what was the role of Resurrection and Judgement? Did souls rest in Abraham's Bosom, as Calvinists believed, while the wicked had a less comfortable waiting place, till the Last Judgement? An even more radical view, 'mortalism' suggested that the soul slept or even died temporarily. It was fiercely condemned by both Calvinists and Lutherans, although Luther himself had accepted the sleep of souls and Thomas Hobbes and John Milton both expounded this doctrine.[16] However, Protestants of all persuasions agreed that the fate of the soul was sealed at death. The actions of the living could have no effect on the dead (nor, officially, could the dead return as ghosts to haunt the living, despite Hamlet's encounters). This created a new relationship between life and death, one which was far more individualistic. The moment of death became more decisive for the dying, particularly since, in a further turn of the Protestant screw, it was essential for salvation to remain perpetually doubtful of your own worthiness.[17] The bereaved were rendered more helpless, with no opportunity to assist the deceased's soul.

The logical outcome of this theological stance was that funerals, having ceased to have any spiritual function for the dead, should be merely secular social events surrounding the practical task of disposing of a corpse. A major move towards this position had been made in the 1552 order for burial, with its drastically shortened service and lack of praying for the dead (see Chapter 5, pp. 141–2). It was this burial order that was revived early in Elizabeth I's reign in The Book of Common Prayer of 1559. However, it was not until A Directory for the Publique Worship of God, established by Parliament in 1644, that the liturgy fully reflected the logic of the theology and prescribed what are tantamount to secular burial rites. The Directory, in a radical move, stated that no minister need be present at a burial; if one should happen to be there, his role was to put those attending 'in remembrance of their duty', which included having the body 'immediately interred, without any ceremony'. However, the Directory included the important caveat that 'civil respects and differences . . . suitable to the rank . . . of the . . . deceased' were still to be observed.[18] This resulted in some extremely lavish funerals during the Interregnum. These secular burials prescribed in the Directory are the forerunners of twentieth-century humanist funerals, although resulting from very different beliefs.

Not surprisingly, these changes both in doctrine and ritual observance were not achieved without a degree of compulsion and some backsliding. Elizabethan bishops attempted to eradicate lingering traces of Roman Catholicism in their dioceses. In 1629 Bishop Potter of Carlisle was still trying to stamp out 'praying for the dead at crosses . . . or any other superstitious use of crosses, with towels, palms . . . or other memories of idolatory at burials'.[19] The remnants of the old burial rites became the folklore practices of early modern England. Among these was the holding of a wake around the corpse, for which food, drink and lights would be provided. At the wake for a Cambridge student in 1618, his fellow scholars also needed perfume to mask the odour of putrefaction and spent 6s. 7d. in total. Wakes sometimes involved horseplay of a ribald nature. Perhaps these games both eased the tension aroused by death and countered the threat of annihilation with jokes about procreation. As anthropologists have noted, in many societies such moments of transition are marked by the inversion of customary rules of propriety.[20] Waking continued at least until the Civil War in

Lincolnshire and even longer in Yorkshire. Other Catholic beliefs and rituals persisted in the north; Edmund Grindal, soon after becoming archbishop of York in 1570, complained of

> those remaining superstitions which have maintained their place more firmly in this part of the country . . . I wish I had found them as well instructed in the true religion as I left my flock in London and Essex to my successor.[21]

It is harder to assess the effectiveness with which the *Directory*'s prescriptions for secular burial were enforced, since the whole apparatus of ecclesiastical record-keeping also fell into abeyance. However, odd glimpses remain; in 1652 John Evelyn managed to have his mother-in-law buried in Deptford church, 'according to the Church Office . . . after it had not been used in that church of 7 years'.[22] Puritan-style funerals had also occurred long before the *Directory*. In 1561 Henry Machyn attended the funeral of a London grocer who was 'carried to the church without singing or clerks and at the church a psalm sung after Geneva and a sermon'.[23] In the case of Mistress Quarles who, with a well-known puritan, had a maidservant buried in an orchard 'without any ceremony and without the communion book', it led to prosecution in the church courts in Essex in 1589.[24]

Deathbeds and dying well

In line with Protestant theology, depictions of deathbeds in early modern England concentrate on worldly, rather than on spiritual matters. The Unton picture gives a graphic account of the futile remedies to which the dying might be subjected by zealous doctors [**plate 11**]. Sir Henry Unton died in France on an embassy from Elizabeth I to Henry IV. The French King visited Unton himself and sent his own doctor, shown taking Sir Henry's pulse. Unfortunately, the remedy for Unton's fever, in line with the currently prevailing theory of humours to explain bodily ills, was bloodletting, in the belief that an excess of blood caused a raised temperature. Bowls of blood may be seen on the table beside Unton's bed. Not surprisingly, this treatment, coupled with tying live pigeons to his body and administering a mixture of musk, amber, gold and ground narwhale horn – supposedly from a unicorn – failed.[25] Watchers pray at Unton's bedside, while his servant, about to lose both master and perhaps employment, sits weeping. Dying is a public spectacle in a crowded room, governed by its own code of conduct.

The dying person had to make a will, an increasingly secular process after the Reformation. Generally, wills were dictated. With the spread of literacy, will-writing was no longer a clerical preserve. While wills usually began with an expression of faith, these were often formulaic, being standard phrases used by the lawyer or scribe rather than the true religious sentiments of the deceased.[26] Unlike many people, Thomas Braithwaite of Ambleside, aged thirty-one, sits up in bed writing his own will, with the pallor of death clearly already upon him [**65**]. His

65] *Thomas Braithwaite of Ambleside making his Will*, by an unknown artist, *c.* 1607. The 31-year-old, on the verge of death, sits up in bed. Behind, inscriptions in English, Latin and French reveal his piety. His friend steadies the paper on which he inscribes his last wishes.

companion helps hold the paper on which he writes; behind him, in-scriptions in English, Latin and French reveal his piety and learning.[27]

Making a will ordering one's earthly possessions was just one ele-ment in preparing 'to die well' in early modern England. It was also necessary to be at peace with God and with one's fellow men. Particu-larly important was to make all the right speeches before one died and, as in previous centuries, to be conscious at death. It was not necessary for a clergyman to be present, but this was the moment for the dying person to display spiritual readiness for the ordeal ahead.[28] When Jane Stephens, a Canterbury servant, was dying in 1602, one of the women with her, having heard 'the passing bell go for her', exhorted 'her to call upon God in her heart and if she were in memory and understanding to hold up her hand in token thereof'; although she then 'sat up Jane in her bed and gave her a little drink', a quarter of an hour later she 'never spake nor stirred more but gave up the ghost'.[29] John Donne was so eloquent in his final sermon that he was described as having 'preached his own funeral sermon'.[30] He also had the rare prescience to predict the exact moment of death and to position his body ready for shrouding [72]. Above all, it was important to be conscious of dying. Instruction manuals were published, the most famous of which was Jeremy Taylor's *The Rule and Exercises of Holy Dying* of 1651 (see Chapter 5 for earlier examples of this genre).

Not everyone managed to achieve the ideal; illnesses which were sudden or involved much pain were especially dreaded, as was dying in one's sleep.[31] When Venetia Digby died unexpectedly one night in 1633 her husband Kenelm was distraught [plate 12] and [71]. His distress was compounded by the knowledge that Venetia's life, before her marriage, had been somewhat irregular and, worse still, by rumours that he himself had poisoned her, though unintentionally, by preparing viper wine for her to drink. Charles I was concerned enough to order an autopsy; all of this amounted to a very bad death indeed. To counter this disaster, Sir Kenelm Digby wove an elaborate fiction to present her as having died well. He wrote a series of letters, which he later had bound and called *In Praise of Venetia*, in which he stressed how well prepared she had been for death – she had received the sacrament, made her will, was even at peace with her mother-in-law and, in short, had 'made her life a practice and school of dying well'.[32]

To reinforce these claims, as well as to capture what remained of his beautiful wife before putrefaction and the surgeon's knife took their toll, he summoned Anthony van Dyck to paint her 'the second day after she was dead'. They 'brought a little seeming colour into her pale cheeks' by 'rubbing of her face'. Seven weeks later, when the painting was delivered, Kenelm declared he could not tell whether she was sleeping or dead, or, indeed, 'whether it were a picture or not', so peaceful did she look. He noted that 'Van Dyck . . . hath altered or added nothing about it, excepting a rose lying upon the . . . sheet', its fallen petals 'a fit emblem to express the state of her body'. The rose also symbolised the Virgin Mary, while pearls were associated with chastity, but did Venetia really wear hers in bed?[33]

Funerals by day and night

Another way to help counteract a bad death was to have a good funeral. To organise a full heraldic funeral was extremely elaborate. When Sir Henry Unton died in France in March 1596 he wanted his body to be returned home for burial [plate 11]. First it had to be embalmed; beneath his tomb in the picture can be seen both his coffin and the upright viscera chest which contained his entrails, removed during embalming.[34] There was, however, a minor revolt against embalming, particularly by various aristocratic women. As Mary, countess of Northumberland wrote in her will in 1572: 'I have not loved to be very bold afore women, much more would I be loath to come into the hands of any living man, be he physician or surgeon'.[35] Such concern over the dead body may be symptomatic of a greater unease about bodily decomposition.

For less wealthy people, the body was simply shrouded; a seventeenth-century winding sheet is shown, tied at head and feet, on John Donne's memorial, although his face has been left uncovered [72]. Often the body was buried just in its shroud; the Book of Common Prayer speaks of the earth being scattered over the body. Some parishes had a communal coffin in which poorer people could at least be carried to the grave. In my study of people before the Civil War sufficiently wealthy to have made wills, coffined burials occurred widely in Kent, about half the time in Berkshire and only infrequently in Lincolnshire. However, the use of coffins increased in all three counties during the first half of the seventeenth century.[36] This increase suggests a greater distance developing between the living and the dead and a growing desire to conceal bodily decay.

With a heraldic funeral, when a considerable time would elapse between death and burial – in Unton's case over three months – the embalmed body would be encased in lead [plate 11]. Unton's corpse had a lengthy journey, as shown in the painting. The ship carrying him across the Channel from Calais to Dover was rigged with black sails. The coffin was loaded on to a cart and draped in black, as were the horses, travelling first to London and then on to his family seat at Wadley in Berkshire.

Funerals of the less wealthy were less protracted. The funeral shown in *London's Lamentation* illustrates many usual features [63]. The grave-digger would receive about 4*d*. for his labour. Burial within the church was considerably more expensive and was in decline during the first half of the seventeenth century.[37] A mixture of concern for hygiene and social discrimination led Bishop Middleton of St David's to order in 1583 that corpses were not to be buried within churches 'for that by their general burying there great infection doth ensue', adding 'except those of the best sort of the parish'.[38]

The minister would charge a few shillings for performing the ceremony, while bell ringing might cost another shilling. As the person lay dying, the passing bell would be tolled, with a stroke for every year of their age. Even for pauper burials these rituals were still performed. All Saints', Newcastle, having abolished the passing bell in 1643 as superstitious, reinstated it again in 1655 because of the loss of revenue. The black pall shown covering the coffin in the engraving would probably be hired from the church [63]; St Botolph's, Bishopsgate, London, had three different grades of pall, costing from 4*d*. to a shilling.[39]

Generally the bearers would be the deceased's friends or family, or sometimes the poor. Particular groups of people had specific bearers. Young women dying before marriage were sometimes carried by other women and any mourning dress would be white, not black, reflecting

66] *The Bride's Burial*, a woodcut of 1621. It shows an unmarried woman carried to her funeral by young women in white, wearing aprons. On the coffin lies a 'maiden's garland' of flowers, which would be hung in the church. This was the extent of funeral wreaths at this period.

the inversion, during a time of transition, of what might customarily be expected. A woodcut of 1621 shows women carrying a coffin on which rests a 'maiden's garland' [66]; the remnants of these occasionally still survive in parish churches. The accompanying verse explains:

A garland, fresh and fair of lilies there was made
In sign of her virginity, and on her coffin laid:
Six maidens all in white did bear her to the
                                              ground.

The mingling of the symbolism of weddings and funerals suggests the close links between the two; the ceremony celebrating the continuation of mankind also conjured up the cessation of life and vice versa. The finality of death could be seen as ritually countered by the rites heralding procreation; although death had removed one potential bride, others remained to carry her to burial.[40] This was a secular, collective consolation in the face of death. The aprons worn by the women in this woodcut might well be a gift from the deceased's estate. Sometimes such women received ribbons, significantly called 'bridelaces', while aprons were occasionally given at men's funerals when members of the same occupational group as the deceased carried him to burial.[41]

An increasingly popular addition to the ceremony in the seventeenth century for those who could afford the cost, generally 10 shillings, was the preaching of a funeral sermon, sometimes on a text specified in the deceased's will. At Henry Unton's funeral the sermon was preached by his chaplain. The text is just legible: 'How are the mighty fallen' [plate 11]. Sermons took a set pattern, with an exposition of a biblical text followed by a eulogy upon the deceased, providing a more individualistic emphasis than the words of the burial service. This second section formed a spiritual biography of the deceased at a time when biographical diaries of a religious nature were encouraged as an aid to spiritual development. Funeral sermons were printed in growing numbers during the seventeenth century, creating a more permanent memorial to the deceased.[42]

The largest item of expenditure at all but the grandest people's funerals was the food and drink served after the burial itself. Often this would account for as much as half the total funeral cost. Some celebration might even take place at the most lowly of burials; after a pauper funeral at Folkingham, Lincolnshire, in 1641, bread and beer costing 7s. was provided.[43] Funerals were commonly well attended, as *London's Lamentation* makes clear [63]. Even if the refreshment was only a 'drinking' it could be for a hundred or more people and often food was provided too. At the drinking following a gentlewoman's funeral in Abingdon in 1641 literally gallons of sack, white wine and claret were served, accompanied by 60 pounds of comfits (a type of sweet), 15 pounds of biscuits and 40 dozen cakes, together with dried fruits, pears, pippins, quinces, plums, almonds, macaroons, marzipan, violet cake and 'green dried lettuce'.[44]

After grander funerals a meal was provided, although it was usually reserved for 'the better sort'. These funeral meals are sometimes referred to as 'entertainments', which aptly suggests their function as a form of social healing, re-establishing bonds within the group fractured by the loss of one of its members. With the drastic reduction, at the Reformation, in the religious element of the burial service, these secular, socially regenerative aspects of the funeral ritual took on a more important role, reflected by the proportion of money and time spent on them.

The Unton memorial picture gives a magnificent illustration of an Elizabethan heraldic funeral. His burial takes up a very large part of the total painting as, with extreme irony, Sir Henry Unton reached his social apogee only at his funeral. Because he had died while Elizabeth's ambassador, the Queen allowed him a baron's burial, two degrees higher than his title, a mere knighthood, would have permitted. As the name suggests, these funerals were orchestrated by the heralds of the College of Arms, the forerunners of the undertaking profession, the rise of which will be discussed in Chapter 7. The tabards they wear bear the arms of the Queen herself, the heralds acting in her name. In the black-clad funeral procession the colour of the heraldry stands out vividly. A heraldic memorandum explained that the royal coat of arms was worn 'not only for the well ordering of the funeral' but also to show 'that the defunct died honourably, without any spot of dishonesty ... [or] dishonour unto his blood', and was a 'good and loyal subject' to the monarch.[45] John Donne, in a sermon, commented on the heralds' association with death:

> Go to the heralds' office, the sphere and element of honour, and thou shalt find those men as busy there about the consideration of funerals as about the consideration of creations; thou shalt find that office to be as well the grave, as the cradle of honour.[46]

The heralds' role at a funeral had more to do with the secular transfer of titles and honours to the heir than with disposing of the dead body. Indeed, the ritual was structured almost to deny that a death had taken place at all. It reflected a traditional view of society in which one person is replaceable by another of the same rank, with little sense of human individuality.[47] The higher up the hierarchy, the more a death threatens social stability. There was therefore a scale as to how many mourners of the same sex and rank must follow the corpse, to show that aristocratic, and ultimately royal, power had not been diminished by the death. Henry Unton, buried as a baron, had seven principal mourners, while earls had nine and dukes, eleven.[48] These rules prevented any spouse from acting as mourner and meant that those singled out in the ritual might often have little or no affection for the deceased.

Once the transfer of power had been carried out, supervised by the heralds, the mourners would leave the church before the body was even buried; only the deceased's servants would remain for the actual interment.

In the Unton memorial picture the mourners, totally enveloped in black robes and hoods, set out from his house to walk to Faringdon Church. The coffin, draped with a pall hung with his coat of arms, is carried by eight men. It is preceded by a herald holding Unton's helmet and crest, which cost 46 shillings.[49] Two more heralds walk in the procession and mourners carry a banner and two pennons. The interest generated by this spectacle is shown by people in the foreground, hurrying to see the procession and climbing on a wall to get a better view. The numbers were often swelled by the promise of a dole of food or money to all who attended. Although prayers for the deceased's soul were no longer solicited from those present, a large crowd at a funeral was a sign of worldly status and much sought after. However, because of possible misinterpretation of doles as payments for prayers, they were disapproved of by the more puritanical Protestant clergy and their use declined during the first decades of the seventeenth century.

Elizabeth I fully realised the political importance of having these displays of royal power at funerals regularly held in all parts of the kingdom. Sometimes an aristocratic subject preferred to hold a funeral in London where it was easier to organise, but the Queen often vetoed such requests.[50]

For Henry Unton's funeral the interior of Faringdon Church was hung in black, decorated with his coat of arms. Generally this black cloth could be hired from the heralds although all the painted shields and the mourning clothes had to be purchased, at considerable expense. Once at the church, the body would be placed inside a hearse, a wooden structure erected in front of the altar. At funerals of members of the royal family, where the disruption to the social fabric was most acute, an effigy of the deceased would be carried in the procession and laid on the coffin within the hearse. Prince Henry Frederick's hearse was decorated with shields, mottoes and his Prince of Wales feathers; his effigy had articulated limbs which 'moved to sundry actions' [67].[51] Some royal effigies of this era still remain in Westminster Abbey.

67] Etching of the hearse of Henry Frederick, Prince of Wales, by an unknown artist, 1612. A hearse, at this date, was still a temporary construction in a church and not transport for a coffin. The Prince's effigy, with moveable limbs, was carried in his funeral procession.

Amazingly, the whole panoply of the heraldic funeral continued right through the Interregnum, so that a country which had cut off

68] Funeral of Robert, earl of Essex, from a broadsheet dated 1646. The Parliamentary commander in the initial battles of the Civil War, he was buried with full military honours, his body borne in a chariot surmounted by the figure of Fame. Parliamentarian funerals were noted for their splendour.

its King's head still appointed a Garter King of Arms.[52] In 1646 the earl of Essex, the Parliamentarian commander at the earlier battles of the Civil War, was buried in Westminster Abbey with great pomp and much firing of guns from all the London forts and pistol volleys from nine regiments [**68**]. The mourners wore the cloaks and hats which had replaced the all-enveloping black mourning garments of the previous century. The body, on which were laid his helmet, sword and gauntlets, merely symbolic accoutrements in the age of firearms, was transported in a chariot by black-plumed horses. A similar ceremony was carried out for General Ireton's funeral in 1652, while at Oliver Cromwell's burial in 1658 there was even a crowned effigy of the Protector. These Interregnum funerals seem to bear out the hypothesis, formulated by an anthropologist, that in times of political and social instability burial rituals increase in grandeur.[53]

Not everyone, however, was prepared to spend such vast amounts on heraldic funerals. The loosening of the royal hold on funeral rituals probably came about in part because King James I, as a Scot, did not appreciate the role played by heraldic burial rites in English social and political control. Soon the heralds were complaining of 'an unusual manner of burying the dead, especially the better sort, by night' which had 'crept into the kingdom'. In fact, it seems that some of the King's own Scottish nobles were among the first to introduce night burial into

England. James himself sanctioned nocturnal rites by reburying his mother, Mary, Queen of Scots, at night by candlelight in Westminster Abbey in 1612. By the time James's son Charles I commanded 'the prohibiting of all nocturnal funerals whatsoever', they were a well-established custom, beyond eradication.[54]

While expense may have been one reason for the adoption of night funerals, another was the ideological framework which underpinned them. This was very different from the traditional replaceability of any-one with another of the same rank, as enshrined in the heraldic funeral. Nocturnal funerals were free of the restrictions imposed by the heralds as to who could be mourners, so spouses could act as each other's chief mourner, as Kenelm Digby did at Venetia's night burial in 1633. Night funerals emphasised sorrow and loss, the darkness and torchlight add-ing to the atmosphere of gloom and reflecting the emotions of grief at bereavement.

The duchess of Richmond and Lenox was buried by night in West-minster Abbey in 1639, as directed in her will [69]. She had been in perpetual mourning for her husband since his death in 1624 and ordered, with more than a hint of eroticism, 'let them wind me up again in those sheets ... wherein my Lord and I first slept when we were married'. She also decreed 'that I may be speedily buried and not opened for so my sweet Lord out of his tender love commanded me that I should not be opened. I may be presently put up in bran, and in lead before I am fully cold'; her burial was to be on the first night a clear twenty-four hours after her death.[55] Night burial was ideal for those who wanted to be rapidly buried, avoiding the horrors of embalming.

The duchess also specified that she should be buried 'without ... any great persons to be invited but if they come of their own good will let them be respectively and dutifully used'. Other provisions in her will make it clear that her reasons for choosing burial by night did not include a desire to save money. She requested that two hundred poor people should attend her funeral and be given 'good cloth gowns' to wear that were 'not too short'; each was to carry a torch. She also willed that the archbishop of Canterbury, four London parsons and her house-hold servants should all receive black garments for her funeral. The cost of the ceremony, together with keeping her house in mourning for three or four weeks, was £2,000.[56] Nocturnal burial allowed her to exercise far more personal control over her funeral ritual than the heralds would have permitted.

From these aristocratic beginnings, night funerals quickly spread down the social hierarchy, although they were always expensive since double fees were charged by the church, reflecting the inconveni-ence of the hour.[57] Few visual records of burial by night survive from this period, although there are plenty of later examples (see [80]). A rare glimpse from the 1630s comes in the background of a page from

plate 12] *Venetia Stanley, Lady Digby on her Deathbed*, by Sir Anthony van Dyck, 1633. On discovering his wife dead, Sir Kenelm Digby [71] sent for his friend Van Dyck to draw her. This painting was completed seven weeks later and played an important role in Kenelm's mourning.

plate 13] Monument to Christopher Roper, second Lord Teynham, died 1622, by Epiphanius Evesham, Lynsted Church, Kent. He lies in death while his wife, in mourning dress, kneels grieving; below, their children pray and weep. Such display of emotion on tombs was an innovation in the early seventeenth century.

69] *Frances Stuart, duchess of Richmond and Lenox*, after Sir Anthony van Dyck, *c.* 1633. Shown in mourning dress, she wears a miniature of her dead husband Ludovick, which is now in the National Portrait Gallery, London. In her grief she cut off her long hair.

George Wither's *Emblems*, where a funeral procession with torches and a gable-lidded coffin wends its way towards a church; in the churchyard an owl, symbolising night, perches on a skull lying on a tombstone [70]. The words 'memento mori' encircle the scene, surmounted by the couplet:

> Whilest thou dost, here, enjoy thy breath,
> Continue mindful of thy Death.

By the 1630s, night burial had become so well established as to be instantly recognised when used in this emblematic manner.

70] Engraving from George Wither's *A Collection of Emblems*, of 1634–35, showing an owl perched on a skull. In the background, a night funeral with torches and a gable-lidded coffin makes its way towards a church. Such visual representations of nocturnal burial are rarely found at this period.

Bereavement and mourning

Frances Stuart, duchess of Richmond and Lenox was well documented as being devastated by the death of her husband, Ludovick, in 1624 [**69**]. As one observer wrote:

> His Lady takes it extreme passionately, cut off her hair that day with divers other expressions of extraordinary grief . . . [His] loss she takes so impatiently and with so much show of passion that many odd and idle tales are daily reported or invented of her.[58]

Her shorn locks can be seen in her portrait; in earlier paintings she has long, flowing hair. She herself said: 'With the loss of my Lord all earthly joys ended with me and I ever computed his funeral day my burial.'[59] Ever afterwards she wore mourning, as shown in her portrait. She wears a black veil, with her duchess's coronet placed beside her. There was also a much bigger style of arched head-dress for mourning, as worn by Lady Teynham on her husband's monument [**plate 13**]. The duchess's ruff is plain and her black dress is hung with pearls.[60]

The duchess's grief was considered excessive by the standards of her day; 'malicious' people suggested that she was really bewailing her loss of position at court, rather than the death of a third husband when she was 'so far past the flower and prime of her youth'.[61] Such lavish mourning was particularly the preserve of rich women and would, of course, have been an unaffordable luxury for most people. Also, since death was the will of God, to rail against it was tantamount to questioning God's divine purpose. It has been argued that it is this which makes seventeenth-century people usually appear, in letters and diaries, to be more accepting of bereavement than people are today. However, there was also a belief that grief could drive the bereaved mad, which certainly suggests no lack of strength in contemporary feeling.[62]

71] *Sir Kenelm Digby*, with a broken armillary sphere, engraved by Robert van der Voerst, *c.* 1636, after Sir Anthony van Dyck. In mourning for his wife [**plate 12**], Kenelm grew long hair and a beard. The broken sphere denotes the shattering of his family circle through Venetia's death.

Like the duchess of Richmond and Lenox, Sir Kenelm Digby was unable to accept with equanimity the death of his spouse [**71**]. One probable reason for this was the suddenness of his wife's death. It was usual for relatives to begin the process of emotional detachment during the final illness of the deceased, but Digby had no such opportunity.[63] It has often been said that grief is a basic human characteristic which does not vary across times or cultures. The case of Sir Kenelm Digby provides confirmatory evidence more than three and a half centuries old; his letters, charting the course of his grief, read almost like a modern text book on bereavement.[64]

Initially, on finding his wife dead, he was stunned as 'amazement . . . for a while supplieth the room of sorrow'. This quickly turned to numbness; in a 'frozen and benumbed condition' he 'for four days together . . . did nothing but weep . . . without intermission'. He became subject to the whole range of often contradictory emotions which are found in bereavement. He suffered mental pain, 'a cruel executioner to torture without mercy', which particularly occurred each week at the time of finding Venetia dead; 'everywhere I carry my hell with me'. He felt guilt at his unfaithfulness to her 'like a worm that incessantly gnaweth at my heart and soul'. He lost all enjoyment of life whose 'contentments' were 'but frothy vanities and wickedness'. His concentration lapsed, being unable to read with 'a broken and afflicted mind'. He also had physical symptoms, losing his appetite and getting 'scarcely . . . an hours slumber in a whole night'. Interestingly, the one emotion mentioned by modern studies of bereavement which he did not share was outward anger at the deceased's death. Instead, he seems to have turned his anger inwards on himself, suggesting 'surely God took her away for punishment of my sins'.[65] This probably reflects the strength of the seventeenth-century taboo against questioning God's will when someone died.

As Sir Kenelm Digby's grief progressed he began to idealise his dead wife, calling her a 'saint'. He also had near hallucinatory experiences:

> I can sometimes fancy to myself particular passages between my wife and me so strongly that methinks they are even then present with me; I see her and I talk with her. When I see they are but vain shadows of what is lost and never can be recovered again, I fall into impatience.

This is actually an extremely accurate description of one twentieth-century view of the process of grieving, with the constant need to reconfirm that the relationship really is over. However, other modern psychologists stress the continuing bond with the deceased, which is also apparent in Digby's words. His endless writing of letters, constructing a biographical account of Venetia's life, was like the need incessantly to talk about the dead person.[66]

Gradually he found the nature of his sorrow began to change. About five months after Venetia's death he described how his grief had become 'familiar and easy to me . . . I wrestled with it . . . but now I lie quietly . . . [and] it lieth gently upon me'. Three months later he could begin to consider the feelings of others and even to see Venetia in a slightly more realistic light, as having some 'human infirmity in her'. During the second year of his bereavement his mourning took a different course. He decided 'to publish unto the world her virtues . . . rather by my actions [than] my words and . . . by my sorrow for the loss of her'. He wore 'a long mourning cloak, a high crowned hat, his beard unshorn, looked like a hermit'. In these garments, though without the hat, he was painted several times by Van Dyck, and later engraved. His pose, with his hand on his heart, is a gesture of melancholy. Although he became involved with other women, Sir Kenelm Digby never remarried and when he died in 1665 he was, at his own request, buried with Venetia.[67]

Memorials and commemoration

The vast majority of people dying in England between 1558 and 1660 were buried in their local churchyard in unmarked graves, as had happened for centuries. During this period there was an increase in memorials to those people wealthy enough to afford burial within the church. Occasionally, provision of a monument would be ordered in the deceased's will. John Brooke of Ash, Kent, writing his will in 1582, not only specified the exact site and wording for his tomb, but added:

> I will that the same stone thus engraved to be laid over me by my executrix [his wife] within two years next after my decease or else she to forfeit twenty pounds to the churchwardens of Ash.[68]

The increasing emphasis on worldly commemoration might be seen as one sign of a developing unease about mortality and an attempt to avoid oblivion.

However, the period also saw a considerable destruction of monuments in the Civil War and its aftermath. For example, fighting around Faringdon Church, shown in the Unton picture, has today left the building without a spire and has reduced the Unton tomb to a single inscription and the figure of Sir Henry's widow, Dorothy [plate 11].

The nature of the commemoration of the deceased on aristocratic tombs also changed as the sixteenth gave way to the seventeenth century. It has been observed, interestingly, that monuments to women, being socially of lesser importance, were often more open to experimentation and innovation than were the tombs of men. Elizabethan monuments, with all religious symbolism forbidden by the dictates of Protestantism, concentrated on the worldly success and social standing of the deceased. The Unton tomb, as it appears in the painting, is a good late example of the type. Sir Henry is shown lying in armour, not dead but supported on his hand, in John Webster's words, as if he 'died of the toothache', with Dorothy kneeling beside him.[69] The use of heraldry is prominent, with the canopied structure surmounted with his helmet and crest while coats of arms flank the figures. Sir Henry Unton's virtues are represented in personified form; Faith and Hope stand in the niches either side of the main figures, while Fame and Victory raise their trumpet and laurels in the central arch. The Latin inscription, which has survived, describes Unton's position within the Elizabethan social hierarchy but gives no sense of personality or feelings. Monuments such as this reflect the same ideology as the heraldic funeral with emphasis on status rather than individuality. They served, at a local level, to reinforce the social hierarchy among those who had to kneel before them in church each Sunday.

A very different type of commemoration is found on the tomb to Christopher, second lord Teynham at Lynsted, Kent [plate 13]. Made by Epiphanius Evesham after 1622, its emphasis is on sorrow and loss rather than continuity. Lord Teynham, dressed in armour, lies in death, while his wife kneels in prayer, her face stricken with grief. Beneath, carved in relief, their daughters openly weep for their father. Although the monument also has the usual heraldic display and allegorical figures, it is the personal feelings which predominate.[70]

Church monuments were only one type of memorial to the dead in early modern England. Paintings such as those of Unton's life, Venetia Digby on her deathbed and the Aston family all commemorated the deceased, although they were far rarer than tomb effigies. Kenelm Digby's letters reveal how he used his wife's picture in his bereavement [plate 12], describing it as

> the only constant companion I now have . . . It standeth all day over against my chair and table . . . and at night when I go into my chamber I set it close to my bedside, and by the faint light of a candle, methinks I see her dead indeed.

72] Monument to John Donne by Nicholas Stone, St Paul's Cathedral, London, c. 1631. Nicholas Stone worked from a painting, commissioned by Donne, of himself in a shroud, on which he had meditated as he lay dying. The monument created a minor fashion for similarly shrouded figures on tombs.

His 'discretest friends' were appalled by this behaviour, which certainly suggests it was considered unusual at the time, and tried to 'direct' Kenelm's 'bootless thoughts from this sad object that can never be recovered'.[71]

John Donne actually commissioned a picture as part of his process of preparing for death, as his biographer described [72]:

> Several charcoal fires being first made in his large study, he brought . . . his winding-sheet in his hand, . . . had this sheet put on him and so tied with knots at his head and feet, and his hands so placed as dead bodies are usually fitted to be shrouded and put into their grave. [He was drawn] with his eyes shut, and with so much of the sheet turned aside as might shew his lean, pale and death-like face.

Donne kept the picture by his bedside 'where it continued and became his hourly object till his death'. Although the painting no longer survives, the image was 'carved in one entire piece of white marble' by the sculptor Nicholas Stone for Donne's monument in St Paul's Cathedral.[72] This tomb started a minor trend in resurrection monuments for the rest of the century (see [83]).

Far smaller and more intimate than such memorials were pieces of jewellery commemorating the deceased. These might well include a miniature portrait, such as that of her husband, Ludovick, in a heart-shaped setting, worn by the duchess of Richmond and Lenox in her painting [69]; the actual miniature still survives in the National Portrait Gallery collection.[73] Many such pictures of the executed Charles I were worn in pendants and rings by his supporters. Often mourning jewellery would be adorned with skulls, skeletons and other emblems of death, fashioned in black and white enamel. It created an interesting dissonance, with images of death and dissolution being used as objects to beautify the wearer and increase sexual allure. Parallels can also be found in seventeenth-century metaphysical verse, where images of death are exploited in love poetry.

Other types of memorial included the writing of poems in the deceased's memory. One of John Donne's finest poems, *The Second Anniversary*, was written to commemorate the death, two years before, of a sixteen-year-old girl, Elizabeth Drury, whom he had never even met, but whose father offered him patronage. In *The First Anniversary*, of the previous year, Donne wrote of the individualism of his contemporaries:

> every man alone thinks he hath got
> To be a phoenix, and that then can be
> None of that kind of which he is, but he[74]

In the same poem, Donne expounded a view of life which was new to England from the 1570s onwards and about which there was considerable intellectual debate in the early seventeenth century – that the world was in terminal decline and dying.[75] This was a very different world-view from that enshrined in traditional rituals such as the heraldic funeral, which presupposed an unchanging social and material order. It is perhaps this shift in thinking which lies behind many of the alterations in attitudes and practices concerning death which have been outlined in this chapter.

Death rituals between 1558 and 1660 were characterised by a mingling of sacred and secular elements. This was apparent, for example, in the typical Elizabethan tomb effigy, with hands clasped in prayer, while heraldry proclaimed lineage and social status. At the deathbed, a major ritual moment, both spiritual and worldly preparations were made for death, though often such preparations were overtaken in practice by extreme pain or loss of consciousness.

The same mixture of sacred and secular can be found in funeral rites. These were the most important and complex of death rituals in early modern England, combining disposal of the corpse, the reintegration of the social group fractured by death and the display of the deceased's status, all within the harsh framework of Protestant doctrine. During the Interregnum this theological position was taken to its logical conclusion with secular burials which foreshadow twentieth-century developments. Only under extreme demographic pressure, such as plague epidemics, did funeral rituals break down; they were maintained even for the poorest members of society. The importance of funeral rituals in early modern England is underlined by their being denied to those deemed outside the Christian community: certain criminals, suicides and infants dying before baptism.

Between 1558 and 1660 important developments occurred in the English funeral, particularly in the south rather than the north of the country, which reveal shifts in the balance of religious and worldly elements and greater emphasis on human individuality. There was increasing use of coffins, reflecting perhaps developing unease about physical decomposition, and a growth in funeral sermons and monuments, pointing to more emphasis on worldly remembrance. Both wakes and doles decreased during the period, under suspicion of being Catholic survivals, while burial in church was discouraged on grounds of hygiene. However, alongside these changes were important continuities, including the socially restorative communal consumpion of food and drink after the burial and the countering of death with symbols of marriage and procreation.

Even more dramatic changes occurred in aristocratic funerals. The heralds' monopoly over funerals of the Elizabethan era, with their emphasis on status and the replaceability of one person by another of the same rank, did not outlast the Queen herself. Gradually night burial came into fashion, allowing spouses to act as each other's mourners and emphasising the irrevocability of death, sorrow and loss. This was paralleled by changes in aristocratic tomb design, accentuating personal grief rather than status. These developments embodied a very different world-view from the unchanging, traditional society of the heraldic funeral.

While these burial rites seem remote from modern practice, the feelings of the bereaved mirrored closely those of the present day. The letters of Sir Kenelm Digby chart an intense grief in intimate detail. Although commissioning a deathbed portrait might seem strange today, the emotions which prompted it are fully recognisable.

Notes

In all references, place of publication is London unless otherwise stated.

1 E.g. N. Llewellyn, *The Art of Death: Visual Culture in the English Death Ritual c. 1500–c. 1800* (1991), pp. 47–8.

2 R. A. Houlbrooke, *The English Family 1450–1700* (1995), pp. 133 and 129.

3 E. A. Wrigley and R. S. Schofield, *The Population History of England: A Reconstruction* (1981), pp. 234–6.

4 P. Slack, *The Impact of Plague in Tudor and Stuart England* (Oxford, 1985), pp. 72–3.

5 C. V. Wedgwood, *The Trial of Charles I* (1966), pp. 192–3.

6 K. V. Thomas, *Religion and the Decline of Magic: Studies in Popular Beliefs in Sixteenth- and Seventeenth-Century England* (Harmondsworth, 1978), p. 527, n. 22.

7 T. B. Howell (ed.), *A Complete Collection of State Trials* (1816–31), vol. II, cols 879–84.

8 J. C. Cox, *The Parish Registers of England* (1910), p. 99.

9 F. G. Emmison, *Elizabethan Life: Morals and the Church Courts* (Chelmsford, 1973), p. 174.

10 Quoted in C. Gittings, *Death, Burial and the Individual in Early Modern England* (1984), pp. 76 and 72.

11 Cox, *Parish Registers*, pp. 114–15.

12 Gittings, *Death*, p. 83.

13 Slack, *Plague*, p. 7.

14 *Ibid.*, pp. 71 and 64–5.

15 Cox, *Parish Registers*, p. 175.

16 P. C. Almond, *Heaven and Hell in Enlightenment England* (Cambridge, 1994), pp. 38–41. N. T. Burns, *Christian Mortalism from Tyndale to Milton* (Cambridge, Mass., 1972).

17 Gittings, *Death*, p. 40. Thomas, *Religion and the Decline of Magic*, p. 721. G. Bennett, *Traditions of Belief: Women and the Supernatural* (1987), p. 158.

E. Disley, 'Degrees of glory: Protestant doctrine and the concept of rewards hereafter', *Journal of Theological Studies*, 42 (1991), 77–105.

18 The Book of Common Prayer (1559). *A Directory for the Publique Worship of God throughout the Three Kingdoms of England, Scotland and Ireland* (1644), pp. 73–4. G. Rowell, *The Liturgy of Christian Burial: An Introductory Survey of the Historical Development of Christian Burial Rites* (1977), pp. 83–93.

19 *Report of the Ritual Commission, Parliamentary Papers*, xxxviii (1867–68), Appendix E, hereafter *Ritual Commission*, p. 508.

20 Gittings, *Death*, pp. 105–7; M. Bloch and J. Parry (eds), *Death and the Regeneration of Life* (Cambridge, 1982); A. Van Gennep, *The Rites of Passage* (Chicago, 1960).

21 H. Robinson (ed.), *The Zurich Letters 1558–1579*, Parker Society (1842), pp. 259–60.

22 E. S. de Beer (ed.), *The Diary of John Evelyn* (Oxford, 1955), vol. III, p. 76.

23 *The Diary of Henry Machyn*, ed. J. G. Nichols, Camden Society 42 (1847), p. 247.

24 Emmison, *Elizabethan Life*, p. 174.

25 R. Strong, 'Sir Henry Unton and his portrait: an Elizabethan memorial picture and its history', *Archaeologia*, 99 (1965), p. 65.

26 R. A. Houlbrooke, 'Death, church and family in England between the late fifteenth and the early eighteenth centuries', in Houlbrooke (ed.), *Death, Ritual and Bereavement* (1989), pp. 29–30.

27 Llewellyn, *Art of Death*, p. 38.

28 L. M. Beier, 'The good death in seventeenth-century England', in Houlbrooke (ed.), *Death, Ritual and Bereavement*, pp. 43–61.

29 E. A. Hallam, 'Turning the hourglass: gender relations at the deathbed in early modern Canterbury', *Mortality*, 1:1 (March 1996), 70.

30 I. Walton, *The Lives of Dr John Donne, Sir Henry Wotton, Mr George Herbert* (1670), hereafter Walton, *Life of Donne*, p. 71.

31 Beier, 'Good death', pp. 46–7.

32 C. Gittings, 'Venetia's death and Kenelm's mourning', in A. Sumner (ed.), *Death, Passion and Politics: Van Dyck's Portraits of Venetia Stanley and George Digby* (1995), pp. 57–60.

33 *Ibid.*, pp. 59–60.

34 J. Litten, *The English Way of Death: The Common Funeral since 1450* (1991), p. 212.

35 L. Stone, *The Crisis of the Aristocracy 1558–1641* (Oxford, 1965), p. 579.

36 Gittings, *Death*, pp. 61 and 114.

37 *Ibid.*, p. 141.

38 *Ritual Commission*, p. 427.

39 Gittings, *Death*, pp. 134 and 116.

40 Bloch and Parry (eds), *Death and the Regeneration of Life*. This functionalist perspective would not be shared by all anthropologists.

41 Gittings, *Death*, pp. 117–18.

42 *Ibid.*, pp. 137–8. D. Cressy, *Birth, Marriage and Death: Ritual, Religion and the Life-Cycle in Tudor and Stuart England* (Oxford, 1997), p. 572, n. 39. R. A. Houlbrooke, *Death, Religion and the Family in England 1480–1750* (Oxford, 1998), pp. 295–330 and 386–7.

43 C. Gittings, 'Funerals in England, 1580–1640: the evidence of probate accounts', unpublished M.Litt. thesis, University of Oxford (1978), p. 133.

44 Gittings, *Death*, p. 157.

45 *Ibid.*, p. 174.

46 J. Donne, 'Sermon V at St Paul's, Christmas Day, 1627', in *The Works of John Donne*, ed. H. Alford (1839), vol. I, p. 90.

47 Bloch and Parry, *Death*, p. 11.

48 Gittings, *Death*, p. 175.

49 R. Strong, *National Portrait Gallery Tudor and Jacobean Portraits* (1969), p. 318.

50 Gittings, *Death*, pp. 168–9.

51 Quoted in Llewellyn, *Art of Death*, p. 55.

52 A. Wagner, *The Heralds of England: A History of the Office and College of Arms* (1967), p. 258.

53 Gittings, *Death*, pp. 229–31, discussing V. G. Childe, 'Directional changes in funerary practices during 50,000 years', *Man*, 45 (1945), pp. 13–19.

54 *Ibid.*, pp. 188–90 and 200. J. Woodward, *The Theatre of Death: The Ritual Management of Royal Funerals in Renaissance England, 1570–1625* (Woodbridge, 1997), pp. 138–41.

55 'Will of Frances Stuart, Duchess of Richmond and Lenox', *Archaeologia Cantiana*, 11 (1877) (hereafter *Arch. Cant.*), pp. 232–50.

56 *Ibid.*, pp. 245–7.

57 Gittings, *Death*, pp. 93–4.

58 J. Chamberlain, *The Letters of John Chamberlain*, ed. N. E. M. McClure (Philadelphia, 1939), pp. 545 and 551.

59 *Arch. Cant.*, p. 247.

60 P. Cunnington and C. Lucas, *Costume for Births, Marriages and Deaths* (1972), plate 59a. L. Taylor, *Mourning Dress: A Costume and Social History* (1983), pp. 93–6.

61 Chamberlain, *Letters*, p. 551.

62 A. Laurence, 'Godly grief: individual responses to death in seventeenth-century Britain', in Houlbrooke (ed.), *Death, Ritual and Bereavement*, pp. 62–76.

63 *Ibid.*, pp. 65–6.

64 Gittings, 'Venetia's death', p. 61.

65 *Ibid.*, pp. 61–2.

66 *Ibid.*, pp. 62–3. The first view dates back to Freud: see B. Raphael, *The Anatomy of Bereavement* (1994), pp. 44–50; for the second view, see D. Klass, P. Silverman and S. Nickman (eds), *Continuing Bonds: New Understandings of Grief* (Washington, D.C., 1988); for constructing the deceased's biography, see T. Walter, 'A new model of grief: bereavement and biography', *Mortality*, 1:1 (1996), 7–25.

67 *Ibid.*, pp. 63–4.

68 Gittings, *Death*, p. 145.

69 *Ibid.*, p. 202; C. Gittings, 'Expressions of loss in early seventeenth-century England', in P. C. Jupp and G. Howarth (eds), *The Changing Face of Death: Historical Accounts of Death and Disposal* (1997), p. 30.

70 B. Kemp, *English Church Monuments* (1980), p. 105; Gittings, 'Expressions of loss', p. 28.

71 Gittings, 'Venetia's death', pp. 59–61.

72 Walton, *Life of Donne*, pp. 11–12.

73 London, NPG 3063.

74 *The Poems of John Donne*, ed. H. J. C. Grierson (1933), p. 214.

75 V. Harris, *All Coherence Gone: A Study of the Seventeenth-Century Controversy over Disorder and Decay in the Universe* (1966).

Select bibliography

Almond, P. C., *Heaven and Hell in Enlightenment England*, Cambridge, 1994.

Cunnington, P., and Lucas, C., *Costume for Births, Marriages and Deaths*, 1972.

Gittings, C., *Death, Burial and the Individual in Early Modern England*, Beckenham, Kent, 1984.

Houlbrooke, R. A., *Death, Religion and the Family in England 1480–1750*, Oxford, 1998.

—— (ed.), *Death, Ritual and Bereavement*, 1989, especially chapters by L. M. Beier, R. A. Houlbrooke and A. Laurence.

Kemp, B., *English Church Monuments*, 1980.

Litten, J., *The English Way of Death: The Common Funeral since 1450*, 1991.

Llewellyn, N., *The Art of Death: Visual Culture in English Death Ritual c. 1500–c. 1800*, 1991.

Slack, P., *The Impact of Plague in Tudor and Stuart England*, Oxford, 1985.

Stone, L., *The Crisis of the Aristocracy 1558–1641*, Oxford, 1965.

Strong, R., 'Sir Henry Unton and his portrait: an Elizabethan memorial picture and its history', *Archaeologia*, 99 (1965), 53–76.

Sumner, A. (ed.), *Death, Passion and Politics: Van Dyck's Portraits of Venetia Stanley and George Digby*, 1995.

Taylor, L., *Mourning Dress: A Costume and Social History*, 1983.

Wagner, A., *The Heralds of England: A History of the Office and College of Arms*, 1967.

Woodward, J., *The Theatre of Death: The Ritual Management of Royal Funerals in Renaissance England, 1570–1625*, Woodbridge, 1997.

Wrigley, E. A., *et al.*, *English Population History from Family Reconstitution, 1580–1837*, Cambridge, 1997.

7 · Ralph Houlbrooke

The age of decency: 1660–1760

'Decency' was one of the keynotes of the century between the Restoration of the monarchy and the accession of George III. The word then embraced more than it does today: appropriateness, fitness, seemliness, order, comeliness, good taste and the avoidance of vulgarity or excess. That epoch was heir to political turmoil, bred, many believed, by fanaticism and superstition. Continuing instability during the first half of the period nurtured the craving for order, balance, harmony and the agreement of reasonable men. The 'Glorious Revolution' of 1688, George I's peaceful accession in 1714, and the defeat of Jacobite rebellions in 1715 and 1745 seemed to make law, property and the constitution more secure. The exclusion of Catholic claimants to the throne, the curbing of High Church pretensions, limited religious toleration and the dissenters' acceptance of quiet respectability took the heat out of religious conflict. Meanwhile, the scientific revolution had given rise to a growing confidence that the physical universe could be understood, and the laws which governed it one day deciphered. The image of a benevolent Supreme Being whose designs were rational, orderly and consistent, and whose revealed Gospel was 'Plain, Practical, and Useful'[1] had an enormous appeal in early-eighteenth-century England.

Demography and disease

The savage indecencies wreaked by Death might seem at first sight hard to reconcile with this picture of growing confidence and optimism. For much of this period, the empire of the 'King of Terrors' was rather more extensive than it had been in the previous century. The population of England fell from just over 5.25 million in 1657 to less than 4,865,000 in 1686. Thereafter it rose, but did not finally move beyond the level of 1657 until 1733. Only after that did steady growth carry the total past the six million mark by 1760. Years of 'crisis mortality' when the death toll rose over 10 per cent above trend were numerous in this period. In six years of '3-star' crisis it rose to over 30 per cent above trend. The first of these was the notorious year 1665–66. In 1665, the plague is believed to have caused nearly 56,000 deaths in

London, more than in any previous outbreak. But London itself had grown, and the proportion of the population dying of plague seems to have been far smaller than in 1563 or 1603. The outbreak of 1665 was to be the last great epidemic of bubonic plague in England, although this was something contemporaries could not know. The remaining five years of exceptionally high mortality during this period were 1680–81, 1727–30 and 1741–42. Bad harvests or dearths in 1678, 1727, 1728 and 1740 may have played a part in these crises. The years 1727–30 were among the most mortal of the early modern period. A variety of diseases were involved, including whooping cough, 'suffocating coughs', smallpox and 'putrid fever'. The period from 1678 to 1685 also stands out as markedly unhealthy. In every year except 1683–84 deaths were more than 10 per cent above trend.[2]

London's population nevertheless grew at a dramatic rate, from about 375,000 in 1650 to 675,000 in 1750. Yet the metropolitan environment became more unhealthy as the population increased. For most of this period well over a third of the babies born in London probably died within a year of birth. The capital's horrifying infant mortality rates were probably more than twice as high as those in the rest of England. Its deaths always outnumbered its births, so that its growth was made possible only by a massive immigration which absorbed much of the natural increase of the rest of the country, and contributed to the demographic stagnation characteristic of much of the period. Many immigrants succumbed to diseases against which they had gained no immunity in their places of origin. An optimism about the divine plan characteristic of the epoch could nevertheless blind one influential commentator, Joseph Addison, to these grim demographic facts. 'A Bill of Mortality', he wrote in *The Spectator* in January 1712, 'is in my Opinion an unanswerable Argument for a Providence; how can we, without supposing our selves under the constant Care of a Supreme Being, give any possible Account for that nice proportion which we find in every great City, between the Deaths and Births of its Inhabitants?' Fifty years before Addison wrote, John Graunt, 'the founder of statistics' (1620–74), had drawn much more accurate conclusions from the same source in his *Natural and Political Observations made upon the Bills of Mortality* (1662), perceiving the grim regularity with which London's burials exceeded its baptisms. Graunt was a pioneer in the discovery of patterns in disease, mortality and life-expectancy. This new understanding reduced the sense of human powerlessness in the face of death. It encouraged such diverse developments as that of life assurance and efforts to curb disease without waiting on Providence.[3]

Bubonic plague was the most terrifying epidemic killer because of the speed with which it despatched its victims and the ways in which it disfigured them. The flight of inhabitants by land and water is vividly represented in an engraving of *c.* 1665 attributed to John Dunstall [73]. Fires were lit in the streets in order to dispel the infected air. The mounting death toll was signalled by the sombre sound of repeated

73] Effects of the plague in London, where of all outbreaks that of 1665 claimed the most victims. We see mass flight by land and water, a coffined victim carried through a deserted square, and others buried by the cartload in newly dug pits.

knells, the ringing of bells before coffins or dead-carts, and harrowing cries of grief from many of the countless afflicted families. The shutting up of infected households, their doors marked with a red cross, condemned whole families to death, but was all too often ineffective, as desperate inmates broke quarantine in attempts to save themselves, sometimes leaving relatives or employers to die alone. The enormous pressure on burial space led to the increasing use of pits in churchyards and sometimes in other open ground. Daniel Defoe imagined the agony and shock with which a man saw the bodies of his wife and children 'shot . . . promiscuously' into the great pit in Aldgate churchyard, 'for he at least expected they would have been decently laid in'. (The fourth picture of Dunstall's engraving presumably shows bodies being 'decently laid in'.)[4]

No other disease caused as much havoc as plague. The high mortality of this period was due to a combination of disorders, including tuberculosis, dysentery and typhus. But after the disappearance of the plague, the most feared and the most contagious of all the diseases of the epoch was smallpox. Its most unpleasant effects were the eruptions which gave it its name. Developing into pustules, they gave off a disgusting smell, and left behind them permanent scars which disfigured many a beautiful face. Smallpox, unlike plague, claimed many of its victims from the upper reaches of society: Queen Mary II died of it in 1694. It was so frightful, even on its first appearance, the governors of the London Smallpox Hospital noted in 1760, and so contagious, that 'families of all degrees are thrown into the utmost confusion when it invades any person amongst them, let his or her station be what it will'.[5] Some families were devastated by this scourge. The Bray family monument at Great Barrington in Gloucestershire [74] records that all save one of the seven children of Sir Edmund Bray died 'of the same fatal distemper to this family'. Sir Edmund's grandson, another Edmund, and his wife Frances, erected the monument, on which the greatest prominence was accorded to their 'dear Children JANE and EDWARD' who both died of smallpox, she in 1711 at the age of seven, he in 1720 at the age of fourteen, ending the family's male line. Both children are being led across the clouds by an angel in a poignant expression of the hope that heartbreaking suffering in this life would be followed by sublime happiness in the next.[6]

74] Monument to Jane and Edward Bray in Great Barrington church, Gloucestershire, probably by Francis Bird. Both died of smallpox, she aged seven (1711), he aged fourteen (1720). Particularly dangerous to children and adolescents, smallpox had already carried off several members of the two previous generations of the Bray family.

Smallpox was the first of the great killers to be curbed by human action. Lady Mary Wortley Montagu encountered the practice of inoculation in Constantinople when she accompanied her husband on his embassy there (1716–18). She had her own son inoculated in Turkey, returned to England a passionate convert and convinced some of the leading physicians, as well as Princess Caroline, wife of the heir to the throne, of the procedure's effectiveness.[7]

Although this period suffered from such a high mortality, there was a growing confidence that disease could be understood and controlled. Quarantine imposed on ships may have played an important part in keeping plague at bay. Inoculation spread only slowly at first, but was soon perceived to be a powerful means of protection against smallpox, even though it remained risky. During the scientific revolution, diseases were more closely observed and carefully categorised than before. Drugs which gained much wider acceptance during this period included opium (as an ingredient of laudanum) and quinine, recently introduced from America. Quinine greatly reduced the debilitating effects of the malaria which was endemic in the marshlands of south-eastern England throughout the century after the Restoration. The foundations for better understanding of the contrasts between London's demographic regime and that of the countryside were laid by John Graunt's *Natural and Political Observations made upon the Bills of Mortality* (1662). The 'eighteenth-century campaign to avoid disease', as one historian has called it, sought to improve environmental conditions as well as personal hygiene. Five general hospitals were established in London between 1720 and 1745, and the London Smallpox Hospital in 1746. The philanthropic merchant Thomas Coram brought about the establishment of the Foundling Hospital in 1741.[8]

Preparation for death

Most people died before they reached old age. Few reached the biblical span of three score years and ten.[9] An enormous quantity of sermons and other Christian advice books was devoted to reminding readers that death could strike at any time. The robust demand for *memento mori* literature is illustrated by the publishing history of two books by John Hayward. *The Horrors and Terrors of the Hour of Death* appeared in twenty-one editions between 1690 and *c.* 1730, and the even more popular *Hell's Everlasting Flames avoided* in thirty-five editions between the mid-1690s and the mid-1730s. A more urbane work, better calculated to appeal to the polite reader, was *A Practical Discourse concerning Death* (1689), by William Sherlock (1641?–1707), Master of the Temple and Dean of St Paul's. Sherlock's main message was often reiterated and pithily expressed. 'This ought to be the Work and Business of our whole Lives, to prepare for Death, which comes but *once*, but that *once* is for Eternity. What unpardonable Folly is it, for any Man to be surprized by Death! To fall into the Grave without thinking of it!' Balance was an outstanding quality of the *Discourse*. While painting the terrors of death in vivid colours for the sensual sinner, Sherlock also sought to comfort and fortify those prone to melancholy and despair. He advised his readers to wean themselves from the enjoyments of the flesh in preparation for the heavenly joys of knowledge and adoration experienced in bodies unimaginably refined. Yet he more than once emphasised that preparation for death was quite compatible with the innocent pleasures of life.[10]

The thirty-second edition of Sherlock's *Discourse* appeared in 1759; it had been reprinted eleven times in England alone during that decade. Joseph Addison believed that few books written in English had been so much perused; he thought this 'Excellent Piece' to be 'one of the strongest Persuasives to a Religious Life that was ever written in any Language'. Not everybody wrote of Sherlock with such respect. Lord Chesterfield flippantly asserted in 1733 that whilst teaching us to die, Sherlock 'cheats us of our living'. This worldly peer was hardly typical of his time. The demand for the literature of preparation for death remained buoyant throughout this century. But Sherlock's work was unique in its outstanding influence and durability down to 1760.[11]

By the 1750s, Hayward's work on death was no longer being reprinted. But Elizabeth Rowe's *Friendship in Death* (1728) went through seven editions during that decade. Its series of imaginary letters from the dead to the living performed in a peculiarly eighteenth-century manner the old tasks of dissuading the worldly from vice or indifference to their eternal fate and consoling the bereaved in their loss. It coated the bitter pill of mortality with elements of romance, descriptions of the 'planetary worlds' and visions of the pleasures 'everlasting, unutterable, and beyond description' of existence in the mansions of the blessed.[12] Edward Young's enormously popular *The Complaint or, Night Thoughts on Life, Death and Immortality* (1742–45), went through twelve editions during the 1750s. Written in about 10,000 lines of blank verse, it addressed a 'worldly infidel', Lorenzo, whom it urged to turn to faith and virtue. It contained a vision of eternity, but its powerful invocation of a spirit of sepulchral melancholy was probably more influential.[13] At the very end of this period, in 1759, William Romaine published *The Knowledge of Salvation is Precious in the Hour of Death*, a sermon he had preached at the funeral of the devotional writer James Hervey. It had an astonishing success, going through twelve editions in England alone by the end of the year. Romaine, an associate of George Whitefield, a strict Calvinist, and a powerful preacher to the poor, is now seen as one of the earliest evangelicals. The immense appeal of his sermon was a portent of a coming change in religious outlook in an influential section of polite society.

Good deaths and bad

The ideal of the 'good death' had originated in antiquity, but the art of dying well had never been so closely observed and analysed as it was during the 150 years following the Reformation. In England, two contrasting models of the good death had developed during the century before the Restoration. Within the 'puritan' tradition, the individual's foremost support in face of death was the inner resource of faith. The dying Christian drew sustenance from the prayers and counsel of those around him or her, godly layfolk as well as ministers. Dying Christians gave reciprocal spiritual comfort to those beside the deathbed, delivered godly exhortations and advice, and surrendered their souls willingly into God's hands. Richard Baxter made notable contributions to this tradition in the directions he wrote for the sick and their friends in *A Christian Directory* (1678). 'Let those that are about you see', he enjoined the sick, 'that you take the life to come for a reality, and that you verily expect to live with Christ in joys for ever.'[14]

The 'sacramental' tradition within the Church of England emphasised the desirability, even the necessity, of making a confession of sins to the clergyman, the comfort imparted by absolution, and the soul-warming succour given by the last Communion, often called viaticum (or food for the last journey). The most famous exponent of this tradition was Jeremy Taylor, in his *Holy Dying* (1651), though its roots can be traced back to the Church's inheritance from medieval Catholicism. In fact elements of both traditions were often combined in practice. Meanwhile, members of the English Catholic community maintained as far as possible the ancient last rites of their faith, including extreme unction as well as absolution and the viaticum, and continued to support masses and prayers for the dead.

Some of the most eloquent descriptions of deathbeds are to be found in funeral sermons. A good example in the 'sacramental' tradition is to be found in the tribute which Thomas Ken, the future non-juror, paid to the pious churchwoman Lady Margaret Mainard (d. 1682). During her last sickness, she suffered doubts and fears in her pains, but these ceased during her intermissions. She prayed continually. When the prayers of the Church were read by her, or during the accustomed hour of her private prayer, she wanted to be placed on her knees, until they would no longer support her. When she received 'the most holy Body, and Blood of her Saviour', it seemed to give her a new transfusion of grace, enabling her to concentrate her thoughts on Heaven 'as if she was teaching her Soul to act independently from the Body', from which it separated shortly after she had received absolution. Compare with this description the account given by John Brine, a famous Baptist minister in London, of the death of Mrs Anne Wildman in 1747. During a serious illness nearly nine years before her death, which had looked as though it might be fatal, God had vouchsafed her an assurance of salvation. Highly conscious of her own unworthiness, she had often described herself as the chief of sinners, with the greatest reason to wonder at God's grace in saving her. She enjoyed great spiritual comfort during a long and tedious last illness. During a visit, Brine found her filled with joy at the thought that death was near. Her dying request was that he should tell the Saints (that is the other members of his congregation gathered to hear him after her death) that the doctrine of free grace which he had preached had been the comfort of her soul. These two examples come from close to the two opposite ends of the spectrum of English Protestantism. But underpinning them both was a faith which had overcome anxiety and given each woman, at the end, an assurance of eternal happiness.[15]

Samuel Wesley, John's elder brother, used the very different medium of heroic verse to present an idealised picture of the good death in his ode to Henrietta, countess of Orrery (d. 1732). He portrayed her as calm and hopeful

> When GOD'S high Summons bade her Virtue try
> That one great Bus'ness of Mankind, to die . . .

untroubled by doubt or guilt, greeting the 'King of Terrors' with a smile. Yet

> Love's stronger Flame, when vital Heat retir'd,
> A while, with Warmth, her dying Breast inspir'd:
> An Husband, Parent, Child, her Soul detains,
> And stops the Chil'ness in her ebbing Veins;
> To these, ev'n then, some pious Thoughts were giv'n;
> These stay'd th'ascending Spirit from its Heav'n.[16]

The presence of the family is prominent in all of this period's more poignant accounts and representations of the deathbed scene. Wesley discreetly captured two elements in the relationship between the dying and their closest relatives. As is still the case today, many of those approaching death felt 'held back' by those they loved. This could be a painful experience for those who had reconciled themselves to the prospect of their approaching end. On the other hand, the imparting of last words of advice, the giving of 'pious Thoughts', helped to give shape and meaning to the last moments of consciousness. This could be invaluable both for the dying, facing their attentive audience, and, especially in retrospect, for those who heard them.

One of the period's outstanding visual evocations of death in the family is the magnificent monument by Caius Gabriel Cibber to Thomas Sackville at Withyham, Sussex, in 1678 [75]. Thomas, who died in his thirteenth year, was the 'thirteenth child and seventh son' of the earl and countess of Dorset. Grief-stricken, they kneel on either side of the altar tomb, their attention focused on their dying child. Lady Dorset holds a handkerchief in her left hand ('What mother would not weep for such a son'). But Thomas, leaning on one elbow, cradling a skull with his other hand, looks heavenwards with a rapt expression, as if already wholly absorbed in the prospect of coming glory. The inscription expresses the hope that the monument will survive

> That the succeeding times to all may tell,
> Here lieth one that lived and died well.[17]

75] Monument to Thomas Sackville at Withyham, Sussex, by Caius Gabriel Cibber (1678). The earl (d. 1677) and countess of Dorset kneel grief-stricken beside their twelve-year-old son. He cradles a skull, emblem of mortality, but looks towards his destination, Heaven, in this powerful evocation of a 'good' death.

The conviction that children as well as adults could 'die well' was widely accepted during this period. It underpinned James Janeway's famous collection *A Token for Children: being an Exact Account of the Conversion, Holy and Exemplary Lives, and Joyful Deaths, of Several Young Children*. Published in two parts in 1671 and 1673, it was almost contemporary with Cibber's Withyham monument. But many of the children who appeared in it were of very different status and background from that of the young Thomas Sackville, belonging as they did to professional, business or artisan families in the middling ranks of society. Most of the children whose ages at death are reasonably clear from Janeway's narratives died in later childhood, between the ages of eight and twelve, and already had a highly developed religious awareness. Some of them had gone through trials and temptations, but according to Janeway they were all convinced of their future happiness by the time they died. In a few cases, indeed, customary roles were reversed, as children tried to comfort their parents.[18]

A specifically Christian ideal of the good death survived throughout this period. But those who had observed many deathbeds knew how hard it often was to realise in practice. The diaries and memoirs of this period contain an unprecedentedly large number of very vivid, immediate and seemingly unvarnished accounts of the painful, messy and tedious last days of close friends and relatives. The manifestations of delirium, and a state of utter prostration and apathy in its intervals, were especially distressing. Diarists such as Samuel Pepys and Lady Warwick, chroniclers of the deathbeds of close relatives, were glad not to have seen the actual moment of death. The traditional expectation was that departing parents would wish to say farewell to their offspring. But Francis Hare, bishop of Chichester, who as a clergyman might have been thought especially likely to regard such an occasion as a valuable opportunity of giving advice, did not wish to see his children during his last illness in 1740, saying that 'he loved them too well to like to see them in his sad condition'. Last farewells could be very distressing both to the dying and to survivors. Benjamin Grosvenor, an eminent London Presbyterian minister, described them as 'very cutting . . . killing formalities of Separation' which were almost fatal to those left behind.[19]

The most perceptive writers on the 'art of dying', including Jeremy Taylor, Richard Baxter and William Sherlock, all warned against reading too much into a person's behaviour on the deathbed. Baxter put this point well: 'Judge not of the state of men's souls, by those carriages in their sickness, which proceed from their diseases or bodily distemper.' Many ignorant people, he continued, judged a man by the manner of his dying. If he died calmly, with clear understanding, and a few good words, they thought this was to die like a saint. But this was not unusual with good or bad people in chronic diseases such as consumption or dropsy, while the very best man might die without the use of reason in a violent fever, frenzy or distraction.[20] The traditional depiction of the deathbed as a trial of virtue in the literature of the *ars moriendi* had tended to give the impression that the outcome would be apparent to spectators. In fact the sorts of caveat expressed by Baxter had been adumbrated long before. But they had never before been as fully or clearly expounded as they were in the later seventeenth century.

Three corollaries followed. First, in judging the individual's performance and its likely outcome, more reliance was to be placed on the record of the life than on comportment in the hour of death. William Archer, a former puritan lecturer, declared nothing on his deathbed in 1670. He was wont to say 'Let the life shew what the man is'.[21] His attitude may have become more widespread as time passed. Despite several outstanding exceptions, there was a marked tendency during the eighteenth century to say less about the final scene in public tributes such as funeral sermons.

If individuals' behaviour in terminal sickness was largely outside their own control, and was not a reliable indicator of their own virtue, it seemed legitimate to attempt to alleviate their suffering. Opium, especially as a constituent of laudanum, was widely employed to this end. It seems likely that it was being used on a much larger scale than in previous centuries, though it is impossible to quantify the growth of supplies with any accuracy. The surviving evidence of its administration in diaries and memoirs is certainly more copious, though writers expressed ambivalent feelings about the drug. It was clearly seen as one which might not only stupefy the patient, but also hasten death.[22]

A third corollary was that sudden death might actually be welcome to the well-prepared Christian. Sudden death had traditionally been regarded as something to be dreaded: it was one of the things from which the Litany besought deliverance (see Chapter 6). Even the writer of the best-known medieval tract concerning the art of dying had nevertheless unobtrusively conceded that a righteous man would be saved if he died suddenly. By 1720 it was possible for the Presbyterian minister Benjamin Grosvenor to devote a whole treatise to developing the proposition that sudden death was a positive boon for the upright. It was an extremely common fate, he asserted, suffered by many good men, which spared both the dying and survivors a great deal of suffering. He who prepared for death properly might say to himself, 'I have nothing to do but wait Orders, to compose my Body to fall decently, and rise gloriously; and my Mind to resigne chearfully and willingly'. Meanwhile, he could enjoy his God, his friends and his comforts of life, with the greater relish. Elizabeth Rowe, the author of *Friendship in Death*, 'often expressed herself desirous of a sudden removal to the skies' which would prevent any indecent behaviour in her last moments. Her wish was granted in 1737.[23]

The Middle Ages had handed down the belief that a bad life might be redeemed on the deathbed: the deaths of all men, however sinful their lives had been, were acceptable and precious in the sight of God, if they died in a state of true repentance and contrition. There were some spectacular instances of deathbed repentance in later seventeenth-century England. The most celebrated of all was that of the earl of Rochester in 1680. This blasphemous wit and notorious rake was snatched by God 'as a brand out of the fire'. It was nevertheless the steadiness of his repentance during several weeks which convinced the preacher of his funeral sermon that it had not been the effect of madness or vapours, and gave grounds for belief that his end had been happy. During this period, a late repentance had to meet fairly exacting criteria if it was to be considered genuine. A 'little outward Grief, or forc'd Sorrow' at the end was no better evidence of true repentance and acceptance than delirious raving was of God's rejection of the righteous Christian. The consistency of Rochester's repentance stood in sharp contrast with the self-dramatising anguish of his friend George Villiers, duke of Buckingham (d. 1687). He finally 'received the Sacrament with all the decency imaginable' a few hours before he died, but only after initial reluctance.[24]

The 'last dying speeches' of condemned malefactors often signalled their repentance and salvation to an expectant audience during the sixteenth and seventeenth centuries. During the eighteenth, dying criminals' efforts to subvert the rituals of punishment by a show of debonair indifference, or their drunken stupor at the gallows, were more likely

76] *THE IDLE 'PRENTICE Executed at Tyburn* (1747). Capital punishment was a popular spectacle in this period. Hogarth's engraving captures a tumultuous fairground atmosphere. A minister exhorts the condemned man to think of Heaven, but the gloomy verse from Proverbs suggests that efforts to assist his salvation may be in vain.

to attract comment. In his description of the imaginary execution of five malefactors, Samuel Richardson described how three of them 'swore, laugh'd, and talked obscenely' under the influence of drink. They ridiculed the attendant clergyman, and a psalm was sung 'amidst the Curses and Quarrelling of Hundreds of the most abandon'd and profligate of Mankind'. After the execution, the friends of the deceased fought with men sent by surgeons to obtain bodies for dissection. William Hogarth's engraving *THE IDLE 'PRENTICE Executed at Tyburn* (1747) depicts the disorderliness of a huge throng of spectators, some of whom are shown joking, squabbling, fighting, tippling, hawking their wares or scrambling for a better view [**76**]. One clergyman waits, perhaps apprehensively, in a coach near the gallows while another, his finger pointed heavenwards, rides in the approaching cart with the condemned man. The latter, sitting with his back to his coffin, has a religious book open in front of him. Accompanying verses from Proverbs 1:27, 28 give a bleak reminder that sinners who have ignored God will in the hour of their distress call on him in vain. It was nevertheless in this grim environment that John Wesley achieved the most striking successes of his early ministry, working on the hearts of some condemned malefactors to such good effect that they went to their deaths in a state of cheerful confidence.[25] During the eighteenth century, despite legislative activity which added considerably to the number of statutory capital offences, there was a continuing decline in the actual incidence of capital punishment. This was due both to a fall in the volume of indictable offences and a lower condemnation rate.

Grief and consolation

Sorrow was recognised as a natural response to the deaths of friends and loved ones. One of this period's best-documented instances of deep grief was caused by an execution. William, Lord Russell, who ascended the scaffold in 1683, was a victim of justice utterly different from Hogarth's Idle Apprentice. But the sort of complicated and aggravated grief described with exceptional fullness in a series of letters written by his widow Rachel [77] may well have been shared by many close relatives of humbler malefactors who lacked her unusual articulateness and powers of self-observation. Russell was condemned for complicity in the Rye House Plot. Husband and wife parted for the last time 'with a composed silence', wishing to spare each other's feelings, and restraining 'the expression of a grief too great to be relieved by utterance'. But Lady Russell's intense pain is sharply reflected in her subsequent correspondence with some eminent divines. She complained of her disordered thoughts and amazed mind, clouded understanding and weak faith. She wanted 'the dear companion of all [her] joys and sorrows' to talk with, to walk with, to eat and sleep with. When she saw her children before her, the memory of the pleasure he had taken in them made her heart shrink. She could not help thinking that Russell might have escaped or been acquitted, had things been differently handled, a reflection which only deepened her dejection. After ten months, she felt that every week that passed made her more and more conscious of the miserable change in her condition. For several years afterwards, her pain intensified around the anniversary of her husband's execution. But as time went on, certain events diverted her from absorption in her own grief. Her son's illness made her realise she still had something left to lose. She contemplated bereavements suffered by other people, like her sister, and Princess Anne, who in 1687 lost her youngest daughter, aged less than nine months. Although Lady Russell's mourning was perhaps exceptional in its depth and length, her expressions of her sense of loss are echoed in several diaries, letters and autobiographies of the period. Many of the symptoms of grief she described

77] *Rachel, Lady Russell* (1636–1723), portrait by Sir Godfrey Kneller. She is in mourning for her husband William, Lord Russell, executed in 1683 for complicity in the Rye House Plot. Lady Russell's complicated and protracted grief is vividly reflected in her correspondence with clergymen to whom she turned for spiritual advice.

in her own case will be familiar to those who have observed or shared in the experience of bereavement. There is in this regard no obvious major contrast between the sensibility of the late seventeenth century and that of the late twentieth.[26]

However, the advice then offered to the bereaved was in certain key respects very different from that given today. Its main themes are well represented in the letters written to Lady Russell by her spiritual advisers. John Fitzwilliam urged her not to let her thoughts dwell too long on her loss, to the prejudice of her body and soul. She must wean herself from the world and meditate on the perfect happiness of Heaven. If God helped her to do this by taking away the person she most loved, she had cause to thank him. God was infinitely more valuable to her than the husband he had given her, who ought to have been dear to her only *in* God. She had been given a bitter potion for her own good. Simon Patrick touched on a theme more familiar to the late twentieth century when he reminded Lady Russell of her duty to take care of herself in order to be able to look after her children. One of the chief consolations for the bereaved during this period was a hope or even confidence of the happiness of the departed soul in Heaven. In the case of a man executed for high treason, this comfort could be mentioned only with some circumspection. But Gilbert Burnet, Russell's intimate friend, expressed the hope that God would give Rachel a powerful sense of his love and wisdom, and of the blessed state to which he had raised that 'dearer part of herself'.[27]

There was a broad consensus among English divines who wrote on the subject that it was unnatural to feel no grief in face of the deaths of loved ones, and indecent to show indifference. But obsessive mourning was equally indecent, and invited divine retribution. God softened the hearts of the bereaved to make them more responsive to his purposes. The ideal of temperate sorrow for dead friends, bounded by religious consolations, was expounded in countless tracts and sermons. *The Decency and Moderation of Christian Mourning* was an eminently suitable title for a funeral sermon preached in 1702 by Zachary Taylor.

Funerals and burial

The sermon had become the centrepiece of the English funeral. Our knowledge of the contents of such sermons is very largely based on those that were published. The printing of funeral sermons reached its highest levels between 1689 and 1714, when the rate of publication was probably running at around 150 per decade. They served to set forth Protestant doctrine concerning death and the afterlife and to offer consolation to the bereaved. Protestants believed that the soul went, on its departure from the body, straight to Heaven or to Hell. The happiness of the saved and the misery of the damned would not however be complete until the reunion of the body and soul and the resurrection immediately before the Last Judgement. But it was the immediate fate of the deceased which concerned their loved ones. The last part of the sermon, in which it was customary to describe the character of the dead person, was awaited with the keenest anticipation. The preacher's task was clearly a delicate one. But by carefully selecting what was good from the life's record, and drawing a veil over the rest, he might usually satisfy the expectations of his audience without violating his own conscience. In many cases, clergy went further, emphasising the grounds for hope of a happy outcome, or even expressing confidence that the deceased had entered a better world. Such sermons usually had to be paid for. Most of the poor probably went to their graves without them.

The chief religious ends of funeral services in Protestant England were to remind participants of their own mortality and to set forth Christian consolations. But clergy of every shade of opinion conceded that funerals also served legitimate social purposes, above all that of showing respect for the dead. 'Decency' was the ideal most frequently specified in connection with all aspects of funerals during this period. When testators referred to their own burial, the word 'decent' was the one they usually employed. The word was useful precisely because it meant so many things, according to context: appropriate to the rank of the deceased, free of ostentation or excess, sober, sufficient, respectful and dignified.

By far the most lavish funeral of this period was Mary II's, in 1695 [78]. The thirty-one-year-old queen had represented, particularly in the eyes of many Tories, the frail thread of legitimate succession which enabled them to reconcile their consciences to the Revolution of 1688–89. Her obsequies were outstanding in many ways: for the presence in her procession of the members of parliament in mourning cloaks; for the performance of a noble dirge specially composed by Henry Purcell; for the splendid processional chariot and 'hearse' under which the body rested in Westminster Abbey, both designed by Sir Christopher Wren; for the use of purple instead of black velvet on the chariot, hearse and canopy; and for its great cost, over £50,000, which made it the most expensive royal funeral celebrated in England since 1625. Several seventeenth-century churchmen taught that a great public loss merited a great public show of mourning. Mary's death was said to have 'spread a *melting Tenderness,* and a *flowing Sorrow* over the whole Nation, beyond any Thing we ever saw'; national mournings had broken out 'in the solemnest as well as in the decentest Manner', beginning in the highest ranks of the nation and spreading downwards.[28]

The stately theatre of Queen Mary's funeral, carefully organised though it was, provided a focus for an unforced national grief. No other royal funeral of the period was nearly so grand. Charles II's in particular was carried out in a relatively economical manner. But even then, his successor James II commanded that mourning be observed with 'that decency that became so great an occasion'. All lords, privy councillors and officers of the late King's household were to cover their coaches and sedan chairs and clothe their livery servants with black cloth.[29]

78] *The Funeral Procession of Mary II* (1695), by Lorenz Scherm after Carel Allard. Costing well over £50,000, this was one of the most expensive funerals ever staged in England. This engraving shows only part of the immense procession as it approached Westminster Abbey, with the great funeral chariot in the foreground.

Great soldiers and sailors who did their kings outstanding service were buried at the Crown's expense. They included during this period George Monck, duke of Albemarle (1670), principal architect of the Restoration; Lord Sandwich (1672), and Lord Stanhope (1721). Sandwich had died in action at sea, and his body was brought up the Thames by a procession of mourning barges saluted by the guns of the Tower. The funeral of the duke of Marlborough (1722) was allegedly paid for by his widow, but in so far as the scale of the procession was concerned, it matched the greatest state funerals. At the head were bands of soldiers, a detachment of artillery, the commander-in-chief of the army and several general officers. Nine dukes and eight earls took part as chief mourner, supporters, assistants and pall-bearers.[30]

Every individual who had a right to bear arms was entitled to the ceremonial of a heraldic funeral, but such observances were becoming increasingly rare during this period. Individuals and families wanted to display arms, a valued mark of status, in the shape of scutcheons or hatchments, but not to have funerals managed by heralds, with their

79] William Boyce's trade card, c. 1680. Undertaking developed as tradesmen supplied a growing range of funeral 'conveniencies' besides their own specialities. Coffin-makers were probably particularly successful as undertakers catering for the lower end of the market, where the coffin was often the most expensive item on the funeral account.

panoply of precedents and perquisites. There were sometimes special reasons for choosing a heraldic ceremony. The magnificent 1736 funeral of the last duke of Buckingham of the Sheffield line was a tribute from his immensely wealthy mother, grieving at her son's tragically early death.[31]

The sumptuous funerals of important people increasingly reflected wealth, taste and personal circumstances as well as rank. Well-off people of middling rank aped the funeral fashions of their social superiors, including even elements of the heraldic funeral. This process of emulation was facilitated by the further decline of the heralds' control and the rise of a new type of commercial funeral manager. The heralds' authority had been seriously weakened by the Interregnum, and was still further undermined by the Glorious Revolution. Gentry unwilling to accept the trouble and expense involved in a full heraldic funeral had long resorted to 'herald painters' to provide them with scutcheons and hatchments. One such painter, William Russell, who in the 1680s took up the additional trade of coffin-maker, has been regarded as the first undertaker by some writers. It was however the upholsterers or upholders who were best placed to act as undertakers to the wealthy. The greater part of the bills for funerals of people of substance consisted of payments for different types of cloth. By hiring, rather than selling, much of what was needed for funerals, undertakers enabled people of comparatively modest means to aspire to a level of funerary ostentation far beyond anything they could hitherto have afforded. But among less well-off tradespeople and artisans in London, the coffin was often the largest single item on the funeral account apart from refreshments, and it therefore made sense for a man like William Boyce, 'Coffinsmaker', to offer 'With all sorts & sizes of Coffins & Shrouds Ready Made . . . all other Conveniencies Belonging to Funerals' [79].[32]

The elements of the 'decent' funeral among the well-born and wealthy included an adequately furnished room for the corpse to lie in before its removal to the church, a decorous, orderly and well-attended procession, and a sufficient distribution of tokens of remembrance to friends and relatives. A large room, or suite of rooms, in the deceased's house, was completely hung with black. The candles on sconces, picking out the bright colours of the heraldic scutcheons, made a brilliant show against the sombre background of the black wall-hangings. The number of coaches bringing up the rear of the funeral procession was often

80] An undertaker's invitation ticket to the funeral of Mrs Sarah Shallett (1720). To the left, a funeral procession wends its way through the dusk; to the right, mourners gather in a candle-lit chamber hung with black. A grieving woman sits with her hand over her face.

mentioned as one measure of the social success of the occasion. On the 1720 invitation to the funeral of Mrs Sarah Shallett [**80**], the right-hand part of the engraving captures the atmosphere of a darkened chamber lit by candles in sconces. To the left, a long, torchlit procession of mourners, some in long cloaks, winds through the dusk, while a coach can be glimpsed in the distance. Rings, silk scarves, hatbands and gloves were distributed to different categories of kinsfolk, friends and acquaintances. The finest gifts distinguished the most valued friends.[33]

Formerly it had been customary to include poor people in the funeral procession, and to give doles of food or money. This tradition had not altogether died out in some places even by the early eighteenth century. But the exclusion of the poor in the interests of sobriety and decorum, and the distribution of money only to carefully selected deserving individuals, were now widespread. One sign of exclusiveness and of the desire to regulate or discourage casual attendance was the custom of sending invitation tickets, some of them, like that for Mrs Shallett's funeral, bearing elaborate and elegant designs. Servants and tenants were not to be excluded from gentry funerals, but their behaviour had to be controlled. 'Let the servants be grave & composed avoiding all confusion them selves, and as far as in them lyes hinder all indecent mirth & noise in others, let them turn out all Children & Rabble'; so ran certain instructions drawn up for the funeral of Mrs Anne Phelips of Montacute in 1707. Hospitable refreshment was still an important part of funeral proceedings, but 'a Small yet decent Collation' was now widely preferred to the feasting and drinking formerly common. It was said to be customary to give guests at London funerals in the 1690s a few glasses of mulled wine both before leaving the deceased's house and on return from the church. The last illustration in Hogarth's *Harlot's Progress* (*c.* 1731) captures the moment before departure to the church [**81**]. The wine releases a variety of emotions, including vanity, amorousness and prurient malice, as well as a somewhat maudlin grief.

81] *The Harlot's Funeral Party*, William Hogarth, *c.* 1731. Moderate refreshment before the burial service was then an established element of 'decent' London funerals. The harlot lies in a well-appointed coffin with lining, plate and grips, the lid drawn back to permit guests a parting look at her.

Sprigs of rosemary, to be carried in the procession and thrown into the grave, lie on a plate in the foreground.[34]

By the eighteenth century, a coffin had come to seem an essential element of the decent funeral, even for the poor. The wealthy went to their graves in increasingly elaborate grave clothes and coffins covered with fabric, fitted with grips and adorned with engraved plates. Statutes of 1667 and 1678 ordered that grave clothes be made of wool. 'Decent and fashionable laced Shifts and Dressings for the Dead made of Woollen' were already being offered by a Mrs Potter in 1678. The 'rich Equipage of the Dead [did] Honour to the Living', according to one foreign observer, when it was viewed by the funeral guests before the final nailing up of the coffin.[35] Hogarth shows us a guest taking a last look at the harlot in her coffin. This receptacle, standing in the middle of the shabby chamber on stools, looks quite elegant, well lined, with a plate on its lid.

Corpses were buried both underneath the church and in the church-yard. The proportion of interments in each, and the social acceptability of burial in the churchyard, depended in large part upon the amount of space available. There was a fairly strong current of disapproval of intramural burial. In 1726, Thomas Lewis went further, publishing a tract with the self-explanatory title *Churches no Charnel-Houses: being An Enquiry into the Profaneness, Indecency, and Pernicious Consequences to the Living, of Burying the Dead in* Churches *and* Churchyards. All nations save Christians, Lewis argued, had been careful 'to bury the Dead in Decent Places, and in a Decent Manner'. The custom of burial in and next to churches had been promoted by superstition, social emulation, and the greed of the clergy. The 'Effluvia of the Dead' and the 'Vapours that continually arise from the Graves' were major health hazards. But it was to be another century, as Chapter 8 will show, before the Anglican near-monopoly of burial space was effectively challenged, and the creation of spacious new extra-parochial suburban cemeteries became common. In the countryside, the prosperous lesser gentry and middling ranks could choose churchyard burial, avoiding the worst of the dangers identified by Lewis. In towns, however, burial under the church continued on a large scale. To avoid the disturbance of recently buried corpses, well-off families resorted to the creation of private burial space in the shape of vaults or brick-lined shafts. The sort of sepulchral honeycomb which could result is well illustrated by the aerial photograph of the excavated church of St Augustine the Less in Bristol [82], where there are over a hundred such burial compartments. London churches erected in accordance with the 'Fifty New Churches Act' of 1711, including the recently excavated Christ Church, Spitalfields, had extensive purpose-built vaults underneath them.[36] Some aristo-cratic families created their own mausolea. The most splendid of these is the Rotunda at Castle Howard, designed by Nicholas Hawksmoor (d. 1736).

82] St Augustine the Less, Bristol. Over a hundred burial vaults and brick-lined shafts were constructed beneath this church between the Reformation period and the mid-nineteenth century. They gave the mortal remains of some wealthier parishioners more protection than was available in a small and intensively used urban churchyard.

Monuments, inscriptions and gravestones

A rich diversity of forms and themes for funeral monuments had developed during the century before 1660. Semi-recumbent, reclining, sitting and standing figures were now more popular than recumbent figures or kneeling families. They offered greater possibilities of rapport between the different individuals represented, and between them and the spectator.[37] Some sculptors used the dramatic potential of these forms to give a vivid representation of Christian hopes. The already mentioned monuments to Thomas Sackville at Withyham and to the Bray children at Great Barrington illustrate this point very well. A powerful imaginative realisation of the actual moment of resurrection is to be found at East Carlton, Northamptonshire [83], where the shrouded figures of Sir Geoffrey (d. 1670) and Lady Palmer step hand in hand out of their burial chamber. They look upwards with awe in their faces. The Latin inscription on an opened door of the monument refers to Sir Geoffrey's dearest wish to sleep together with his wife 'in vrna Conjugali' and to his awakening again with her. In a very different vein is Louis François Roubiliac's monument to Lady Elizabeth Nightingale and her husband [84], completed in 1761, just after the end of this period. Lady Elizabeth died in premature childbirth brought on by a flash of lightning in 1731, and it was the couple's only son who by his will ordered the monument's erection. Lady Elizabeth's distraught husband attempts in vain to ward off a blow from the dart wielded by a horribly realistic and grimly purposeful figure of Death in the shape of a shrouded skeleton. Death with his dart had appeared on several seventeenth-century funeral monuments and brasses, sometimes carrying in his other hand a victor's Crown in intimation of coming glory. His macabre representation on the Nightingale monument, which conveys only the pain and horror of parting, was exceptional in the mid-eighteenth century. Yet John Wesley, harbinger of religious revival, thought highly of this powerful composition, writing that it was 'one tomb which showed common sense' and that 'Here indeed the marble seems to speak'.[38]

Such dramatic representations were in truth somewhat atypical of the period. Urbanity and serenity were much more characteristic of its grand monuments. Sometimes they struck an incongruous note. Joseph Addison complained that Grinling Gibbons's monument to Sir Cloudesley Shovell (d. 1707) in Westminster Abbey represented this 'brave rough *English* Admiral . . . by the Figure of a Beau, dress'd in a

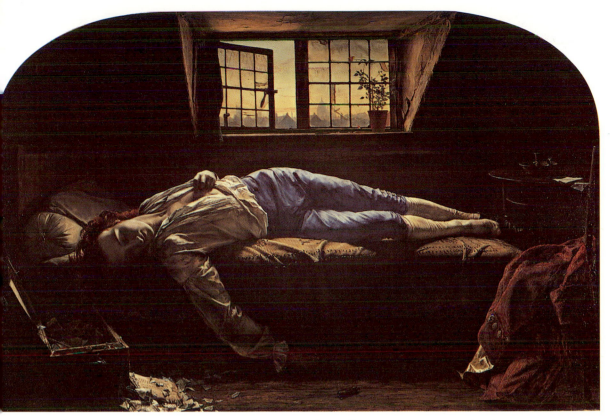

plate 14] *The Death of Chatterton* (1856), by Henry Wallis. Wallis's painting represents the glamour attached to suicide during the Romantic period, and the lingering influence of death of the young poet. Note the scattered fragments of manuscript and the arsenic bottle.

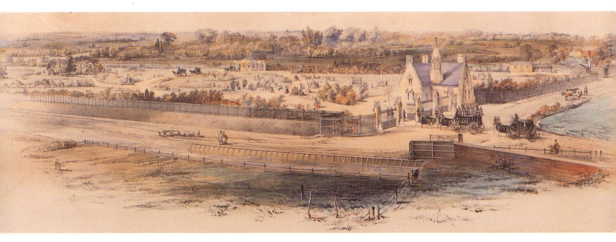

plate 15] *To the Chairman and Directors of the Hull General Cemetery Company* (1846). Print of cemetery. Particularly from the 1840s, cemeteries – secure, elegantly landscaped and located out of towns – wrestled away from the Church its virtual monopoly over the place of burial. Offering attractive locations for burial, cemeteries were also fashionable places in which to promenade.

plate 16] *The Last Judgement* (1853), by John Martin. This spectacular painting depicts God sitting in judgement on the deceased, surrounded by 24 saints, with the sinners tormented in Hell on one side and the pious who are saved in Heaven on the other. This is a Protestant Last Judgement; the saved include Wyclif, Luther, Milton and Nicholas Ridley who was the painter's ancestor.

83] Monument to Sir Geoffrey (d. 1670) and Lady Palmer, at East Carlton, Northamptonshire. At the moment of resurrection, the amply shrouded couple, risen from their funeral urns, pause in wonder at the door of their tomb. Their clasped hands show that their love has survived the grave.

right **84**] Monument in Westminster Abbey to Lady Elizabeth Nightingale (d. 1731) and her husband, by Louis François Roubiliac (1761). Death, horrifyingly vivid, aims his dart at Lady Nightingale, ignoring her anguished husband's attempt to shield her. Despite its power, and hints of incipient Romanticism, this composition inspired no imitative vogue.

long Perriwig, and reposing himself upon Velvet Cushions under a Canopy of State'. A simple bust or portrait in low relief might seem more decent and less extravagant than a grandiose monument. The memorial at Acton Round (Salop), showing Richard Acton (d. 1703) and his wife hand in hand, half turned towards each other, expresses feeling with elegance and dignity.[39]

But text alone was widely preferred to any visual representation of the dead, and epitaphs or simple descriptive inscriptions were by far the most popular memorials of this period. The finest of them 'hang' on the walls of churches on framed tablets or cartouches. One magnificent example is Peter Scheemakers' memorial to John Rudge (d. 1740) at Wheatfield, Oxfordshire [**85**]. Of delicately veined marble, flanked by Corinthian columns and surmounted by a broken pediment, it is faithful to classical models in its relative restraint and simplicity. It pays tribute to Rudge's public service, especially as a member of parliament.

195

Apart from that it is a bare record of his marriage and those of his surviving children: it makes no mention of other outstanding virtues, and concludes by telling us when he 'departed this Life', though the decoration of the frame consists of symbols of immortality (urn, cherubs, laurel wreath and palms). His arms occupy a fairly unobtrusive position just below the pediment. By this time, English was probably the most popular language for epitaphs. In the later seventeenth century, very many of them, especially ones commemorating gentry and clergy, had been written in Latin. Besides admiring the elegance and economy of Latin prose, those who commissioned and composed such tributes may possibly have wanted to hide their contents from the eyes of the vulgar.

Within churches, wall monuments were outnumbered by inscriptions in stone or marble set into the floor. Very many epitaphs celebrated private virtue as well as, or rather than, public careers, virtue exerted, as Dr Johnson remarked, 'in the same Circumstances in which the Bulk of Mankind are placed, and which, therefore, may admit of many Imitators'.[40] One of thousands such was dedicated to Mrs Hannah Randall, of Cerne Abbas, who died in 1733, at the age of seventy-seven, in the thirtieth year of her widowhood.

85] Hanging wall monument to John Rudge (d. 1740), at Wheatfield, Oxfordshire, by Peter Scheemakers. An epitaph concerning Rudge's distinguished public service, marriage and surviving children, occupies the central space. But the eye dwells on the superb classical framework, with its Corinthian columns, broken pediment and symbols of immortality.

> She adorn'd the Several Relations of Life
> She was Engag'd in with the utmost
> Integrity and Good Nature.
> As a Wife, she was Affectionate & Discreet.
> As a Parent: the most Carefull, & Indulgent.
> And as a Friend the most Sincere & Constant.
> For as nothing could gain her Esteem, but
> Vertue & Good Sense so nothing could forfeit
> it but Baseness or Folly.

Far more numerous, however, were inscriptions which said nothing at all about the personal qualities of the deceased, but simply provided the basic facts of age at, and date of, death together with place of residence and names of closest relations.

Churchyard monuments seldom if ever during this period matched the elegance and sophistication of the best work within the church. It was not customary for them to include portraits of the deceased. But some monuments carried a wealth of symbolic figures. On the side of the Knowles chest tomb (c. 1707?) at Elmore, Gloucestershire [**86**], for example, appear Time with his hourglass and Death with his shovel, flanking what look like cherubs blowing trumpets (who are however

86] The Knowles tomb (*c.* 1707?), at Elmore in Gloucestershire, a county where an exceptionally large number of fine early churchyard monuments survives. Death, Time, angels and a Book of Life held open by robed figures are the most prominent elements of a crowded and rather naive yet majestic apocalyptic scene.

decently clad!) and robed figures holding open the scriptures. The popularity of skeletal figures and skulls as decorative motifs gradually declined during the eighteenth century. Much commoner than elaborate monuments such as the Knowles chest tomb were headstones. The stone which records the last resting place in Standish churchyard, Gloucestershire, of Judith Androwes, who died in December 1695 at the age of thirteen, with its primitive and largely abstract vernacular decoration, is exceptionally well preserved.

To judge from surviving examples, and from the chronological spread of the inscriptions and headstones recorded by the Gloucestershire antiquary Ralph Bigland (d. 1784) and his helpers from the 1750s onwards, it was during the later seventeenth century that more durable or substantial churchyard monuments first began to be erected in relatively large numbers.[41] Social emulation in the middling ranks of society was probably an important reason for this development. In one case we can glimpse the process at work. In 1740, Samuel Collier of Reading, a former bargemaster, requested that a 'Monument with Iron Rails' be set up in Swallowfield churchyard in memory of him and his wife, 'and made after the manner and as good as that placed up in St Giles Churchyard in memory of Mr William Greenaway'.[42] St Giles's was an urban parish where new styles were probably adopted earlier than in the rural community of Swallowfield. The prosperous middling ranks of society were seeking during this period not only to protect the bodies of their relatives by means of more durable and substantial coffins but also to preserve their memories in stone. These were two manifestations of standards of politeness and decency which were shared by an increasing proportion of the population.

Early eighteenth-century England cherished an ideal of decency. Yet it tolerated abuses which some contemporary critics found highly indecent, including intramural burial, overcrowded churchyards, a massive waste of infant life, especially in London, and the treatment of capital punishment as popular entertainment. The rational religion, free of cant, superstition and enthusiasm, practised by a large portion of the ruling class, and regarded by its adherents as a bulwark against the recurrence of civil strife, resembled a foundation of sand in the eyes of some observers. In a highly charged sermon delivered in 1746, one evangelical preacher made a caustic reference to 'the reputable, the honourable, the polite, the self-righteous, good Christians of this Age . . . (whose Religion may be summed-up in that *formal decency*, which the *Apostle* calls *the Form of Godliness without the Power)*'.[43]

In 1760 there lay ahead a period during which the hard-won equilibrium of Hanoverian Britain would be severely tested by the social and environmental consequences of industrial revolution, and by a demographic explosion which would treble the English population in the space of a hundred years. Decency would demand growing public intervention in the fields of sanitation and public health. Even more profound in their effects on the psychological climate, successive religious movements, heralded by the missionary work of John Wesley and his associates from the 1730s onwards, would attack secularism and unbelief in the last great Christian revival of recent British history, bringing a renewed earnestness of moral purpose.

Notes

In all references, place of publication is London unless otherwise stated.
1 B. Hoadly, *A Sermon Preach'd at the Funeral of Mrs. Elizabeth Howland* (1719), p. 17.
2 E. A. Wrigley and R. S. Schofield, *The Population History of England 1541–1871: A Reconstruction* (1981), pp. 532–3, 333–5, 664–9, 680–5; P. Slack, *The Impact of Plague in Tudor and Stuart England* (Oxford, 1985), p. 151; R. B. Outhwaite, *Dearth, Public Policy and Social Disturbance in England, 1550–1800* (Basingstoke, 1991), pp. 57–8.
3 A. L. Beier and R. Finlay (eds), *London 1500–1700: The Making of the Metropolis* (Harlow, 1986), pp. 2–4; J. Landers, *Death and the Metropolis: Studies in the Demographic History of London, 1670–1830* (Cambridge, 1993), pp. 98–101, 170; *The Spectator*, ed. D. F. Bond, 5 vols (Oxford, 1965), III, p. 27; W. F. Wilcox (ed.), *Natural and Political Observations . . . by John Graunt* (Baltimore, Md., 1939), p. xiii, cited by P. Laslett, 'Natural and political observations on the population of late seventeenth-century England: reflections on the work of Gregory King and John Graunt', in K. Schurer and T. Arkell (eds), *Surveying the People: The Interpretation and Use of Document Sources for the Study of Population in the Later Seventeenth Century* (Oxford, 1992), p. 10; L. Prior, 'Actuarial visions of death: life, death and chance in the modern world', in P. C. Jupp and G. Howarth (eds), *The Changing Face of Death: Historical Accounts of Death and Disposal* (Basingstoke, 1997).
4 *The Shorter Pepys*, selected and ed. by R. Latham (1985), pp. 494, 500, 506, 509, 513, 515–16, 519, 522, 527; D. Defoe, *A Journal of the Plague Year*, ed. A. Burgess and C. Bristow ([1722,] Harmondsworth, 1966), pp. 67–82 (esp. p. 80), 89, 91, 130–1, 166–7, 172–3, 177–8; V. Harding, 'Burial of the plague dead in early

modern London', in J. A. I. Champion (ed.), *Epidemic Disease in London*, Centre for Metropolitan History Working Papers Series 1 (1993), pp. 53–64. Concerning Defoe's reliability, see Slack, *The Impact of Plague*, p. 337: 'There have been various opinions as to the historical accuracy of *A Journal of the Plague Year*. No one would now use it as primary evidence for what happened in 1665, although there is more to be said in its favour than against it, granted the limitations of Defoe's sources: the printed literature of 1665 and 1721, contemporary recollections and the known topography of London.'

5 Cited by A. Hardy, 'The medical response to epidemic disease during the long eighteenth century', in Champion (ed.), *Epidemic Disease*, p. 68.

6 Inscription printed in R. Bigland, *Historical, Monumental and Genealogical Collections relative to the County of Gloucester*, ed. B. Frith, Bristol and Gloucestershire Archaeological Society, Gloucestershire Record Series, 2, 3, 5, 8 (1989–95), I, p. 136.

7 R. Halsband, *The Life of Lady Mary Wortley Montagu* (Oxford, 1956), pp. 71–2, 80–1, 104–5, 109–12.

8 Slack, *Impact of Plague*, pp. 323–6; P. Razzell, *The Conquest of Smallpox* (Firle, 1977), W. C. Gibson (ed.), *British Contributions to Medical Science* (1971), pp. 8–9, 23, 123, 205–7, 243, 284–5; A. G. Debus (ed.), *Medicine in Seventeenth Century England* (Berkeley, Cal., 1974), pp. 87–8, 101, 133, 155–7, 176–8, 234, 259, 263, 276, 351; J. C. Kramer, 'Opium rampant: medical use, misuse and abuse in Britain and the West in the 17th and 18th centuries', *British Journal of Addiction*, 74 (1979), 377–89; C. Creighton, *A History of Epidemics in Britain*, 2nd edn, 2 vols (1965), II, pp. 315–26; M. J. Dobson, 'History of malaria in England', *Journal of the Royal Society of Medicine*, 82, supplement no. 17 (1989), 3–7, esp. 4; J. C. Riley, *The Eighteenth-Century Campaign to avoid Disease* (Basingstoke, 1987); Hardy, 'Medical response', p. 68; R. McClure, *Coram's Children: The London Foundling Hospital in the Eighteenth Century* (New Haven, Conn., 1981).

9 Wrigley and Schofield, *Population History*, pp. 250, 528–9; Landers, *Death and the Metropolis*, pp. 98–101.

10 W. Sherlock, *A Practical Discourse concerning Death*, 23rd edn (1739), pp. 43–53, 95, 129, 181–2, 219–20, 233–6, 291–2.

11 *Spectator*, III [1712], p. 29; *The New Oxford Book of Eighteenth Century Verse*, ed. R. Lonsdale (Oxford, 1984), p. 275.

12 E. Rowe, *Friendship in Death, in Twenty Letters from the Dead to the Living* (1814), pp. xxiii–xxv, 4–8, 11–12, 15–18, 33–5.

13 E. Young, *Night Thoughts*, ed. S. Cornford (Cambridge, 1989). See Introduction, p. 17, for its contribution to 'a secular cult of sepulchral melancholy'. Young's work helped to inspire, in a subsequent period, the garden cemetery pioneers. See Chapter 8 below and J. S. Curl, 'Young's "Night Thoughts" and the origins of the garden cemetery', *Journal of Garden History*, 14:2 (1994), 92–118.

14 N. L. Beaty, *The Craft of Dying: A Study in the Literary Tradition of the 'Ars Moriendi' in England* (New Haven, Conn., 1970); *The Practical Works of the Rev. Richard Baxter*, ed. W. Orme, 23 vols (1830), IV, p. 439.

15 T. Ken, *A Sermon preached at the Funeral of the Right Honourable the Lady Margaret Mainard*, in C. H. Sisson (ed.), *The English Sermon*, II: *1650–1750* ([1682], Cheadle, 1976), pp. 187–8; J. Brine, *The Chief of Sinners, saved thro' Jesus Christ: A Sermon occasioned by the Death of Mrs. Anne Wildman* (1747), pp. 44–6.

16 S. Wesley, 'On the death of the Right Honourable Henrietta, Countess of Orrery', in J. Wilford, *Memorials and Characters, together with the Lives of Divers Eminent and Worthy Persons* (1741), pp. 694–6.

17 The epitaph is printed in T. W. Horsfield, *The History, Antiquities and Topography of the County of Sussex* (Lewes, 1835), I, p. 395.

18 J. Janeway, *A Token for Children: being an Exact Account of the Conversion, Holy and Exemplary Lives, and Joyful Deaths, of Several Young Children*, 2 parts in 1 vol. (1676), I, pp. 36–7, II, pp. 85–7.

19 J. Evelyn, *The Life of Mrs Godolphin*, ed. H. Sampson (Oxford, 1939), pp. 77–8; diary of Samuel Woodforde in Oxford, Bodleian Library, MS Eng. misc. fo. 381,

fos 56–62; *Shorter Pepys*, pp. 365–6; *English Family Life, 1576–1716: An Anthology from Diaries*, ed. R. Houlbrooke (Oxford, 1988), pp. 80–7; *Fourteenth Report of the Royal Commission on Historical Manuscripts, appendix ix* (1895), p. 258; B. Grosvenor, *Observations on Sudden Death. Occasion'd by the Late Frequent Instances of it, both in City and Country* (1720), p. 29.

20 *Practical Works of Baxter*, IV, p. 449.

21 *Two East Anglian Diaries 1641–1729: Isaac Archer and William Coe*, ed. M. Storey, Suffolk Records Society 36 (Ipswich, 1994), p. 122.

22 Kramer, 'Opium rampant'; R. Porter, 'Death and the doctors in Georgian England', in R. Houlbrooke (ed.), *Death, Ritual and Bereavement* (1989), pp. 91–3; *Two East Anglian Diaries*, pp. 95–6.

23 Grosvenor, *Observations on Sudden Death*, p. 22; Wilford, *Memorials and Characters*, p. 753.

24 R. Parsons, *A Sermon preached at the Funeral of the Right Honourable John Earl of Rochester* (Oxford, 1680), pp. 33–4; J. Ellesby, *The Great Danger and Uncertainty of a Death-bed Repentance* (1693), p. 16; Winifred, Lady Burghclere, *George Villiers, Second Duke of Buckingham 1628–1687: A Study in the History of the Restoration* (1903), pp. 397–9.

25 J. A. Sharpe, '"Last dying speeches": religion, ideology and public execution in seventeenth-century England', *Past and Present*, 107 (1985), 141–67; S. Richardson, *One Hundred and Seventy-Three Letters written for Particular Friends, on the Most Important Occasions*, 7th edn (1764), pp. 239–42; J. Wesley, *The Journal of the Rev. John Wesley A. M., sometime Fellow of Lincoln College, Oxford*, ed. N. Curnock, 8 vols (1909–16), II. pp. 100, 338–40.

26 Lord John Russell, *The Life of William Lord Russell, with Some Account of the Times in which he lived*, 2nd edn, 2 vols (1820), II, p. 100; *The Letters of Lady Rachel Russell: From the Manuscript in the Library at Wooburn Abbey*, 4th edn (1792), pp. 244–6, 254–63, 273–8, 283–308, 322, 329–40, 352–6, 368, 372–3, 400. Compare C. M. Parkes, *Bereavement: Studies of Grief in Adult Life*, 2nd edn (Harmondsworth, 1986).

27 *Letters of Lady Rachel Russell*, pp. 247–53, 263–71, 279–81, 310–12, 344–6.

28 P. S. Fritz, 'From "public" to "private": the royal funerals in England, 1500–1830', in J. Whaley (ed.), *Mirrors of Mortality: Studies in the Social History of Death* (1981), pp. 65–8; C. Gittings, *Death, Burial and the Individual in Early Modern England* (1984), pp. 136, 222, 227; G. Burnet, *An Essay on the Memory of the Late Queen Mary*, reprinted in *The Historical Register*, 23:91 (1738), 252.

29 British Library, London, Harleian MS 6309, fo. 15.

30 *Ibid.*, fos 14v, 33; Gittings, *Death, Burial and the Individual*, pp. 231–2, citing F. Sandford, *The Order and Ceremonies used for and at the Solemn Interment of . . . George Duke of Albemarle* (1670); W. Coxe, *Memoirs of the Duke of Marlborough, with His Original Correspondence*, rev. J. Wade, 3 vols (1896), III, pp. 423–5.

31 *Historical Register*, 21:81 (1736), 70–5.

32 Perhaps the best account of the complicated story of the attempts by the heralds to maintain their position is the (unpaginated) tract 'On funerals', in J. Edmondson, *A Complete Body of Heraldry*, 2 vols (1780), I. See also Sir Anthony Wagner, *Heralds of England: A History of the Office and College of Arms* (1967), chapters vi–x. On the rise of the undertakers, see P. Fritz, 'The undertaking trade in England: its origins and early development, 1660–1830', *Eighteenth-Century Studies*, 28:2 (1994–95), 241–53.

33 *The Autobiography of the Hon. Roger North*, ed. A. Jessopp (1887), p. 229; R. Houlbrooke, '"Public" and "private" in the funerals of the later Stuart gentry: some Somerset examples', *Mortality*, 1:2 (1996), 170–4.

34 *Ibid.*, 172–4; Somerset Record Office, Taunton, MS autobiography of John Cannon, pp. 61, 129, 143; H. Misson, *Memoirs and Observations in His Travels over England* (1719), p. 91. Misson's classic description of a middle-class English funeral is conveniently reprinted in J. Litten, *The English Way of Death: The Common Funeral since 1450* (1991), pp. 143–6.

35 P. Cunnington and C. Lucas, *Costume for Births, Marriages and Deaths* (1972), p. 161; Misson, *Memoirs and Observations*, pp. 90–1.

36 Lewis, *Churches no Charnel-Houses*, pp. 3–5, 37–60; *Shorter Pepys*, ed. Latham, p. 367; Litten, *English Way of Death*, pp. 3–5, 37–60; E. Boore, 'The Church of St Augustine the Less, Bristol: an interim statement', *Transactions of the Bristol and Gloucestershire Archaeological Society*, 104 (1986), 211–13; J. Reeve, M. Adams, T. Molleson and M. Cox, *The Spitalfields Project*, 2 vols, Council for British Archaeology Research Reports 85 and 86 (1993), vol. I: *The Archaeology: Across the Styx*, esp. pp. 65–7; M. Cox, *Life and Death in Spitalfields 1700–1850* (York, 1997).

37 An excellent survey of the period is in B. Kemp, *English Church Monuments* (1980), pp. 106–41.

38 Quoted in J. W. Blundell and J. Physick, *Westminster Abbey: The Monuments* (1989), p. 119, where the date of death given on the monument for Lady Elizabeth is also corrected.

39 *Spectator*, I [1711], pp. 110–11; Kemp, *English Church Monuments*, p. 117.

40 Anon. [S. Johnson], 'An essay on epitaphs', *The Gentleman's Magazine*, 10 (1740), 595.

41 This suggestion is based on the examination of a large number of churchyard surveys and transcriptions of epitaphs in county record offices at Aylesbury, Cambridge, Exeter and Warwick, and the Local Studies Library in Reading Central Library, as well as on Bigland's transcriptions and dated lists of individuals named on simpler churchyard memorial stones.

42 Berkshire Record Office, Reading, Berkshire Archdeaconry Wills, D/A1/59/159.

43 H. Piers, *True Wisdom from Above: Or, Christianity the Best Understanding* (1746), p. 17.

Select bibliography

Almond, P. C., *Heaven and Hell in Enlightenment England*, Cambridge, 1994.

Cressy, D., *Birth, Marriage and Death: Ritual, Religion, and the Life-Cycle in Tudor and Stuart England*, Oxford, 1997.

Defoe, D., *A Journal of the Plague Year*, ed. A. Burgess and C. Bristow [1722,] Harmondsworth, 1966.

Dobson, M. J., *Contours of Death and Disease in Early Modern England*, Cambridge, 1997.

Houlbrooke, R. A., *English Family Life, 1576–1716: An Anthology from Diaries*, Oxford, 1988.

——*Death, Religion, and Family, 1480–1750*, Oxford, 1998.

Kemp, B., *English Church Monuments*, 1980.

Landers, J., *Death and the Metropolis: Studies in the Demographic History of London, 1670–1830*, Cambridge, 1993.

Lonsdale, R. (ed.), *The New Oxford Book of Eighteenth Century Verse*, Oxford, 1984.

McManners, J., *Death and the Enlightenment: Changing Attitudes to Death in Eighteenth-Century France*, Oxford, 1985.

Porter, R., *Disease, Medicine and Society in England 1550–1860*, Basingstoke, 1987.

Riley, J. C., *The Eighteenth-Century Campaign to avoid Disease*, Basingstoke, 1987.

Scodel, J., *The English Poetic Epitaph: Commemoration and Conflict from Jonson to Wordsworth*, Ithaca, N.Y., 1991.

Walker, D. P., *The Decline of Hell: Seventeenth-Century Discussions of Eternal Torment*, 1964.

Wrigley, E. A., and Schofield, R. S., *The Population History of England 1541–1871: A Reconstruction*, 1981.

8 · Julie Rugg

From reason to regulation: 1760–1850

By 1850, death was acquiring many of the features familiar to the modern experience of mortality: a doctor at the bedside, concerned to ease the pain of death; undertakers operating wholly on commercial lines, beginning to mass-produce funerals for anyone prepared to pay; burial increasingly in a cemetery rather than a churchyard; and the death recorded and logged by the state. A key element of the emerging modern experience of death was the loosening of the Church's hold on sepulchral matters, being edged out of death tableaux on a number of levels. The centrality of the church building to death ritual was undermined by the increased use of secular burial places where pagan symbolism could hold sway; and a shift in attention to the feelings of the bereaved over the spiritual fate of the deceased reduced the importance of a clerical presence at the deathbed.

Although a growing secularity in the experience of death remains a constant theme throughout this chapter, its remit covers a broader range of material. The four sections deal with the period in roughly chronological order, although some strands are prevalent over more or less all the period. The late eighteenth and early nineteenth centuries formed a time of great movement in thought and feeling. The Enlightenment, Romanticism and Evangelicalism are all discussed with respect to their impact on attitudes towards death. The chapter also addresses more prosaic concerns such as population growth and urbanisation, and presents an exploration of ritual, respectability and class division. The transition towards a more secular experience of death was not a smooth one. The chapter concludes with a brief discussion of the Gothic Revival and its critique of a lack of spirituality in death ritual.

The Enlightenment, neoclassicism and a respite from death's terror

The second half of the eighteenth century was characterised by a scientific and philosophical energy that sought to cast light on areas of ignorance, superstition and intolerance. 'The Enlightenment', as this movement came to be known, was pervasive in its influence. Although traditional studies have focused on Enlightenment thinkers in France, such as Voltaire, Diderot and D'Alembert, the movement and its impetus towards social improvement were evident throughout Europe.[1] The expression of enlightened thought in England tended to lack the radical nature of its European counterpart, and had a more self-congratulatory edge. Indeed, the English were often heralded as the most enlightened nation in Europe, celebrated by Voltaire himself.[2] Enlightenment in England was manifest in a revelling in the freedom to explore intellectual and scientific boundaries – often through provincial clubs and societies – and the acknowledgement that the age was benefiting from a vastly improved store of knowledge. Enlightened thought offered many challenges to traditional views on death, but this chapter will focus on only two: the way in which scientific progress in medicine began to naturalise death; and a diminution of the traditional stress on eternal hellfire and damnation. Both these trends tended to remove the terror from death, which – in contrast to its baroque counterpart – was portrayed as a more restful and serene experience. Shifting attitudes towards death were complemented by a radical change in aesthetics which consciously rejected the overblown emotionalism of the baroque. Neoclassicism was characterised by elegance and restraint, and had 'sleep' as its key allegory for mortality.[3]

Enlightenment faith in the value of rational exploration of all aspects of life transformed the medical arena. Medicine became increasingly scientific, and a growing number of conditions and diseases could be anticipated by professionalised doctors, surgeons and apothecaries. Enlightenment tenets decreed that medical knowledge should be freely available to all. Medical texts for wide audiences included William Buchan's *Domestic Medicine* of 1769. Endlessly reprinted, *Domestic Medicine* aimed to overturn popular superstitions regarding health and the treatment of diseases, and to show men 'what was in their own power' to prevent and cure illness.[4] In promoting education about the causes of disease and ill health, it became possible for more people to understand, anticipate and even prevent unnecessary mortality. Even though the eighteenth century may still be characterised as 'the Age of Agony', there was room for optimism. Life expectancies were rising, the population was increasing, and there had been no incidence of plague for decades. Medical science had produced a smallpox vaccine that was much safer than inoculation – Jenner started his work on vaccination in 1796 – and it was possible that further advances would eradicate other diseases. Death could be viewed as a natural phenomenon, over which man appeared to have increasing control.

Advances in medical knowledge and a more widespread trust placed in the medical profession also led to a transformation of the deathbed. The doctor was becoming a common presence for upper- and middle-class families around the time of death, and the second half of the eighteenth century saw a heavy reliance on opiates to ease the pain of the dying. William Heberden, the celebrated physician who had attended George III, considered that one of the most important roles of the physician should be to 'try and disarm death of some of its terrors', so that life could be taken away 'in the most merciful manner'.[5] The use of opium, laudanum, alcohol and paregoric was not confined to the wealthier patients. Such medicines were freely available in patent formulas such as Dover's Powders and Godfrey's Cordial. In 1808 one Nottingham chemist noted that 'upwards of 200lbs of opium and above 600 pints of Godfrey's Cordial are retailed to the poorer classes in the year'.[6] By 1800, through the use of this sort of drug, death could easily resemble a gentle slipping away or falling asleep.

As a greater understanding of medicine and use of opiates removed terror of the arbitrary incidence of death and the deathbed agony, Christian teaching on the afterlife could take a gentler tone. The God of the Enlightenment was a rational being, distant, benevolent, tolerant and unmysterious. The image of such a God did not sit happily with the notion of eternal damnation and hellfire, and this aspect of the afterlife tended to be underplayed. Perhaps the most telling image of death during this period is that conveyed in the work of the sculptor John Flaxman. Although Flaxman was a principal exponent of what was often largely secular neoclassical design, he imbued his images with a gentle Christian piety. Flaxman was deeply influenced by the writings of the Swedish visionary Emanuel Swedenborg, who claimed to have seen an afterlife in which angels assured humanity of an easy passage to eternal life.[7] In *Come, thou blessed*, a monument to Agnes Cromwell who died aged eighteen, Flaxman's ideas are clearly expressed. In a beautifully elegant sculpture, completed in 1798 and combining high and low relief, Flaxman describes the ascent of a figure borne upwards by two angels, whilst a third angel floats above [87]. Other common death images in Flaxman's works included a seated, pensive figure representing 'Resignation'. This stoicism was a further aspect of a more rational response to death. The attitude is typified in the comment made in 1813 by Joseph Banks, botanist and president of the Royal Society, in a note to the bereaved Lady Somerset: 'May the gracious & divine Bounty which sustains us all, Grant to your grace the inestimable Gift of Patience which alone can blunt the arrows of Pain & deprive Fortune of its Sting'.[8] Death was an event to be faced with equanimity, not dominated by fear of a life in eternal damnation.[9]

Enlightened theories that removed the terrors from death were in perfect accord with the neoclassical aesthetics that were all-pervasive in the visual arts of the late eighteenth and early nineteenth centuries. During the 1760s, two publications played a significant part in popularising the art of ancient Greek civilisation. In 1762, James Stuart and Nicholas Revett, financed by the Society of Dilettanti, were sent to Greece. The resulting sketches were published as *The Antiquities of Athens* and included details of Greek ruins, so providing material on which English neoclassical design could be based. In 1765, further inspiration came with the translation and publication of *Reflections on the Paintings and Sculpture of the Greeks* by Johann Winckelmann, the

COME THOU BLESSED

SACRED TO THE MEMORY OF
AGNES SARAH HARRIET,
DAUGHTER OF HENRY CROMWELL ESQ⸢ᵉ⸣ CAPTAIN R.N.
AND MARY HIS WIFE
WHO DIED ON THE 30ᵀᴴ DAY OF NOVEMBER 1797
IN THE 18ᵀᴴ YEAR OF HER AGE.

87] *'Come, thou blessed'* (1798). John Flaxman's memorial sculpture in Chichester Cathedral. Flaxman's memorial sculpture for Agnes Cromwell, completed in 1798, demonstrates the unthreatening nature of Enlightenment death: passage to Heaven was assured by the ministration of tending angels.

88] *Death of Germanicus* (1774). Thomas Banks's sculpture at Holkham Hall, Norfolk. Death was represented in the first truly neoclassical sculpture, executed by Thomas Banks in 1774. The *Death of Germanicus* demonstrates that, in this period, death was coming to be viewed as a serene experience, akin to sleep.

German antiquarian. For Winckelmann, Greek aesthetics comprised a 'noble simplicity and calm grandeur in gesture and expression'.[10] Winckelmann particularly noted that ancient Greek representation of death eschewed a revelling in skeletal imagery. In 1766, his dictionary of iconography described the Homeric conceit of 'Death' as being the twin brother of 'Sleep'. Gotthold Lessing was in agreement: 'I do not see what should prevent our artists from abandoning the hideous skeleton and again availing themselves of a better image. Scripture itself speaks of an angel of death. What artist ought not rather to aim at portraying an angel than a skeleton?'[11] Painters and sculptors were encouraged by academies and patrons to choose classical themes: for example in 1761 the French Academy proposed the death of Germanicus as its sculpture subject. Germanicus Julius Caesar, frequently compared to Alexander the Great in terms of charisma and popularity, had met a mysterious death by alleged poisoning in AD 19. Thomas Banks took the death of this classical hero as his theme in 1774, so producing what one scholar[12] has considered to be the first truly neoclassical sculpture, *Death of Germanicus* [88]. Germanicus is shown surrounded by mourning figures, carved in high relief against a plain background. His pose in death is elongated and languid and his body is represented as perfect and unmarked. Death by poisoning has left no signs of agony on the hero's serene features.

Until aesthetics began to reflect Gothic Revivalism in the 1840s, neoclassical symbols and images dominated representations of death.

89] *Invitation to the Funeral of Sir Joshua Reynolds*, a funeral card by Bartolozzi (1792). Common neoclassical imagery attached to death is illustrated by the funeral card designed by Bartolozzi to mark the death of Sir Joshua Reynolds. The reclining, mourning figure and the draped urn are represented.

Symbolism included the draped urn, the willow, the veiled and weeping mourner and the broken column. According to one historian, this symbol had first been prominent in a memorial designed by Thomas King of Bath in memory of Lt. Colonel Robert Walsh, who had died in 1788.[13] In that case, the broken column designated early death and a family line that would not be continued. Since the broken column could also symbolise the ephemeral nature of earthly glory, it soon became a popular monument type even where life had not been cut short. Other popular images were the cut lily or flower for the death of a child, maid or young wife. The symbols were not only represented on funerary monuments. Mourning jewellery such as rings also displayed urns and willow branches, as did funeral cards.[14] Francesco Bartolozzi's design for a card for the funeral of Sir Joshua Reynolds in 1792 shows a draped and mourning woman ('Genius'), resting against a tomb decorated with willows and being consoled by Fame [89].

Neoclassical aesthetics were also reflected in architecture. The Royal Academy received 164 designs for mausolea between 1768 and 1820, 70 of which were built. The mausoleum offered the possibility of a 'pure' representation of classical design ideals, since such structures did not need to include basic domestic utilities such as windows. One of the most striking mausolea built during this time was that designed by James Wyatt for the first earl of Yarborough in 1787. The mausoleum, on the earl's estate at Brocklesby Park near Great Limber in Lincolnshire, was to contain the remains of, and commemorate, Sophia,

90] Joseph Nollekens' memorial in the Yarborough mausoleum on the Brocklesby Park estate, Great Limber, Lincolnshire (1794). The design of mausolea was a common late-eighteenth-century architectural exercise. This mausoleum, designed by Wyatt and erected following the death of Lord Yarborough's wife, indicates the acceptability of death celebrated outside the aegis of the Church. The sculpture it contains, executed by Nollekens, underlines the idea of repose attached to mortality during this period.

who had been married to the earl for sixteen years before dying of a brain fever in 1786. The mausoleum is circular in construction with a domed ceiling, and has studiously neoclassical detail. The monument contains a sculpture by Nollekens, reflecting the common theme during this period of the virtuous wife, elegantly draped and serene in repose with her chin delicately resting on her hand as she leans against a tree trunk [90]. The mausoleum and its sculpture, completed in 1794, reflect the quiet mood of neoclassical death, contrasting with the often frenzied nature of the baroque of previous decades as typified by the Nightingale monument [84] discussed in Chapter 7.[15]

The use of mausolea shifted memorialisation of the dead to areas outside the confines of the church building. In France from the 1770s there was considerable discussion of the need for new places in which to bury the dead which would celebrate civic virtue rather than spiritual worth. Jacques-François Blondel, writing in the 1770s, considered the ideal cemetery to be an area of arcaded cloisters with cenotaphs of civic worthies.[16] In England a shift away from the spiritual worth of the deceased is best reflected in the neoclassical treatment of civic and military heroes. Representations of the death of Admiral Lord Nelson in 1805 during the Battle of Trafalgar are perhaps a good example. There had been considerable discussion about the need for appropriate symbols and monuments to the naval hero. The comments of Benjamin West, president of the Royal Academy, reflected the need for a monument that would excite 'awe and veneration'.[17] The sculpture by John Flaxman in St Paul's Cathedral includes images of naval battle, a figure representing Minerva as a symbol of war, and Britain as a lion. The inscription bears no Christian reference, but instead records 'a life spent in the service of his country, and terminated in the moment of victory by a glorious death'.[18] The monument contained no direct representation of death. Similarly, Benjamin West's own *Apotheosis of Nelson*, painted in 1807 [91] celebrated the maritime achievements of the admiral, and indicated that immortality could be attained through remembrance of his victories. West's painting was highly popular, and attracted thousands of visitors to the artist's home. The image

91] *Apotheosis of Nelson* (1807), painting by Benjamin West. The death of Nelson was marked by debate on the best way in which to commemorate the naval hero. Much of the imagery attached to representations of the death of Nelson lacked a Christian symbolism, as in West's *Apotheosis*, painted in 1807.

shows Nelson, in a Christ-like pose, being borne out of the sea by Neptune into the arms of Britannia and Victory.

Thus, by the end of the eighteenth century, a combination of Enlightenment theory, medical advances and neoclassical aesthetics had begun to rob death of both its terror and its Christian symbolism. The move towards a more secular experience of death had begun, but was by no means a smooth transition. As the next section will demonstrate, the hellfire and damnation preaching that characterised sections of the Evangelical revival revisited the notion of eternal torment, although these images were offset to a large degree by strong sentiments attached to heavenly reunion.

Romanticism and Evangelicalism: loss, love and Hell revisited

The concept of Romanticism – like the Enlightenment – has taxed the powers of historians wanting to summarise succinctly a movement of thought that expressed itself in diverse cultural developments on an international level. Some historians consider that Romanticism can be interpreted, in part, as a revolt against the high value placed on rationality which was characteristic of the Enlightenment. By contrast, Romanticism – in full flower by the end of the eighteenth century and dominating most of the nineteenth – placed faith in moral passion over intellectual analysis. Most strikingly, Romanticism also comprised a new obsession with the individual. The Genevan philosopher, Jean-Jacques Rousseau, was perhaps the most important figure in formulating some of the key precepts of Romanticism. His autobiography – *The Confessions* – began with the startling announcement: 'I am made unlike any one I have ever met; I will even venture to say that I am like no one in the whole world. I may be no better, but at least I am different.'[19] The value placed on the individual, and a new respect for individual experience, framed attitudes towards death for much of the period covered in this chapter. In this section three main themes will be drawn out: sentiment, love and grief; the attraction of melancholy in appropriately lugubrious settings; and romantic suicide. A fourth theme counterpoints romantic images of the reunion of families and lovers in Heaven with the hellfire and damnation message of many Evangelical preachers.

Although it would be unreasonable to claim that romantic love was not experienced before the second half of the eighteenth century, the stress placed by the Romantic movement on the uniqueness of the individual and the value of sentiment engendered a period in which love was openly celebrated. Of particular note was the move towards the establishment of smaller, nuclear families, ideally characterised by openly affectionate relationships between husband and wife, and between parents and children.[20] The work of the French historian Phillipe Ariès underlines a shift taking place in attitudes towards death during this time, which saw a movement away from concerns with the death of the self, and towards a stress on loss, and death of 'the other'.[21] At a time when 'feeling' was paramount, the almost wild expression of grief at the loss of a member of the family was considered to be appropriate and laudable. In 1793, Thomas Banks exhibited a monument to Penelope Boothby, the child of Sir Brooke Boothby [92]. This was, according to some historians, the first significant monument to a child in eighteenth-century England, and perhaps the first truly Romantic sculpture.[22] Penelope had died in 1791, and her father, in deep despair, wrote a volume of verse entitled *Sorrows*. The monument, simple in design and beautiful in execution, depicts a dead or sleeping child in peaceful repose. Its sentimentality provoked tears from Queen Charlotte at its showing in the Royal Academy.[23] Romantic attachments between

92] Monument to Penelope Boothby (1793). Thomas Banks's memorial in Ashbourne Church, Derbyshire. This beautiful monument of a dead/sleeping child by Thomas Banks is reckoned by some historians to be the first Romantic sculpture. The pure sentimentality of the memorial provoked tears from Queen Charlotte at its showing in the Royal Academy.

husbands and their wives were also celebrated in memorial sculpture for much of the first half of the nineteenth century: the depiction of wives in domestic or saintly poses was a common motif. As the period progressed, however, there was a tendency for such images to slide into excessive pathos. Landseer's depiction in 1837 of *The Old Shepherd's Chief Mourner* [93] is one example of a revelling in loss following sentimental attachment – in this case between a shepherd and his dog. Far from being considered excessively maudlin, the picture was singled out for gushing praise by art critic John Ruskin, who noted 'the convulsive clinging of the paws' of a dog in "utter hopelessness"'.[24]

Rousseau's influence was perhaps most strongly expressed in the Romantic concept of Nature. Landscapes were capable of reflecting and even promoting emotions which were required of a fashionable person of feeling. This trend already had a strong precedent. For much of this period, the Graveyard school of poets showed continued popularity. Although most of their works were produced in the early part of the eighteenth century, continued republication was evidence of their enduring attraction. Works such as Robert Blair's *The Grave*, Thomas Gray's *Elegy in a Country Churchyard* and James Hervey's *Meditations among the Tombs* revelled in the enjoyable melancholy that could be experienced by contemplation of death in appropriately gloomy surroundings. Edward Young's *Night Thoughts* – a remarkably popular

93] *The Old Shepherd's Chief Mourner* (1837), painting by Edwin Landseer. Landseer was a favourite Victorian painter, whose representation of the death of an old shepherd was hugely popular. It indicates a maudlin and perhaps overly sentimental attitude towards death that became common by the mid-nineteenth century.

devotional work during this period – became a seminal publication in this cult of largely secular sepulchral melancholy, despite Young's intention to convey an explicitly Christian message.[25] The value of natural surroundings to the expression of grief was expressed in its most significant fashion in the tomb erected for Rousseau following his death in 1778. The tomb, surrounded by poplars, was built on an island in a lake on a private estate at Ermenonville [94]. Girardin, the friend with whom Rousseau spent his last years, intended to build a monument appropriate to 'the friend of nature and truth'. Although the 'natural' features surrounding the tomb were quite painstakingly reconstructed by landscape designers, the island and its tomb were celebrated by thousands of pilgrims who enjoyed its melancholy. There are reports of one Englishman actually swimming the lake in order to weep at the tomb. Girardin was finally compelled to restrict access to the island, which was in danger of becoming little more than a tourist attraction.[26] The consideration of what might be considered appropriate surroundings for the expression of grief fed into the design of new cemeteries in Britain from the 1820s.

One almost inevitable outcome of a passion for melancholy was the Romantic obsession with suicide. Genius and suicide – or, at the very least an early and tragic death from natural causes – were closely associated in literary circles. This trend was driven by two principal exemplars: Goethe's enormously popular hero, Werther; and the death of the young poet Thomas Chatterton. Werther, the hero of *Young Werther* (1774), chronicles the emotional turmoil of a sensitive young man who is driven to suicide by, amongst other things, an unhappy love affair. *Werther* caused a sensation in England, with foppish young men affecting sensitivity and even dressing in the characteristic Werther style of blue tailcoats and yellow waistcoats. Suicide became fashionable, and it was recorded that one such 'New Werther' prepared himself by opening his copy of the book to the appropriate page and being sure of an audience before shooting himself through his right eye.[27] The suicide of Thomas Chatterton in 1770 also caused a sensation, and by the beginning of the nineteenth century he was being heralded as the poet with the most supreme Romantic death. Chatterton's poetry was of small consequence measured against the manner of his demise at the age of seventeen by taking arsenic. His body was found surrounded by his manuscripts, torn into minute fragments. The vivid portrayal by Henry Wallis in 1856 demonstrates the poet's lingering influence [**plate 14**]. The passion for suicide was caricatured by a satire in the periodical *Bentley's Miscellany* in 1839. The 'London Suicide Company' offered its shareholders all assistance in hastening their departure: the services of John Ketch, the hangman, are promised to

94] Rousseau's tomb at Ermenonville (*c.* 1780–85), monument designed by Hubert Robert and sculpted by Le Sueur. The great Romantic philosopher was buried in a tomb surrounded by poplars on an island in a private estate. This was a fitting end for a philosopher whose works exhorted the union of people and nature. By the 1820s in Britain, greater consideration was being given to appropriate surroundings for grief, as was evident in attention given to new cemetery design.

> instruct such shareholders as shall be desirous in the easiest and most elegant way of tying themselves up. The proprietors of Vauxhall Gardens have proffered the use of their extensive grounds for the exercise of their part of the Company's business; and the Directors will, at their own expense, throw open a view of the Penitentiary at Millbank, for the purposes of deepening the gloomy feelings of such of the subscribers who may not have completely made up their minds.[28]

Thus Romanticism popularised the obsession with suicide as a fashionable indicator of sensitivity and feeling, a theme which by the end of the period was open to parody.

The stress placed on family and sentimental love during the Romantic period also found echoes in changing attitudes towards the nature of Heaven.[29] Images of Heaven increasingly lost their stress on an eternity of worship in the presence of God. Rather, Heaven became a place where lovers and families reunite, giving rise to the sombre Victorian cliché – 'Not lost, but gone before'. For the afterlife to be meaningful, love must continue after death. This is a theme that appears in art, producing erotic images of dead and romantic lovers, and is also common throughout much of the literature of the period. Goethe's

95] *Epitome of Hervey's 'Meditation among the Tombs'* (c. 1820–25), by William Blake. Blake's representation of Heaven – in an illustration from a popular work of the 'Graveyard' school of poets – contradicts earlier theology that death saw an end to earthly union. Blake's Heaven is a return to the embrace of families and lovers.

Werther dies in order to be with his lover Charlotte; and Rousseau's heroine, Julie, dies before her lover, claiming 'I do not leave you – I go to await you'. Perhaps its most extreme expression lies in the desire of *Wuthering Heights'* Heathcliffe to be buried with Cathy, so time can dissolve their bones into an eternal embrace.[30] Where he chose to depict the afterlife, the paintings of William Blake are dominated by the theme of reunion. In his *Epitome of Hervey's 'Meditation among the Tombs'*, produced in the early 1820s [95], Blake consciously rejects Hervey's assumption of a severing of earthly connections at death. In his Heaven, Blake envisages joyous meetings between children and their parents, and husbands and wives. This picture of Heaven offered no challenge to the respite from death's terror that had been offered by enlightened thought.

However, new images of Hell that were common to some Evangelical preachers could undermine optimism and revisited a fear of hell-fire and damnation. This sort of preaching checked – albeit temporarily – the passage towards more benign views of the afterlife that were to re-emerge in the second half of the nineteenth century. The nature of the relationship between Romanticism and Evangelicalism – a new religious fervour which became increasingly potent from the end of the eighteenth century – is not always clear. It is certain, however, that Evangelicalism, like Romanticism, placed a stress on individual experience. Evangelicalism considered that everyone was an heir to the sins of Adam, and each would spend an eternity in Hell unless they experienced a personal conversion.[31] For many Evangelical preachers, alluding to the pains of Hell was a certain way to provoke such a conversion. For example, John Leifchild of the Craven Congregational Church was famed for his depictions of the torments of Hell 'as realistically as the sufferings of a convict stretched on a rack by a human torturer'.[32]

Children were not protected from this rhetoric. In *Jane Eyre*, Charlotte Brontë, with the character of Mr Brocklehurst, parodies the use of Hell to control errant children. However, the infant Jane is too sharp for Brocklehurst and declares that she will avoid falling into a pit of flames and burning there forever by keeping in good health, and not dying.[33] The torrid deathbed agonies of the sinful, who were certain to spend eternity in Hell, were common moral fare through much of the first half of the nineteenth century. However, by the 1850s, an increasing unease was attached to preaching eternal punishment, and debate began in attempts to explain away the precept.[34]

Death counted and the dead contained

The first half of the nineteenth century saw the beginning of trends that were to secularise death further, re-creating death as a statistical and disposal issue that was considered more appropriately the responsibility of local government authorities. By the end of the period the Church had lost its virtual monopoly in providing accommodation for the dead. The reasons for this were varied, but one key factor was the massive growth in population which meant that in urban areas traditional places of burial were simply unable to cope with the increasing numbers of the dead. This section will explore population and mortality in the period, and describe the inadequacy of traditional modes of burial. The chapter will then discuss the emergence of a new response to this problem: the development of large-scale extra-mural (out of town) cemeteries, which introduced a secular option for the burial of the dead.

The Registration Act 1836 established the General Register Office, which oversaw the compulsory notification of deaths. These statistics were collated and presented with information on births and marriages in an abstract annually laid before Parliament. This counting of the dead by the state was the beginning of a process that would eventually re-create dealing with death as a municipal and medical function, increasingly hidden from the general population. Although steady population growth had been a feature of British society for centuries before the middle of the eighteenth century, the decades from 1760 to 1850 saw startling increases especially in urban areas. Between 1741 and 1801, the population of England and Wales rose from 6 to 8.9 million, and the following half-century saw the growth accelerating to 17.9 million. In 1801 only 20 per cent of the population lived in towns with more than 5,000 residents. By 1851, this proportion had reached 54 per cent. Indeed, ten towns in excess of 10,000 residents were accommodating around a quarter of the population of England and Wales.[35] Historians are generally undecided as to the key factors underlying population growth during this period, but most recent studies have tended to highlight increased fertility rates. Although house building for the middling and upper classes of society kept pace with the expansion, there was a lack of affordable accommodation for the poor. Chronic overcrowding was inevitable, as was the rapid spread of disease. A great deal could be said about the causes of death during this period, but this section will discuss two features: the high incidence of death amongst babies and children; and the prevalence of epidemic disease.

The sentimentality attached to the death of children was a poignant one, given the high death rate amongst babies and infants for much of the nineteenth century. Rowlandson, in his series of sketches, *The Dance of Death*, which were drawn during 1814–16, includes 'Death' visiting a large family, where children cluster around a meal table whilst their mother suckles a further child. Death, in an attached couplet, says ''Twere well to spare me two or three/Out of your num'rous family' [96].[36] Edwin Chadwick, using mortality figures from nine different locations in 1840, calculated that in these places on average one in five children of the gentry and professional persons had died. There was substantial variation, with death rates higher for poor children and children in the northern industrial cities. For the children of labourers, artisans and servants, Chadwick's death figure was one dead in two.[37]

96] *The Family of Children* (1814–16), by Thomas Rowlandson. High fertility and high mortality rates amongst children were a marked feature of population change during the first half of the nineteenth century, as underlined in this watercolour from Rowlandson's *The Dance of Death* series from 1814–16.

Amongst the poor, the causes of death amongst the very young were frequently connected with malnutrition, often caused by exhausted and themselves malnourished mothers, and an upbringing in cold, germ-ridden environments.

Accounts of epidemic disease in the first half of the nineteenth century tend to be dominated by discussion of the cholera epidemics of 1831–32 and 1848–49. These epidemics struck intensely and violently, resulting in 32,000 deaths in the earlier and 62,000 in the later episode. Cholera inspired panic because of the very suddenness with which it appeared and spread. Apparently healthy people could contract the disease and be dead within a matter of hours, as reported in the *Methodist Magazine* in 1832:

> To see a number of our fellow creatures, in a good state of health, in the full possession of their wonted strength, and in the midst of their years, suddenly seized with the most violent spasms, and in a few hours cast into the tomb, is calculated to shake the firmest nerves, and to inspire dread in the stoutest heart.[38]

Similarly, James Kay-Shuttleworth, as Secretary to the Manchester Board of Health, reported the death from the disease of an Irish labourer living in a two-roomed house with his wife and three children. The body was removed from the house, and the wife and children taken to hospital, none with symptoms of cholera. Within hours they all began

St Mary's Burial Ground

St Mary's churchyard

Holy Trinity churchyard
Independent Chapel
Holy Trinity Burial Ground

Wesleyan Chapel

97] *Kingston-upon-Hull and the Environs* (1842). Burial could be a gruesome and inescapable feature of urban life. During the 1830s and 1840s in Hull, the burial grounds and vaults marked on the map comprised the inadequate destination of more than a thousand bodies a year.

to show signs of the disease, and within the day 'the whole family was extinct'.[39] Although cholera appeared to strike in a particularly severe and intensive way, it was by no means a major cause of death during this period. Indeed, statistics indicate that none of the years in which cholera epidemics struck between 1760 and 1850 were above average in terms of national mortality rates. Cholera, although intensive, was highly localised. Taking a wider, national view, the biggest 'crisis years' for high mortality were at the very beginning of the period in 1762–63 when the death rate was 24 per cent above average, as a consequence of a raging influenza epidemic. Influenza was to strike significantly four more times in the period, in each case increasing the average death rate by at least 10 per cent.[40]

Growth in population had one inevitable consequence: whatever the cause of death the disposal of the dead was a necessary task, the dimensions of which were also increasing at a rapid rate. In 1760–64, the number of deaths in England was around 885,000. By the end of the century, the number of deaths counted in five-year periods consistently totalled well over a million, and by 1845–49, deaths per five years had reached 1,900,000.[41] Since the eighth century, the dead had traditionally been accommodated in local churchyards, later and modestly supplemented by private grounds, family vaults and Nonconformist graveyards. By the beginning of the nineteenth century, it was clear that this provision was under severe pressure, and evidence grew of the inadequacies of burial grounds to accommodate the newly massing dead.

For example, a report sent by James Smith to the General Board of Health in 1850 detailing the sanitary condition of Hull contained an appendix showing what effect the pressure of population had exerted on the town's graveyards [97]. Hull was largely reliant on the Holy Trinity Burial Ground at Dock Green, situated in the heart of the town. The 3-acre ground had been opened relatively recently – in 1783 – and still had space for burial. The interment of cholera victims in the ground and its proximity to the most heavily populated areas of the town were felt to be cause for alarm, however, because of the supposedly detrimental effects of graveyard 'miasmas'. The parish of St Mary's also had a burial ground of half an acre, located on Trippet Street, again a densely housed neighbourhood. The Holy Trinity Church, at the Market Place, also had a burial ground attached, of nearly 1.5 acres. This ground had been in use since about 1300, and was so full that its surface was well above the level of the street. The St Mary's churchyard was in a similar condition. The St James Church on Mytongate had only a limited graveyard around it, but burial vaults beneath the church had accommodation for over five thousand coffins. Vaults were also available at the Wesleyan Chapel on Humber Street, and the Independent Chapel on Fish Street, again in the centre of town. These burial places accommodated almost all the deaths in the town, which between 1838 and 1845 averaged 1,136 a year.[42] Hull was not distinctive in having unsatisfactory burial places; the situation was true of the majority of towns in Britain. In the memorable words of Dickens, in *Nicholas Nickleby*, the dead 'lay cheek by jowl with life; no deeper down than the feet of the throng that passed there every day, and piled high as their throats'.[43]

For much of the period, tolerance for poor burial conditions was remarkably high. However, from the end of the 1830s, the situation changed, and a radical occurrence broke the habit of finding this overcrowding acceptable. Credit for this change is due to the work of Dr George Alfred Walker. Walker's *Gatherings from Graveyards* (1839) treated its readership to an exposé of burial conditions of such force that it transformed the language then used to describe graveyards, and allowed an almost Gothic relish of the worst conditions which accelerated demand for change. *Gatherings* contained a history of burial, gave examples of the public health consequences of overcrowded graveyards and offered descriptions of a selection of the burial grounds in London. What was radical about Walker's approach was the language used. All his medical case studies were drawn out with sickening detail, and his descriptions of conditions in graveyards dwelt unremittingly on stench and gore. For example, in describing a graveyard in Southwark, Walker noted that

> a body partly decomposed was dug up and placed on the surface, at the side slightly covered with earth; a mourner stepped upon it, and the loosened skin peeled off, he slipped forward and had nearly fallen into the grave.[44]

Although his writing was at times melodramatic, Walker's conclusions were rarely questioned. Periodicals and provincial newspapers reproduced extracts from his work, and the *Lancet*, itself publishing corroborating stories and articles, declared that Walker had 'succeeded in awakening an unusual degree of public attention to the subject of intramural [inner city] interments'.[45]

Ecclesiastical authorities proved unwilling to establish new burial sites on a scale sufficient to deal with the problem. Fortunately, the power of provincial Nonconformity coupled with a typically nineteenth-century approach to finance had set a precedent. Cemetery companies had been growing in popularity since their first establishment in the early 1820s. These laid out cemeteries financed through the sale of shares, and had proved to be a successful response by Dissenters to their own growing congregations and the unwillingness to submit to burial in churchyards according to Church of England tenets. By the 1830s, the innovation had become attractive to speculators who were particularly successful in London, laying out cemeteries such as Highgate, Nunhead and West Norwood. By the 1840s, galvanised by Walker's purple prose, communities could use the sale of shares to secure for themselves adequate burial space in which sanitary principles could be applied.

In many of the new cemeteries the concern was expressed to make burial affordable. The sanitary reformer Edwin Chadwick had stressed that the key to the interment problem was the inability of the poorer classes to afford quick and hygienic interment, away from the heart of the city. Thus many of the public health cemetery companies offered to the poorer classes burial at cost. Board of Health inspectors generally found that these companies were doing 'good service' in offering sanitary burial 'at moderate charges', successfully drawing burials away from the overcrowded town churchyards. Hull's new cemetery, opened in 1846, drew particular praise from the inspectors, as providing 'ample accommodation, with every necessary precaution as to the public health, and at moderate charges, for the interment of the dead in the town of Hull'[46] [**plate 15**]. By 1850, the dead were becoming contained. A series of Burial Acts, established through the 1850s, built on the success of the cemetery companies by permitting the establishment of Burial Boards. These new local agencies had the powers to raise funds through the rates to finance cemeteries and, crucially, to apply for the closure of insalubrious churchyards. The Church's virtual monopoly on provision for the dead had been irredeemably shattered.[47]

Respectability, ritual and class divisions

Previous chapters have demonstrated that the ritual attached to death has frequently been used as a medium to display worth and status. During the late eighteenth and early nineteenth centuries, two factors contributed to the growth and intensification of the attachment of such symbolism to funerals. The period saw the expansion in size and confidence of a self-conscious middle class, eager to demonstrate its importance; and the concomitant growth and increased commercialism of the undertaking trade which both met and fed demand for elaborate funerary display. Relatively high levels of spending on funerals were not restricted to families of the middling classes. The poor also endeavoured to give an appropriate funeral to their loved ones, and so avoid the stigma of death on the parish. This tendency was given a significant fillip by the passage of the Anatomy Act 1832, which decreed that the bodies of unclaimed paupers could be given to medical science for anatomical purposes.[48]

The filtering down the classes of aristocratic funerary rituals had been taking place at least since the seventeenth century. Industrialisation and a tremendous energy poured into commercial activity brought increased wealth to the middle classes. The drive to acquire riches was matched in its passion by the wish for social advancement, or at the very least to be considered 'respectable'.[49] Death was an event which could demonstrate respectability on a number of levels: it was a vehicle for affirming gentility through the correct adherence to mourning etiquette; the funeral could reinforce an individual and family's place in society; and expenditure on funerary materials comprised conspicuous consumption indicating financial worth.[50] Commentators during the early part of the eighteenth century had been critical of the middle-class affectation of status through the purchase of mourning dress. The late eighteenth and early nineteenth centuries saw no diminution in this trend, and indeed, as cloth suitable for mourning wear became cheaper and more readily available, the custom spread. There was a wish to be in tune with Court customs on the issue of mourning, which occasioned hurried letters between family members in London and in the provinces requiring exact detail on the current mourning fashions. The spread of fashion magazines during the course of the nineteenth century meant that such information was more readily available, and probably contributed to the regulation of mourning etiquette that was to create anxiety on its exacting niceties for much of the nineteenth century.[51] The supremacy of mourning dress during this period was demonstrated by the death of Princess Charlotte in 1817, which pitched the entire nation into black in a gloomy precursor of the widespread mourning that was to follow the death of Prince Albert.

Funerary ritual proved an admirable medium through which individuals and families could demonstrate their place in society. It was increasingly the case through the nineteenth century that death in certain communities would elicit a significant turnout from neighbours and colleagues, in forming part of the procession and lining the streets of the procession route. In part, such display denoted solidarity. The funeral of a trade-union member was often met with a high attendance from fellow union members. For example, the death of a linen operative in 1834 was reported in the trade-union newspaper the *Pioneer* as consisting of 1,500 marchers, all wearing rosettes and carrying union insignia – 'How elated did every spectator appear, and with what amazement did they gaze upon the whole movement.'[52] Similarly, funerals of middle-class civic worthies were often heavily attended with a strong contingent of peers of the deceased in the actual procession, and with turnout from the more general population acting as an indicator of civic worth.[53]

The increased professionalisation of undertaking fed the demand for funerary display that was appropriate to the actual, and in cases aspired-for, status of the deceased. By the second quarter of the nineteenth century, undertaking was becoming a highly competitive activity – an indicator perhaps of its profitability. In the 1843 London Post Office Directory, 640 businessmen advertised undertaking services, which largely comprised arranging delivery of the vast range of services required for funerals at that time.[54] New technical processes permitted the reproduction of coffin furniture on a large scale: from 1770, metalworkers in Birmingham were producing coffin plates and handles for wholesale purchase. Thus funerals, even for the middling classes, could be an elaborate affair, as demonstrated by the account of the funeral of a Mrs Sarah Hurlin in 1839, as recalled by her grandson in 1908:

On the day of the funeral, an hour before it occurred, the two men called 'mutes' took their places outside the front door, one on each side of it. They were dressed in black, and had a black silk sash over one shoulder, and

98] *The Dance of Death, c.* 1814–16, by Thomas Rowlandson. Elaborate funerary ritual was a feature of the first half of the nineteenth century, as Rowlandson's satire on a funeral cortège from *The Dance of Death* demonstrates. Death is shown carrying a lid of feathers. This image contrasts with the lack of death ritual afforded poorer members of society (see [**99**]).

across the breast low down on the other side. Each had a broad black silk band on his hat with the ends of it, about 18 inches long, hanging down behind. In the hand furthest from the door, they each held a black staff about four and a half feet long, with a cross piece about a foot long on top of it, over which was laid a piece of black silk about eight feet long, which was bound close to the staff about two feet from the top, and its folds hung loose about two feet lower.

When the mourners were assembled, the undertaker dressed them, the men in long black cloth coats and black gloves, and a broad black crepe band around their hats, the ends of which hung down about 18 inches; and the women in a long black scarf with a hood attached to it which covered their heads, and also with black gloves.[55]

The funeral procession itself comprised the undertaker followed by the mutes, a man carrying a board of black ostrich feathers, the hearse, also decorated with ostrich feathers, mourning coaches and various black-clad attendants. Rowlandson satirises a funeral cortège of *c.* 1814–16, complete with its large numbers of attendants and tray of ostrich feathers – an invention of undertakers during this period [**98**]. Dickens parodied the elaborate nature of such ritual in *Martin Chuzzlewit*, describing the funeral of old Mr Chuzzlewit. Mr Mould the undertaker is delighted to find that the 'affectionate regret' of Chuzzlewit's son has 'positively NO limitation':

> I have orders, sir, to put on my whole establishment of mutes; and mutes come very dear . . . not to mention their drink. To provide silver plated handles of the very best description, ornamented with angel heads from the most expensive dies. To be perfectly profuse in feathers. In short, sir, to turn out something absolutely gorgeous.[56]

This level of display constituted what might be considered a 'respectable' funeral, and its elements were reproduced still further down the social class. For 2d. a week, burial societies assured members of an elm coffin decorated with two rows of black japanned nails, coffin plate and handles, a velvet pall, three gentleman's cloaks, hatbands, hoods and scarves, six pairs of gloves, two porters and an attendant.[57]

By contrast, during this period, the funeral of the pauper reached levels of degradation deliberately calculated to contribute to the 'less eligibility' ethos of poor relief, whereby assistance would be so unpleasant and humiliating that the poor would be discouraged from applying. Paupers had always been afforded a funeral 'on the parish'. In some areas, these funerals – even up to the early nineteenth century – bore some resemblance to the rituals attending other members of the community. Thus, for example, the death of a poor, unknown deaf-mute in custody in Oxford in 1775 met with the civic response of a burial in the churchyard, with the coffin carried by bearer, refreshment for those involved and a peal of the bells.[58] As the period progressed, however, the punitive nature of poor relief removed such niceties. Poor-law unions ordered pauper coffins – of deliberately cheap and inferior quality – and in some cases enforced use of a pall marked 'pauper'. Dickens again gives perhaps the best flavour of a pauper funeral in *Oliver Twist*. Mr Sowerberry the undertaker arranges the funeral of a poor woman on the parish. In this case, the mourning dress is 'an old black cloak' lent to the husband and mother of the deceased woman by the undertaker, and smartly removed immediately after the burial; the funeral procession includes the bare coffin, carried by bearers recruited from the workhouse, and is completed at trotting pace; and burial itself takes place in an 'obscure corner of the churchyard where the nettles grew', after a delay of an hour during which time the mourners sat in drizzle whilst local boys 'played a noisy game of hide and seek among the tombstones, or varied their amusements by jumping backwards and forwards over the coffin'.[59]

In 1832, a further level of degradation was added to the pauper funeral, with the introduction of Warburton's Anatomy Act. The Act was passed following the scandal that was increasingly attached to the activity of body-snatchers, who stole cadavers for sale to anatomy schools. Although there are no statistics on the incidence of bodies stolen, there was clearly a public perception that body-snatching was a frequent occurrence. The insecurity felt by communities when faced with the threat of body-snatching or 'resurrectionist' activity was reflected in increased attention to the security of the corpse. Double and triple coffins were popular during this period, as were a range of gadgets designed to prevent the levering off of the coffin lid.[60]

It is important to understand the strength of feeling that was connected to the notion of a body being taken for dissection. Generally, anxiety was expressed on three counts. First, the dissection of the corpse was held to have serious consequences for the spiritual state of the dissected. Christian belief in the physical resurrection of the whole body after death was still commonplace, and the dismemberment of the corpse was thought to be detrimental to this process. Such belief was supplemented by more indefinable solicitude for the corpse, deeply rooted in folklore.[61] The activities of resurrection men in dragging corpses out from their coffins by ropes around their neck was enough in itself to violate this feeling, even without dissection taking place. Second, dissection was associated with the worst crimes. Without recourse to body-snatchers, anatomists could only make use of the corpses of executed felons, and dissection was often specified as part of the punishment. The final source of anxiety about disinterment and dissection was occasioned by its sexual connotations. The notion of the body of a mother, sister or wife 'subjected to the gaze of lads learning to use the incision knife' was deeply harrowing, with dissection being thought akin to sexual assault.[62] A number of ineffectual attempts were made by reformers to dispel the fear of anatomical treatments after death. Perhaps the most notable example was the dissection and display of the remains of Jeremy Bentham, the philosopher of Utilitarianism, following his death in 1832.[63] Bentham's carefully dressed and posed cadaver is still open to view in a cabinet at University College, London.

Warburton's Anatomy Act was intended to remove the general fear of body-snatching activity, by ensuring an alternative supply of cadavers: the unclaimed bodies of paupers dying in hospitals and workhouses. The act was successful in undermining the profitability of body-snatching, but its consequence in cultural terms was an intensification in the fear of death on the parish. An illustration from *Punch* in 1845 shows death as *The Poor Man's Friend* – an old man praying to die so that he does not end his days in the workhouse, with his body given to anatomists after his demise [99]. One response to this fear was the use of burial clubs and societies, which proliferated during this period. These clubs attracted the attention of the sanitary reformer Edwin Chadwick, who detailed many aspects of burial and the funeral business in his report *Interment in Towns* published in 1843. Chadwick noted that the clubs were often run by undertakers or publicans on sometimes quite an arbitrary basis, with weekly contributions anywhere between one-half and two pence a week. It was reckoned that between six and eight million pounds were held in various burial clubs.[64] This was a trend that did not abate over the nineteenth century: by 1897 burial-club membership had reached 4.3 million.[65] The operation of the

99] *The Poor Man's Friend* (1845). Illustration from *Punch*. Death on the parish – passing without ritual and with the prospect of dissection by anatomists – led many poor people to save in burial clubs or, as in this sketch from *Punch* in 1845, to pray that death took place before they would have to move into the workhouse.

Anatomy Act continued to be felt as the ultimate indignity afforded to the poor, whose funerals on the parish were a deliberately inverted reflection of 'respectable' ritual. Perhaps at no time in the modern period has the contrast been so marked between the death of the rich and the death of the poor: as the middle classes purchased often massive memorials to mark the passage of their loved ones, the poor were deprived even of a body over which to mourn.

The Gothic Revival: looking back to Christian death

Much of this chapter has demonstrated the way in which secularity took hold on the experience of death in the late eighteenth and early nineteenth centuries. That this shift had taken place was not lost on contemporary commentators. In the last decade of this period, moves were afoot to reclaim death for the Church. One of the more active publications in this arena was *The Ecclesiologist*, which frequently published articles on funerary practice, offering recommendations for change that would encompass a renewed stress on Church ritual.[66] For example, in 1845, *The Ecclesiologist* set out its ideals for cemeteries and cemetery chapels. It was considered that the chapel should be fitted for the celebration of Communion, a ritual that *The Ecclesiologist* writer considered essential to the burial service. The cemetery entrance should comprise a lichgate 'of unusual size and elaboration', decorated with sculptured figures. In particular, 'scrupulous care must be taken to exclude all allusion to heathen rites or heathen notions'.[67]

For the most part, these moves had symbolic and aesthetic rather than legislative consequences. The particular high-minded religious seriousness that characterised the mid-Victorian period had its most eloquent expression in Gothic style. The Gothic Revival looked back to an idealised medieval period, when spirituality was expressed in all aspects of civic life, and when the population showed a natural veneration for the Church. What was not revived in architecture and tomb sculpture, unsurprisingly, was the medieval representation of the macabre (Chapter 5). Instead, this suffused the literature of Gothic horror, as in Mary Shelley's *Frankenstein* (1818).[68]

The architect and designer Augustus Welby Pugin was a principal proponent of Gothic style, and was particularly critical of the way in which the experience of death was losing its spiritual nature. In

plate 17] *The Plains of Heaven* (1853), by John Martin. This amplifies the vision of Heaven in the Last Judgement. Jeremy Maas, *Victorian Painters* (1969) describes it as 'a paean of rapturous serenity with its Brucknerian mountains, translucent blue skies, langorous groups of seraphic damsels basking in forest glades'.

plate 18] *The Doubt: 'Can These Dry Bones Live?'* (1855), by Henry Alexander Bowler. This painting was intended to illustrate Alfred, lord Tennyson's great poem *In Memoriam*, depicting the struggle and ultimate triumph of faith over doubt concerning traditional Christian beliefs about life after death.

Contrasts, published in 1836, Pugin compares medieval practices with current fashions. His town of 1840 has replaced a graveyard with a 'pleasure ground'; and the poor – afforded a full burial service in the medieval period – were now bundled up for sale to students for dissection.[69] Pugin's *Apology for the Revival of Christian Architecture in England* of 1843 continued the critique, as he parodied the amalgam of Egyptian and neoclassical styles that were evident in the new cemeteries of the day.[70] By 1850, the popularity of Gothic style as an expression of Victorian spirituality was evident in cemetery building [**plate 15**] and individual monuments. Crosses, which for decades had been considered a popish symbol, re-emerged as a popular memorial type.[71]

Thus, the late eighteenth and early nineteenth centuries heralded changes that were to remain as components of the modern experience of death. The centrality of the Church was threatened by the incursion of secular imagery associated with death, and which endured for much of the nineteenth century. Doctors began to take the place of ministers as essential figures at middle-class deathbeds, and death increasingly became an individual, family experience, so minimising the involvement of the congregation or community. Professionals began to take a hold on death, both secularising and concealing its processes. Funerals began to be mass-produced, and disposal of the dead took on the flavour of a sanitary, public health measure. Towards the end of the period, criticism was made of the lack of spirituality in much of contemporary funerary practice. As the next chapter shows, the second half of the nineteenth century saw a heightened spirituality attached to death. However, this trend was only temporary: as Chapter 10 demonstrates, the move towards the secular remained the more constant long-term trend.

Notes

The author would like to thank Roger Bowdler for valuable discussions about late-eighteenth-century memorials. Thanks are also given to David Bebbington for essential guidance in key theological areas. In all references, place of publication is London unless othewise stated.

1 See, for example, R. Porter and R. Teich, *The Enlightenment in National Context* (Cambridge, 1981).
2 See, for example, Voltaire, *Lettres philosophiques ou Lettres anglaises* (1733).
3 H. Honour, *Neoclassicism* (Harmondsworth, 1991).
4 W. Buchan, *Domestic Medicine*, 22nd edn (1826), p. xxv.
5 D. Porter and R. Porter, *Patient's Progress: Doctors and Doctoring in Eighteenth Century England* (Cambridge, 1989), p. 151.
6 *Ibid.*, pp. 149–51.
7 D. Bindman, 'John Flaxman: art and commerce', in Bindman (ed.), *John Flaxman, RA* (1979).
8 J. Gascoigne, *Joseph Banks and the English Enlightenment* (Cambridge, 1994), p. 46.

9 See, for example, P. C. Almond, *Heaven and Hell in Enlightenment England* (Cambridge, 1994).

10 M. Whinney, *Sculpture in Britain 1530–1830* (Harmondsworth, 1964), p. 281.

11 Honour, *Neoclassicism*, p. 148.

12 Whinney, *Sculpture in Britain*, p. 176.

13 N. Penny, *Church Monuments in Romantic England* (New Haven, Conn., 1977), p. 29.

14 N. Llewellyn, *The Art of Death: Visual Culture in the English Death Ritual c. 1500–c. 1800* (1991).

15 Penny, *Church Monuments*.

16 D. Watkin, 'Monuments and mausolea in the Age of Enlightenment', in G. Waterfield (ed.), *Soane and Death* (1996).

17 H. von Effra and A. Stanley, *The Paintings of Benjamin West* (New Haven, Conn., 1986), p. 222.

18 D. Irwin, 'Sentiment and antiquity: European tombs 1750–1830', in J. Whaley (ed.), *Mirrors of Mortality* (1981), p. 134.

19 J. J. Rousseau, *The Confessions*, ed. J. M. Cohen (Harmondsworth, 1971), p. 17.

20 L. Stone, *The Family, Sex and Marriage in England 1500–1800* (Harmondsworth, 1979).

21 P. Ariès, *The Hour of our Death* (Harmondsworth, 1983).

22 Whinney, *Sculpture in Britain*, p. 179.

23 Penny, *Church Monuments*, p. 115.

24 C. Lennie, *Landseer, the Victorian Paragon* (1976), p. 91.

25 Edward Young, *Night Thoughts*, ed. S. Cornford (Cambridge, 1989). See also James Stevens Curl, 'Young's "Night Thoughts" and the origins of the garden cemetery', *Journal of Garden History*, 14:2 (1994), pp. 92–118.

26 R. Etlin, *The Architecture of Death* (Cambridge, Mass., 1984); J. McManners, *Death and the Enlightenment* (Oxford, 1981).

27 A. Alvaraz, *The Savage God* (Harmondsworth, 1979).

28 'The London Suicide Company', *Bentley's Miscellany*, VI (1839), p. 541.

29 C. McDannell and B. Lang, *Heaven: A History* (1988).

30 As discussed in Ariès, *Hour of Our Death*, pp. 442–6.

31 D. W. Bebbington, *Evangelicalism in Modern Britain: A History from the 1730s to the 1980s* (1989).

32 M. R. Watts, *The Dissenters*, vol. II (Oxford, 1985), p. 79.

33 C. Brontë, *Jane Eyre* (1847), chapter 4.

34 M. R. Watts, '"The hateful mystery": Nonconformists and Hell', *Journal of the United Reformed Church History Society*, 2:8 (1981), pp. 248–58.

35 A. S. Wohl, *Endangered Lives* (1983).

36 J. Baskett and D. Snelgrove, *The Drawings of Thomas Rowlandson in the Paul Mellon Collection* (1977), p. 32.

37 E. Chadwick, *Report on the Sanitary Conditions of the Labouring Population of Great Britain*, ed. M. W. Flynn (Edinburgh, 1965), p. 228.

38 As quoted in Wohl, *Endangered Lives*, p. 119.

39 J. Carey, *The Faber Book of Reportage* (1987), pp. 307–8.

40 E. A. Wrigley and R. S. Schofield, *The Population History of England: A Reconstruction* (1981), pp. 332–5.

41 *Ibid.*

42 J. Smith, *Report to the General Board of Health on a Preliminary Inquiry into the Sewerage, Drainage and Supply of Water, and the Sanitary Condition of the Town and Borough of Kingston upon Hull* (1850); G. Milner, *On Cemetery Burial: or Sepulture Ancient and Modern* (Hull, 1846).

43 C. Dickens, *Nicholas Nickleby* (1838–39), chapter 62.

44 G. A. Walker, *Gatherings from Graveyards* (1839), pp. 201–2.

45 *Lancet*, 1 (1840), 366.

46 Smith, *Report . . . on . . . Kingston upon Hull*.

47 J. Rugg, 'The emergence of early cemetery companies in Britain 1820–53', unpublished Ph.D. thesis, University of Stirling (1992).

48 R. Richardson, *Death, Dissection and the Destitute* (1987).
49 W. E. Houghton, *The Victorian Frame of Mind 1830–1870* (New Haven, Conn., 1976).
50 T. Laqueur, 'Bodies, death and pauper funerals', *Representations*, 1:1 (1983), pp. 109–31.
51 L. Taylor, *Mourning Dress: A Costume and Social History* (1983).
52 Laqueur, 'Bodies, death and pauper funerals', p. 117.
53 L. Davidoff and C. Hall, *Family Fortunes* (1987).
54 J. Reeve and M. Adams, *The Spitalfields Project*, vol. I: *The Archaeology: Across the Styx* (York, 1993).
55 *Ibid.*, p. 134.
56 C. Dickens, *Martin Chuzzlewit* (1843–44), chapter 19.
57 Laqueur, 'Bodies, death and pauper funerals'.
58 *Ibid.*
59 C. Dickens, *Oliver Twist* (1838–39), chapter 5.
60 Richardson, *Death, Dissection and the Destitute*.
61 See, for example, B. Puckle, *Funeral Customs: Their Origin and Development* (1926).
62 *The Times*, 9 December 1822.
63 Richardson, *Death, Dissection and the Destitute*, pp. 159–60.
64 E. Chadwick, *A Supplementary Report on the Results of a Special Enquiry into the Practice of Interment in Towns* (1843).
65 P. H. J. H. Gosden, *The Friendly Societies in England 1815–75* (Manchester, 1961).
66 G. Rowell, 'Nineteenth-century attitudes and practices', in G. Cope (ed.), *Dying, Death and Disposal* (1970).
67 *The Ecclesiologist*, January (1845), p. 10.
68 Irwin, 'Sentiment and antiquity', p. 141.
69 M. Belcher, 'Pugin writing', in P. Atterbury and C. Wainwright (eds), *Pugin: A Gothic Passion* (New Haven, Conn., 1994).
70 J. Morley, *Death, Heaven and the Victorians* (1971).
71 Rowell, 'Nineteenth-century attitudes'.

Select bibliography

Alvarez, A., *The Savage God*, Harmondsworth, 1979.
Ariès, P., *The Hour of Our Death*, Harmondsworth, 1983.
Chadwick, E., *A Supplementary Report on the Results of a Special Enquiry into the Practice of Interment in Towns*, 1843.
Honour, H., *Neoclassicism*, Harmondsworth, 1991.
Laqueur, T., 'Bodies, death and pauper funerals', *Representations*, 1:1 (1983), 109–31.
Llewellyn, N., *The Art of Death: Visual Culture in the English Death Ritual, c. 1500–c. 1800*, 1991.
McDannell, C., and Lang, B., *Heaven: A History*, 1988.
Penny, N., *Church Monuments in Romantic England*, New Haven, Conn., 1977.
Reeve, J., and Adams, M., *The Spitalfields Project*, vol. I: *The Archaeology: Across the Styx*, York, 1993.
Richardson, R., *Death, Dissection and the Destitute*, 1987.
Rowell, G., 'Nineteenth-century attitudes and practices', in G. Cope (ed.), *Dying, Death and Disposal*, 1970.
Rugg, J., 'A new burial form and its meanings; cemetery establishment in the first half of the nineteenth century', in M. Cox (ed.), *Grave Concerns: Death and Burial in England, 1700 to 1850*, York, 1998.
Stone, L., *The Family, Sex and Marriage in England 1500–1800*, Harmondsworth, 1979.
Taylor, L., *Mourning Dress: A Costume and Social History*, 1983.
Wrigley, E. A., and Schofield, R. S., *The Population History of England: A Reconstruction*, 1981.

9 · Pat Jalland

Victorian death and its decline: 1850–1918

This chapter examines the chief features of domestic death in Victorian England, its myths and its realities, and also analyses the major causes of significant change by 1918. An exploration of visual images of the Victorian way of death powerfully illuminates the cultural and spiritual chasm between the nineteenth century and the present. The most famous Victorian images of death and mourning may readily be misinterpreted or misunderstood by the modern viewer. This is true of Walton's *The Last Moment of HRH The Prince Consort*, Henry Peach Robinson's *Fading Away*, Henry Bowler's *The Doubt* and Luke Fildes's *The Doctor*, among other images discussed in this chapter.

This process of cultural change is well illustrated by the history of John Martin's astonishing trilogy portraying the Last Judgement, Heaven and Hell — subjects of profound significance in the mid-nineteenth century [**plates 16** and **17**]. The three vast paintings went on tours around British galleries for many years after Martin's death in 1854, creating an intense effect on spectators; as one impressed visitor remarked, 'all seemed to be carried away from worldly thoughts, and, as it were, intoxicated by the solemn, the lofty, and the majestic inspirations of the master mind of the great artist'.[1] By contrast, by the end of the century Martin's paintings hung neglected in Alexandra Palace, and were later stored until they were sold in 1935 for less than £7, at the low point of Martin's reputation. The trilogy now dominates one large wall of a gallery in the Tate, where visitors appear baffled and bemused rather than awed and inspired. Most visitors no longer comprehend the Victorian meanings ascribed to Heaven, Hell and the Last Judgement, so the paintings lose their original spiritual significance. As we shall see, the same process of cultural change has in various ways altered the meanings attributed to many important Victorian images of death. By studying these images in the nineteenth-century context we can learn much about the meaning of death for many Victorians.

The author of *The Victorian Celebration of Death* published in 1972 claimed that 'ostentatious displays of grief were very much required by Victorian Society'.[2] The familiar images of Queen Victoria in black

100] Queen Victoria at the wedding of Edward, Prince of Wales and Princess Alexandra, 1863. Two years after her husband's death, Victoria was still in full mourning. She chose to commemorate her eldest son's wedding by grouping her family around a bust of Albert while she showed her younger children pictures of their dead father.

widow's weeds have contributed to this misleading view of the Victorian way of death [100]. Victoria has been represented as the archetypal Victorian mourner, whose influence on nineteenth-century mourning behaviour was 'supreme'. The image of Queen Victoria as the eternal widow of Windsor has been so pervasive that she has been seen as representative rather than exceptional. One historian describes the Queen as 'the middle-class ideal of Christian widowhood' who turned her mourning for Albert 'into a cult which dominated most of the rest of her life. Her example was admired, respected and copied . . . by many Victorian ladies.'[3] Another argues that 'the excessive concentration of [Victorian] mourning . . . condemned [the bereaved] to spend their remaining years more obsessed with death than was either necessary or healthy – as exemplified most spectacularly in the case of Queen Victoria'.[4]

The Queen's influence on behaviour and attitudes to death and grief has been substantially overstated, though she certainly affected upper-class mourning and dress etiquette. Queen Victoria's practice of widowhood was neither widely admired nor highly respected, nor was it representative of her people in all their diversity. Her mother's death in March 1861 led to a 'nervous breakdown' precipitated by 'unremitting' grief and guilt. Only nine months later her beloved husband, Prince Albert, died suddenly of typhoid. Victoria mourned Albert as if he might return from the dead at any moment, leaving his rooms and belongings just as they were, with his clothes carefully laid out each day. At the age of forty-two she withdrew from public life, afraid that the combined pressure of grief and royal business would drive her insane. She mourned Albert for nearly two decades, rather than the two or three years which her subjects considered normal, while the press condemned her seclusion and neglect of royal duties. The campaign against her unnatural behaviour reached its climax eight years after her bereavement, followed by a slow recovery in the 1870s.[5]

Queen Victoria clearly suffered intensely for twelve years or more from prolonged depression, chronic grief, an obsessive preoccupation with her dead husband, persistent 'nervous' ill-health and numerous physical maladies. Even her doctor, Sir William Jenner, believed that 'these nerves are a form of madness', and those around her considered her mad or neurotic, rather than a role model for widowhood. Modern psychologists see Queen Victoria as a classic case of pathological chronic grief, which was probably more unusual among Victoria's subjects than it is today. Queen Victoria was an 'exemplar of chronic grief', criticised by her own subjects for her extreme behaviour, not the model widow nor the typical Victorian mourner.[6]

Characteristics of the Victorian way of death

EVANGELICAL CHRISTIANITY AND THE 'GOOD DEATH'

Religion played a powerful role in the lives of most middle- and upper-class Victorians, for whom church attendance was usually more than just a matter of convention; half the working classes still attended church in 1851. From the late eighteenth century the Evangelical movement strengthened Christianity in Britain through its part in the development of Methodism, while it also transformed the Church of England. Large elements of the population were affected by the Evangelical impulses of seriousness, piety, discipline and duty. Evangelicalism reached the peak of its social and spiritual dynamism and influence in the 1850s and 1860s, starting to decline from the 1870s. It has been called 'the religion of the heart', encouraging men as well as women to show the intensity of their grief on the deaths of loved ones by weeping together. Death evoked intense emotions, expressed through the art, literature and poetry of the Romantic movement which largely coincided with the Evangelical revival.[7]

The Evangelical movement had enormous influence on deathbed behaviour through its revival of the Christian ideal of the 'good death', which can be traced back to the medieval tradition of the *ars moriendi*, the Christian art of dying well. This ideal of the good Christian death was still exceptionally powerful in 1850 among the middle and upper classes; it was disseminated for popular moral instruction by Evangelical tracts and journals, which in turn influenced the depiction of deathbed scenes in Victorian art and fiction. The good death required piety and lifelong preparation, as well as fortitude in the face of physical suffering. It should take place in a good Christian home, surrounded by a loving and supportive family, with the dying person making explicit farewells to family members, comforted by the assurance of future family reunion in Heaven. There should be time, and physical and mental capacity, for the completion of temporal and spiritual business. The dying person should be conscious and lucid until the end, resigned to God's will, able to beg forgiveness for past sins and to prove worthy of salvation.

It was far more difficult in life, than in art or literature, to achieve the good Christian death, and it was almost impossible for the poor and the unbelievers. Realisation of the ideal varied enormously according to class, age, gender, disease, religion and family circumstances. Deathbed scenes in art were usually romanticised occasions which represented the Christian ideal rather than the historical reality. Two famous images of the Victorian deathbed are included here to illustrate the gulf between ideal and reality, and to show how Victorian images can mislead the modern viewer.

The well-known coloured lithograph of *The Last Moments of HRH The Prince Consort* by William Walton is a formal portrait depicting twenty-one people standing, sitting and kneeling around the bed of Prince Albert in 1861 [101]. The attendants, who appear to have been there for some considerable time, include Queen Victoria, the royal family, several politicians and the four doctors. But such a formal portrait of a royal deathbed scene gave a misleading impression of a large 'crowd' of onlookers and family participants, because royal births and deaths required statesmen and doctors as witnesses. Noble and bourgeois deathbeds had indeed been occasions of public ceremony in seventeenth-century France and England, but the custom of dying in public at the centre of a crowded scene had been abandoned by the nineteenth century. Victorian middle- and upper-class deathbed scenes were private family affairs which were usually limited to a very small number of members of the immediate family, together with a nurse or a servant and occasionally a doctor. Deathbed attendants usually increased in number for an hour or so only for the final farewells, the sacraments and sometimes for the last vigil; otherwise they were restricted to one or two people.

Walton's depiction of Prince Albert's death is also misleading because it is an idealised Christian death, with Albert looking surprisingly alert for a man in the 'last moments' of a sudden death from typhoid. The uninformed observer might assume that Albert had said his farewells to family, doctors and politicians, and completed his spiritual business.

101] *The Last Moments of HRH The Prince Consort* (1862), lithograph by William I. Walton. Prince Albert was dying of typhoid surrounded by a large cast of attendants appropriate to a royal deathbed, including politicians and doctors.

But in practice sudden deaths from rapid infectious diseases were seen as bad deaths for Christians in 1861, because they allowed no time for spiritual preparation and repentance. Fever of all kinds, including typhoid, struck terror into the families of the afflicted because they knew there was no cure, and it usually prevented meaningful final communications and farewells between the family and the sufferer.[8]

Henry Peach Robinson's *Fading Away* of 1858, is probably closer to historical reality but it can also mislead the modern viewer. It portrays a young woman dying of tuberculosis and was a very popular photograph at Victorian exhibitions [102]. It illustrates the way this dreadful death was romanticised by early- and mid-Victorian artists, including D. G. Rossetti, W. Holman Hunt, C. F. Watts and John Everett Millais. Works by these artists and, for example, Verdi's opera *La Traviata* depicted consumptives as young, beautiful, innocent and usually female. It seems paradoxical to us today that a disease which was a product of poverty, overcrowding and unsanitary conditions should have been idealised. Tuberculosis was a painful, debilitating disease which could neither be cured nor prevented until streptomycin was isolated in 1943. Poor working-class families did not romanticise this dreaded disease because they were too familiar with the painful reality of its debilitating effects. 'As a fundamental destructive social force it was rivalled among illnesses only by the venereal diseases and insanity.'[9]

102] *Fading Away* (1858), by Henry Peach Robinson. This was a popular print at exhibitions – a combination made from five negatives, depicting a young woman dying of tuberculosis.

Two reasons might be suggested for the Victorian idealisation of such a terrible disease. First, consumptives usually fitted the romantic stereotype because of their youth, and the disproportionate number of young women who were rendered delicate and emaciated by the wasting disease. Until 1865 many more young females than males died of pulmonary tuberculosis, leading to the pre-Raphaelite images of a disease which killed young, innocent and beautiful women. Second, slow consumptive deaths of young women were also sometimes idealised by Evangelical clergymen and doctors wishing to represent the 'Good Christian Death' as a blessing in disguise which allowed time and mental clarity for spiritual preparation. According to one clergyman, consumption encouraged 'the better traits of human character and develop(ed) the graces of the Christian life'.[10] But the vast majority of consumptive victims, especially those from poor families, would have shared the *Lancet's* opinion that the romantic view of tuberculosis 'seems to us as false as can well be'.[11]

HEAVEN, HELL AND REUNIONS THEREAFTER

For early- and mid-Victorian Christians, death and suffering were acts of divine providence to be accepted with submission as a test of their Christian faith. They were chiefly concerned about bad deaths in the spiritual sense of concern for the unrepentant or unprepared sinner judged at the moment of death and doomed to the eternal punishment of hellfire. Protestant theology was far tougher than that of Roman Catholics since it excluded the Catholic hope of Purgatory where the prayers of the living could slowly purify repentant sinners. Protestants had only two stark alternatives: God's judgement at death determined whether souls ascended to Heaven, or joined the majority of sinners to burn in Hell for all eternity.

The doctrines of Judgement and Hell provided preachers and theologians with abundant material for terrifying sermons on the horrors of eternal torment and the urgent need for repentance. They are spectacularly illustrated by John Martin's extraordinary trilogy of huge oil canvasses painted in the early 1850s, depicting the Last Judgement, Hell and Heaven, inspired by the Book of Revelation [**plates 16** and **17**].[12] *The Last Judgement* represents God sitting in judgement on the deceased, surrounded by twenty-four saints; the sinners who are damned appear in a lurid coloured Hell on the right, and the pious who are saved on *The Plains of Heaven* are on the left. The other two fantastic paintings of the trilogy amplify the panoramic visions of Hell and Heaven. Heaven is depicted as a celestial landscape in bright blues and golds, which was ridiculed by more progressive Protestants like the Congregationalist Revd James Baldwin Brown in 1885 as 'a restful and self-centred vision of immortality' with its selfish souls 'mooning on the mount'.[13] Despite unfavourable critical reviews, the grandeur of Martin's trilogy attracted awed and admiring crowds when it was first exhibited in London in 1854, when Judgement and Hell still held profound meaning for many.

Hell and Judgement were transformed in the minds of many more liberal Victorian Protestants between 1850 and 1918.[14] From the seventeenth century some theologians saw the concept of everlasting torment as incompatible with a just and loving God, and the doctrine of Hell was slowly eroded.[15] More progressive Victorian Protestants increasingly believed in some sort of intermediate state, where spiritual progress was possible before the Last Judgement, and interpreted Hell as meaning the absence of God.

Heaven was also transformed, though the traditional view of Heaven as a static, peaceful place of eternal worship of God was still strongly held by Anglicans and Catholics. Their vision of Heaven as 'unspeakable bliss', depicted in *The Plains of Heaven*, was ridiculed by more liberal Protestants who placed increasing emphasis on two quite different concepts of Heaven. One was a progressive view of Heaven as a place of dynamic progress and 'fruitful sunlit activity', where the Victorian work ethic could extend to the afterlife. Ideas of this sort were largely confined to more progressive Nonconformist clergymen who preached to unenthusiastic congregations. Far more popular (see Chapter 8) was the idea of Heaven as a happy home where earthly families would be reunited. It was increasingly taken for granted that Christian families would meet again in the next life, without the earlier Victorian need to justify salvation by a detailed account of a pious earthly life.

The concepts of heavenly love and marriage were increasingly con-doned by clergymen like William Branks, who argued in *Heaven our Home* in 1861 that personal recognition of family in Heaven would be combined with continuing affection for those remaining on earth. Branks described Heaven as 'a home with a great and happy and loving family in it'.[16]

'As Hell ceased to be a fiery furnace, Heaven became a cosy fireside where long-lost loved ones congregated.'[17] Family condolence letters show that the primary consolation on the death of a loved one was the expectation of family reunion in Heaven, without too many details of the precise nature of Heaven. As Emma Lee noted on the death of her friend's father in 1870, 'It takes away all the mystery and horror of the grave, to think that when we die we shall only pass from the loving hearts and arms here, to the arms of those who have gone before us'.[18] The central consolation offered to Christians in the late nineteenth century was the concept of immortality in an afterlife shared with God and also with the beloved earthly family 'gone before'.

THE DEATHS OF BABIES AND CHILDREN

The statistics for infant mortality record a grim story of a high death rate throughout the nineteenth century, with little change until after 1900. Since one-quarter of all nineteenth-century deaths were of in-fants dying before their first birthday, every mother had to face the possibility that at least one child would die at birth or soon after. The death rate in England and Wales per 1,000 live births for infants under one year varied remarkably little up to 1900, standing at 154 in 1840 as well as in 1900. All classes were affected by the high mortality rate for infants and children, but poor working-class children in large indus-trial cities such as Liverpool and Manchester suffered most.[19] The turn-ing point in this appalling child mortality rate was not reached until the first decade of the twentieth century when a slow decline in the death rate began, largely caused by the dramatic reduction in deaths from infectious diseases, which mainly affected the young.[20]

It is sometimes argued that parents in earlier centuries limited their emotional investment in young children because of high infant mortal-ity, allowing them to accept their losses more easily than we do today.[21] High child mortality rates did not necessarily result in reduced parental affection. A recent historian finds little change in levels of affection between parents and children in England and America between 1500 and 1900.[22] My own research into family archives in Britain between 1830 and 1920 supports the argument that most parents were dis-tressed and anxious at the illnesses and deaths of their children, re-gardless of their expectations for their survival. Most Victorian parents did not feel that several remaining children would compensate for the loss of any one, however alarming the child mortality statistics.

The deaths of babies and children were devastating for parents and almost impossible to explain in Christian or any other terms.

The churches produced a mass of consolation literature attempting to explain the meaning of such deaths in Christian terms, showing why a just God would allow innocent children to die so young.[23] The tracts insisted that children's deaths were a spiritual trial intended to teach parents the lesson of submission to God's will, and that a benevolent God had removed these children early from an unhappy world of pain, sin and temptation. These sentiments were repeated hundreds of times in condolence letters by grieving families, carrying varying degrees of conviction and comfort.

Above all, the belief in family reunions with the lost children in Heaven gave some meaning to otherwise futile premature deaths. Many Christian parents found their dominant source of consolation in the belief that 'we have one of our own in heaven, ready to welcome us when we are there'.[24] One consolation tract reassured parents of the Bible's revelation that 'your dear child is now a glorious, happy spirit . . . in heaven'.[25] The anonymous mother who wrote *Comfort for Bereaved Mothers* in 1863 after the loss of her own three children, assured her readers that 'there would be a blessed and glorious reunion in a brighter and happier world . . . Each and every member of many dear families will be there, all safely gathered.'[26] These comforting concepts were often represented in such magazines as *Sunday at Home* and *The Children's Friend* by images of 'the angel of death' carrying off a sleeping child to a happier existence in Heaven.

A plethora of Victorian children's literature on the subject of death served two major purposes. The Evangelical didactic aim was 'to frighten the young reader or listener into good behaviour, "to edify by recording pious deaths"'. These stories taught children that since death was omnipresent and could wipe out entire families, they must always be prepared for it.[27] But the stories might also help to reduce children's fears by their emphasis on death as the entry to a happier life in Heaven where they might join beloved siblings 'gone before'. Bible stories and children's literature on the subject of death could teach them to cope with death more readily among their own siblings or friends. Children regarded death as a fact of life, knowing that if one family member died from an infectious disease, others might well follow, including themselves.

Children were expected to participate in the process of death and grief, if they were considered old enough to understand. Children of all classes were often taken by their parents to view the bodies of close family members, including siblings, except in infectious cases. A drawing [103] shows three working-class boys in 1857 taken by their mother to see their father's body in the family home in a coffin supported by wooden trestles. Occasionally siblings and young friends, dressed in white to symbolise innocence, would act as coffin-bearers at a child's funeral [104]. Children also frequently accompanied their parents on regular visits to the newly established cemetery to pray by the graves of their loved ones or simply to remember them (see Chapter 8).

103] *'Look, Bairn, at thy Father once more'*, *The British Workman*, 1857. Drawing by J. Knight. Three working-class boys taken by their mother in 1857 to see their father's body in a coffin supported by wooden trestles.

104] *Her First Born* (1876), by Frank Holl. Four young girls act as coffin-bearers at the funeral of a baby. White is the colour traditionally used at the burials of children.

Therapeutic medicine had a very limited power to cure disease before the advent of the sulphonamide drugs in the 1930s. The medicine of the Victorian general practitioner was not much more advanced than that of his predecessor two centuries earlier, because he had few effective medications.[28] Medicine could do little in the face of infectious diseases such as cholera, typhus and scarlet fever, as the doctors themselves understood only too well. Most working-class people could not afford doctors in any case, relying instead on druggists and 'sixpenny doctors' who were cheap but completely untrained, or self-medication with traditional herbal medicines. Despite the limitations on their scientific knowledge, Victorian doctors were highly regarded by the middle and upper classes, a paradox perhaps reflecting that the doctor's concern for the patient's personal life and general well-being varied inversely with his ability to cure.[29]

Yet Victorian doctors compensated for their limited power to cure with a remarkably good record of terminal care and palliative management. Victorian physicians such as William Munk may be seen as the forerunners of the modern hospice movement and have much to teach twentieth-century doctors about care of the dying. If the doctor could do little to cure disease, at least he could provide invaluable assistance in reducing the pain, discomfort and fear associated with dying. At times of death in the family, gratitude to the doctors far outweighed any criticism. When Dorothea Palmer was dying of tuberculosis in 1851 she thanked Dr Peter Latham for his 'care, kindness and attention . . . I quite love Dr Latham – he was like a father', even though he could not prevent her death.[30]

The best-known artistic representation of the Victorian medical profession at the deathbed is Sir Luke Fildes's famous 1891 painting in the Tate Gallery entitled *The Doctor* and described by *The Times* as 'the picture of the year' [**105**]. This was one of the most popular paintings by an English artist for many years, with copies hanging in countless homes and doctors' waiting-rooms. *The Doctor* can mislead the modern visitor to the Tate Gallery in several respects. Its setting in a poor fisherman's cottage on the Devonshire coast implicitly but inaccurately suggests that the working classes had ready access to benevolent physicians at their deathbeds. The little girl lies on pillows propped across two chairs, and appears to be dying peacefully, while the doctor sits close by her makeshift bed, having done all he could, and the weeping mother is comforted by her husband. The doctor appears compassionate and gentle but resigned as he maintains his long vigil in the face of approaching death. The painting was inspired by Fildes's gratitude for the devotion of the doctor who attended his own son Phillip while he died of an infectious disease in 1877. The Tate Gallery's present-day caption interprets the grey dawn light showing through the window as a symbol of hope for the child's survival; but this late-twentieth-century reading is in stark contrast to that of the Victorians, for whom the

105] *The Doctor* (1891), by Sir Luke Fildes. A compassionate doctor maintains his vigil by the bedside of a dying child in a fisherman's cottage. A popular painting which hung in numerous homes and doctors' waiting-rooms.

dawn light more likely signified the hope of eternal life, than worldly life, given the 1891 child mortality statistics. Moreover, the painting is idealised, in portraying the child's death as peaceful, when so many children's deaths from infectious diseases were agonising.[31] Of course, if Fildes had been closer to most people's reality, the painting would have been rejected by the Royal Academy.

At their best Victorian doctors were more than a friend of the family and source of invaluable moral support. When patients were dying they provided a caring management, combined with improved palliative care. They used the term 'euthanasia' in the classical Greek sense of a peaceful, easy and painless death, to express their aim and role with dying patients. The nineteenth-century physician lacked the technological or medical means to prolong life, but he could make the terminal stage easier, without any sense of failure at his admission that death was inevitable. Dr C. J. B. Williams observed in 1862 that his colleagues were often at their best in ministering to the dying and they received more gratitude from making death more comfortable and dignified than from effecting a cure.[32]

The most influential Victorian text on terminal care was Dr William Munk's *Euthanasia: or Medical Treatment in Aid of an Easy Death* published in 1887. Munk was the Victorian equivalent of modern specialists like Elizabeth Kübler-Ross, John Hinton and Cicely Saunders, anticipating their work to a remarkable degree. Munk emphasised that when death was approaching 'we dismiss all thought of cure, or of the prolongation of life', to concentrate instead on the relief of pain and discomfort. He offered practical advice on alleviating restlessness and difficulty in breathing and stressed the need to regulate the temperature and ventilation of the room and the administration of food and alcohol.[33] Munk paid tribute to the supreme role of opiates in the control of pain, since opiates allowed sufferers to die with dignity, offering tranquillity to the mind as well as soothing 'corporeal pains and complaints'. The correct dosage should be measured by the relief afforded, as addiction was not considered a problem when a disease was terminal.[34]

The change from a Christian ideal of a good death to a medical model was a very slow process which was not completed until the modern 'miracle' drugs of the 1930s produced cures for a broad range of diseases. In the early-Victorian period doctors and patients were likely to be Christians who assumed that death was ordained by the will of God. By the late nineteenth century increased religious doubt and Evangelical decline coincided with a revised view of disease, as death was more often attributed to particular diseases than divine providence. The balance swung gradually away from primary concern with the state of the soul at the deathbed towards a greater emphasis on freedom from pain and suffering.

REFORM OF FUNERALS AND UNDERTAKING

Earlier historians tended to focus on the 'ostentatious displays of grief' and the vulgar 'madness' of the excessive funerals of the Victorians.[35] However, this criticism needs to be seen in a broader context and balanced against the therapeutic advantages of funerals for many mourners. Extravagant aristocratic funerals can be traced back through the centuries, but from the late seventeenth century the vogue spread downwards to the growing ranks of the middle classes. Extravagance was well entrenched long before Victoria ascended the throne, though the number of middle-class families able to afford more expensive funerals substantially increased.[36] Edwin Chadwick's 1843 *Report on the Practice of Interment in Towns* found that the average funeral expenses of the aristocracy in London varied from £500 to £1,500. A London undertaker testified before the inquiry that an 'ordinary' middle-class funeral would cost from £50 to £70, and that most funerals were too expensive. Undertakers with a direct financial interest in the outcome advised families as to 'customary' requirements, keeping their prices very high and arousing the criticism and anger of the public.[37]

Public ceremonies on the deaths of famous people were often the occasion for ostentatious display up to the 1870s. The duke of Wellington's funeral in 1852 was the high point of Victorian extravagance, with a triumphal funeral car which alone cost £11,000. Lord Palmerston's funeral in 1865 at Westminster Abbey was another occasion of great pomp and magnificent ceremony. *The Illustrated London News* [106] shows the feather tray and black draped staves, the hearse decorated with colourful armorial bearings, and the pall of black velvet and white satin making a powerful contrast with the striking crimson coffin. The duke of Northumberland's funeral procession to Westminster in

106] Lord Palmerston's funeral in 1865 at Westminster Abbey showing the pomp and ceremony of a state funeral, including the black-draped staves and feather tray.

1865 included numerous mutes on horseback, 2 pages with a lid of black feathers, a horseman carrying the ducal coronet on a crimson velvet cushion, a hearse and 6 horses accompanied by 12 pages, and 15 mourning-coaches.[38]

But these were extraordinary state occasions for exceptional people. To achieve a balanced picture we must acknowledge that the Victorians were themselves responsible for significant funeral reform. Edwin Chadwick's 1843 *Report* made a powerful case for the reform of funeral ceremonies, concluding that over £4 million was 'annually thrown into the grave at the expense of the living'. The awakening concern for public health was strengthened by the revelations of the noxious 'emanations' from overcrowded and insanitary churchyards. The Metropolitan Interment Act 1850 was a landmark in funeral and burial reform, closing urban churchyards, and stimulating the development of public cemeteries (see Chapter 8).

Funeral reform inevitably involved a major attack on the perceived greed of undertakers who were exploiting the bereaved at their most vulnerable, especially the working classes afraid of a pauper's burial. Charles Dickens's satire in such novels as *Martin Chuzzlewit* and *Great Expectations* had been most powerful in its critique of squalid lower-middle-class or working-class funerals which lacked the funds to imitate

107] *The Starved-Out Undertakers.* This *Punch* cartoon (1850) illustrates the reform campaign against greedy undertakers who were obliged to reduce their extravagant funeral paraphernalia, including plumes of black feathers and hatchments, and offer cheaper funerals.

their betters in style.[39] The press and influential Victorian periodicals such as the *Quarterly Review* took up the cry for reform. *Punch* in 1850 depicted four undertakers in all their sombre black finery with black scarves and hat-bands and plume of black feathers; their undertaker's hatchment depicted a coat of arms showing glasses of beer and wine with the inscriptions 'All up!' and 'We have been reduced by common-sense' [107].

The churches were responsible for the creation of societies such as the National Funeral and Mourning Association in the 1850s to encourage simplicity and moderation. The undertakers were obliged to reduce their extravagant funeral paraphernalia and offer simpler and cheaper funerals over the next half-century. The middle and upper classes from the 1840s increasingly expressed in their wills a desire to be buried simply and at limited expense. By 1894 the *Lancet* rejoiced that funeral reform had been achieved with the cost of funerals greatly reduced: 'the expenditure of £10 to £15 will allow of everything being completed in good taste and reverence, but without any excess'.[40] Undertakers further responded to pressure for funeral reform by forming protective associations, notably the British Undertakers Association in 1905. Ironically, however, while the middle and upper classes simplified their funerals, the working classes were more reluctant to abandon their cheaper versions of the respectable Victorian funeral. 'Decent' burials only became accessible to poorer members of society comparatively late in the century through weekly payments to burial clubs, which helped to combat fear of pauper burials.[41]

MOURNING RITUALS AND MEMORY

Modern psychologists argue that mourning rituals meet the psychological needs of the bereaved by structuring death within an accepted system of values, whilst also rallying the support of family, friends and community to comfort the bereaved.[42] Victorian rituals provided opportunities for the bereaved to express their sorrow in a manner that made the grieving experience easier to endure and to complete. Protestant Christianity still provided the dominant Victorian belief system to console the bereaved.

The funeral began the process of working through grief, affirming the reality of the loss through public recognition of the death and bringing together a supportive and sympathetic gathering of family, friends and community to share the sorrow. The more devout Christians found spiritual edification or consolation in the funerals of their loved ones. The burial service was a legal requirement for funerals of the Church of England in churchyards up to 1880, with its emphasis on the resurrection consoling believers with the prospect of reunion in Heaven. John Callcott Horsley, a devout Anglican and a popular portrait painter, experienced his wife's funeral in 1852 as a valuable ceremony of prayer for the purification of his own soul, to enable him to join her in Heaven. Less devout Christians often found funerals a painful but necessary duty to show respect to those they loved and confirm the reality of their deaths. But Christian funerals were religious ceremonies which could make unbelievers feel uncomfortable and alienated because of their emphasis on resurrection and atonement, with their implications for the unhappy fate of unrepentant sinners. Thomas Huxley, the agnostic scientist, was profoundly shocked in 1860 as he listened carefully to the funeral service for his three-year-old son, since he rejected the Christian doctrines of Hell and resurrection with their offensive implications for unbelievers.[43]

If the supreme Christian consolation on the death of a loved one was the belief in the resurrection of the body, then the continuing memory of the deceased was an almost equally important consolation which was open to believers and unbelievers alike. The memory of the dead was central to the grieving process for mourners of all faiths and none. Psychiatrists have emphasised the importance of memory in the dynamics of grief, as a painful process takes place in which the mourner reviews all memories of the lost relationship. The bereaved might find comfort in talking through such memories, over and over again, especially with relatives and friends who also knew the deceased. As Rebecca Kenrick reassured her cousin on the death of her father in 1845, 'The memory of the just and good is indeed a blessing to the survivors'.[44] Victorians seemed to understand the value of reliving their memories of the past and talking about their dead loved ones as an aid to mourning.

They also found consolation in writing lengthy family memorials on the life and death of the deceased, as a precious recollection for the family and as therapy for the writer. To the families who treasured these accounts they were not sentimental effusions but soothing memories which sustained their closeness to the deceased as well as helping them through the grieving process.

Modern critiques neglect the significant role of visible symbols of remembrance in the grieving process, but the Victorians understood this very well. They perpetuated the memory of dead loved ones through paintings, photographs, death-masks and busts of the deceased, as well as through monuments, mourning jewellery and grave-visiting. Victorians viewed these as therapeutic aids in the process of grieving, where many people today see these Victorian practices as morbid and distasteful. External symbols represented the physical memory of the deceased which was especially important in the 'searching' period of grief, following the shock of death. In the initial period of deep grief Victorian mourners sought to keep their loved one's memory alive as vividly as possible. The wealthy could afford to pay portrait painters to memorialise dying relatives in their final months of a terminal illness or on their deathbeds, while the less wealthy relied on drawings or photographs. Three months before Ada Lovelace's painful death from cancer in 1852, her husband arranged to have a portrait painted, though she was already 'wasted almost to a beautiful shadow'. Ada's young daughter was pleased at this prospect as she saw her dying mother 'like what I should imagine an angel to be'.[45]

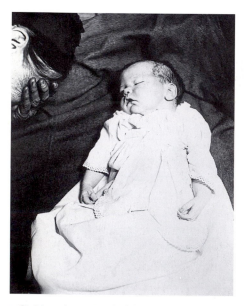

Photographs, drawings or portraits of the recently deceased, sometimes lying in the coffin, were another common form of remembrance which brought comfort to the bereaved family, however macabre they seem to some late-twentieth-century eyes. John Callcott Horsley, the artist, attached great importance to recording the likenesses of the recently dead, especially when they were babies and children. In 1852 he noted in his diary that he went 'to make a drawing of a dead child, thinking it a duty so to do', since the family would otherwise have no likeness. Two years later John Callcott Horsley made a plaster-cast of the head and shoulders of his own three-year-old son Harry, who died of scarlet fever, and he kept the cast on a table in his dressing-room as a constant reminder.[46] This emphasis on the memorial significance of a likeness of a dead baby or child helps to explain why so many photographs and lithographs have survived of dead babies in coffins, or apparently sleeping peacefully in cribs [108].

108] *Mourning a Dead Child*, photograph *c.* 1895. Many of these nineteenth-century photographs of babies, posed as if sleeping, would pass unrecognised as images of the dead in the twentieth century.

Lucy Cavendish, niece of W. E. Gladstone, found comfort in dwelling on her memories of her husband Lord Frederick Cavendish, who was murdered by Irish extremists in Dublin in 1882. She found 'such a deep comfort' in 'the dear beautiful photographs of sleeping Freddy' which were taken in the Dublin hospital immediately after his murder and organised by the Irish Viceroy as a surprise for her [109]. Lucy found one so consoling that she sent copies to relatives and friends, some of whom doubtless framed it in silver or velvet. Lord Spencer had also cut off a lock of Frederick's hair for Lucy, a very tangible reminder, and she liked the idea of his 'dear hair . . . being enshrined in a beautiful diamond locket'.[47] Locks of hair were sometimes bequeathed in wills, together with mourning-rings, brooches or lockets, designed before death to hold the hair and left to named relatives.[48]

The grave in the cemetery became a site for remembrance and for meditation for many Victorian families, helping to evoke a sense of closeness to the deceased and to perpetuate their memory. Much care was taken in the choice of an appropriate tombstone to mark the burial place and provide the site for future remembrance, especially on anniversaries. Visiting these graves was a vital source of consolation for many bereaved, especially when the new garden cemeteries outside city centres provided a peaceful rural setting. Plots were carefully maintained with plants, and photographs or drawings of the grave sent to those relatives unable to visit in person. Gertrude Gladstone in 1891 found the photo of her husband's grave 'a great comfort to me, it looks so quiet and peaceful, and makes one long so to be lying there too, with all one's great misery ended'.[49]

109] A photograph of Lord Frederick Cavendish after his assassination in Dublin in 1882. 'The dear beautiful photograph of sleeping Freddy', taken in the Dublin Hospital immediately afterwards, brought comfort to his widow who sent copies to relatives and friends.

The two major motors of change in relation to death between 1850 and 1918 were the decline of Christian belief and the significant demographic transformation caused by the death-rate decline, both clearly marked from the 1870s. The First World War reinforced and accelerated these processes.

A new demographic pattern was established from about 1870 which had a fundamental impact on the history of death. The death rate in England and Wales fell from 21.8 per 1,000 per year in 1868 to 18.1 in 1888, 14.8 in 1908 and 11.7 in 1928. This decline affected different age cohorts in stages, starting with children between one and fifteen who benefited from the 1870s, followed by young adults and the middle-aged ten years later. Children in their first year and people over fifty-five had to wait for improvement until after 1900.[50] This decline in mortality can be explained by public health reforms, better diet and living standards and the natural fall in mortality from infectious diseases. Life expectancy at birth in England and Wales increased from about 40 years in 1850 to 52 for males and 55 for females by 1911–12.[51] Thus the commonest time of death began to shift from infancy to old age between 1850 and 1918. Within half a century death began to be perceived as the monopoly of the elderly and society's preoccupation with death receded (see Chapter 10).

The gradual decline in Christian faith between 1850 and 1918 was the second fundamental motor of change in the history of death, grief and mourning. From the 1870s church attendance ceased to keep pace with population growth and Evangelicalism had passed its peak by the 1880s. Victorians faced the combined theoretical challenges of biblical criticism, geological discoveries and Darwinian evolutionary theory, as well as profound economic and social changes. Religious doubt was insidious but the process was very slow and gradual. Alfred, lord Tennyson's great poem *In Memoriam* was published in 1850, nine years before Darwin's *Origin of Species* which explained the origins of all animal and plant species through a system of natural selection. Tennyson's poem charted his own struggle for the divine assurance that his friend Arthur Hallam had found immortality rather than extinction on death. Tennyson's faith initially faltered in the face of the scientific and geological challenges to Christianity, but his hope of a future life finally triumphed over doubt.

Henry Bowler's painting, *The Doubt*, in the pre-Raphaelite style, first exhibited at the Royal Academy in 1855, was intended to illustrate Tennyson's poem and reached the same conclusion [**plate 18**]. Bowler's painting shows a young woman leaning against a gravestone, contemplating the exhumed skull and bones of a man named John Faithful, and asking the question 'Can these dry bones live?' The answer is provided in the painting in symbolic form which would have a powerful meaning for educated Victorians. The skull and bones signify the reality of death, but the symbols of faith and hope in the painting are more powerful; the butterfly is a traditional symbol of the resurrection, and the word 'Resurgam' is inscribed on the gravestone, meaning 'I shall rise again'.[52] Bowler's *The Doubt* and Tennyson's famous poem both emphasised that religious doubt was not uncommon in the early 1850s, even before the *Origin* was published in 1859. But faith was more likely to triumph at the death of a loved one in the 1850s than twenty or thirty years later, when religious doubt had become more firmly entrenched. Late-Victorian unbelievers could be isolated in their grief. They lacked the Church and community support which sustained Victorian Christians, and they had rejected the system of beliefs and rituals which helped to deal with grief. They were steadily losing the biblical language of consolation, so heavily dependent on Christian beliefs.

There were some unexpected related effects of the growth of unbelief between 1870 and 1918, notably the increase in support both for spiritualism and for cremation. Some people looked to spiritualism as an alternative belief system which might help in dealing with the death of loved ones but which might be reconciled with a nebulous form of Christianity. The movement began in the United States in the 1840s and spread in Britain from the 1860s, with private seances and home circles, a parlour pastime for some and a religion for others. Spiritualism taught the immortality of the soul and the possibility of communication through mediums with the spirits of the dead. In 1882 a group of distinguished Cambridge scientists and philosophers established the Society for Psychical Research to use scientific methods to establish the validity of the physical phenomena produced by mediums. Some prominent members of the Psychical Society, such as F. W. H. Myers and Henry Sidgwick, were Christians haunted by religious doubt, still seeking empirical evidence of immortality thirty years after Bowler's *Doubt* and Tennyson's *In Memoriam*.[53]

The rise of cremation as an alternative to burial from the 1870s was also linked with declining Christian belief. Cremation societies were first established in the 1870s in Italy, Germany, Holland, Belgium and the United States. Sir Henry Thompson, a prominent surgeon and President of the Cremation Society of England, which he had established in 1874, presented the sanitary and materialist arguments for cremation. It would end the graveyard pollution of air and water which spread infection and raised death rates; it was cheaper than burial and would reduce extravagant ceremonial, while instant destruction of the body appealed to those terrified of premature burial. Thompson demonstrated his new cremation oven in 1874, but when the Cremation Society experimentally cremated a horse at its first crematorium in Woking in 1879, the ensuing community outcry obliged the Home Secretary to threaten prosecution [110].[54] A favourable legal ruling in 1884 led to the building of crematoria in Woking, Manchester and Glasgow over the next decade, while the Cremation Act 1902 legalised the practice of cremation in Great Britain.

110] Sir Henry Thompson demonstrates a cremation oven in 1874 in his campaign to promote the sanitary and medical case for cremation. The first legal cremations took place in 1885 and the Cremation Act was passed in 1902.

Yet cremation was only very slowly accepted in Britain and was still no more than tolerated by 1918 when 0.3 per cent of funerals involved cremation. There were only about eight hundred cremations a year in Britain by 1908, and half of those who died were still buried even in the 1960s. This very slow pace of change can be explained by examining the two main forces of opposition to cremation. Sir Francis Seymour Haden, another leading surgeon, proposed to abolish burial abuses, not by cremation, but by safe, fast burial in perishable 'earth to earth coffins' made of wicker. The debate between the two surgeons raged for years in the weekly periodicals and no doubt Haden's arguments helped to reassure many Christians that reformed burial could indeed be safe and sanitary.

More significant than the sanitary and materialist arguments against cremation in the longer term were the deeply held Christian objections of the majority of the community, including those who had ceased attending church but retained residual beliefs. Thompson and Haden, as surgeons, concentrated on medical and sanitary arguments, almost entirely ignoring two thousand years of Christian burial tradition and an emotional distaste for cremation. Dr Wordsworth, Bishop of Lincoln, spoke for many Christians when he declared in 1874 that the 'barbarous and unnatural' heathen practice of cremation would destroy popular faith in the resurrection of the material body, leading to social revolution.[55] Even the *Lancet*, a medical journal predisposed to support the sanitary case for cremation, acknowledged in 1892 that burial 'still holds the public mind with a power little if at all abated'.[56] A diffuse, residual Christian sentiment caused passive resistance to cremation which was strong enough to influence even the medical profession.

Support for cremation was strongest among the upper and middle classes, notably amongst the literary and scientific intelligentsia, and weakest among the working classes. That minority of people who chose cremation before 1918 were often unbelievers influenced by the public health argument, whose mourners were usually hesitant at the unusual prospect of attending a cremation ceremony. In 1903 Kate Courtney found Herbert Spencer's cremation less unpleasant than anticipated, though 'English society' ignored it: 'There was nothing repellent as I feared about the business part of the ceremony – it was simple and reverent.'[57]

The impact of the First World War

Finally, the First World War reinforced and accelerated those secular and demographic changes already under way. Church attendance and religious belief went into steeper decline as Christian ministers faltered in explaining God's purpose in the war when consoling families after terrible war deaths. Christian doctrines of immortality were further compromised by clerical concessions that soldier heroes killed in a just war would advance directly to Heaven. As organised religion weakened, the spiritualist movement was energised by the desperate desire of countless bereaved relatives to contact lost soldier sons and husbands in the spirit world. The number of spiritualist societies doubled in the six years after 1914, despite the press publicity attracted by fraudulent mediums.[58]

The reform of mourning rituals and funeral ceremonies was also advanced by the Great War. The simplification of mourning dress and the rejection of black crape were accelerated by the fear that thousands of widows in formal widows' weeds would demoralise the nation. Moreover families were reluctant to perform grand ceremonial funerals for individual civilians when soldiers who died for their country could not be repatriated or even, in many cases, identified for foreign burial. Advocates of cremation seized the opportunity to demand that cremations for all with 'everyday clothes' should replace 'funeral gloom' and all its dismal rituals.[59]

But the First World War was also a major turning-point in the history of death in its own right, since it shattered what remained of the Victorian way of death for many bereaved families. Vast numbers of violent and unnatural deaths of adult sons killed prematurely could not be mourned in the traditional manner by individual families. It is estimated that one man in eight was killed of the six million British soldiers: 'the individuality of death had been buried under literally millions of corpses'.[60] The terrible trauma of so many grieving families was unprecedented. Burial and identification were impossible for vast numbers of soldiers blown to bits or lost in 'no man's land' – horrible facts which added immensely to the awful reality of violent deaths far from

111] *Part of the Battlefield of Third Ypres.* The photographer's original caption reads: 'corpse, water-filled shell hole, elephant iron, wire, pill box, tree stumps'. The First World War with its massive loss of life hastened the decline of traditional Christian beliefs, and simplified both funerals and memorials.

home [111]. It was a world away from the Victorian ideal of a good Christian death which had rarely been attainable even in peacetime.

Without seeing the body of their soldier-son or participating in his funeral, bereaved families could find the reality of death almost impossible to accept. Even where bodies were recovered and buried behind the trenches, relatives could be haunted by 'the most terrible recurring nightmares that he had not been killed but was lost somewhere, insane and helpless'. After 1916 it became even harder as the numbers of dead increased while the early idealism and heroic rhetoric waned. Where soldiers were missing, presumed dead, for months or years the 'long-drawn-out agony' of waiting and uncertainty must have been appalling.[61] Any normal process of mourning was often impossible and traditional burial and mourning rituals were seen as inadequate and irrelevant.

Commemoration of lost soldier sons became even more significant when bodies were never found, identified or buried, and so a new form of national civic memorial was required, to mourn the dead rather than celebrate war. This helps explain the immense popular appeal of the Cenotaph, the tomb of the Unknown Soldier and the ritual of Armistice Day. 'The Unknown was understood to represent all his dead comrades, but especially the Missing, the huge numbers of men blown to pieces or rotted in mud or otherwise unrecognisable . . . Bereaved people gave dead soldiers, as nearly as they could contrive, the funeral they never had.'[62] It has been suggested that the mass outpouring of sorrow during and after the Great War was a 'cult of the dead' on a mass scale by a whole community suffering chronic, unresolved grief.[63]

The Victorian way of death was itself buried under the weight of mass deaths in war, and also undermined by the decline of Christian beliefs, and the increasing association of death with old age. This complex process of change eroded the social and cultural supports which had made death meaningful and grief endurable for many Victorians. Even the advantages of a medical focus on palliative care were reduced by the new preoccupation with a curative model of medicine. There was no cultural replacement for the Victorian way of death; only a fragmentation of belief, and a contraction of the cultural and social space to which death was increasingly restricted in postwar Britain.

Notes

In all references, place of publication is London unless otherwise stated.

1 William Feaver, *The Art of John Martin* (1975), pp. 188–204, quotation p. 200; *Great Victorian Pictures*, Arts Council of Great Britain (1978), p. 57.

2 J. S. Curl, *The Victorian Celebration of Death* (1972), pp. 7, 20; Bertram Puckle, *Funeral Customs: Their Origin and Development* (1926), pp. 87, 253–4.

3 Lou Taylor, *Mourning Dress: A Costume and Social History* (1983), pp. 61, 122, 154–5.

4 David Cannadine, 'War and death, grief and mourning in modern Britain', in Joachim Whaley (ed.), *Mirrors of Mortality: Studies in the Social History of Death* (1981), pp. 190–1.

5 See e.g. E. Longford, *Victoria R. I.* (1964); M. Ponsonby, *A Memoir* (1927); *Letters of Queen Victoria*, ed. A. C. Benson and Viscount Esher (1908), III.

6 See Pat Jalland, *Death in the Victorian Family* (Oxford, 1996), chapter 16 (see the forthcoming paperback edition). On chronic grief, see Colin Murray Parkes, *Bereavement: Studies of Grief in Adult Life*, 3rd edn (Harmondsworth, 1996).

7 On the Evangelical movement, see David Bebbington, *Evangelicalism in Modern Britain: A History from the 1730s to the 1980s* (1989).

8 Jalland, *Death in the Victorian Family*, chapter 2, 'Revival and decline of the good Christian death', pp. 39–58.

9 See F. B. Smith, *The Retreat of Tuberculosis 1850–1950* (1988), p. 1 (an excellent study of the history of consumption).

10 Daniel C. Eddy, D.D., *The Angel's Whispers ... (Sermons) designed to console the Mourning Husband and Wife* (1885), pp. 121–2.

11 *Lancet*, 30 September 1882.

12 See *Great Victorian Pictures*, p. 57; Jeremy Maas, *Victorian Painters* (1969), p. 34.

13 Revd J. Baldwin Brown, 'The soul and future life', *Nineteenth Century*, 2 (October 1887), 511–17.

14 Geoffrey Rowell, *Hell and the Victorians* (Oxford, 1974).

15 P. C. Almond, *Heaven and Hell in Enlightenment England* (Cambridge, 1994).

16 William Branks, *Heaven our Home* (Edinburgh, 1861), pp. iii, iv, viii; Rowell, *Hell and the Victorians*, pp. 9–10; Robert Bickersteth et al., *The Recognition of Friends in Heaven* (1866). See also Colleen McDannell and Bernhard Lang, *Heaven: A History* (New Haven, Conn., 1988); Michael Wheeler, *Death and the Future Life in Victorian Literature and Theology* (Cambridge, 1990), chapters 2–4 (abridged edition published as *Heaven, Hell and the Victorians* (Cambridge, 1994).

17 Boyd Hilton, *The Age of Atonement: The Influence of Evangelicalism on Social and Economic Thought 1795–1865* (Oxford, 1988), pp. 335–6.

18 Emma Lee to Maria Sharpe, 13 June 1870, Sharpe Papers 139/6, University College, London.

19 R. C. Ansell, *On the Rate of Mortality* (1874), pp. 69, 71.

20 B. R. Mitchell and Phyllis Deane, *Abstract of British Historical Statistics* (Cambridge, 1962), pp. 36–7; Rosalind Mitchison, *British Population Change since 1860* (1977), pp. 49–52.

21 Lawrence Stone, *The Family, Sex and Marriage in England 1500–1800*, 2nd edn (1977), pp. 651–2.

22 Linda A. Pollock, *Forgotten Children: Parent–Child Relations from 1500 to 1900* (Cambridge, 1983).

23 See e.g. *Our Children's Rest; or Comfort for Bereaved Mothers* (1863); *To a Christian Parent, on the Death of an Infant*, Religious Tract Society 351 (*c.* 1852).

24 W. M. Smith to Emily Giberne, on the death of his baby son, 7, 10 February 1866, Hambleden MS E/1.

25 *To a Christian Parent, on the Death of an Infant*, pp. 3, 5.

26 *Our Children's Rest; or Comfort for Bereaved Mothers*, pp. 63, 78–9.

27 James Walvin, *A Child's World: A Social History of English Childhood 1800–1914* (1982), pp. 29–44.

28 See e.g. Roy Porter, *Disease, Medicine and Society in England 1550–1860* (1987), pp. 54, 61–5; F. B. Smith, *The People's Health 1830–1910* (1979).

29 Edward Shorter, 'The history of the doctor–patient relationship', in W. F. Bynum and Roy Porter (eds), *Companion Encyclopedia of the History of Medicine* (1993), II, pp. 791–4.

30 Dorothea Palmer to her brother, Revd William Palmer, 13 September 1851, Selborne Papers, MS Eng. misc. c. 690, fo. 105, Bodleian Library, Oxford.

31 See Raymond Lister, *Victorian Narrative Painting* (1966), pp. 128–9; *Great Victorian Pictures*, p. 36; C. E. Gifford, 'Fildes and "The Doctor"', *Journal of the American Medical Association*, 224 (1973), pp. 61–3; Sherwin B. Nuland, *How We Die* (1994), p. 9.

32 *Lancet*, 5 April 1862.

33 William Munk, *Euthanasia: or Medical Treatment in Aid of an Easy Death* (1887), pp. 4–8, 18–26, 65–105.

34 *Ibid.*, pp. 68–85.

35 Puckle, *Funeral Customs*, pp. 87, 253–4; Curl, *The Victorian Celebration of Death*, pp. 7, 20; see also John Morley, *Death, Heaven and the Victorians* (1971), pp. 19–31.

36 Julian Litten, *The English Way of Death: The Common Funeral since 1450* (1991).

37 Edwin Chadwick, *Report on the Practice of Interment in Towns* (1843), pp. 50–1, 48–9; see Jalland, *Death in the Victorian Family*, chapters 9 and 10; Morley, *Death, Heaven and the Victorians*, chapter 2.

38 *The Times*, 27 February 1865.

39 See Morley, *Death, Heaven and the Victorians*, chapter 2.

40 Jalland, *Death in the Victorian Family*, pp. 200–2; *Lancet*, 20 January 1894.

41 Glennys Howarth, 'Professionalising the funeral industry in England 1700–1960', in Peter C. Jupp and Glennys Howarth (eds), *The Changing Face of Death: Historical Accounts of Death and Disposal* (Basingstoke, 1997), pp. 120–8.

42 See e.g. John Hinton, *Dying* (1979); Beverley Raphael, *The Anatomy of Bereavement* (1984); Parkes, *Bereavement*.

43 See Jalland, *Death in the Victorian Family*, chapters 10 and 17.

44 Rebecca Kenrick to her cousin, Lucy Sharpe, March [1845], Sharpe Papers, 122/13, University College, London.

45 Lord Lovelace to his son Ralph King, 13 August 1852, MS dep. Lovelace Byron 167, fo. 80, Bodleian Library, Oxford.

46 John Horsley's diary, 24 April 1852, Horsley Papers, MS Eng. c. 2200, fo. 58, Bodleian Library, Oxford.

47 Lavinia Talbot to Mary Gladstone, 18 May 1882, Mary Gladstone Drew Papers, British Library, Additional MS 46236, fo. 137.

48 P. Cunnington and C. Lucas, *Costumes for Births, Marriages and Deaths* (1972), p. 253.

49 Gertrude Gladstone to Herbert Gladstone, 7 October 1891, Glynne–Gladstone Papers, MS 47/10, St Deiniol's Library, Hawarden.

50 B. R. Mitchell and Phyllis Deane, *Abstract of British Historical Statistics* (Cambridge, 1962), pp. 36–7; Michael Anderson, 'The social implications of demographic change', in F. M. L. Thompson (ed.), *The Cambridge Social History of Britain 1750–1950*, 2 vols (Cambridge, 1990), II, pp. 15–16; Rosalind Mitchison, *British Population Change since 1860* (1977), pp. 39–57.

51 *Ibid.*

52 See Christopher Wood, *The Pre-Raphaelites* (1981), p. 68; Lister, *Victorian Narrative Painting*, p. 84; Wheeler, *Death and the Future Life*, pp. 59–61.

53 On spiritualism, see e.g. G. K. Nelson, *Spiritualism and Society* (1969); Ruth Brandon, *The Spiritualists: The Passion for the Occult in the Nineteenth and Twentieth Centuries* (1983).

54 On cremation, see e.g. Jennifer Leaney, 'Ashes to ashes: cremation and the celebration of death in nineteenth-century Britain', in R. Houlbrooke (ed.), *Death, Ritual and Bereavement* (1989), pp. 118–35; Peter C. Jupp, 'Why was England the first country to popularize cremation?', in K. Charmaz, G. Howarth and A. Kellehear (eds), *The Unknown Country: Death in Australia, Britain and the USA* (Basingstoke, 1997), pp. 141–54.

55 *Lancet*, 16 May 1874, 11 July 1874.

56 *Lancet*, 27 August 1892.

57 Kate Courtney to Margaret Courtney, 16 December 1903, Courtney Collection, vol. IX, fos. 37–8, British Library of Political and Economic Science, London.

58 Alan Wilkinson, *The Church of England and the First World War* (1978), pp. 174–84; Nelson, *Spiritualism and Society*, pp. 155–64; Cannadine, 'War and death', pp. 228–9.

59 Litten, *The English Way of Death*, p. 171; C. E. Lawrence, 'The abolition of death', *Fortnightly Review*, 101 (February 1917), 326–31.

60 J. M. Winter, *The Great War and the British People* (1987), pp. 71–2, 92, 99, 305.

61 Mary Wemyss, *A Family Record* (privately printed 1932), pp. 337, 399–403.

62 Ken Inglis, 'War memorials: ten questions for historians', *Guerres mondiales*, 167 (1992), 13; Cannadine, 'War and death', pp. 217–26. See also K. S. Inglis, *Sacred Places: War Memorials in the Australian Landscape* (Melbourne, 1998).

63 Inglis, 'War memorials', p. 12; Cannadine, 'War and death'.

Select bibliography

Cannadine, David, 'War and death, grief and mourning in modern Britain', in Joachim Whaley (ed.), *Mirrors of Mortality: Studies in the Social History of Death*, 1981, pp. 187–242.

Curl, J. S., *The Victorian Celebration of Death*, Newton Abbot, 1972.

Houlbrooke, Ralph, (ed.), *Death, Ritual and Bereavement*, 1989.

Jalland, Pat, *Death in the Victorian Family*, Oxford, 1996.

Jupp, Peter C., and Howarth, Glennys (eds), *The Changing Face of Death: Historical Accounts of Death and Disposal*, Basingstoke, 1997.

Litten, Julian, *The English Way of Death: The Common Funeral since 1450*, 1991.

McDannell, Colleen, and Lang, Bernhard, *Heaven: A History*, New Haven, 1988.

Morley, John, *Death, Heaven and the Victorians*, 1971.

Nelson, G. K., *Spiritualism and Society*, 1969.

Parkes, Colin Murray, *Bereavement: Studies of Grief in Adult Life*, 3rd edn, Harmondsworth, 1996.

Richardson, Ruth, *Death, Dissection and the Destitute*, 1987.

Rowell, Geoffrey, *Hell and the Victorians: A Study of the Nineteenth-Century Theological Controversies concerning Eternal Punishment and the Future Life*, Oxford, 1974.

Smith, F. B., *The People's Health 1830–1910*, 1979.

Walvin, James, *A Child's World: A Social History of English Childhood 1800–1914*, Harmondsworth, 1982, chapter 2: 'Death and the Child'.

Wheeler, Michael, *Death and the Future Life in Victorian Literature and Theology*, Cambridge, 1990.

The healthy society: 1918–98

On 11 November 1918, the streets of London and many cities were filled with people celebrating the Armistice. The four years of exceptional mortality, strain and restraint were over. The war, however, had accelerated changes in so many attitudes, social conditions and institutions that had existed before August 1914[1] that future patterns in human mortality would change, and change more speedily than in any previous period. This chapter selects nine specific areas: the impact of war, health and longevity, changes in funeral arrangements, the rise of cremation, the abolition of capital punishment, belief in an afterlife, the good death, grief and high-profile deaths.[2] It presents a view of the twentieth century which challenges the popular journalistic cliché of death as the ultimate taboo subject of modern society.

The impact of war

The impact of war on attitudes to death was profound throughout the inter-war period. The historian David Cannadine has even argued that, 'Inter-war Britain was probably more obsessed with death than any other period in British history'.[3] One-eighth of the six million British combatants had been killed; one and a half million were disabled. Survivors were never able to forget their experiences of degradation and horror. Elite social groups suffered proportionately greater losses. Stanley Baldwin, Prime Minister in 1923–29 and 1935–37, was convinced that 'he was in command only because better men lay underground . . . He held power by the sufferance of the dead.'[4]

Yet how might the grief of ordinary people be estimated? For Cannadine, these are to be glimpsed through public responses to the Armistice Day rituals that developed: the first Two Minutes Silence in 1919 [112]; the Burial of the Unknown Warrior [113] and the permanent Cenotaph, both in 1920; and Poppy Day from 1921. The key to the extraordinary success of the Silence, for example, was that 'it made public and corporate those unassuageable feelings of grief and sorrow which otherwise must remain forever private and individual'.[5]

112] Road-workers in London's Regent Street raise their hats for the first Two Minutes Silence, 11 November 1919. The first Two Minutes Silence, in 1919, marked the anniversary of the Armistice. The Silence was enormously effective in uniting the nation in commemoration. Inter-war Remembrance rituals were not without controversy. From 1945, it was moved to the nearest Sunday, and organised by churches and the British Legion.

Another historian has more recently revealed a far more complex situation, drawing on local as well as national materials.[6] His analyses of Armistice Day controversies are particularly revealing. In 1925, the *Daily Mail*, opposed by the *Daily Express*, led a successful campaign to curb the merry-making of 'Victory Balls' as disrespectful to the dead and bereaved. The next year, in the 'medals controversy', relatives insisted – against the Forces' preferences – on wearing the medals won by their dead. In the 1930s, Armistice Day was celebrated in the context of growing unemployment at home and war abroad: the Prince of Wales twice sought, to no avail, to minimise the presence of the military. Pacifists encouraged the 'White Poppy' movement. In 1938, an ex-Serviceman interrupted the Silence at the Cenotaph ritual with shouts of 'All this hypocrisy!' There is, as yet, no history of twentieth-century grief in peacetime. Yet studies like these, even whilst they show the continual interaction of different groups in forming public rituals, have revealed how the private feelings of ordinary people may be gauged from their reactions to public events.

The Second World War lifted the 'pall of death'. Principally, people felt that the experiences of loss and bereavement were more widely

113] The coffin of the Unknown Warrior on HMS *Verdun* en route for Dover, 9 November 1920. This unidentified soldier, exhumed from the Flanders battlefields, was carried into Westminster Abbey by leaders of the three services. The congregation was primarily widows and bereaved mothers. Together with the unveiling of the Cenotaph, the event had a huge impact on the nation.

shared. Some 300,000 servicemen died, the majority in the final year of the war, and 60,000 civilians died, most in bombing raids between September 1940 and May 1941. This nourished the popular image of 'the people's war', sustained by the different nature of the war: not only were there extended periods of service leave, but about four-fifths of the military occupied largely non-combatant roles.[7] Military service lasted until 1960. All this may help explain why images like the 'lost generation' and 'war experience' of 1914–18 did not recur after 1945. The 1945 election unrolled a red carpet towards a new social order offering employment and prosperity and removing wartime restrictions and the prospect of sudden death.

Longer life and better health

In 1918, the prospect of a healthier society was far from apparent. The great influenza pandemic of 1918–19 caused 150,000 deaths in Britain. Many influenza victims were young adults. The paradox, according to one historian, was that Britain, with one of the most sophisticated public health mechanisms in the world, mounted the least effective response. Doctors were overconcerned to defend their professional status, and credit for any success should properly be given to local public health

plate 19] The resurrection of the body. *The Resurrection, Cookham* by Stanley Spencer, 1923–27. Spencer's painting is one of a series representing traditional themes in contemporary settings. Belief in bodily resurrection was severely challenged by the Great War, as were beliefs in Judgement and in Hell. During the century, popular concepts of the afterlife became much more liberal and heterodox.

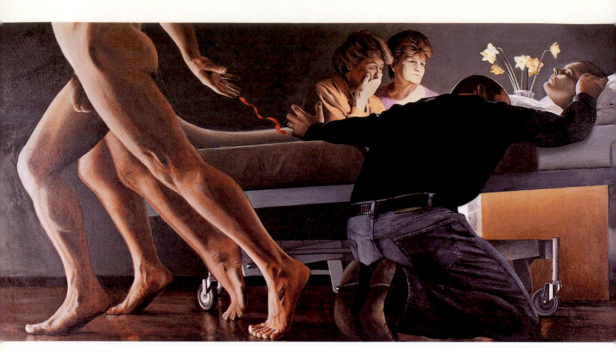

plate 20] *Philip Munro, my partner, died 13.1.89, aged 34,* painted by Gary Sollars. Exhibited in 1995, the picture drew an enormous and sympathetic response. When HIV/AIDS first came to England in the early 1980s, homosexuals were feared to be especially at risk. Unlike most killer diseases of the twentieth century, its victims were mostly in the prime of life.

plate 21] Flowers outside the gates of Kensington Palace in tribute to Diana, Princess of Wales, September 1997. Millions of flowers were laid outside the London home of Diana, Princess of Wales. Her sudden death was a shock throughout the world and the rituals it inspired may change the 'British way of grief'. London had not seen such mourning crowds since the burial of the Unknown Warrior.

authorities.[8] Thereafter, public health and medical services combined with political and social change to provide the population with its best ever opportunities for good health.

In 1911 England's population totalled 33,650,000. By 1991, it reached 46,161,000. Yet, from 1911 on, there was a dramatic decline in population growth.[9] This happened largely in two decades, the 1910s (when population growth dropped below half that in each nineteenth-century decade) and the 1970s (when population growth fell below replacement levels for the first time since the Black Death). England became a society where dying was largely deferred to old age. By the 1990s the country faced increasing problems of healthy longevity, exacerbated by social and geographical mobility. A 1997 survey revealed that more public funds were expended on people during the last two years of their lives than in all their previous years.

In the twentieth century, life expectancy for people in England increased enormously. In the period 1915–19 it had been 58.8 for males and 65.7 for females. By 1990 it had increased, respectively, to 73.0 and 78.5. The bulk of improvements for children occurred before 1950, but it was only after 1950 that increases in life expectancy began for the over-45s. While the crude annual death rate stabilised during the 1930s and 1940s, it dropped sharply in the 1950s, with a further decline in the 1980s.[10]

The increase in nineteenth-century life expectancy had largely been the result of declining mortality rates for children, adolescents and young adults. In the twentieth century, infant death rates continued to decline, from 154 deaths per 1,000 live births in 1900, to 75 in 1925, 30 in 1950 and 8 in 1990.[11]

By contrast, however, the decline in maternal mortality lagged behind. For each 10,000 live births in 1920, 41 mothers died. The rate rose to 46 in 1934, then dropped sharply to 28 in 1940 and 8 in 1950. According to a Ministry of Health report in 1929, half the deaths could have been prevented by better antenatal care, better training of midwives and improved obstetrics and antiseptic methods. Most babies at this time were home-delivered. Some people argued that better quality of birth care needed to be provided by the birth-attendant. Others felt that poverty and diet were to blame: what expectant mothers most needed was 'a herd of cows, not a herd of specialists'.[12] Conditions were enhanced by the Midwives Act 1936, and the situation improved rapidly as the country moved out of recession and into a wartime economy where fairer shares of food and health were guaranteed by the state.

The inter-war years revealed increasing connections between mortality and social class. The First War had uncovered the nation's poor health: two-thirds of prospective servicemen were found to be unfit for service. That only one-third of recruits was unfit in 1939 indicates the general rise in the physical health of young men. For the most part, these pre-1939 health improvements were not so much attributable to better medical care, as to the rising standards of public health, new

housing and slum clearance, water and sanitation, better maternity care, old-age pensions and medical inspection of school children.

Inter-war surveys examined the links between mortality rates and diet. A 1936 survey calculated that one-fifth of all children were seriously undernourished.[13] A 1937 survey showed how the diet and the death rates of the poor varied by region, by occupation and through unemployment.[14] The social critic and novelist George Orwell brought home the nature of inter-war poverty to many readers with his *Down and Out in London and Paris* (1933) and *The Road to Wigan Pier* (1937). The situation became even more apparent to middle-class families who opened their homes to evacuees in 1939.

What was lacking was access to health services, although by 1938 National Insurance, founded in 1911, provided a free General Practitioner service for 20 million people. Throughout the inter-war period, successive reports made recommendations about hospitals, insurance schemes, maternity benefits and dental treatment. Long before the Beveridge Report of 1942, there was a growing consensus for a National Health Service (NHS), finally introduced by the postwar Labour government in 1948 [114].

114] The Rt. Hon. Aneurin Bevan, political pioneer of the National Health Service, attends Golders Green Crematorium for the funeral of Foreign Secretary Ernest Bevin, 18 April 1951. As Labour's Health Minister, Aneurin Bevan introduced the National Health Service (NHS) in 1948. The NHS has contributed enormously to longer life and better health in the UK. Bevan opposed capital punishment and helped promote cremation. Both Bevin (1951) and Bevan (1960) died of cancer, the most feared disease of the postwar years.

How had the twentieth century achieved better health? Between the 1900s and the 1950s falling death rates were due to the demise of communicable, infectious diseases as the primary cause of death. Two-fifths of the decline was in air-borne diseases – bronchitis, diphtheria, influenza, measles, pneumonia, scarlet fever, smallpox and respiratory tuberculosis. One-fifth was in the decline of water-, insect- or food-borne diseases like cholera, diarrhoea, dysentery, typhoid or typhus. As these had been most prevalent among the young, the effect upon survival and longevity is obvious.

By 1950, infectious diseases as the primary cause of death were being replaced by non-communicable, degenerative conditions, like heart disease and cancer. Such degenerative diseases had always been a significant cause of death, particularly among manual working families in industrial areas and the inner cities.[15] However, their postwar prominence was heightened by general health and prosperity: hence the term 'diseases of affluence'. Cannadine commented in 1981, 'The reason why so many people seem to die today of heart attacks, strokes and cancer is that there is, literally, nothing else to die of'.[16]

The factors accounting for the reduction in infectious diseases and the rise in longevity are still hotly debated, probably because no one factor was sufficiently effective in isolation from the others: all were interlinked. In addition to public health – already discussed – major credit is also claimed for both improved diet and better medical treatment. While some historians champion the role of diet above everything else,[17] most take less radical views. For the inter-war period, whilst diet undoubtedly improved, so did a range of environmental conditions as well as medical innovations.[18]

The relationship between death rates and diet, income and unemployment has, of course, been further complicated by other postwar developments. The contribution is well established, for example, of alcohol not just to alcohol-related diseases but also to road deaths, of fat-eating to heart conditions and of smoking to lung cancer, coupled with the unhealthy effects of eating saturated fats and red meats and low-fibre convenience foods, and lack of physical exercise. The picture is further complicated by gender, class and regional differences.

The third factor contributing to increased longevity is the development of medical services: institutions, personnel, techniques and research. The Second World War accelerated both treatment and prevention. Without the war, mass production of Fleming's 1928 discovery of penicillin would not have occurred so soon. The war stimulated the blood transfusion service and the first mobile X-ray units. Plastic surgery for burns was improved. The development of antibiotics in the 1940s enabled mass BCG immunisation campaigns. A. B. Hill's development of randomised trials hugely enhanced the effectiveness of drugs.[19]

From 1948, the impetus of the NHS worked in parallel with the rapidly growing pharmaceutical industry to produce a whole series of drugs, including antibiotics, antihistamines, steroids and anticoagulants. Cancer treatments, with first radiation and then chemotherapies, raised patients' chances of recovery. Heart surgery was stimulated after the first transplant operation in 1967. Successful renal transplants followed. There were new surgical techniques from hip replacements in the 1970s to keyhole surgery in the 1980s. All these factors helped to prolong life and enhance its quality. Meanwhile, an old concern had resurfaced.

The founders of the NHS had sought to provide equal prospects of health. Yet, exasperatingly, mortality rates continued to vary by social class, actually becoming less equal than in 1918. The higher status groups benefited most from improvements in health. In 1977, the Labour government commissioned *The Black Report*. It showed that the poorer health experience of the lower social groups extended to all stages of life.[20] The failing was not one of access to health services but inequality in a wider range of factors affecting health: education, income, housing, work and employment. The new Conservative govern-ment of 1979 resisted *The Black Report* on grounds of cost. In 1986, *The Health Divide*[21] revealed a widening chasm between the classes, with all the killer diseases affecting the poor more than the rich: 'Such inequity is inexcusable in a democratic society which provides itself on being humane.'[22] In the 1990s, new health strategies were developed, with specific health targets which in *The Health of the Nation* (1992) included sexual health and HIV/AIDS.[23] Five years later, the new Labour government proposed four national targets, to reduce deaths from heart disease and stroke, cancer, accidents and suicide.[24] Yet Labour rapidly discovered that funding the NHS and reversing health inequality were almost insuperable challenges.

From undertaking to funeral directing

Deaths, however they occur, mean funerals. During this century, the funeral-directing industry took a dominant hold over families' arrange-ments.[25] The decline in the death rate before 1914 had increased com-petition between undertakers. Middle-class families were limiting funeral expenses. The pinch was felt by full-time undertakers whose profit-share was challenged by part-time rivals like the draper undertaker, the specialist coffin-manufacturer and the carriage-master who loaned horses which were essential for reaching distant cemeteries. Up to the 1950s most families kept dead bodies at home until the funeral. Basically, undertakers supplied families with coffins and transport. In 1935, the British Undertakers Association, keen to exchange the Dickensian image for higher professional status, signalled these aspirations with a change of name – the National Association of Funeral Directors (NAFD). Crucial in their gaining control over funeral arrangements were develop-ments in four areas: chapels of rest, embalming, motor transport and cremation.[26]

With the new NHS, hospitals steadily replaced the home as the place for dying. Until 1958, most deaths took place in the home, so control of the body remained with the family.[27] Previously, the only alternative had been the public mortuary, generally 'regarded as pro-vided by the State for the bodies of unfortunate outcasts'.[28] There were several strands to the process whereby the home became no longer fitting for a corpse. In 1926, the Births and Deaths Registration Act and the Coroners (Amendment) Act combined to increase the number of postmortem examinations, and thus the need for more public mor-tuaries. Increasingly during the 1930s, undertakers began to provide private mortuaries, 'chapels of rest'.[29] Families in the new suburbs probably welcomed this development. It was aided by growing demands for privacy in working-class homes.[30]

As hospitals became the main context for dying, funeral directors discarded the local neighbourhood layers-out.[31] Their control over the corpse was also enhanced by their adoption of embalming. Embalming offered hygienic safeguards, and facilitated storage, consequent economies of scale and opportunities for better presentation.[32] Not until the 1990s was embalming criticised, by funeral reform groups like the Natural Death Centre[33] and by cemetery staff concerned about embalming fluid polluting soils and atmosphere.[34]

Growing use of motor hearses and crematoria also increased funeral directors' control over funerals. The most popular horse had been the (Dutch) Belgian Black, whose supply ceased in 1939. Cheaper and faster, motor hearses became a necessity for crematoria journeys, enabling four or more funerals in a day. Now responsible for the transport both of the body and of the mourners, funeral directors' control over the funeral process was almost complete. The larger firms, with centralised facilities for coffin storage, embalming and client-reception, were able to reap considerable economies of scale.[35]

The Co-operative movement moved into undertaking in the 1920s. With its advantages of a large capital base and existing customer networks, the Co-ops' growth helped discourage many of the part-time undertakers, whose trade had often been based on the old neighbourhoods dispersed by bombing and rehousing. In Nottingham, for example, there were 300 listed undertakers in 1939; in 1950, 30.[36]

In the 1970s, a cemetery company, the Great Southern Group, began to buy up funeral-directing firms. Acquisition fever was heightened by Howard Hodgson in the 1980s.[37] In 1989, several small companies broke away from the NAFD and formed the Society of Allied and Independent Funeral Directors (SAIF). After 1994, further reorientations occurred. First, many Co-operative societies left the NAFD, formed the Funeral Standards Council and set up the Funeral Ombudsman Scheme. Second, Service Corporation International (SCI), an American company, bought both the Great Southern and the combined Hodgson–Kenyon–Pompes Funèbres group. The rivals' market share was then approximately: Co-operatives 25 per cent, SCI 14 per cent and independents 61 per cent. These moves galvanised the funerals industry, consumer groups and the media, most attempting to resist 'the American way of death'.[38] SCI proved adept at marketing pre-paid funeral plans. By 1998, it had sold 70 per cent of existing plans, worth about £200 million.

With such amounts of money involved, the government's interest in the whole funerals industry increased. Public concern about funerals in general was also raised by a series of media articles, with radio and television documentaries. Specific proposals for funeral reform have come from the Natural Death Centre, promoting DIY funerals and woodland burials, from The National Funerals College with *The Dead Citizens Charter* and The Institute of Burial and Cremation Administration (IBCA) with *Charter for the Bereaved*.[39] Such groups aimed to shift control over death, dying and disposal away from professionals and back towards individuals.

115] Peterborough crematorium, opened in 1959 as the New Town was being developed. Peterborough crematorium is representative of the 161 crematoria built in the 1950s. Following the Cremation Act 1952, local authorities heavily promoted cremation which was less expensive than burial. People settling in such New Towns had moved far from their traditional family burial grounds. After 1967, the number of cremations exceeded that of burials.

From burial to cremation

For nine hundred years, since the Anglo-Saxons, the English had buried their dead. In 1919, 99 per cent of English funerals were burials. In 1998, 28 per cent of the 600,000 funerals that year involved burial while 72 per cent used the 233 available crematoria [115].[40] The preference for cremation proved significant in terms of urban land use, lower funeral costs and patterns of family remembrance: until the 1990s, most ashes were scattered.[41]

In 1918, there were 13 crematoria, ten owned by local government authorities. Cremation thereafter was promoted by pressure groups in increasing alliance with institutional interests. In 1924, the Cremation Society set up the Federation of Cremation Authorities, which became autonomous in 1937. The Federation itself started joint conferences in 1931 with the National Association of Cemetery and Crematorium Superintendents, later called the IBCA.

All three groups recommended cremation as an economy for local authorities, for whom pressure for new cemetery land increasingly conflicted with inter-war needs for housing and open space. Captain Ellison, MP, expressed this in 1935 with the comment, 'the London County Council wants a green belt. Currently our cities have a white belt of cemeteries.'[42] His phrase 'either cemeteries or playing-fields' became a motto for crematorium planners after 1945. The Births and Deaths Registration Act 1926, by insisting on the registration of deaths *before* burial, placed burial and cremation on a more equal footing. Incidentally, it was this Act which, when infanticide was at last a fading social problem, enforced the registration of stillbirths.[43] Cremation regulations were steadily simplified, though not until 1965 did new regulations transfer the decision as to burial or cremation from dying people to their next of kin.

Before 1945, cremation was an expensive option. Cremation Society membership had always included free cremation, although it was not always claimed. In 1965 the Society informed the government that the late Sir Winston Churchill, as a Society member, was entitled to free cremation; Churchill was, however, buried. At the other end of the social scale, the 1902 Act had forbidden local authorities to provide cremation for pauper funerals, which accounted for 11 per cent of London funerals in 1938.[44] One popular stratagem for cheaper funerals was the 'public reading time' by which several bereaved families could share one burial ceremony. This option persisted until the late 1950s.

The economics of crematoria were brought home to local authorities during the Depression. By 1939, there were fifty-eight crematoria, the majority being council-owned, and the cremation rate had risen to nearly 4 per cent. Thus, whilst crematoria were largely a post-1945 phenomenon, their value to local government was established before 1939. This process helped conclude the era of private cemeteries which had commenced in 1821 (see Chapter 8). In 1945, the Labour government began to implement Beveridge's Welfare State proposals. These included funeral reform: benefits for widows and death grants to ease funeral costs were introduced in 1946. The government also sought to phase out 'Industrial Assurance', funeral assurance sold by doorstep salesmen, reckoned to number 65,000 part-timers in 1943.[45] Local councils sought government support for building crematoria to reduce the financial subsidies required by cemeteries.

In 1948, Aneurin Bevan, as Minister both for Housing and Health, approved the building of more crematoria [115]. The government's Interdepartmental Cremation Committee (1947–51) reported the doubling of the cremation rate to 9.1 per cent. By then, a consensus for cremation had been established between government and local authorities, the Church, doctors, funeral directors and the public, who all benefited from the new arrangements. Cremation was now priced lower than burial. This was an added incentive for families who, increasingly subject after 1945 to geographical mobility for better work and housing, were distanced from their traditional family burial grounds. With social mobility and a decline in religious observance, people saw less value in traditional burial and grave rituals. The mutual relationship between the popularity of cremation and rejection of belief in the resurrection of the body has not yet been clearly assessed.[46]

The Church of England officially accepted cremation in 1944. Two decades later, in 1965, the Vatican Council reversed the 1886 decision outlawing cremation for Catholics. By 1967 the cremation rate in England reached 50 per cent. During the next twenty-five years, it continued to rise, though more slowly. Traditional Catholicism, eastern

Orthodoxy and Judaism, together with newly arrived Islam, ensured that local authorities still had to provide facilities for burial.

During the inflationary period of the 1980s, the cost of funerals came under public scrutiny. London's Westminster City Council caused an outcry when it sold three cemeteries for 15p. Their forced repurchase cost £2 million. The Environmental Protection Act 1990 precipitated higher cremation costs by insisting on stricter pollution controls. In 1995, the Conservative government, seeking to accelerate compliance with the Act, initiated a new era of privately owned crematoria. It thereby challenged the tradition of local-government responsibility for the disposal of the dead, begun in the 1850s (see Chapter 8).

Environmental concerns in the 1990s also revived interest in burial, further stimulated by the lower costs of family-organised funerals and the long-held distaste for the 'conveyor-belt' ethos of crematoria. The new recognition of the grave in mourning, including the burial rather than the scattering of ashes, was also partly fostered by the bereavement support groups which had grown since the 1950s. A new breed of cemetery and crematorium staff, increasingly supported by academic researchers, looked for different burial arrangements which would be cheaper, aid 'the grieving process' and make best use of existing land. By 1998, there was even talk of 'the revival of burial'.

The abolition of capital punishment

Capital punishment had a long, slow decline. After 1868, executions ceased to be tumultuous public spectacles. Hanging continued to be carried out within the confines of prisons, but even the 'improved' form of ritual gradually came under increasing criticism.[47] In the twentieth century the argument against capital punishment had two main strands – the fundamental immorality of taking human life and, pragmatically, the impossibility of reversing the sentence if a miscarriage of justice was later discovered.

Campaigners against capital punishment were sidelined during the Great War. However, there was considerable public indignation over wartime executions of soldiers for crimes like cowardice. Campaigns for posthumous pardons by soldiers' descendants continued throughout the century. After 1918, the movement to abolish capital punishment recommenced, partly due to penal reformers within the emerging Labour Party, notably Stephen Hobhouse and Fenner Brockway. In 1921, the Howard Association and the Penal Reform League joined forces. In 1922, there was a minor but overdue victory, the Infanticide Act. However, no woman had been executed for killing her baby since 1849 and this Act, urged by child-protection reformers for sixty years, was passed when the problem was fast fading.[48]

Public sympathy against the death penalty was evoked by the Thompson–Bywaters case of 1922–23. Thompson's husband had been murdered by her lover, Bywaters. Many thought she was executed as much for adultery as for murder. Bishop William Temple, prominent as a social reformer, emerged as one of the comparatively few abolitionists in the senior ranks of the Church of England. The Quakers consistently fought for abolition, with Margery Fry and Roy Calvert prominent. Calvert helped promote a private member's bill for abolition in 1928. It did not receive a third reading but it revealed a significant shift in parliamentary opinion. The new Labour government set up a Select Committee in 1930, the majority voting for an experimental abolition for five years, but the government fell in 1931.

Hanging was rare. Even during the Second World War, when crime increased overall, there were just thirteen hangings a year. Before 1939, humanitarian motives for abolition were coloured by the realisation that most murders were domestic, and that deterrence was not therefore an issue. The coarsening effect of the war upon the character of English murder was noted in 1946 by George Orwell.[49] Abolitionists expected much from the 1945 Labour government. The abolitionist Sydney Silverman, MP, secured a Commons amendment to suspend the death penalty for five years. The Lords rejected this, with strong backing from the Lord Chief Justice and the Archbishop of Canterbury. The Labour Government resorted to a Royal Commission. In seeking to limit the liability for murder, the 1953 Gowers Report rejected 'degrees' of murder, and proposed leniency for mental deficiencies.[50]

Meanwhile, three murders had reawakened public concern. In 1952, Christopher Craig and Derek Bentley were accused of murdering a policeman during a robbery. Craig fired the shot but, being under age, was only imprisoned. Bentley, aged eighteen but mentally younger, was hanged. Bentley's family challenged home secretaries for over forty years, success finally coming in 1998. In 1953, J. H. Christie was arrested when six bodies were found beneath his London house. Three years before, Timothy Evans had been hanged for the murder of his own wife and daughter at the same address. Christie had then been the main prosecution witness. Now he was found guilty and was hanged. In 1955, Ruth Ellis was convicted of shooting the man whose violence had caused her miscarriage. In this *crime passionel* the public was hugely supportive of Ellis. The crowd outside the prison before her execution chanted, 'Evans, Bentley, Ellis!' [116].

The pressure of the abolitionists, together with these three trials, forced the government to respond. The Homicide Act 1957 recognised mental conditions with a definition of 'diminished responsibility'. It also allowed for degrees of murder whereby, for example, the use of a gun was more serious than that of a knife. The logical absurdities of this did not recede.

The new Labour government of 1964 contained two leading abolitionists, the Lord Chancellor, Gerald Gardiner, and Lord Longford. Capital punishment was abolished in 1965. Ever since, Parliament has resisted public opinion favouring the restoration of hanging. Successive Conservative governments have regularly introduced free, but unsuccessful, votes for restoration.

116] Mounted police ride among the thousand-strong crowd outside London's Holloway Prison, after the execution of Ruth Ellis, 13 July 1955. Ellis was hanged for the murder of her lover, David Blakely. The Ellis case intensified the campaign against capital punishment, following the controversial trials of Timothy Evans (1949) and Derek Bentley (1953). Capital punishment was abolished in 1965. Ellis was the last woman to be executed in Britain. Years later, Evans and Bentley were posthumously pardoned.

Meanwhile, the Suicide Act 1961 had reformed a far more tragic and widespread form of violent death. In the ten years following the war, there were just under 45,000 cases of attempted suicide known to the police. Postwar research increasingly supported the growing public perception that medical help, not legal sanctions, was a more appropriate response to suicide attempts. One lawyer commented in 1961, 'Many moral matters formerly governed by public law must today be left in the private sphere, either permanently or until society re-formed by persuasion is prepared to re-admit them to the public order'.[51] With the Suicide Act 1961 it was no longer an offence to take one's own life, or to attempt to do so.

The afterlife

Popular religious beliefs changed considerably during the twentieth century yet, in its latter decades, surveys indicated that half the English still believed in an afterlife. This was somewhat less than the seven out of ten who said they believed in God, but much more than the tiny minority (11 per cent) who regularly attended church. Though there was a strong statistical correlation between belief in an afterlife and other measures of religiosity, there was considerable flexibility in the content of what the English believed.[52]

The first two-thirds of the twentieth century were characterised by unprecedentedly long marriages, the result of unprecedentedly low rates of adult mortality. In this demographic context, the nineteenth century hope of reunion with the soul of the beloved continued to flourish. There was a sharp rise in the divorce rate towards the end of the century, reducing the average length of marriage (sundered by divorce) to that of the mid-nineteenth century (sundered by death). It is still too early to say to what extent this will undermine belief in the reunion of souls, but at the end of the century reunion remained popular with the generation that enjoyed those long marriages, and notably elderly widows.

Very marked was the decline in belief in Hell, down to around 25 per cent towards the millennium. This is one of the clearest differences in religious belief between England and more religious societies such as Ireland (North and South) and the USA. For reasons documented in Chapter 9, Hell was much weakened by the Great War; subsequent funeral liturgies spoke less of worms, sin and Hell, and more of comfort: out with the *Dies Irae*, in with the twenty-third Psalm.[53] Hell continued to be taught in Catholic and conservative Evangelical churches until the 1960s, after which there was a studied silence on the matter even in these circles. Catholics who took the contraceptive pill, deemed sinful by the Vatican, could not believe they would go to Hell for this, so they continued with the pill and dropped Hell.[54] Evangelical theologians eventually came to consider that unbelievers went not to eternal flames, but simply ceased to exist – hardly a terror for those unbelievers who believed this was what would happen anyway.[55] Devout Christians became more concerned with the secular evils of this world than with the supernatural terrors to come. Mrs Mary Whitehouse, a 1970s campaigner for conservative Christian morality, commented, 'What do I believe happens when I die? To tell the truth this is something I think about hardly at all.'

Belief in a physical resurrection of the body [**plate 19**] steadily declined through the century. In the 1920s, two Christian churches debated the doctrine furiously: the Methodist Leslie Weatherhead, a former Army chaplain, and the Anglican H. D. A. Major, a college principal, were charged unsuccessfully with heresy. Both controversies revealed that the doctrine was being increasingly discarded by many ordinary people. If this belief had not utterly collapsed as the year 2000 approached, it was partly due to the 2 per cent of the English who were Muslims. Meanwhile, other non-corporeal ideas of the afterlife have flourished. After 1914, spiritualism changed from a prewar elite intellectual interest in the evidence for life after death to a movement that appealed particularly to women who had lost sons in the war. By the mid-1930s it was estimated there were over 2,000 local spiritualist societies and over a quarter of a million committed members, but it declined thereafter [**117**].[56] Interest nevertheless continued among all social classes throughout the second half of the twentieth century, not least among bereaved mothers.

117] Communicating with the spirits of the dead, a scene from *Blithe Spirit*.
Characters in Noel Coward's film *Blithe Spirit* seek to make contact with the dead
at a seance. Mass bereavements during the Great War stimulated the revival of
spiritualism, especially among grieving mothers and widows. Spiritualist societies
claimed 250,000 members, but the movement declined thereafter in the different
war conditions of 1939–45.

Towards the end of the century, ghost beliefs were popular and –
unusually among religious beliefs – more popular among those aged
under 44 and more popular in England than in the USA.[57] Between a
fifth and a quarter of the English told pollsters they believed in reincarnation, as many as believed in Hell. Quite what this means remains
uncertain, but it is clear that many showed an interest in reincarnation
who had not been obviously influenced by eastern religious ideas and
who were not New-Agers. Immigration from the Indian sub-continent
and elsewhere has created a much more multiracial England but absolute
numbers are low: no more than 3 per cent of the English population
believed in reincarnation because this was the traditional belief of their
ethnic community. Spiritualist and Theosophical ideas emanating from
the nineteenth century may have been as important as recent immigration in shaping ideas about reincarnation.[58]

The late twentieth century saw considerable publicity given to near-
death experiences (NDEs). It seems likely that, due to modern resuscita-
tion techniques, these may have been occurring more often, or at least
occurring more often to people who lived to tell the tale. Typically,
reported NDEs entail a journey through a tunnel and/or to an enticing
source of light, are deemed positive experiences and subsequently reduce the fear of death in the person involved. Though debate about the

cause and meaning of NDEs continues, a number of people take NDEs as evidence of life after death.[59]

The decline of traditional Christian doctrines such as Hell, a Last Judgement and the resurrection of the body, and the rising interest in heterodox concepts such as ghosts, reincarnation and NDEs, may be explained as follows. The rapid decline in Sunday School attendance from the 1950s, along with other aspects of secularisation, has produced a society that is uninformed about Christian dogma and increasingly sceptical of Church authority. By the 1970s, however, environmental scares were inducing a similar scepticism in the authority of science. This has encouraged people to toy with ideas without submitting them either to the touchstone of religious orthodoxies or to the rigours of empirical scientific verification. The unverifiable life hereafter is particularly prone to this kind of post-Christian, post-rational speculation.

The good death

In previous centuries, the commonest form of death was from an infectious disease or from infection following what today might be seen as a minor accident. Such deaths typically occurred weeks or days after falling ill and – although related to social class and living conditions – could easily be perceived as random.[60] Hence all those *memento mori* images of the grim reaper threatening the apparently healthy farmer.[61]

The twentieth century saw very different patterns of dying, as discussed above. This helped create an impression that death had been conquered, and that medicine would sooner or later find cures for everything, available to all through the NHS. Hospitals and doctors were now oriented to cure, not to death and dying. The hospital increasingly replaced the home as the typical place of death, so that by 1995 54 per cent died in hospital, 18 per cent in nursing and residential homes and only 23 per cent at home. In hospital, the dying were all too likely to be perceived as a medical failure and embarrassment, ignored by medical and nursing staff.[62] Chapter 9 showed how in the nineteenth century doctors knew they could not cure most illnesses of any seriousness, but were able to use opiates to relieve pain. By the mid-twentieth century the situation had been reversed, with both doctors and public expectations focused on cure, so that the incurable were all but abandoned.

People lived longer. By the second half of the century, non-communicable degenerative diseases began to hold out a very different prospect for the individual, the prospect of months or years between diagnosis and eventual death. Developments in medicine amplified this, especially with heart disease, cancer and a new communicable disease of the late twentieth century, HIV/AIDS. Medicine could diagnose these diseases earlier and earlier, and could treat them in such a manner as to prolong life, but ultimate cures remained elusive. If the traditional last rites of Christendom were geared to the fast dying of earlier centuries,

118] The logo of the first modern hospice, St Christopher's, 1967. The saint carries the Christ child across the river. Dame Cicely Saunders pioneered the hospice movement. The logo symbolises the aid given to terminally ill patients as they cross the river of death. Unlike earlier centuries, twentieth-century death was usually a long-drawn-out affair. The hospice and palliative care movement has helped provide a new model of death.

a new *ars moriendi* was required for the increasingly slow deaths of the late twentieth. People were taking longer to die, but doctors oriented to cure did not know what to do with them. By around 1960, helping people die well was off nearly everyone's agenda.

It was in this situation that the modern hospice movement emerged. The logo of St Christopher's Hospice [118] depicts St Christopher carrying the Christ child over a river, symbolising the care given by the hospice to those travelling across the river of death. The hospice, or palliative care movement, rediscovered and developed techniques of pain and symptom control that enabled many people with cancer and, later, AIDS to enjoy a much improved quality of life in the time remaining to them. The movement is an English innovation, pioneered from the 1950s by Cicely Saunders who in 1967 set up St Christopher's.[63] By the millennium, there were four hundred hospice and palliative care units in the British Isles, and the concept had been exported internationally. As Saunders originally intended, the emphasis is increasingly on good palliative care, not inside specialist hospice buildings but in people's homes and in ordinary hospitals.

Many people – had they the choice – would like to 'go out like a light', to go to bed feeling fine, then die in their sleep. Unfortunately, few people are dying this way. Thus the hospice movement's 'good death' is better geared to the physical reality of deferred death. Theirs is a death in which, though people may be comatose at the end, their preceding days, months or years are very much lived consciously. 'Adding life to years, not years to life' is the effective motto of palliative care. Meanwhile, dying people can conclude 'unfinished business' with friends and family, and come to terms with the ambitions they must abandon. This is a time less for making peace with one's maker as in traditional Christian dying than making peace with oneself and one's family.[64]

This new 'good death' has spawned a considerable literature, including first-person accounts,[65] and some painting and other visual media. With AIDS, the combination of palliative care with a highly creative gay community created a particularly fertile soil for the generation of artistic expression [plate 20]. Cancer, however, was a far more common disease in late-twentieth-century England. In 1998, BBC TV concluded a series on the human body with a film on the peaceful dying at home, from cancer, of a man in his sixties. His wife nursed him to the end, helped by their local doctor and a palliative care nurse-adviser, with friends and neighbours calling to say farewell. This also represents the good hospice death [119]. Cancer, once 'The Big C', the unmentionable disease whose name conjured up images of unavoidable, prolonged and intractable pain, now provides the setting for a new, heroic form of dying.[66] The literature of the palliative care movement is not only changing the reality of dying, it is doing for the image of cancer what grand opera did for tuberculosis: turning it into the most romantic of deaths. Reality is not always like the image.

119] A dying patient at St Christopher's Hospice, London, talks with the Head of Medicine, Dr Nigel Sykes, *c.* 1998. The modern hospice movement began when St Christopher's Hospice opened in 1967. By the millennium Britain had 400 hospices and palliative care units. Palliative care provided the late twentieth century with new models of 'the good death': dying either in hospices or, nursed by family and professionals, at home.

Not all can, or do, die the good hospice death. Not all cancer pain can be controlled. The widow in the TV film is statistically likely to live another twenty-five years and to die on her own, possibly in an old people's home, probably with a degree of dementia. Other people die in accidents, or of diseases where heroic efforts at cure persist to the end, eroding the quality of life in the meantime. Others linger on after series of strokes, as virtual vegetables not allowed to die. The dreaded death is, perhaps, no longer cancer, but the stroke that takes months to kill; or perhaps lingering on into an extreme old age, *sans* teeth, *sans* eyes, *sans* taste, *sans* memory, *sans* everything that made life worth living: a social death in a body that refuses to die.[67]

Grief

If the Victorian era had its romantic image of dying, it also had one of grief.[68] The era that celebrated the familial bonds between spouses and between parents and children envisaged grief as the continuation of that bond beyond death. Letting go of the dead, for example by remarriage, was often seen by the mourner (and the relatives) as betraying the dead. This romantic notion of everlasting grief continued throughout the twentieth century in the private experience of many people, not least among those shrouded by the inter-war 'pall of death'.

But many, especially after 1945, wanted to leave their memories of loss and trauma behind. The terms in which some intellectuals discussed grief had already made an about turn. Freud's essay 'Mourning

273

and melancholia' (published in German in 1917 and in English in 1925) defined grief as the process of letting go of attachments to the dead, an idea which came to dominate twentieth-century psychologies of grief, especially after the 1940s. By the 1970s, British psychiatrists Colin Murray Parkes and John Bowlby were among the leading world authorities on bereavement. Their influence, along with that of a hospice movement whose concept of total care included care of survivors, meant that England became a pioneer in bereavement care. The experts' emphasis on 'working through' grief so one would 'let go' resonated with a popular culture that, after two devastating world wars, wished to leave the dead behind and get on with life. Secularism, rationalism and an emphasis on youth, progress and consumerism blocked those channels, such as grave-visiting and spiritualism, through which people between 1850 and 1939 had maintained their bonds with the dead.[69]

Bereavement experts did not, however, commend what they perceived as a popular English culture that inhibited the shedding of tears: experts deemed these an important part of what they termed the 'grief process'. It would be incorrect, however, to think that popular twentieth-century English culture totally repressed grief; rather, it suppressed it in public – suppression being a conscious choice, very different from unconscious psychological repression. It was expected that bereaved people keep themselves together whilst in public – at work, shopping, at the funeral or entertaining visitors – but it was also expected that privately they would be grieving deeply. As one upper-class etiquette book advised in 1926:

> The ladies of a bereaved family should not see callers, even intimate friends, unless they are able to control their grief. It is distressing alike to the visitor and the mourner to go through a scene of uncontrolled grief. Yet it is difficult to keep a firm hold over the emotions at such a time, and it is therefore wiser to see no-one if there is a chance of breaking down ... relatives should remember that the bereaved ones will want to be by themselves, and that solitude is often the greatest solace for grief.[70]

In other social classes it was important that in public there be a quiver of the lips, a temporarily moist eye, a catch in the voice that revealed that, deep down, one was grieving deeply, even though one had the courtesy to hold oneself together when others were around.[71] We may see this portrayed in the following *in memoriam* notice in a northern newspaper from the 1970s:

> No-one knows my sorrow
> Few have seen me weep
> I cry from a broken heart
> While others are asleep.

By placing this verse, the mourner made it clear to everyone that, despite appearances, she was grieving deeply. We also see it in the press photograph of the police constable on duty at the funeral of brutally murdered two-year-old James Bulger in 1993 [120]. Whilst remaining on duty and in charge, he dabs a single tear from his eye; we guess that he too may have young children, and we respect his remaining in control at the very moment he contemplates the worst tragedy that could befall any family. Increasingly, however, this 'private grief' was being challenged by the more 'expressive grief' advocated by most 1990s books and experts on grief.[72]

120] A policeman wipes away a tear at the funeral of the murdered two-year-old, James Bulger, Sacred Heart Church, Kirkby. When James Bulger was murdered by two older children, the nation was shocked. This policeman, officially on duty, yet overcome by his own emotion, symbolises the changing culture of grief in the late twentieth century, as 'silent' grief – trying to let go of the dead – is challenged by more expressive forms.

In the nineteenth century, the gendered division of grief had been explicit. Bereaved men were expected to bury themselves in work; women to absent themselves from social life and – assuming they had the leisure, which most did not – stay at home to grieve.[73] Grief thus became the property of women, hidden behind closed doors – at least as far as the public gaze of men was concerned. In the last three decades of the twentieth century, the women's movement together with increasing involvement in paid work outside the home has given women more confidence to speak publicly of their own inner experiences, including expressions of grief. The overwhelming majority of late-twentieth-century autobiographical accounts of grief are by middle-class women.[74] Their grief has come out into the open, encouraging other women to explore and express their own grief, at precisely the time – and for the same reasons – that most would-be female comforters and listeners are not there: they are out at work, and too busy. Hence the demand for professional, or semi-professional, help.

From the 1950s a number of groups were set up, like Cruse-Bereavement Care in 1958 (originally offering volunteer counselling for widows), The Compassionate Friends (a self-help group for those who had lost a child, set up in 1969) and the National Association of Widows.[75] These have grown dramatically, along with a wide range of other support groups. The demand for their help has a number of sources. Formal Victorian mourning had been abandoned, largely because people wanted to be free to grieve in their own way.[76] This, however, left people with little guidance as to the nature of grief. Many who now seek counselling or join a bereavement group do so because their suffering seems to have no end and there is no one to turn to. Even when other family members survive, they may not want to discuss the dead, or to witness tears. With a counsellor, or in the group, tears and endless talk about the dead are allowed.[77]

By the end of the century, one message was being delivered increasingly clearly by many bereaved women, especially in The Compassionate Friends: grief does not necessarily end, grief does not necessarily entail 'letting go', it does not necessarily get resolved. This was being said on both sides of the Atlantic. Romantic nineteenth-century notions of grief were making a comeback.

High-profile deaths

Dying people are today far more likely to want the doctor than the priest; cremation and burial are organised according to the precepts of public health rather than of safe transport to the next world; and counselling is concerned with the psychological health of the bereaved, not the spiritual health of the departed. To these frames by which dying, disposal and bereavement are managed, the twentieth century has provided an important new frame within which the *meaning* of death may be negotiated, the mass media.[78]

Local newspapers report the deaths of many ordinary citizens, and print funeral and *in memoriam* notices in which popular ideas of the afterlife may be readily observed.[79] National news media, however, discuss the deaths only of famous people, or of people made famous by the violent or bizarre manner of their deaths. Gruesome murders are as popular media material now as in Victorian times. Mass deaths, or disasters, are particularly high-profile. In 1930, the R101 airship crashed, killing the Secretary of State for Air; in 1958, the Munich air disaster killed several members of the Manchester United football team; in 1987, thirty-two people died in a fire which swept King's Cross underground station in London; two years later, ninety-four fans of the Liverpool football team died whilst watching a game at Hillsborough, which was being televised live. Welsh and Scottish tragedies have been reported in the English papers and on television, and affected the English as if the events had happened within their own borders: the 1966 Aberfan disaster, when an unstable coal tip engulfed a primary school, killing 116 children; the 1971 Ibrox football crush in Glasgow; the 1989 Lockerbie disaster, when a plane sabotaged by a terrorist bomb crashed upon a Scottish town; the shooting of sixteen primary-school children and their teacher in Dunblane in 1996. Mass killings in Northern Ireland, however, when the 'troubles' settled in the 1920s re-emerged in 1968, have been seen by many English people as something 'other', only forcing themselves directly upon the English consciousness when there are bomb attacks on the mainland. Television's incongruous juxtaposition of such deaths with trivial advertisements, sit-coms and soap operas is arguably the source of the many 'sick' jokes that invariably follow such disasters.[80]

Throughout the century, news media coverage of disasters has typically focused on a number of themes: initial depiction of the carnage, followed by personalised pictures and accounts of survivors and the grief of victims' families, along with the search for the human or technical cause of the disaster. Attempts at explanation can draw press attention until the findings of an official inquiry are universally accepted.

121] Mourners lay flowers in memory of the ninety-four people crushed to death at the Hillsborough disaster, April 1989. The game was being televised live and thus affected many people watching at home. The rituals developed that week for mourning the dead – especially the laying of flowers and cathedral services – have been copied at many subsequent disasters. Today flowers are often laid at the site of traffic accidents.

Indeed, after the initial news of the disaster, grief and the search for causes *become* the news stories. One consequence of this is that the evolving folk response to mass death increasingly relies on media portrayals of other mourners. How do I learn how to behave when there is a tragedy? In part through observing how the media portray other people behaving. The origins of the laying of flowers, or of teddy bears and other mementoes at the scene of an accident are unknown, but it is clear that this became far more widespread after the televising of the mourning for the Hillsborough victims [121]. In the week following the tragedy, around one million people visited Liverpool's home stadium, Anfield, to lay flowers and footballing regalia, notably scarves.[81] Thereafter, the number of flowers and other gifts at the scene of accidents and crimes has risen markedly.

Other public mourning rituals increased in the 1990s. In 1945, Armistice Day and its Two Minutes Silence fell on a Sunday: thereafter, it was shifted to the nearest Sunday as Remembrance Sunday.[82] Silence in the middle of an already quiet English Sunday morning clearly downplayed the effect of this ritual. In 1995, however, the British Legion succeeded in reinstating the Silence on 11 November as well as on Remembrance Sunday, observed increasingly thereafter in many workplaces and supermarkets. One minute's silence in the weekends following the Hillsborough disaster, the Dunblane shooting and the death of Diana, Princess of Wales, was also widely observed.

Following the death of Winston Churchill in 1965, 300,000 people filed past his coffin at the lying in state. Twenty million Britons and 350 million worldwide watched the funeral on television. But the highest profile English death of the century was that of the Princess of Wales in 1997. This sensational story – involving royalty, romance, mystery, a young mother, a car chase and sudden, violent death – prompted huge levels of mourning throughout Britain and the world. For three weeks, the millions of flowers left at Kensington Palace, her London home, became London's major tourist attraction [**plate 21**]. True to form, the media covered the crash, the emotional response and the search for the cause of the accident. Unusually for tragedy, but usual for the deaths of royal and political leaders, the funeral – or, rather, the memorial service not the burial itself – was televised live, generating the largest live audience to date.[83] Diana was buried on a private island. Whilst this decision was reminiscent of Rousseau's Romantic island (see Chapter 8), its main purpose was to keep her admirers at bay.

The twentieth century was healthier and safer for the English than all previous centuries. It saw radical changes in the visibility of death. Death is no longer all around us; plagues do not descend randomly on rich and poor, pious and sinful; most children now survive childhood without witnessing the death of a parent or sibling; it is now possible to grow up without direct experience of human mortality. And yet children witness thousands of deaths, indirectly, on the television. Since 1945, England has not been involved in total war, yet through the Cold War we lived under the abstract threat of nuclear annihilation. We have more control over nature than ever before, yet have spent the last decades anxious about ecological catastrophe, or about catching some potentially fatal disease from the eggs and beef that form our staple diet.

Most English people die in old age, out of sight, in hospital or nursing and residential homes. These are the all-too-frequent unseen deaths of the confused elderly, victims of strokes, or in coronary care or suffering Alzheimer's. Meanwhile, virtually everyone has close friends, family or neighbours who have survived cancer treatment, a heart attack or HIV. Even these can only say – however clean a bill of health their doctor has given them – that they have survived *so far*. Others with these conditions know their time is up, yet modern palliative care enables them to live actively at home and in the community for months or years. Death is nowhere to be seen, but it is everywhere. Death is no longer random, but it remains everybody's lot.

Notes

In all references, place of publication is London unless otherwise stated.

1 For a study stressing continuity as well as change, see G. J. DeGroot, *Blighty: British Society in the Era of the Great War* (1996).

2 The first five sections were written by Peter C. Jupp, the last four by Tony Walter.

3 D. Cannadine, 'War and death, grief and mourning in modern Britain', in J. Whaley (ed.), *Mirrors of Mortality: Studies in the Social History of Death* (1981), p. 189.

4 K. Middlemas and J. Barnes, *Baldwin: A Biography* (1969), pp. 53–5, quoted by Cannadine, 'War and death', pp. 199–200.

5 Cannadine, 'War and death', p. 222.

6 A. Gregory, *The Silence of Memory: Armistice Day 1919–1946* (Oxford, 1994).

7 *Ibid.*, pp. 212–15.

8 S. M. Tomkins, 'The failure of expertise: public health policy in Britain during the 1918–1919 influenza epidemic', *Social History of Medicine*, 5 (1992), 435–54.

9 N. L. Tranter, *British Population in the Twentieth Century* (Basingstoke, 1996), pp. 1 ff.

10 *Ibid.*, pp. 62–6.

11 J. M. Winter, 'The impact of the First World War on civilian health in Britain', *Economic History Review*, 30:3 (1977), 489, 493–4; and 'Infant mortality, maternal mortality and public health in Britain in the 1930s', *Journal of European Economic History*, 13:2 (1979), 443.

12 Quoted by I. Loudon, 'On maternal and infant mortality 1900–1960', *Social History of Medicine*, 4:1 (April 1991), 35.

13 J. B. Orr, *Food, Health and Income*, 1936.

14 G. C. M. M'Gonigle and J. Kirby, *Poverty and Public Health* (1937).

15 J. M. Winter, 'The decline of mortality in Britain, 1870–1950', in T. Barker and M. Drake (eds), *Population and Society in Britain, 1850–1980* (1982), p. 143.

16 Cannadine, 'War and death', p. 189.

17 J. M. Winter, 'Some aspects of the demographic consequences of the First World War in Britain', *Population Studies*, 30:3 (1976), 539–32.

18 I. Loudon, 'Maternal mortality: 1880–1950. Some regional and international comparisons', *Society for the Social History of Medicine* (1988), part 2, 185–228.

19 Later, Hill and Doll established the connection between lung cancer and smoking.

20 D. Black, J. N. Morris, C. Smith and P. Townsend, in P. Townsend and N. Davidson (eds), *The Black Report* (Harmondsworth, 1980).

21 M. Whitehead (ed.), *The Health Divide* (1988).

22 *Ibid.*, p. 217.

23 Department of Health, *The Health of the Nation: A Strategy for Health in England* (1992), Cm 1986.

24 Department of Health, *Our Healthier Nation: A Contract for Health* (1998), Cm 3852.

25 B. Smale, 'Deathwork: A Sociological Analysis of Funeral Directing', unpublished Ph.D. thesis, University of Surrey (1985); M. J. A. Page, 'Funeral Rituals in a Northern City', unpublished Ph.D. thesis, University of Leeds (1989); G. Howarth, *Last Rites: The Work of the Modern Funeral Director* (Amityville, N.Y., 1996); B. Parsons, 'Change and Development of the British Funeral Industry in the 20th Century with Special Reference to the Period 1960–1994', unpublished Ph.D. thesis, University of Westminster (1997).

26 Howarth, *Last Rites*.

27 B. Parsons, 'Supply or demand? Perspectives on the increase in the practice of embalming during the 20th century', *The Embalmer*, 40:4 (Autumn 1997), 7.

28 B. S. Puckle, *Funeral Customs: Their Origin and Development* (1926), p. 28.

29 G. Howarth, 'Professionalising the funeral industry in England 1700–1960', in P. C. Jupp and G. Howarth (eds), *The Changing Face of Death: Historical Accounts of Death and Disposal* (Basingstoke, 1997), pp. 130–1.

30 E. Roberts, 'The Lancashire way of death', in R. Houlbrooke (ed.), *Death, Ritual and Bereavement* (1989).

31 S. Adams, 'A gendered history of the social management of death and dying in Foleshill, Coventry, during the inter-war years', in D. Clark (ed.), *The Sociology of Death: Theory, Culture, Practice* (Oxford, 1993).

32 Parsons, 'Supply or demand?'.

33 N. Albery, G. Elliott and J. Elliott, *The Natural Death Handbook for Inexpensive, Green, Family-Organised Funerals*, 2nd edn (1997), pp. 174–5.

34 Institute of Burial and Cremation Administration, *Charter for the Bereaved* (1996), pp. 65–6.

35 B. Parsons, 'The changing role of the funeral director', *Journal of the Institute of Burial and Cremation Administration*, 65:4 (Winter, 1997), 34–9.

36 G. Rose, 'The direction of funeral directing', unpublished paper given to the first Anglo-European Funerary Congress, organised by the Memorial Advisory Bureau, 1991.

37 H. Hodgson, *How to Become Dead Rich* (1992).

38 For a 1995 overview, see The Monopolies and Mergers Commission, *Service Corporation International and Plantsbrook Group plc: A Report on the Merger Situation* (1995), Cmd 2880.

39 N. Albery, G. Elliot and J. Elliot, *The Natural Death Handbook*; The National Funerals College, *The Dead Citizens Charter*, 2nd edn (Bristol, 1998); The Institute of Burial and Cremation Administration, *Charter for the Bereaved.*

40 P. C. Jupp, 'The Development of Cremation in England 1820–1990: A Sociological Analysis', unpublished Ph.D. thesis, University of London (1993).

41 B. G. Friar, 'The disposal of cremation ashes', *Journal of the Institute of Burial and Cremation Administration*, 50:2 (Summer 1982).

42 *Pharos*, 2:1 (October 1935), p. 6.

43 L. Rose, *The Massacre of the Innocents: Infanticide in Britain 1800–1939* (1986), pp. 134–5.

44 A. Wilson and H. Levy, *Burial Reform and Funeral Costs* (Oxford, 1938).

45 J. S. Clarke, *Funeral Reform* (n.d., probably 1943).

46 J. D. Davies, *Cremation Today and Tomorrow* (Nottingham, 1990).

47 H. Potter, *Hanging in Judgement: Religion and the Death Penalty in England from the Bloody Code to Abolition* (1993).

48 Rose, *Massacre*, p. 182.

49 G. Orwell, *Decline of the English Murder and Other Essays* (Harmondsworth, 1965).

50 *The Royal Commission on Capital Punishment* [the Gowers Commission] (1953), Cmd 8932.

51 N. St John Stevas, *Life, Death and the Law* (1961), p. 1.

52 T. Walter, *The Eclipse of Eternity: A Sociology of the Afterlife* (Basingstoke, 1996); see also D. Davies and A. Shaw, *Reusing Old Graves: A Report on Popular British Attitudes* (Crayford, Kent, 1995), pp. 86–101, and D. Davies, 'Contemporary belief in life after death', in P. C. Jupp and T. Rogers (eds), *Interpreting Death: Christian Theology and Pastoral Practice* (1997).

53 E. Duffy, 'An apology for grief, fear and anger', *Priests & People*, 5:11 (1991), 397–401.

54 M. Hornsby-Smith, *Roman Catholic Beliefs in England: Customary Catholicism and Transformations of Religious Authority* (Cambridge, 1991); D. Lodge, *How Far Can You Go?* (1981).

55 D. L. Edwards and J. Stott, *Essentials* (1988), pp. 313–20.

56 Cannadine, 'War and death', p. 229; G. K. Nelson, *Spiritualism and Society* (1969); J. Winter, *Sites of Memory, Sites of Mourning: The Great War in European Cultural History* (Cambridge, 1995).

57 Walter, *Eclipse*, p. 42; G. Bennett, *Traditions of Belief: Women and the Supernatural* (Harmondsworth, 1987).

58 T. Walter and H. Waterhouse, 'A very private belief: reincarnation in contemporary England', *Sociology of Religion*, 60 (1999), 187–97.

59 A. Kellehear, *Experiences near Death: Beyond Medicine and Religion* (Oxford, 1996).

60 L. Prior and M. Bloor, 'Why people die: social representations of death and its causes', *Science as Culture*, 3 (1992), 346–74.

61 L. Prior, 'Actuarial visions of death: life, death and chance in the modern world', in Jupp and Howarth (eds), *The Changing Face*.

62 M. Mills *et al.*, 'Care of dying patients in hospital', *British Medical Journal*, 309 (1994), 583–4.

63 S. du Boulay, *Cicely Saunders* (1984).
64 D. Field, 'Awareness and modern dying', *Mortality*, 1:3 (1996), 255–65.
65 E.g. M. de Hennezel, *Intimate Death* (1997), serialised on BBC Radio 4, July 1998.
66 C. Seale, *Constructing Death* (Cambridge, 1998).
67 M. Mulkay, 'Social death in Britain', in D. Clark (ed.), *The Sociology of Death* (Oxford, 1993).
68 M. Stroebe *et al.*, 'Broken hearts or broken bonds: love and death in historical perspective', *American Psychologist*, 47 (1992), 1205–12.
69 T. Walter, *On Bereavement: The Culture of Grief* (Buckingham, 1999).
70 Lady Troubridge, *The Book of Etiquette* (Kingswood, Surrey, 1926), pp. 57–8.
71 T. Walter, 'Emotional reserve and the English way of grief', in K. Charmaz, G. Howarth and A. Kellehear (eds), *The Unknown Country: Experiences of Death in Australia, Britain and the USA* (Basingstoke, 1997).
72 Walter, *On Bereavement*.
73 P. Jalland, *Death in the Victorian Family* (Oxford, 1996).
74 J. Holloway, 'Bereavement literature: a valuable resource for the bereaved and those who counsel them', *Contact: Interdisciplinary Journal of Pastoral Studies*, 3 (1990), 17–26.
75 M. Torrie, *My Years with Cruse* (Richmond, Surrey, 1987); P. Clarke, *Twenty-five Compassionate Years: The Story of The Compassionate Friends* (Bristol, 1994).
76 G. Gorer, *Death, Grief and Mourning in Contemporary Britain* (1965).
77 C. M. Parkes, M. Relf and A. Couldrick, *Counselling in Terminal Care and Bereavement* (Leicester, 1996).
78 T. Walter, M. Pickering and J. Littlewood, 'Death in the news: the public invigilation of private emotion', *Sociology*, 29:4 (1995), 579–66.
79 S. Adams, 'Women, death and *in memoriam* notices in a local British newspaper', in Charmaz, Howarth and Kellehear (eds), *The Unknown Country*; J. Davies, 'Vile bodies and mass media chantries' in G. Howarth and P. C. Jupp (eds), *Contemporary Issues in the Sociology of Death, Dying and Disposal* (Basingstoke, 1996).
80 C. Davies, 'Jokes on the death of Diana', in T. Walter (ed.), *The Mourning for Diana* (Oxford, 1999).
81 T. Walter, 'The mourning after Hillsborough', *Sociological Review*, 39:3 (1991), 599–625.
82 Gregory, *The Silence of Memory*, pp. 215–22.
83 Walter (ed.), *Mourning for Diana*. For views dissenting from mourning for the Princess, see I. Jack and P. Marlow, *Granta*, 60 (Winter 1997).

Select bibliography

Black, D., Morris, J. N., Smith, C., and Townsend, P., *The Black Report* (first published 1980) and Whitehead, M. (ed.), *The Health Divide* (1988), published together as *The Black Report and the Health Divide*, Harmondsworth, 1988.
Cannadine, D., 'War and death, grief and mourning in modern Britain', in J. Whaley (ed.), *Mirrors of Mortality: Studies in the Social History of Death*, 1981.
Charmaz, K., Howarth, G., and Kellehear, A. (eds), *The Unknown Country: Death in Australia, Britain and the USA*, Basingstoke, 1987.
Froggatt, K., and Walter, T., 'Hospice logos', *Journal of Palliative Care*, 11:4 (1995).
Gorer, G., *Death, Grief and Mourning in Contemporary Britain*, 1965.
Gregory, A., *The Silence of Memory: Armistice Day 1919–1946*, Oxford, 1994.
Howarth, G., *Last Rites: The Work of the Modern Funeral Director*, Amityville, N.Y., 1996.
Landscape Design: The Journal of the Institute of Landscape Architects, 119 (August 1977) and 187 (October 1989) (special issues on cemeteries).
Loudon, I. (ed.), *Western Medicine: An Illustrated History*, Oxford, 1998, especially chapters by J. Lewis, S. Lock and E. M. Tansey.
Potter, H., *Hanging in Judgement: Religion and the Death Penalty in England from the Bloody Code to Abolition*, 1993.

Prior, L., *The Social Organisation of Death: Medical Discourse and Social Practices in Belfast*, Basingstoke, 1989.

Tranter, N. L., *British Population in the Twentieth Century*, Basingstoke, 1996.

Walter, T., *On Bereavement: The Culture of Grief*, Buckingham, 1999.

Wilson, Sir A. T., and Levy, H., *Burial Reform and Funeral Costs*, Oxford, 1938.

Winter, J., *Sites of Memory, Sites of Mourning: The Great War in European Cultural History*, Cambridge, 1995.

Index

Abbreviations used in the index are: A-S for Anglo-Saxon; B Age for Bronze Age; I Age for Iron Age; lMA for late Middle Ages; med for medieval; Neand for Neanderthal; Neol for Neolithic; R-B for Romano-British; 12c for twelfth century, 14c for fourteenth century etc. Subentries are arranged chronologically, according to the different eras. Page references in italics indicate illustrations and captions.